SEEING & WRITING 3

SEEING & WRITING 3

Donald McQuade
University of California, Berkeley

Christine McQuade
Queens College, City University of New York

Bedford/St. Martin's
Boston, New York

FOR BEDFORD/ST. MARTIN'S

Executive Editor: Alanya Harter
Developmental Editor: Genevieve Hamilton Day
Senior Production Editor: Bridget Leahy
Senior Production Supervisor: Joe Ford
Marketing Manager: Karita dos Santos
Editorial Assistant: Joanna Lee
Text and Cover Design: 2x4
Copyeditor: Barbara Bell
Photo Research: Sally McKissick
Composition: Monotype, LLC
Printing and Binding: R.R. Donnelly & Sons, Inc.

President: Joan E. Feinberg
Editorial Director: Denise B. Wydra
Editor in Chief: Karen S. Henry
Director of Marketing: Karen Melton Soeltz
Director of Editing, Design, and Production: Marcia Cohen
Managing Editor: Elizabeth M. Schaaf

Library of Congress Catalog Card Number: 2005927796

1 0 9 8 7 6
f e d c b a

For information, contact: Bedford/St. Martin's,
75 Arlington Street, Boston, MA 02116
617-399-4000
bedfordstmartins.com

ISBN: 0-312-43429-4
EAN: 978-0-312-43429-8

ACKNOWLEDGMENTS

Introduction

Verbal Texts

Robert Frost. "In White." From *The Dimensions of Robert Frost* by Reginald L. Cook. Copyright © 1958 by Reginald L. Cook. Reprinted by permission Henry Holt & Company, LLC. "Design." From *The Poetry of Robert Frost*, edited by Edward Connery Latham. Copyright © 1964 by Lesley Frost Ballantine, 1936 by Robert Frost, 1969 by Henry Holt & Company. Reprinted by permission of Henry Holt & Company, LLC.

David Ignatow. "My Place." From *Against the Evidence: Selected Poems 1934–1994*. © 1994 by David Ignatow. Reprinted by permission of Wesleyan University Press.

Visual Texts

Untitled drawings. Peter Arkle. © Peter Arkle, 2005.

Dean College, The Way There. Courtesy of Dean College, Franklin, MA.

Subway Passengers, New York, NY. Walker Evans. The Metropolitan Museum of Art, Gift of Arnold H. Crane, 1971. (1971.646.18) © 1999 The Metropolitan Museum of Art.

Man Turning into a Barcode. Graphis Student Design.

Life in Hell. Matt Groening. © 1985 by Matt Groening.

Untitled cartoon. Marshall Hopkins. © 2004 The New Yorker Collection, 2004 Marshall Hopkins from cartoonbank.com. All Rights Reserved.

Poverty Is a Crime, and Our People Are the Victims [*after Migrant Mother, Nipomo, California*]. Malik. Courtesy the Dorothea Lange Collection, Oakland Museum of California.

Migrant Mother, Nipomo, California series. Dorothea Lange. Courtesy the Dorothea Lange Collection, Oakland Museum of California.

Mountain Lakes, New Jersey, 1977. Arno Rafael Minkkinen, Courtesy of Arno Rafael Minkkinen.

12-23-97 5:09 PM; 3-3-98 6:25 PM. Richard Misrach. Courtesy of Richard Misrach.

Down and Out in Discount America cover, by *Nation* magazine, January 3, 2005. Reprinted with permission from *Nation* magazine. www.thenation.com.

Natural Resources, February 16, 2005. Nerilicon. Copyright by Nerilicon and Cagle Cartoons. All rights reserved.

Overhead view of cloverleaf. Photodisc Collection/Getty Images.

American Gothic. Gordon Parks. Courtesy Gordon Parks/Corbis.

Image of Homelessness. Mark Peterson. Courtesy of Redux Pictures.

Warren Avenue at 23rd St., Detroit, Michigan, October 1993. © Joel Sternfeld. Courtesy of the artist and Luhring Augustine.

It's Your Life. Courtesy of Visa.

For Susanne and Marc

PREFACE FOR INSTRUCTORS

Our work on the third edition of *Seeing & Writing* began with a series of conversations with instructors and students across the nation. We are very grateful to those who took the time to meet with us and to write to us—and especially for their willingness to share their experiences working with the book. These conversations have taught us a great deal about the current state of composition classrooms, and have reaffirmed our conviction that *Seeing & Writing* ought to be grounded in a simple pedagogical premise: Invite students to give words and images equal attention. *Seeing &Writing 3* remains, at its core, a first-rate collection of engaging verbal and visual texts to inspire students to see, think, and write with clarity and conviction. Instructors across the nation—from Trident Technical College (South Carolina) to Diablo Valley College (California)—have reported that *Seeing & Writing* generates lively classroom discussions and strong writing exercises.

As teachers and editors, we are grateful to, and inspired by, the number of colleagues who have responded so eagerly to the founding principle of the book—that learning to see well helps students to write well. We have designed this third edition to help students improve their writing by sharpening their perception. This pedagogical principle informs the book's three goals: (1) to provide opportunities for composition students to think critically about compelling visual and verbal representations of American culture; (2) to help students write effectively about how they perceive themselves, especially in relation to the images and words that compete for their attention; and (3) to give instructors the flexibility to work with these materials in ways best suited to the interests and abilities of their students.

Grounded in our decades of experience on both sides of the instructional desk, *Seeing & Writing 3* illustrates the pedagogical principle that instructors ought to start where students are able. Our experience suggests that undergraduates are thoroughly familiar—although often in a passive and uncritical way—with the myriad visual elements of contemporary American experience. We believe that undergraduates are sufficiently conversant with the subjects and strategies of a wide range of visual images (including advertisements, photographs, paintings, and comic art) and related nonfiction prose, short stories, and poems to want to write about them—and the questions and issues they prompt—in original, coherent, and convincing terms. We believe that providing students with opportunities to move fluently within and between these visual and verbal worlds will improve their analytic and compositional skills.

New to This Edition

In addition to confirming for us the many ways in which *Seeing & Writing* works in the classroom, the instructors we talked with gave us concrete suggestions for improvement, suggestions that have been the driving force behind this revision. While urging us to preserve the core strengths of the text, many instructors recommended that we make *Seeing & Writing* an even more effective tool for the composition classroom by focusing our revision on the following features:

— **A redesigned and more teachable general introduction.** In Writing Matters, the introduction to *Seeing & Writing 3*, we've integrated the verbal and visual to guide students through the processes of reading, thinking, and writing— from drafting to making observations and drawing inferences to revising and editing. We've added more visual examples, model analyses of visual and verbal texts, and opportunities for students to develop practiced confidence in critical reading and writing skills.

— **More models of strong expository writing.** We have included an even greater number of excellent expository essays. The list of authors new to this edition includes John Updike, E.B. White, Bharati Mukherjee, and Brian Doyle.

— **New images, and more of them.** This new edition offers a wider range of visual compositions. Classic and contemporary art (photographs, paintings, sculpture, and graphic art) are juxtaposed with cultural artifacts (web sites, ads, movie posters and stills, and icons) to expand teaching possibilities.

— **Additional attention to context helps students read challenging texts.** We have increased the number of both interviews with artists and writers, and cultural and historical documents; and we have as strengthened the connections between and among texts. Our goal: to help students read challenging texts by providing more access points to complex essays and images.

— **New opportunities for students to create visual compositions.**

— **Increased attention to thematic issues such as race, gender, class, global perspectives, and spirituality.**

Teaching *Seeing & Writing 3*

Paradoxically, one of the most important changes in *Seeing & Writing 3* is not in the book but in the instructor's guide that accompanies it. This comprehensive manual—*Teaching Seeing & Writing 3*—offers suggestions on how to teach the material in the new edition, paying respectful attention to different institutional settings and instructional purposes. It now includes the contributions of two dozen teachers who have used *Seeing & Writing* successfully in their composition courses, each of whom shares his or her most effective surefire classes or assignments. In addition, fourteen of these members of the *Seeing & Writing* Community offer snapshots of their colleges and universities, their students, and themselves.

Each chapter of this "field-tested" compendium of teaching resources includes generous helpings of the following elements:

— **Surefire Classes and Assignments:** Instructors from around the country on their teaching strategies and surefire methods for working with the images and verbal texts in *Seeing & Writing 3*.

— **Generating Class Discussion and In-Class Writing:** A thorough assessment of how to work imaginatively and productively with each text in class to stimulate discussion and in-class writing, which may motivate students to write engaging, coherent, and convincing essays about the text and the issues and themes it articulates.

— **Additional Writing Topics:** Two or three additional topics for each selection that involve informal and personal writing, descriptive and narrative essays, expository and argumentative papers, or research assignments.

— **Connections with Other Texts:** Activities that link each selection to other texts in the chapter or book, along with suggestions about how to encourage students to discover connections among texts on their own.

— **Suggestions for Further Reading, Thinking, and Writing:** A list of supplemental materials for classroom use—including print, web, and audiovisual resources—along with recommendations on how to use them to reinforce instructional goals.

Additionally, there is seeingandwriting.com, a book-related web site that includes guided exercises on reading visual images; web-based research activities; annotated research links to sources on the artists, writers, and thematic and compositional issues in the textbook; and doorways to visual resources, virtual museums, and much more.

A Note about the Design

Our colleagues who have worked with previous editions of *Seeing & Writing* consistently praise the design of the book as one of its strengths. The success of the book's design has also received recognition beyond academia. *Seeing & Writing* was featured in an exhibition of the outstanding work of its designers, 2x4, at the San Francisco Museum of Modern Art in 2005.

In the third edition we wanted our colleagues to recapture the sense of seeing the book for the first time. Perhaps the most visible example of this effort is the striking cover illustration by acclaimed artist Peter Arkle. The drawing, which was commissioned for this edition, highlights the interrelatedness of the visual and the verbal. The collaborative work of Peter Arkle, 2x4, and the editors represents a new stage in the relationship of pedagogical form and function, and redefines authorship in composition textbooks. The design of this third edition remains true to the spirit and substance of the previous two editions while offering a fresh look and a more intense expression of the relationship between seeing and writing.

The design of *Seeing & Writing 3* creates an attractive and engaging environment in which students can reflect on, and see reflections of, contemporary American culture. The double purpose of the design is to prompt inquiry into the similarities and differences between images and verbal texts, and to encourage conversation about the ways in which they are connected reinforces our goals. By integrating visual and verbal texts, juxtaposing them, and giving both equal importance on the page, the book's design both facilitates discussion and reflects the complex nature of the multimedia environment in which we all function.

Acknowledgments

From its inception to this third iteration, *Seeing & Writing* has been the product of conversations and collaborations—with each other, our colleagues, our family and friends, the Bedford/St. Martin's team, the design firm 2x4, and a growing community of instructors and students.

The genesis of the book can be traced to innumerable conversations Don McQuade had over more than twenty years with Charles H. Christensen, the now-retired publisher of Bedford/St. Martin's and an extraordinary patron and developer of teaching ideas. Throughout this long collaboration and friendship, Chuck and Don talked about creating a book that draws on undergraduates' familiarity with the visual dimensions of American culture to develop their skills as readers, thinkers, and writers.

When Chuck Christensen, Joan Feinberg (now president of Bedford/St. Martin's), and Don began to talk seriously about bringing this vision to fruition in 1996, Don began a series of dinner-table conversations with his family—his wife, Susanne, and their two children, Christine and Marc—about the relationships between the visual and the verbal in the writing classroom and in contemporary American culture. Christine had returned home for the holidays from New York City, where she had completed the fall season dancing with the STREB modern dance company. Marc was home from the University of California, Berkeley, where he had finished his first semester as an architecture major. We batted around questions like these: Which has a more powerful impact on people— an image or a word? What place do images have in a writing classroom? How is writing visual? How do nonverbal learners learn to write? Those early conversations, and Marc's thoughts on the relationship between word and image in particular, were—

and continue to be—the central impetus for the development of the book. We were immediately struck by the value of a cross-generational conversation about an inter-disciplinary subject.

Having studied American popular culture as a history major and served as a writing tutor at Berkeley's Student Learning Center, Christine was eager to investigate and re-think the teaching of writing in a visual age. Her ideas about relating visual and verbal texts immediately drew her father's attention and encouragement; and she was eager to apprentice with him in the craft of creating textbooks. Our work together began spontaneously and grew organically. We would like to take this opportunity to thank each other for the continuing conversation.

Our work together is only one part of the collaborative effort behind *Seeing & Writing*. In preparing the third edition we relied more than ever on instructors around the country who took time from busy schedules to meet with us to share their experiences teaching the first and second editions, and many others who generously offered critiques of the book during its various stages of development. We are enormously grateful for their insight, enthusiasm, and honesty. Those conversations guided our planning for this revision; they also revealed a growing community of passionate instructors who share our commitment to starting where students are able and improving the analytical and compositional skills of students by having them see, read, think, and write about the visual and verbal dimensions of American culture. We hope that we have responded effectively to their numerous suggestions for improving the pedagogical strengths of *Seeing & Writing*. For their many thoughtful and helpful recommendations, we would like to thank the following:

Lisa Albers, Pierce College

Susan Al-Jarrah, Southwestern Oklahoma State University

Sherrie Amido, California Polytechnic State University

Paul Bogard, University of Nevada, Reno

Rebecca Burns, Southern Illinois University Edwardsville

Terry Cole, LaGuardia Community College

Dan Coleman, Trident Technical College

Melanie Conroy, State University of New York at Buffalo

Dan Cross, Southwestern Illinois College

Kirk Davis, University of Wisconsin–Madison

Dànielle Nicole DeVoss, Michigan State University

Judy Donaldson, Paul Quinn College

Keri DuLaney, Diablo Valley College

Ernest Enchelmayer, Louisiana State University

Lise Esch, Trident Technical College

Laury Fischer, Diablo Valley College

Katharine Gin, WritersCorps

Heidi Goen-Salter, Diablo Valley College

Kim Haimes-Korn, Southern Polytechnic State University

Christine Hamel, University of Arizona

Carolyn Handa, University of Alabama

Troy Hicks, Michigan State University

Matt Hinojosa, University of Arizona

Charles Hood, Antelope Valley College

Samantha Howsden-Hubbard, Walnut Middle School, Nebraska

Debbie Jacob, International School of Port of Spain

Jill Jones, Southwestern Oklahoma State University

Jean Kaufmann, Southwestern Illinois College

Dan Keller, University of Louisville

Winnie Kenney, Southwestern Illinois College

Paul Knox, University of Nevada, Reno

Joshua Kretchmar, University of Texas at Arlington

Ann Krooth, Diablo Valley College

Martha Kruse, University of Nebraska at Kearney

Rich Lane, Clarion University

Norman Lewis, Queens College–CUNY

Jon Lindsay, Southern Polytechnic State University

Rachel Losh, University of Michigan–Ann Arbor

Thomas Lovin, Southwestern Illinois College

Jennifer Lutman, University of Michigan–Ann Arbor

Elizabeth MacDaniel, Clarion University

Andrew Maness, California Polytechnic State University

Ann McDonald, Trident Technical College

Kara Moloney, University of Nevada, Reno

Barbara Morningstar, California Polytechnic State University

Maureen Ellen O'Leary, Diablo Valley College

Jeff Orr, Southern Polytechnic State University

Ann Parker, Southern Polytechnic State University

Dara Perales, Mira Costa College

Jean Petrolle, Columbia College Chicago

Nick Plunkey, University of Nevada, Reno

Fred W. "Skip" Renker, Delta College
Sherrie Rheingans, California Polytechnic State University
Priscilla Riggle, Truman State University
Lilly Roberts, The Cambridge School of Weston
Jerald Ross, Southwestern Illinois College
Albert Rouzie, Ohio University
Alison Russell, Xavier University
Sue Ruth, Trident Technical College
Nicola Schmidt, Southern Illinois University
Jack Stack, University of Minnesota
Joyce Stoffers, Southwestern Oklahoma State University
Tina Stover, Southwestern Illinois College
Lilla Toke, State University of New York at Stony Brook
Rebecca Walsh, Southern Illinois University
Heidi Wilkinson, California Polytechnic State University–
    San Luis Obispo
Donna Williamson, State University of New York at Potsdam

Behind this collaborative effort also stand a large number of friends and colleagues who have graciously allowed us into their already crowded lives to seek advice, encouragement, and assistance since the first edition. We would like to underscore our continuing gratitude to Elizabeth Abrams of the University of California, Santa Cruz; Tom Ahn; Austin Bunn; Eileen O'Malley Callahan of the University of California, Berkeley; Beth Chimera; Mia Chung; Lee Dembart; Duncan Faherty of Queens College; Kathy Gin; Sandra and Yuen Gin; Justin Greene; Anne-Marie Harvey; Eli Kaufman; Aileen Kim; Laura Lanzerotti; Joel Lovell; Greg Mullins of Evergreen College; Barbara Roether; Anjum Salam; Shayna Samuels; Elizabeth Streb and the dancers of STREB; Matthew Stromberg; and especially Darryl Stephens of the University of California, Berkeley, who brought inestimable intelligence, writing skill, and pedagogical care to the second edition.

We are especially grateful to Andrew Beahrs, whose superb reading skills and admirable sensitivity to teaching matters strengthened the questions following many selections. Andy is a first-rate writer and teacher, and we thank him for his thoughtful and generous assistance.

Special thanks, too, to Michael Hsu for reading and rereading the drafts and for his general encouragement and support. His generous and rigorous intelligence, as well as his energy and patience, have strengthened *Seeing & Writing 3* in innumerable ways.

It quickly became clear that *Seeing & Writing* would be a book that needed a particularly sophisticated designer's eye. We are grateful to Irwin Chen for introducing us to the design firm 2x4. Michael Rock and Katie Andresen of 2x4 have been invaluable in helping us not only to expand our imagination of how this book could look and function but also to sharpen our own abilities to think visually. During the preparation of this third edition, Katie once again turned a chaotic collection of materials into an elegant and useful instructional tool. Her discerning eye and imaginative intelligence are everywhere evident in this book—especially to those who, like us, have the pleasure of working with and learning from her.

Katie Andresen also deserves special thanks for leading us to Peter Arkle, a brilliant illustrator whose art provides fascinating portraits and social commentary on contemporary American life. We are delighted that Peter accepted our invitation to collaborate with us on accentuating the relationship between seeing and writing in engaging and memorable ways. His cover art and illustrations provide an eminently teachable series of classes in their own right and serve as complementary expressions of connections between words and images. For those interested in seeing more of Peter's work, we urge you to explore his web site at peterarkle.com.

We remain grateful to Esin Goknar for opening the door to new sources of photography and other visual media in the first edition. With great skill and patience, Naomi Ben-Shahar widened our lenses even further as we worked with her on selecting images for *Seeing & Writing 2*. A distinguished photography teacher, artist, and photoresearcher, Naomi brought the best of each of these perspectives to the project, as well as her passion for teaching and learning. For *Seeing & Writing 3* we would especially like to thank Sally McKissick for her outstanding work on our behalf, mining the world of images with an unfailingly astute sensibility and an admirable alertness to the pedagogical possibilities of linking seemingly disparate images. We appreciate her thoroughly professional approach to her work, and we will always be grateful for all that she has taught us about seeing carefully.

Dan Keller of the University of Louisville has skillfully prepared *Teaching SEEING & WRITING 3*. We are grateful to have had the opportunity to work with and learn from him again as well as to have the benefit of his accomplishments as an outstanding teacher and writer. His understanding of the practical applications of the book's vision continues to strengthen *Seeing & Writing* and to reinforce our belief in what is teachable of the principles and practices that inform this book. He has been an invaluable collaborator throughout the revision process—from our earliest conversations about what might be the shape of the third edition to our numerous, and more recent, discussions about the pedagogical possibilities of an illustrated cover. In addition to crafting *Teaching SEEING & WRITING* with great insight and sensitivity to what works best in the classroom, Dan has skillfully interwoven commentary on the numerous contributions from instructors across the nation. Dan has been the intellectual and pedagogical driving force behind what

is a groundbreaking instructor's manual. We are grateful for his presence in our lives and in our classrooms.

We would once again like to extend special thanks to the kind people of Bedford/St. Martin's. Barbara Bell copyedited the manuscript with first-rate skill as well as sensitivity to and respect for our instructional purposes. We also would like to thank Jan Cocker for her skilled proofreading and Joanna Lee for her fine work on preparing the index. Joanna Lee deserves special praise—and thanks—for her exemplary work on virtually every aspect of this project. She has set a new standard for excellence in editorial assistance. Stefanie Wortman managed the preparation of *Teaching SEEING & WRITING 3* with remarkable skill and attentiveness, and we would like to recognize her dedicated assistance in organizing the Surefire Classes and Assignments and the profiles that highlight the new edition of the instructor's manual.

Susan Doheny and Sandy Schecter managed with great skill and determination the complex project of securing permissions to reprint the visual and verbal materials the book. We'd also like to thank Nick Carbone and Kim Hampton for their professional work on revising the web site for *Seeing & Writing 3* so effectively. Bridget Leahy somehow managed to figure out the logistics of producing this edition with an admirable blend of intelligence, energy, imagination, patience, and goodwill. We are fortunate to have had the opportunity to work with her again.

We would like to thank marketing manager Rachel Falk for her work in communicating the vision of *Seeing & Writing*. We are also enormously grateful to Rachel, Kevin Feyen, Jane Betz, Colleen Brady, Karita dos Santos, Richard Rosenlof, Marjorie Adler, Paul Coleman, Sandy Manly,

Jimmy Fleming, Dennis Adams, and Benjamin Yots for effectively and graciously facilitating our meetings with instructors around the country.

More generally, we would like to underscore our gratitude to the superb sales representatives of Bedford/St. Martin's for the invaluable insights they so generously offered to us about the pedagogical strengths and weaknesses of the second edition of *Seeing & Writing*. These colleagues also played a central role in helping us to discover—and to make more visible in *Teaching SEEING & WRITING*—the community of teachers who have found working with *Seeing & Writing* both pleasant and effective as they seek to improve the seeing, thinking, and writing of their students.

We continue to be indebted to Joan Feinberg, a perceptive, encouraging, and compelling voice of reason and impeccable judgment. Her vision of the book's potential and her critiques of our work stand as models of intellectual and professional integrity. Chuck Christensen offered wise and energizing support well beyond his retirement. His thoughtful encouragement and confidence in us and what we are seeking to achieve made each sentence easier to write.

Genevieve Hamilton Day contributed her keen editorial eye and sensitivity to pedagogical responsibility, along with a generous dose of good judgment, to every aspect of developing this third edition. She did so with an uncommon blend of intelligence, rigorous reading, encouragement, and good cheer—all the while preparing to deliver her own work of art, Flora Simone Day, born in the midst of this revision. We'd like to underscore our thanks to Genevieve for so generously making room for us in her busy life and for her steadfast support and dedication to improving this teaching tool.

We also would like to thank our editor, Alanya Harter. She is a remarkably skillful and accomplished reader and writer, someone who balances good judgment, tact, and taste with knowledge and resourcefulness. She is the kind of editor every author hopes to work with and write for. Her animated and rigorous intellectual presence is everywhere evident to us in this final version of *Seeing & Writing 3*; and we would like to express our gratitude for her hard work, intelligent promptings, insightful suggestions, and patience. Without her engaging intelligence, *Seeing & Writing 3* would be less than it is.

Genevieve Hamilton Day and Alanya Harter often served as tag-team editors on this project, and they invariably made these trade-offs seamlessly and successfully. They juggled a remarkable number of responsibilities with ease, and they remain our most important collaborators on this project. Individually and as a team, Alanya and Genevieve strengthened our work, discovered first-rate selections, carefully considered the most pedagogically engaging themes and forms for the apparatus, and helped us grapple with the most important design questions. We are most fortunate to work so effectively with these outstanding editors. Their patience, clearmindedness, intellectual integrity, and good humor helped create the kind of supportive conditions in which every writer can thrive.

Finally we would like to acknowledge Susanne and Marc McQuade. This project would never have been possible without their questions, ideas, encouragement, and, most important, their inspiring intellectual curiosity.

Merci vu mou!
Donald McQuade and Christine McQuade

HOW THIS BOOK WORKS

Each of the selections and exercises in this book asks students to take a closer look at the objects, people, places, identities, ideas, and experiences that make up the varied expressions of American culture—to pay closer attention to, interpret, and then write about what they see.

The seven chapters that follow are filled with images and words that will help students think critically and write convincingly about increasingly complex themes and issues: observing "ordinary" objects; exploring what makes a space a place; considering the ways in which we record personal and public memories; decoding the many different icons that surround us; and confronting challenging images, both questioning what they represent and forcing ourselves to look closely at pictures that make us uncomfortable. Two new chapters focus on gender and difference, exploring how we embody and express sex and sexuality, and how race and class figure in our personal and public Americas.

Generally we have designed each chapter to progress from the concrete to the abstract, from shorter to longer texts, and from works with a limited and readily accessible frame of reference to works that are complex. The overall organization of the book reflects a similar progression—from practicing skills of observation and inference, to working with description and narration, and then to applying exposition, argumentation, and other rhetorical forms. Yet because each chapter is self-contained and begins with an exercise in observation and inference, instructors can sequence subjects and themes to best address their own instructional needs as well as the interests and backgrounds of their students.

Accompanying each selection are a headnote that provides background information about the writer or artist and text and suggested questions for "Seeing" and "Writing." The Seeing and Writing questions will help you focus carefully on each of the selections. Seeing questions help you generate careful observations and think through—and beyond—your initial response; writing questions help you identify compositional issues such as how the author or artist has chosen to assemble the elements of the piece. New "Responding Visually" prompts offer you the opportunity to create nontraditional assignments in response to certain selections.

Starting on the facing page are thumbnails of the special features and sample selections in this book. A brief description of each recurring feature runs below its thumbnail. These give you a sense of the pedagogical, visual, and textual architecture that underpins *Seeing & Writing 3*—each page of which, we hope, will reward your students' closer attention.

OPENING PORTFOLIO
A provocative collection of images opens each chapter, jumpstarting students' engagement with the chapter's theme.

PAIR
Images juxtaposed with a poem or short prose piece ask students to think about the relationship between verbal and visual strategies.

EXERCISES
Re: Searching the Web and Talking Pictures exercises look at texts you see on screen—computer, TV, and film—and how they shape information and inform our culture.

RETROSPECT
Visual timelines graphically show students how time has changed the face of the ads we're shown, the movies we see, and the magazines we read.

PORTFOLIO
Collections of paintings, photographs, or mixed-media texts by a single artist or on a single theme ask students to consider style, theme, and vision.

INTERVIEW
Artists and writers talk about the creative process — sharing both general strategies and specific stories about compositions included in the book.

VISUALIZING COMPOSITION
Key concepts for writers—such as tone, structure, purpose, and audience—are given concrete shape.

CONTEXT
Cultural and historical documents and images give additional context for challenging readings.

LOOKING CLOSER
A sharply targeted collection of visual and verbal texts invites students to focus attention on a specific question about each chapter's larger topic.

CONTENTS

Introduction

Writing Matters

3
Writing Matters
EXERCISE: Walker Evans, *Subway Passengers, New York, NY*

6
Making Observations
EXERCISE: Mark Peterson, *Image of Homelessness*

8
Drawing Inferences
EXERCISE: David Ignatow, *My Place*

12
Drafting
EXERCISE: Peter Arkle

14
Revising
EXERCISE: Robert Frost, *In White* and *Design*

16
Composition Toolkit
Purpose
Structure
Audience
Point of View
Tone
Metaphor
Context
EXERCISE: Joel Sternfeld, *Warren Avenue at 23rd Street, Detroit, Michigan, October 1993*

1 Observing the Ordinary

 27

 90

 126

2 Coming to Terms with Place

3 Capturing Memorable Moments

4 Projecting Gender

374

396

401

5 Examining Difference

6 Reading Icons

 516

 526

 586

7 Challenging Images

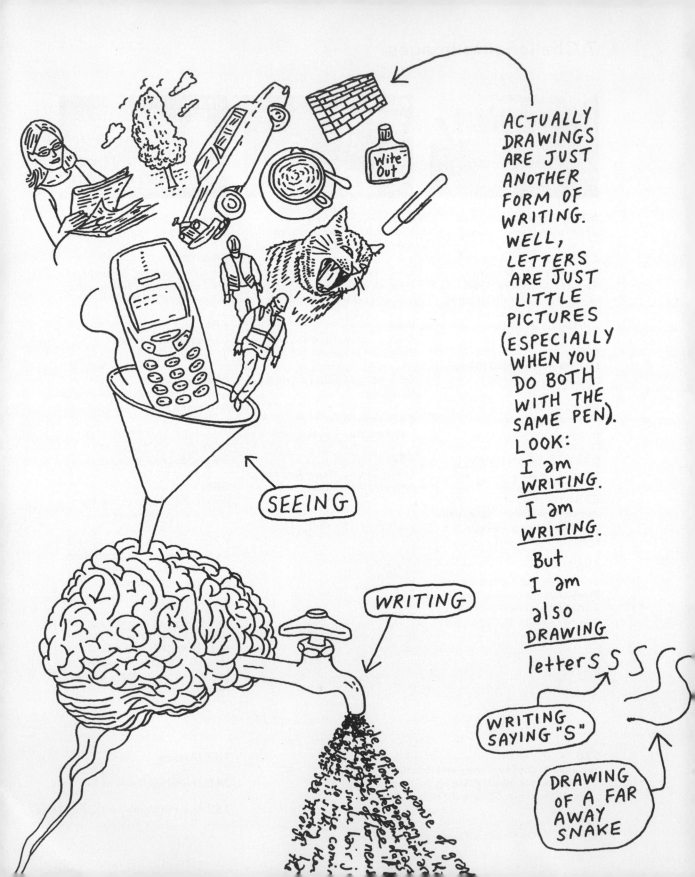

WRITING MATTERS

"THE REAL VOYAGE OF DISCOVERY CONSISTS NOT IN SEEKING NEW LANDSCAPES BUT IN HAVING NEW EYES." *MARCEL PROUST*

What does seeing have to do with writing? You may be asking this question as you begin working with this book. Seeing and writing seem—on the surface—to have very little to do with each other. We tend to regard seeing as an effortless, reflex-level activity. Think of common phrases such as *take a quick glance* or *give something a look-see*. They suggest speed, lightness, and ease. Writing, on the other hand, is more frequently associated with careful thought, weight, and labor. The idiom *writer's block* is an example: Think of the classic image of a writer staring at a blank page, crumpled papers overflowing a nearby trash can. Few writers of any age or level of experience have not lived through some version of this frustration.

In this book we will show you that seeing and writing have more in common than you might think. They are inextricably bound: Learning to see more carefully will help you write more easily and successfully. The more your eyes are open and alert, the more you will have to write about and the more you will write with conviction and clarity.

This book provides you with opportunities to sharpen your perception and develop your ability to write with clarity and insight. In the following pages you will find a wide range of visual and verbal "snapshots" from contemporary culture: words, pictures, and combinations of the two taken from our increasingly multimedia world. You will be invited to pay as much attention to, say, an advertisement for Pirelli tires as to the more traditional essays and arguments you will read and write in most of your college courses. We hope you will consider virtually everything around you to be a potential text for serious reading, discussion, and writing—from a movie poster for the latest box-office hit to a wall with graffiti scrawled on it; from an advertisement for building a stronger body to an essay about immigrating to the United States from Puerto Rico; from the clothes you buy to the jingles you hear on television commercials. Some may be familiar, some unfamiliar. Some might inspire, others unsettle. Our hope is that you will use these selections to draw on your own experience with contemporary culture and to recognize—and practice—your skills as an effective thinker and writer.

We believe that anyone interested in becoming an articulate and confident writer needs to "cross-train," to learn from the different ways in which serious thinkers see the world and express their distinct perspectives on it. The strategies artists and photographers employ to capture and direct the viewer's attention, make a point, or create an effect are not very different from the strategies writers use to achieve the same effects, albeit in a different medium. For example, you might think of a writer's choice of word to be akin to a painter's brushstroke. A dot of bright color (say, red), like a single word (say, *smash*), doesn't do much on its own: It's the combination of different elements, the composition of a text, that gives the audience something to read, respond to, admire, and remember.

Thinking carefully about visual and verbal strategies will improve your own skills as a reader and writer. We want to help you become more aware of—and develop more practiced confidence in—the skills identified with both verbal and visual literacy. These skills will enable you to learn, recognize, understand, and create compelling and convincing messages for audiences within and beyond the halls of higher education. You are already a member of several distinct communities; mastering the skills of critical reading and writing will enable you to contribute your ideas—to make your voice heard—in these and other communities with which you choose to associate.

Whatever your field of study in college, you will be asked to make observations and draw inferences about what you read, and you will be expected to formulate these inferences as assertions about an idea or a text. And you will be expected to support your claims with evidence. Such moves—from observation to inference, from concrete to abstract—form the cornerstone of all academic inquiry. This book provides you with opportunities to practice these fundamental skills.

This introduction offers you a set of concrete intellectual tools to help you practice the skills of seeing more clearly and writing more effectively about the world around you—the people, objects, images, events, ideas, and commercial appeals that compete for your attention and seek to gain your endorsement and loyalty.

"Stare. It is the way to educate your eye, and more. Stare, pry, listen, eavesdrop. Die knowing something. You are not here long."
WALKER EVANS

"Seeing comes before words."
JOHN BERGER

"No method nor discipline can supersede the necessity of being forever on the alert. What is a course of history, or philosophy, or poetry, or the most admirable routine of life, compared with the discipline of looking always at what is to be seen? Will you be a reader, a student merely, or a seer?"
HENRY DAVID THOREAU

Much like the woman pictured here staring blankly into space, many of us tend to look without really noticing. How carefully do you pay attention to the details of your everyday environment? How specific could you be, for example, if you were asked to describe a street corner you pass every day?

Walker Evans, *Subway Passengers, New York, NY*, 1938

EXERCISE

Draw—from memory—what a penny looks like. Then compare your description of a penny with an actual coin. Write a paragraph or two descibing the differences between your drawing and the penny. What elements did you leave out of the drawing? What elements did you add that are not on the coin?

EXERCISE

The word *literacy* has spawned numerous variations in recent years. Educators now speak of computer, visual, and media literacy, for example. What variations on the term *literacy* have you encountered? What does being literate mean in the 21st century? Take a few moments to write your own definition of the word *literate*, being sure to support each point you make with an example. Then discuss your definition with your classmates.

Making Observations

A useful place to begin with any text—visual or verbal— is to jot down your first impressions. Answer these questions: What details do I notice? What parts of the text stand out to me more than others? It is important to allow yourself to react "purely" to a text before you begin analyzing it. What are your initial instincts about the text?

Whenever you read anything, you bring to that activity the sum total of your experience and your identity—how you define yourself in terms of race, class, gender, sexuality, and politics. You should also acknowledge your predispositions to, or prejudices about, the text in question.

Once you've attended to your first impressions, look again and write down a set of more careful observations about the text. An observation is a neutral, nonjudgmental, and verifiable statement.

Making notes on what you observe involves recording the obvious. **Observations** are concrete; they describe things that everyone can see in a text. It's easy to make assumptions about something you're looking at or reading without taking the time to base your statements on what you can actually see.

Making initial observations when responding to a text will enable you to build confidence in your ability to read it carefully and insightfully. Reading with an eye on making observations also best prepares you to write effectively about what you see in a text.

We urge you to write down as many statements as possible about whatever you are observing. Whenever you encounter a new text, always begin by writing out or typing your thoughts.

Observation: 1. (a) The act, practice, or power of noticing. (b) Something noticed. 2. (a) The fact of being seen or noticed; the act or practice of noting and recording facts and events, as for some scientific study. (b) The data so noted and recorded. 3. A comment or remark based on something observed.

"The best writing advice I've ever received is: 'Facts are eloquent.'"
NORRIE EPSTEIN

EXERCISE

Take a few moments to write down as many observations as possible about this photograph by Mark Peterson. What exactly do you notice?

Mark Peterson, *Image of Homelessness* (page 180)

Drawing Inferences

One of the most productive ways to approach understanding and appreciating any text involves a two-step process: Make observations, and then draw reasonable and verifiable **inferences** from those observations. This pattern of observing and inferring—what we regard as the cornerstone skills of careful reading and writing—can be applied to any question you ask about a text in terms of its purpose, structure, audience, metaphor, point of view, and tone, or the context within which it was written or produced.

How can you know whether the inferences you have drawn from your observations are reasonable? What makes an inference reasonable is whether specific evidence in the text warrants the intellectual leap you've made. When drawing an inference, be careful not to rush to judgment and formulate a conclusion, even a provisional one, before you have carefully examined the details of the evidence under consideration.

Remember to verify each interpretive claim you make with *specific details* from the text. Providing ample, detailed evidence to support each of your assertions also ensures that you don't develop the habit of believing that you can say whatever you want about a text, that you can read, as one student put it, "almost anything into a text."

Observation and inference are the fundamental building blocks of academic inquiry. Any time you write an essay, carry out a scientific experiment, or investigate an historical question, you must make observations and draw inferences, find evidence and make assertions. Observations and inferences provide the basic material you need to write an essay. Essays are pieces of writing that support the assertions they make. Assertions are articulated in a thesis, and your evidence forms the body of the essay. In the next section we explore the process of moving from note-taking to drafting an essay.

Inference: An intellectual leap from what one sees to what those details might suggest.

What inferences can you draw about Mark Peterson's photograph (page 7) based on your observations? Now think about how you might apply the same process of making careful observations and drawing inferences to a verbal text. Take a few moments to read the poem by David Ignatow below. Then write down as many observations and inferences as possible.

MY PLACE
David Ignatow

I have a place to come to.
It's my place. I come to it
morning, noon and night
and it is there. I expect it
to be there whether or not   5
it expects me — my place
where I start from and go
towards so that I know
where I am going and what
I am going from, making me   10
firm in my direction.

I am good to talk to,
you feel in my speech
a location, an expectation
and all said to me in reply   15
is to reinforce this feeling
because all said is towards
my place and the speaker
too grows his
from which he speaks to mine   20
having located himself
through my place.

OBSERVATIONS AND INFERENCES: A STUDENT'S RESPONSES

We've reprinted a series of observations and inferences one student made about Mark Peterson's photograph and David Ignatow's poem. How do they compare with your own findings? those of your classmates?

Observations

1. I notice that there are cardboard boxes strapped to a sidewalk bench with three different kinds of twine or fabric.

2. I notice a Burger King sign in the top left of the image.

3. I notice that there are pieces of cardboard boxes on the ground.

4. I notice that there are dead leaves on the ground.

5. I notice that there are four people in the background.

6. I notice that the words HANDLE WITH CARE are written on the box in the bottom left corner of the photograph.

7. I notice that there is a pillow and at least two blankets visible through the opening of the box.

8. I notice that the diagonal line of the fence behind the bench divides the image in two.

9. I notice that the background street scene is blurry but that the foreground bench part is in focus.

Inferences

1. Based on the observations I made, I infer that this is a place where someone has set up a place to sleep.

2. The way the photographer framed this shot helps emphasize the juxtaposition between the life of a homeless person and the rest of bustling city life in New York City.

3. Based on the photograph's subject, the way it is framed or cropped, and the prominent inclusion of the Burger King sign and the text HANDLE WITH CARE, I infer that Peterson is making an ironic statement about the severity of the homelessness problem.

MY PLACE
David Ignatow

I have a place to come to.
It's my place. I come to it
morning, noon and night
and it is there. I expect it
to be there whether or not   5
it expects me—my place
where I start from and go
towards so that I know
where I am going and what
I am going from, making me   10
firm in my direction.

I am good to talk to,
you feel in my speech
a location, an expectation
and all said to me in reply   15
is to reinforce this feeling
because all said is towards
my place and the speaker
too grows his
from which he speaks to mine   20
having located himself
through my place.

Observations

1. I notice that the word *place* is repeated five times in this poem, in addition to the title.

2. I notice that Ignatow uses *I*, the first person.

3. I notice that this poem is made up of two parts, or stanzas.

4. I notice that there are 11 lines in both parts of the poem.

5. I notice that the longest line in the poem is six words long.

6. I notice that Ignatow uses simple, relatively short words in this poem.

7. I notice that the first stanza is made up of two sentences; the second stanza is made up of one sentence.

Inferences

1. Based on the observations I made, I infer that Ignatow is not referring to an actual, physical place in this poem but rather to an idea of place.

2. Ignatow's use of simple words, short lines, and stanzas of equal length help reinforce the simplicity of the poem's message.

3. The balanced form of the poem helps convey an overall feeling of being centered, or "at home."

Drafting

Composing is a **recursive** process of seeing and writing. Taking a closer look around you not only gives you subjects and ideas to write about (which are the initial ingredients in writing) but also leads to effective writing. Careful seeing is an intellectual equivalent of breathing in; writing is a form of intellectual exhaling—expressing an idea in clear, convincing, and memorable terms. Writing, in turn, can also help you see and understand your subject more clearly.

Writing rarely proceeds neatly from one phase to the next. Rather the phases often overlap, making the process somewhat messy. Many writers revise what they have written as soon as they see the word or sentence on the page. Others wait until they have a complete draft and only then go back through it. Each writer participates in the writing process in a different way, at a different pace, and with a different result.

The term *draft* is used across disciplines to describe a first take, a first focused and sustained effort at completing a piece of writing or artwork. In the first phase of the writing process, a writer usually chooses a subject to write about (or one may be assigned), identifies a purpose for writing about that subject, develops observations and inferences about the text(s) in question, generates a thesis—a controlling idea—about the subject, considers the audience to be addressed, and then expands that idea in brainstorming or freewriting exercises, in an outline, or in some other form that provides the basis for a first draft of the essay.

Exercises like brainstorming and freewriting help writers search for and then decide on a subject to write about. These exercises are excellent confidence builders, especially if you are a relatively inexperienced writer, because they can help you produce a great deal of writing in a short time. They also enable you to see rather quickly just how much you have to say about a subject while resisting the urge to edit your work prematurely.

We believe that there is no single way to write, no fail-proof formula to produce successful essays. Anyone who is seriously interested in learning to write can benefit not only from listening carefully to what other writers and artists have to say about the challenges and pleasures of the composing process, but also, and more importantly, from a willingness to practice the skills regularly.

Writing is, after all, a skill; and skills develop over time with frequency of practice. Like throwing the perfect pitch, drawing a portrait, or playing a piano sonata, writing with clarity and ease requires daily practice. Making writing a habitual, daily activity reduces the anxiety and tension about whether you're writing correctly. Too many people focus on writing to avoid making mistakes rather than on articulating the ideas they want to convey. The best method to build confidence as a writer starts out with seeing carefully.

Recursive: From the Latin *recursus*, "to run back." A term adapted from mathematics to describe a process of writing in which the writer loops back to a preceding point in order to move forward with an idea.

"When you sit down to write, tell the truth from one moment to the next and see where it takes you."
DAVID MAMET

To create illustrations for the cover and inside of this book, artist Peter Arkle began by sketching his take on the processes of seeing and writing. Reprinted here is an early draft of the image that appears on page 2 of this introduction. What differences do you notice? What issues and concerns might have prompted Arkle's revisions?

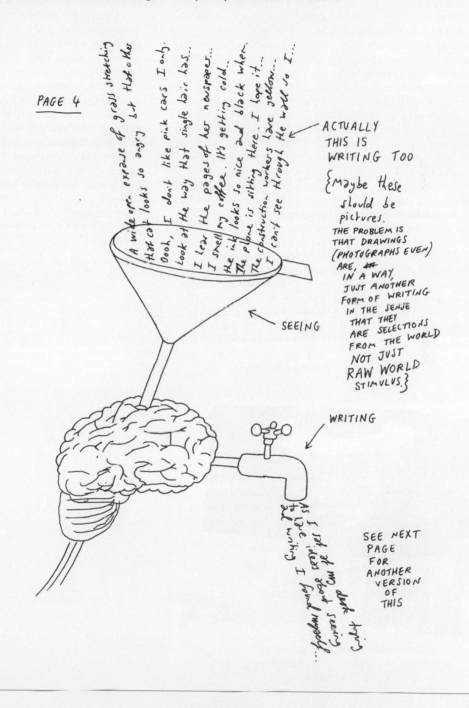

Revising

Many writers appreciate the power and permanence that revision can give to the act of writing. When writers revise, they reexamine what they have written with an eye to strengthening their control over ideas. As they revise, they expand or delete, substitute or reorder. In some cases they revise to clarify or emphasize. In others they revise to tone down or reinforce particular points. More generally, they revise either to simplify what they have written or to make it more complex.

Revising gives writers an opportunity to rethink their essays, to help them accomplish their intentions more clearly and fully. Revising also includes such larger concerns as determining whether the essay is logical and consistent, whether its main idea is supported adequately, whether it is organized clearly, and whether it satisfies the audience's needs or demands in engaging and accessible terms. Revising enables writers to make sure that their essays are as clear, concise, precise, and effective as possible.

Revising also allows writers to distance themselves from their work and to see more clearly its strengths and weaknesses. This helps them make constructive, effective decisions about the best ways to produce a final draft. Some writers revise after they have written a very quick and very rough draft. Once they have something on paper, they revise for as long as they have time and energy. Still other writers require more distance from their first draft to revise effectively. Thinking about an audience also helps writers revise, edit, and proofread their essays.

When writers proofread, they reread their final drafts to detect misspellings, omitted lines, inaccurate information, and other errors.

"When speaking aloud, you punctuate constantly—with body language. Your listener hears commas, dashes, question marks, exclamation points, quotation marks as you shout, whisper, pause, wave your arms, roll your eyes, wrinkle your brow. In writing, punctuation plays the role of body language. It helps readers hear you the way you want to be heard. Careful use of those little marks emphasizes the sound of your distinctive voice and keeps the reader from becoming bored or confused.... [Punctuation] exists to serve you. Don't be bullied into serving it."
RUSSELL BAKER

"Don't embarrass me again, spell-checker."

Marshal Hopkins, *Don't Embarrass Me Again, Spell-Checker*, 2004

Reprinted here are two versions of a poem by Robert Frost. The first, "In White," was written in 1912; the second, "Design," was published in 1936. Write an essay in which you discuss the differences between these two poems. How does the speaker's tone of voice lead the reader to respond differently to each poem? Point to specific changes in diction and metaphor that help characterize the change in voice the second poem has undergone. See pages 21 and 22 for definitions of tone and metaphor. What happens in the revision?

IN WHITE

A dented spider like a snow drop white,
On a white Heal-all, holding up a moth
Like a white piece of lifeless satin cloth—
Saw ever curious eye so strange a sight?—
Portent in little, assorted death and blight   5
Like the ingredients of a witches' broth?—
The beady spider, the flower like a froth,
And the moth carried like a paper kite.

What had that flower to do with being white,
The blue prunella every child's delight.   10
What brought the kindred spider to that height?
(Make we no thesis of the miller's plight.)
What but design of darkness and of night?
Design, design! Do I use the word aright?

DESIGN

I found a dimpled spider, fat and white,
On a white heal-all, holding up a moth
Like a white piece of rigid satin cloth—
Assorted characters of death and blight
Mixed ready to begin the morning right,   5
Like the ingredients of a witches' broth—
A snow-drop spider, a flower like a froth,
And dead wings carried like a paper kite.

What had that flower to do with being white,
The wayside blue and innocent heal-all?   10
What brought the kindred spider to that height,
Then steered the white moth thither in the night?
What but design of darkness to appall?—
If design govern in a thing so small.

Composition Toolkit

All texts and images are composed. By *composition* we mean both the process of creating a text and the way in which a text is put together. This section will help you sharpen your understanding and appreciation of the compositional techniques used by the authors and artists you encounter. The more confident you become in your own capabilities as a writer, the more you will exercise compositional strategies and techniques in your own prose. We encourage you to think about the following seven features of composition in particular. As you look closely at an image or text, you should establish a wider lens for viewing and looking at the overall composition of the text, on how the details and the elements of the work are put together to form a whole.

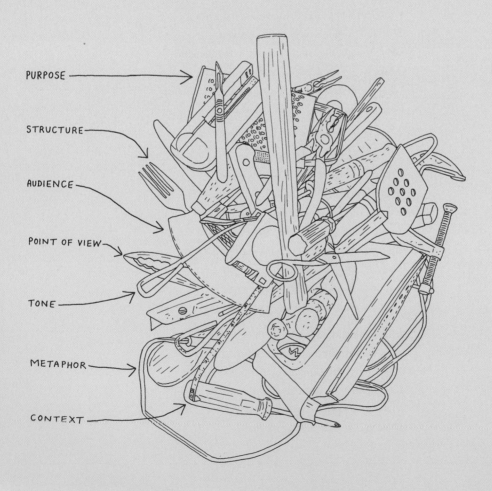

PURPOSE

STRUCTURE

AUDIENCE

POINT OF VIEW

TONE

METAPHOR

CONTEXT

Purpose

Determining your purpose means making decisions about what to say and how to say it. The first of these concerns establishes the general content and overall goal of the essay. The second focuses on the writer's style, on choices in such aspects of writing as structure, diction, and tone. For many writers, the principal purpose can be as simple as wanting to narrate or describe an experience, recall a concert, remember a family story, advocate a certain social cause, argue on behalf of freedom of speech, or recount the pleasure of reading a book or seeing a film or a play. Just as there is no surefire way to succeed at writing, there is no single definition of an appropriate subject or purpose in writing.

What compositional purpose does this particular text serve? Does the text explain? describe? tell a story? entertain? convince you of an argument? persuade you to engage in an action? move you to laughter or tears? do something else? These questions may be difficult to answer quickly, and you will no doubt need to work closely with details in the text and then infer reasonable answers. Likewise, when you sit down to write your own text, we hope that you'll be motivated to draft a paper with a clear purpose in mind, something other than earning a good grade.

EXERCISE

Both images below focus on the American flag. What compositional purpose do you think each one serves?

Gordon Parks, *American Gothic*, 1942 (page 515)

Matt Groening, *Life in Hell*, 1985 (page 594)

Structure

Every text has a shape of its own. Images are built through subject, color, texture, light, line, and focus, or patterns of color or shape, to name just a few structural variables. Written texts use ideas, words, details, voice, and other tools as their structural building blocks. The most polished texts are hard to pull apart. If you're having trouble describing the structure of a text, make a list of the work's constituent parts and only then think about how they contribute to the whole.

When you are working carefully with an image, begin by breaking the image into visual fields. Find its horizontal or diagonal line. Sometimes this line is self-evident, as in the image below, where the highway forms horizontal lines that divide the frame. Lines like these direct the viewer's attention up or down or across; they also provide smooth movement within an image, which is important for the visual perception of most viewers. Familiar objects offer excellent picture possibilities and a chance to exercise your imagination.

EXERCISE

What structure do you see in the photograph below? How do the highway lines divide the frame? Where is your eye drawn?

Overhead View of a Cloverleaf

Audience

Audience refers to the reader(s) you have in mind when you write an essay or create a visual text. Most first-year college writers assume—mistakenly—that they are writing *solely* for their instructors rather than a larger audience beyond their classroom. Identifying the audience for a specific text is important because certain audiences have certain expectations. Consider, for example, television shows. *The Ashlee Simpson Show* is written and performed for one group of people, and *The NewsHour with Jim Lehrer* is produced for a different group.

Trying to picture the intended audience helps writers articulate what they want to say and how to say it. Writers usually ask some version of the following questions: Who is my reader? What do I have to do to help that person understand what I want to say about my subject? The first question addresses the knowledge, background, and predispositions of the reader toward the subject. The second points to the kind of information or appeal to which the reader is most likely to respond.

Thinking about their readers helps writers make decisions about appropriate subjects, the kinds of examples to include, the type and level of diction and tone to use, and the overall organization of the essay. Every writer wants to be clear and convincing.

EXERCISE

What audiences did the creators of each of these ads have in mind? What choices in imagery and language did the creators employ to "speak" to their audiences?

Visa, *It's Your Life* (page 46 *l*)

Dean College, *The Way There*

Point of View

Point of view is a term used to describe the angle of vision, the vantage point from which the writer or artist presents a story or a description or makes a point. The term also applies to the way in which the writer or artist presents readers with material.

How is the image or text framed? What's included within the frame? What's been left out? What is the point of view from which the subject is seen? It can be difficult to determine what is not included in an image or an essay, but occasionally what is excluded can be more important than what you see.

You should consider point-of-view choices when you read a verbal text as well as a visual one. For example, if you are reading a classmate's essay about going to college that talks about the friendship she developed with her roommate, you might reasonably ask how using this event to describe her university days—rather than, say, the classes she took or what she learned in them—contributes to the overall effect of the essay.

EXERCISE

Consider Dorothea Lange's famous photograph of a migrant mother and her children. Notice what happens when the same subject is framed in a different way. What are the effects of Lange's decision to focus on the faces of her subjects rather than to take their picture from farther away? How do these framing choices change Lange's point of view?

Dorothea Lange, *Migrant Mother, Nipomo, California,* 1936, three views (pages 537, 532, and 537)

Tone

Tone is a widely used term that has slightly different meanings in different disciplines. In its simplest sense, *tone* refers to the quality or character of sound. As such, tone usually describes the sound of one's voice, what Robert Frost called "the hearing imagination." Frost was talking about our natural ability to detect the tone of voice a person is using in a conversation, even if that conversation is going on behind closed doors and we are not able to hear precisely what is being said.

In music, *tone* refers to sound; in art, *tone* indicates the general effect of light in a painting or photograph. In everyday language, the word also can evoke images of the muscles in the body. In speaking and writing, *tone* is the feeling—joy, anger, skepticism—the writer uses to convey his or her expression. It also describes the degree of formality in a written work.

EXERCISE

The point of view in the Misrach photographs below is consistent; the only thing that varies is the time of day. How would you describe the tone of each of the images?

Richard Misrach, *12-23-97 5:09 PM* (page 139)

Richard Misrach, *3-3-98 6:25 PM* (page 141)

Metaphor

In writing, a metaphor is a word or phrase meaning one thing that is used to describe something else in order to suggest a likeness or analogy. *She's drowning in money* uses a metaphor of money as water to suggest an infinite quantity; it's far more descriptive than simply saying *She has more money than she needs*.

Metaphor can work in visual texts as well. Here the artist uses an image that we accept as having one meaning in a way that suggests a likeness to something completely different. Many symbolic images, or icons, in our culture have shared meaning: the American flag, Elvis Presley, the bar code. When we see these images in a context we recognize—the flag flying over the White House for example, or the bar code on the back of this book—most of us would agree that it means something in particular: a symbol for the United States; a code that marks commercial products, tracks inventory, and denotes prices. But if these symbols are used to describe something else, as in *Man Turning into a Bar Code*, they suggest something completely different (the loss of individuality in a consumer culture). When you read verbal and visual texts, pay close attention to the way the texts use symbolic language or imagery to suggest relationships.

EXERCISE

Look carefully at the three images below. What metaphors are being used in these images? What kind of relationship is suggested in each?

Nerilicon, *Natural Resources*, 2005

Arno Rafael Minkkinen, *Mountain Lakes, New Jersey, 1977*

Man Turning into a Bar Code

Context

Visual and verbal texts are not composed and published in a vacuum. As you practice reading and writing about texts, we encourage you to consider the various contexts within which they function. Gather information about the circumstances behind the original composition: Who created the text? Who was the intended audience? Where was it originally published? For what purpose? To what extent does this contextual information deepen your reading of the text?

To widen your perspective on a text, consider the larger cultural and historical context in which it was created. What cultural assumptions do you think the artist or author relied on? Asking questions about the larger cultural context of a particular text or image means recognizing the assumptions that are made about a shared body of knowledge on the part of the audience. You as a reader—with your own set of assumptions, values, knowledge, and experience—are also part of every text's larger context. What value(s) and code(s) of conduct does the writer of the text encourage you to adopt?

Context is an essential aspect of both understanding and practicing the art of composition. Asking questions about the relationship between a text and its context—or the relationship of a part to the whole—is another way to see clearly and write well.

EXERCISE

Dorothea Lange's *Migrant Mother* is one of the recognizable images in American history. What observations and inferences can you make about the context of each of the three images below? What is the bigger picture behind the three uses of the same image? For more information on Lange's *Migrant Mother*, see pages 532–44.

Dorothea Lange, *Migrant Mother*, 1936 (page 532)

Cover of *The Nation*, January 3, 2005 (page 484)

Back cover of *The Black Panthers' Newsletter*, December 7, 1972

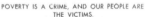

EXERCISE

Take a moment to practice the skills of seeing and writing discussed in this introduction. What do you notice first about this photograph by Joel Sternfeld? What initial observations and inferences can you make? Now consider the compositional strategies used: How would you describe the structure of the image? the photographer's point of view? the use of metaphor? Read the biographical note about Sternfeld on page 200 for contextual information on the artist and this photograph. Then write the first draft of an essay in which you make an assertion about the overall impact of this photograph based on your observations of Sternfeld's compositional strategies. Make sure to support your assertions with detailed evidence from the image.

Joel Sternfeld, *Warren Avenue at 23rd Street, Detroit, Michigan, October 1993*

1

OBSERVING THE ORDINARY

Roe Ethridge, *Kitchen Table*, 2000

Imagine the following scene: It's Thanksgiving, well into the second night of a long holiday weekend visiting your parents. You have two papers due on Monday and an exam on Tuesday. It's been only two hours since you savored the delights of a home-cooked alternative to dorm food. Yet for the third time tonight, you stand at the open refrigerator door and stare blankly inside.

What are you doing? You are looking without actually noticing. That's the kind of attention many of us give to the ordinary in our lives. Staring into the refrigerator is a common example of what might be called *passive looking*—seeing without recognizing, looking without being aware of what we're looking at. How accurately, for example, can you describe the objects most familiar to you: a penny? your favorite pair of shoes? the blanket on your bed? the food you ate this morning for breakfast? Most of us need to have ordinary things physically in front of us to describe them in detailed and accurate terms. Even if we all had the same object before us, our descriptions would likely be different, depending on who we are, the perspective from which we view the object, and the details we find important in it. *Refrigerator,* one of the series of

Roe Ethridge, *The Jones's Sun Room*, 2003

Roe Ethridge, *Ryder Truck at the Jones's*, 2003

photographs in this introduction, provides an opportunity to practice examining the messages ordinary objects can convey, messages read by photographer Roe Ethridge as a family's "values, allegiances, and memories." If we practice examining commonplace objects with both attention to and an awareness of what makes every individual's perspective unique, we can begin to characterize who we are and what we are like for ourselves and others. By *actively seeing* the details of the ordinary, we hone our skills of observation, the first step toward becoming a confident writer.

Observing the ordinary with fresh eyes sharpens our skills of description; it also helps develop our ability to draw inferences. Indeed, drawing reasonable inferences from accurate observations involves seeing more than what is actually visible. Inferences are discoveries—of something we can't immediately see from what we can see. Look at Ethridge's *Refrigerator* again. From the photographs of children and children's drawings posted on the refrigerator, we can infer that children live in the household or are an important part of this family's life.

Observing the ordinary is both the simplest skill to start exercising as a writer and a practical means

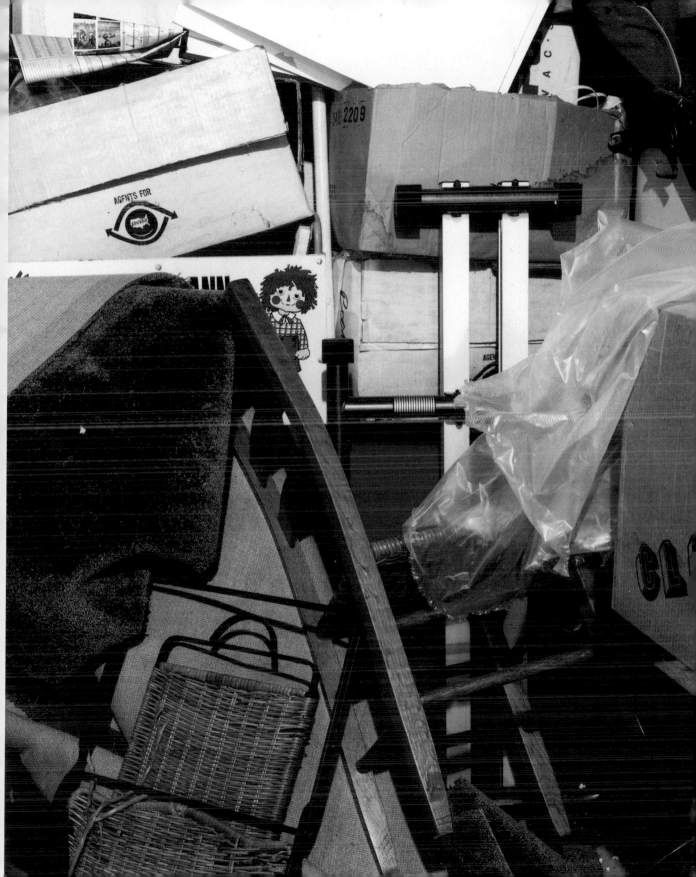

Roe Ethridge, *Basement Carpet*, 2004

of training ourselves to think and write analytically. When we are actively looking at the ordinary, we realize that what seems ordinary can be more complicated than what we might at first have recognized. What might be regarded by some as ordinary may well be viewed by others as exceptional. Consider, for example, a car. Some people take owning a car for granted; for others, it is a luxury they can't afford. (Can you identify things that you view as ordinary in your own life that certain classmates would likely regard as exceptional?) We also invest ordinary objects with private and public meanings. Each of us might relate to an ordinary object— a toothbrush, a coffee cup, a pencil—in different ways, yet we are likely to share at least some of the public significance attributed to these ordinary objects in American culture.

As you practice writing descriptions that will make your readers see what is extraordinary in your everyday life, you'll also be practicing active seeing, seeing the world around you more carefully. To be an effective thinker and writer, you need to bring all of your sight—and insight—to bear on what is around you. If you notice and attend to the ordinary, if you devote focused and sustained attention to it, you increase the likelihood of becoming someone on whom, as the novelist Henry James once said, "nothing is lost."

Each of the selections in this chapter presents the ordinary in some extraordinary way. The work of Roe Ethridge and of other photographers throughout the chapter conveys the clarity of attention a photographer gives an object through the lens of a camera; the paintings by Alfred Leslie and others show what can result when high art meets mundane subjects; and the essays by Larry Woiwode, John Updike, Brian Doyle, Annie Dillard, K. C. Cole, and others demonstrate how writing can make us see something clearly that we would not otherwise have noticed.

ROE ETHRIDGE

Roe Ethridge (b. 1969), received a BFA from the Atlanta College of Art. Today he lives and works in New York. He moves easily between photographic genres and venues, from landscapes to commercial portraits, without regard for traditional distinctions between high and low art, fine and commercial art, and documentary and staged images. Working in color, with a large-format camera, Ethridge frequently photographs album and book covers for emerging musicians and writers, and contributes to magazines like *Tokion* and *Purple* as well as the *New York Times Magazine.* Much of his work, like this collection of photographs, reflects a contemporary culture in which commercialized images abound. "Everything is involved in production and distribution," he says in a *Contemporary* magazine interview. Yet his cluttered still lifes and messy domestic scenes with beer bottles, garbage bags, and plastic buckets suggest the harmonious composition of their fine-art precedents even as they reject them.

Since 2000, Ethridge has had three solo exhibitions at the Andrew Kreps Gallery in New York City and in other galleries. He also has been included in group shows at PS 1 (New York), the Barbican (London), and Art/35/Basel.

Visit seeingandwriting.com for an interview with Roe Ethridge.

SEEING

1. How would you describe each of Ethridge's photographs of ordinary scenes to someone who has not seen them? What specific words and phrases would you use to characterize what you see in these photographs? Which details—textures, colors, objects, shapes—stand out the most to you? Why? Choose one of Ethridge's photographs. What story (or stories) does the photograph suggest to you? If, for example, you chose *Refrigerator,* what relationship do you see between and among the objects on the refrigerator door?

2. Choose one of Ethridge's photographs and comment on the framing of the image. How does Ethridge frame the refrigerator, for example? What particular patterns link the items on the refrigerator door to what can be seen in the rest of the kitchen? What are the effects of Ethridge's having taken this picture as the family dog crossed his line of sight? How does the appearance of the dog add to—or detract from—the image captured in the photograph? How would the image have changed if Ethridge had waited for the dog to be fully visible in the picture?

WRITING

1. Consider Ethridge's photograph *Refrigerator* as an artistic statement of a family's "values, allegiances, and memories." Choose two or three words that you think accurately describe what is being communicated by this photograph. Write a descriptive paragraph on each of these words, using evidence from this photograph to illustrate your choice. How would seeing *Refrigerator* in a different context—in an advertisement, for example— change the way you read it?

2. Look through a popular magazine and make notes about the kinds of ordinary objects presented in its advertising and editorial content. What images of the ordinary do you find there? How are the images of these objects presented, and for what purpose? Choose one presentation of ordinary objects and compare it with Ethridge's photographs of ordinary objects (pages 28–34). Write an essay comparing and contrasting the methods the magazine uses with those Ethridge uses to present the experience of observing the ordinary.

Abelardo Morell, *Pencil, 2000*

Pair: Morell & Petroski

THE PENCIL
Henry Petroski

HENRY DAVID THOREAU SEEMED TO THINK OF everything when he made a list of essential supplies for a twelve-day excursion into the Maine woods. He included pins, needles, and thread among the items to be carried in an India-rubber knapsack, and he even gave the dimensions of an ample tent: "six by seven feet, and four feet high in the middle, will do." He wanted to be doubly sure to be able to start a fire and to wash up, and so he listed: "matches (some also in a small vial in the waist-coat pocket); soap, two pieces." He specified the number of old newspapers (three or four, presumably to be used for cleaning chores), the length of strong cord (twenty feet), the size of his blanket (seven feet long), and the amount of "soft hardbread" (twenty-eight pounds!). He even noted something to leave behind: "A gun is not worth the carriage, unless you go as a huntsman."

Thoreau actually was a huntsman of sorts, but the insects and botanical specimens that he hunted could be taken without a gun and could be brought back in the knapsack. Thoreau also went into the woods as an observer. He observed the big and the little, and he advised like-minded observers to carry a small spyglass for birds and a pocket microscope for smaller

objects. And to capture the true dimensions of those objects that might be too big to be brought back, Thoreau advised carrying a tape measure. The inveterate measurer, note taker, and list maker also reminded other travelers to take paper and stamps, to mail letters back to civilization.

But there is one object that Thoreau neglected to mention, one that he most certainly carried himself. For without this object Thoreau could not have sketched either the fleeting fauna he would not shoot or the larger flora he could not uproot. Without it he could not label his blotting paper pressing leaves or his insect boxes holding beetles; without it he could not record the measurements he made; without it he could not write home on the paper he brought; without it he could not make his list. Without a pencil Thoreau would have been lost in the Maine woods.

According to his friend Ralph Waldo Emerson, Thoreau seems always to have carried, "in his pocket, his diary and pencil." So why did Thoreau—who had worked with his father to produce the very best lead pencils manufactured in America in the 1840s—neglect to list even one among the essential things to take on an excursion? Perhaps the very object with which he may have been drafting his list was too close to him, too familiar a part of his own everyday outfit, too integral a part of his livelihood, too common a thing for him to think to mention.

Henry Thoreau seems not to be alone in forgetting about the pencil. A shop in London specializes in old carpenter's tools. There are tools everywhere, from floor to ceiling and spilling out of baskets on the sidewalk outside. The shop seems to have an example of every kind of saw used in recent centuries; there are shelves of braces and bins of chisels and piles of levels and rows of planes—everything for the carpenter, or so it seems. What the shop does not have, however, are old carpenter's pencils, items that once got equal billing in Thoreau & Company advertisements with drawing pencils for artists and engineers. The implement that was necessary to draw sketches of the carpentry job, to figure the quantities of materials needed, to mark the length of wood to be cut, to indicate the locations of holes to be drilled, to highlight the edges of wood to be planed, is nowhere to be seen. When asked where he keeps the pencils, the shopkeeper replies that he does not think there are any about. Pencils, he admits, are often found in the toolboxes acquired by the shop, but they are thrown out with the sawdust.

In an American antique shop that deals in, among other things, old scientific and engineering instruments, there is a grand display of polished brass microscopes, telescopes, levels, balances, and scales; there are the precision instruments of physicians, navigators, surveyors, draftsmen, and engineers. The shop also has a collection of old jewelry and silverware and, behind the saltcellars, some old mechanical pencils, which appear to be there for their metal and mystery and not their utility. There are a clever Victorian combination pen and pencil in a single slender, if ornate, gold case; an unassuming little tube of brass less than two inches long that telescopes out to become a mechanical pencil of twice that length; a compact silver pencil case containing points in three colors—black, red, and blue—that can be slid into writing position; and a heavy silver pencil case that hides the half-inch stub of a still-sharpened yellow pencil of high quality. The shopkeeper will proudly show how all these work, but when asked if she has any plain wood-cased drawing pencils that the original owners of the drafting instruments must certainly have used, she will confess that she would not even know what distinguished a nineteenth-century pencil from any other kind.

Not only shops that purport to trade in the past but also museums that ostensibly preserve and display the past can seem to forget or merely ignore the indispensable role of simple objects like the pencil. Recently the Smithsonian Institution's National Museum of American History produced "After the Revolution: Everyday Life in America, 1780–1800," and one group of exhibits in the show consisted of separate worktables on which were displayed the tools of many crafts of the period: cabinetmaker and chairmaker, carpenter and joiner, shipwright, cooper, wheelwright, and others. Besides tools, many of the displays included pieces of work in progress, and a few even had wood shavings scattered about the work space, to add a sense of authenticity. Yet there was not a pencil to be seen.

While many early American craftsmen would have used sharp-pointed metal scribers to mark their work, pencils would also certainly have been used when they were available. And although there was no domestic pencil industry in America in the years immediately following the Revolution, that is not to say that pencils could not be gotten. A father, writing in 1774 from England to his daughter in what were still the colonies, sent her "one dozen Middleton's best Pencils," and in the last part of the century, even after the Revolution, English pencils like Middleton's were regularly advertised for sale in the larger cities. Imported pencils or homemade pencils fashioned from reclaimed pieces of broken lead would have been the proud possessions of woodworkers especially, for carpenters, cabinetmakers, and joiners possessed the craft skill to work wood into a form that could hold pieces of graphite in a comfortable and useful way. Not only would early American woodworkers have known about, admired, wanted to possess, and tried to imitate European pencils, but also they would have prized and cared for them as they prized and cared for the kinds of tools displayed two centuries later in the Smithsonian.

These stories of absence are interesting not so much because of what they say about the lowly status of the wood-cased pencil as an artifact as because of what they say about our awareness of and our attitudes toward common things, processes, events, or even ideas that appear to have little intrinsic, permanent, or special value. An object like the pencil is generally considered unremarkable, and it is taken for granted. It is taken for granted because it is abundant, inexpensive, and as familiar as speech.

Yet the pencil need be no cliché. It can be as powerful a metaphor as the pen, as rich a symbol as the flag. Artists have long counted the pencil among the tools of their trade, and have even identified with the drawing medium. Andrew Wyeth described his pencil as a fencer's foil; Toulouse-Lautrec said of himself, "I am a pencil"; and the Moscow-born Paris illustrator and caricaturist Emmanuel Poiré took his pseudonym from the Russian word for pencil, *karandash*. In turn, the Swiss pencil-making firm of Caran d'Ache was named after this artist, and a stylized version of his signature is now used as a company logo.

The pencil, the tool of doodlers, stands for thinking and creativity, but at the same time, as the toy of children, it symbolizes spontaneity and immaturity. Yet the pencil's graphite is also the ephemeral medium of thinkers, planners, drafters, architects, and engineers, the medium to be erased, revised, smudged, obliterated, lost—or inked over. Ink, on the other hand, whether in a book or on plans or on a contract, signifies finality and supersedes the pencil drafts and sketches. If early pencilings interest collectors, it is often because of their association with the permanent success written or drawn in ink. Unlike graphite, to which paper is like sandpaper, ink flows smoothly and fills in the nooks and crannies of creation. Ink is the cosmetic that ideas will wear when they go out in public. Graphite is their dirty truth. ○

ABELARDO MORELL

Born in Cuba in 1948 and raised in New York City, Abelardo Morell is an internationally recognized photographer whose work has been collected by many major museums, among them the Museum of Modern Art in New York City and the Art Institute of Chicago. Currently a professor at the Massachusetts College of Art, Morell received a Guggenheim Fellowship in 1993 and has published several books, including *Retrospective Photographs* (2005). He is best known for his radical use of *camera obscura,* a technique in which the image of an object is received through a small opening or lens and focused on a natural surface rather than recorded on a film or plate. Morell's body of work also includes many large-format black-and-white photographs of everyday objects. "I am really rebelling against—maybe rebelling is too strong a word—the standard way in which things are supposed to be looked at," Morell said in an interview with writer-photographer Robert Birnbaum in 2003.

In *Pencil, 2000,* Morell transforms a commonplace object using only light, shadow, and a long exposure time. Among his other vivid images of ordinary things are a looming stack of toy blocks seen from a child's perspective, the deep black interior of an empty grocery bag, and a pan full of swirling soapy water. As the writer David Levi Strauss has said of these simple but powerful images, "Though they take time to astonish, astonish they do."

HENRY PETROSKI

Henry Petroski (b. 1942), the Aleksandar S. Vesic Professor of Civil Engineering and a professor of history at Duke University, has been called "America's poet laureate of technology." He chose the pencil as the subject of his 1990 book, *The Pencil: A History of Design and Circumstance,* from which this excerpt is taken, because he considers it the perfect vehicle to explain engineering methods. In the March–April 2000 issue of *American Scientist,* Petroski describes how he was inspired to write the book after a visit to Walden Pond because "[Thoreau] believed in the value of the microcosm as a means of making the seemingly inaccessible complexities of the world accessible."

In addition to *The Pencil,* Petroski has published many other books, including *Design Paradigms: Case Histories of Error and Judgment in Engineering* (cited as the "best general engineering book published in 1994" by the Association of American Publishers), *Remaking the World: Adventures in Engineering* (1997), and *Pushing the Limits: New Adventures in Engineering* (2004).

Petroski has received numerous awards, including a Guggenheim Fellowship, and is a member of the American Academy of Arts and Sciences. He writes regular engineering columns for *American Scientist* and *ASEE Prism.*

SEEING

1. What is your first impression of Abelardo Morell's photograph *Pencil, 2000*? What characteristics of the pencil does Morell seem to emphasize? With what effect(s)? How is your overall understanding of the photograph after studying it different from your initial impression? What senses in addition to sight does the photograph evoke? With what effect?

2. Now turn your attention to Henry Petroski's prose account of the pencil. To what extent does invoking Henry David Thoreau reinforce the overall impression he is trying to create in his account of the origins of the pencil?

3. Compare and contrast the effectiveness of Morell's photograph and Petroski's words as projections of the importance of the pencil. Which artistic vision of the pencil do you find more appealing? Why? What can descriptive writing accomplish that photography cannot? And what can a photograph do that words cannot?

WRITING

1. Morell's photograph and Petroski's prose account of the pencil offer two very different perspectives on an ordinary object. Choose another ordinary object—a ballpoint pen, a stapler, a paper cup, for example—and write the first draft of an essay in which you make as many observations as possible about the object. Then use your description as a basis for drawing inferences about the object's distinctive character.

2. Morell and Petroski use different artistic strategies to focus their audience's attention on the importance of the pencil. What artistic tools can Morell draw on in his photograph that are not available to Petroski in his prose account of the pencil? Write an essay in which you analyze the nature and extent of the different effects produced by a photograph and an essay.

character: The combination of features or qualities that distinguishes one person, group, or object from another.

Ode to an Orange

Larry Woiwode

OH, THOSE ORANGES ARRIVING IN THE MIDST OF the North Dakota winters of the forties—the mere color of them, carried through the door in a net bag or a crate from out of the white winter landscape. Their appearance was enough to set my brother and me to thinking that it might be about time to develop an illness, which was the surest way of receiving a steady supply of them.

"Mom, we think we're getting a cold."

"*We?* You mean, you two want an orange?"

This was difficult for us to answer or dispute; the matter seemed moved beyond our mere wanting.

"If you want an orange," she would say, "why 5 don't you ask for one?"

"We want an orange."

"'We' again. *'We want an orange.'*"

"May we have an orange, please."

"That's the way you know I like you to ask for one. Now, why don't each of you ask for one in that same way, but separately?"

"Mom..." And so on. There was no depth of 10 degradation that we wouldn't descend to in order to get one. If the oranges hadn't wended their way northward by Thanksgiving, they were sure to arrive before the Christmas season, stacked first in crates at the depot, filling that musty place, where pews sat back to back, with a springtime acidity, as if the building had been rinsed with a renewing elixir that set it right for yet another year. Then the crates would appear at the local grocery store, often with the top slats pried back on a few of them, so that we were aware of a resinous smell of fresh wood in addition to the already orangy atmosphere that foretold the season more explicitly than any calendar.

And in the broken-open crates (as if burst by the power of the oranges themselves), one or two of the lovely spheres would lie free of the tissue they came wrapped in—always purple tissue, as if that were the only color that could contain the populations of them in their nestled positions. The crates bore paper labels at one end—of an orange against a blue background, or of a blue goose against an orange background— signifying the colorful otherworld (unlike our wintry one) that these phenomena had arisen from. Each orange, stripped of its protective wrapping, as vivid in your vision as a pebbled sun, encouraged you to picture a whole pyramid of them in a bowl on your dining room table, glowing in the light, as if giving off the warmth that came through the windows from the real winter sun. And all of them came stamped with a blue-purple name as foreign as the otherworld that you might imagine as their place of origin, so that on Christmas day you would find yourself digging past everything else in your Christmas stocking, as if tunneling down to the country of China, in order to reach the rounded bulge at the tip of the toe which meant that you had received a personal reminder of another state of existence, wholly separate from your own.

The packed heft and texture, finally, of an orange in your hand—this is it!—and the eruption of smell and the watery fireworks as a knife, in the hand of someone skilled, like our mother, goes slicing through the skin so perfect for slicing. This gaseous spray can form a mist like smoke, which can then be lit with a match to create actual fireworks if there is a chance to hide alone with a match (matches being forbidden) and the peel from one. Sputtery ignitions can also be produced by squeezing a peel near a candle (at least one candle is generally always going at Christmastime), and the leftover peels are set on the stove top to scent the house.

And the ingenious way in which oranges come packed into their globes! The green nib at the top, like a detonator, can be bitten off, as if disarming the orange, in order to clear a place for you to sink a tooth under the peel. This is the best way to start. If you bite at the peel too much, your front teeth will feel scraped, like dry bone, and your lips will begin to burn from the bitter oil. Better to sink a tooth into this greenish or creamy depression, and then pick at that point with the nail of your thumb, removing a little piece of the peel at a time. Later, you might want to practice to see how large a piece you can remove intact. The peel can also be undone in one continuous ribbon, a feat which maybe your father is able to perform, so that after the orange is freed, looking yellowish, the peel, rewound, will stand in its original shape, although empty.

The yellowish whole of the orange can now be divided into sections, usually about a dozen, by beginning with a division down the middle; after this, each section, enclosed in its papery skin, will be able to be lifted and torn loose more easily. There is a stem up the center of the sections like a mushroom stalk, but tougher; this can be eaten. A special variety of orange, without any pits, has an extra growth, or nubbin, like half of a tiny orange, tucked into its bottom. This nubbin is nearly as bitter as the peel, but it can be eaten, too; don't worry. Some of the sections will have miniature sections embedded in them and clinging as if for life, giving the impression that babies are being hatched, and should you happen to find some of these you've found the sweetest morsels of any.

If you prefer to have your orange sliced in half, as some people do, the edges of the peel will abrade the corners of your mouth, making them feel raw, as you eat down into the white of the rind (which is the only way to do it) until you can see daylight through the orangy bubbles composing its outside. Your eyes might burn; there is no proper way to eat an orange. If there are pits, they can get in the way, and the slower you eat an orange, the more you'll find your fingers sticking together. And no matter how carefully you eat one, or bite into a quarter, juice can always fly or slip from a corner of your mouth; this

happens to everyone. Close your eyes to be on the safe side, and for the eruption in your mouth of the slivers of watery meat, which should be broken and rolled fine over your tongue for the essence of orange. And if indeed you have sensed yourself coming down with a cold, there is a chance that you will feel it driven from your head—your nose and sinuses suddenly opening—in the midst of the scent of a peel and eating an orange.

And oranges can also be eaten whole—rolled into a spongy mass and punctured with a pencil (if you don't find this offensive) or a knife, and then sucked upon. Then, once the juice is gone, you can disembowel the orange as you wish and eat away its pulpy remains, and eat once more into the whitish interior of the peel, which scours the coating from your teeth and makes your numbing lips and tip of your tongue start to tingle and swell up from behind, until, in the light from the windows (shining through an empty glass bowl), you see orange again from the inside. Oh, oranges, solid *o*'s, light from afar in the midst of the freeze, and not unlike that unspherical fruit which first went from Eve to Adam and from there (to abbreviate matters) to my brother and me.

"Mom, we think we're getting a cold."

"You mean, you want an orange?"

This is difficult to answer or dispute or even to acknowledge, finally, with the fullness that the subject deserves, and that each orange bears, within its own makeup, into this hard-edged yet insubstantial, incomplete, cold, wintry world. ○

LARRY WOIWODE

Larry Woiwode (b. 1941) grew up in North Dakota and Illinois. After moving to New York City in his twenties, he began to publish poems and stories in *The New Yorker, The Atlantic, Harper's,* and other prestigious magazines. Among his books are the highly acclaimed novels *What I'm Going to Do, I Think* (1969) and *Beyond the Bedroom Wall* (1975). In 1978 he moved back to North Dakota, where he lives on a small farm and continues to write. Woiwode published a memoir, *What I Think I Did,* in 2001.

Woiwode uses precise observation and a sense of place to open up his fictional worlds. He notes that there "seems to be a paradox in writing fiction. For some reason the purest and simplest sentences permit the most meaning to adhere to them. In other words, the more specific a simple sentence is about a place in North Dakota, let us say, the more someone from outside that region seems to read universality into it." Although "Ode to an Orange" focuses on an object rather than a place, the same principle applies. In engagingly detailed sentences, Woiwode remembers specific experiences but evokes a universal romance with an ideal orange. This selection first appeared in *Paris Review* in 1985.

SEEING

1. Larry Woiwode lingers on the special qualities of what most of us would view as an ordinary piece of fruit. What impression of an orange does Woiwode create? When, how, and why does he draw on each of the five senses to create this overall effect?

2. In addition to description, what other techniques does Woiwode use to evoke such a vibrant orange? What does he mean when he says that the oranges of his youth signified "the colorful otherworld" (para. 11)? What range of associations do the oranges of his youth evoke in Woiwode now? He was a child in the 1940s and 1950s, the same time that labels like "Have One" (page 48) were used to promote the fruit. If you consider the essay and the crate label together, does the way you see each one change? Why or why not?

WRITING

1. Consider Woiwode's title: "Ode to an Orange." How does his essay satisfy the expectations usually associated with the word ode? Write your own ode to a piece of fruit. The goal is to evoke longing in your readers.

2. Woiwode uses each of the five senses—touch, sound, sight, smell, and taste—to convey the appeal of an orange. Imagine that only four senses were available to you. Which sense would you give up? Write the first draft of an essay explaining your choice and using examples from Woiwode's work to support your argument.

ode: A formal lyric poem, usually written in an elevated style and voice, usually praising a person or thing.

Sequoia Citrus Association, *Have One*, 1920s

California Orange Growers, *Orange Crate Labels*, early 20th century

SEQUOIA CITRUS ASSOCIATION

From the late 1880s through the 1950s, California citrus growers and farmers relied on colorful paper labels to promote the fruits and vegetables they shipped in wooden crates throughout the United States. Designed primarily to attract wholesale buyers in distant markets, these distinctive examples of commercial art also helped to promote an idealized image of California and to lure seekers of sunshine and fortune. Many early labels accentuated the image of California as a land of plenty, innocence, and beauty. Pastoral images and allegorical scenes soon yielded to the accelerated pace and more sophisticated look of urban life: bolder typography, darker colors, and the billboard-like graphics associated with automobile advertisements.

The use of paper labels ended when corporate interests overshadowed individual and family enterprises, when small private groves were consumed by cooperatives or turned into sites for tract-home communities, and when cardboard cartons replaced wooden crates.

The orange crate label for the Have One brand, which appeared in the 1920s, and the other labels reprinted here from the early twentieth century offer striking examples of the graphics and themes used to identify brand names through easily remembered images.

SEEING

1. The label used by the Sequoia Citrus Association to identify its oranges looks simple: a hand, an orange, a brand name. But as you examine the label more carefully, do you notice anything that makes the image more complicated? What about the hand makes it distinct? How does its placement reinforce—or subvert—the invitation to have an orange? What are the advantages—and the disadvantages—of using an imperative in the headline ("Have One")? Is anything being sold here besides an orange?

2. Look at each of the graphic elements in the label. What do you notice about the placement of the forearm and hand? What effects does the artist achieve by superimposing the forearm and hand on the image? What aspects of the fruit does the artist highlight to call attention to the orange? What other graphic elements help focus the viewer's attention on the orange and its succulence? In what ways does the typography used in the name of the brand reinforce or detract from the effectiveness of this graphic design?

have: (1) to possess a thing or a privilege, as in *to have permission;* (2) to receive, as in *I had some news;* (3) to feel an obligation to do, as in *to have a deadline;* (4) to aquire or get possession of a person or thing, as in *I had him where I wanted him;* (5) to be characterized by a certain quality, as in *I have blue eyes;* (6) to use or exercise a quality, as in *to have pity;* (7) to trick or fool, as in *I was had;* (8) to be forced to do something, as in *I have to go.*

WRITING

1. What products are most often identified with the community in which you live or attend college? Choose one product that interests you, and conduct preliminary research on its earliest commercial representations. (You might check the holdings in the periodical and rare-book sections of your library, or you might visit the local historical society.) Focusing on one example of commercial art used to promote this product, write an analytical essay in which you show how the graphic elements and language borrow from or help reinforce the identity of this particular community.

2. Cryptic advertising imperatives that never explicitly name the product they are promoting (e.g., "Just do it" or "Enjoy the ride") are used in many contemporary ads and commercials. Which is more effective in these ads—the image or the language? Choose a cryptic ad or commercial for any product, and write an expository essay about why you think the ad or commercial does or does not work.

LEONG KA TAI

Leong Ka Tai is an award-winning journalist whose photographs have appeared in *National Geographic, Life, Time,* and *Fortune.* Born in Hong Kong in 1952 and educated at Rice University in Houston, Texas, Leong is a founding member of the Hong Kong Institute of Professional Photographers. He has published many books, including *Macau Gardens and Landscape Art* (2000) with one of Portugal's leading landscape architects, Francisco Caldeira Cabral.

Leong took this photograph of the Wu family in Shiping, Yunan Province, China, on November 26, 1993. He was one of sixteen photographers at work on a project to identify "statistically average" families in thirty countries. Each of the photographers lived with, photographed, and videotaped a representative family for a week. At the end of that week, the family was photographed outside its home with all its worldly goods on display.

Heading up the project was photojournalist Peter Menzel. In the Afterword to *Material World: A Global Family Portrait* (1994), Menzel explains his decision to profile average families around the world: "I thought the world needed a reality check. Newspaper, magazine, and television stories almost always deal with the extremes: famine, flood, mass killing, and, of course, the lifestyles of the rich and famous."

SEEING

1. In *Material World,* what is essentially a collection of family portraits is juxtaposed with statistics and bulleted lists of the objects and people represented, as reproduced here. How does the accompanying information influence how you read the photographs? How might you read the photos differently if, instead of statistics, the pictures were "explained" by quotations from Guo Yu Xian about cooking for her family or other aspects of their daily lives?

2. Cover up the list of objects in the first photo (pages 54–55) and make your own list of everything you can identify. Then compare your list with the "official" one. How many things did you miss? Why, if the objects are so important, do you think the photographer chose to capture the family in three spaces—boat, courtyard, and river bank—relatively empty of things?

WRITING

1. Imagine that you and your family have been asked to participate in a contemporary version of the Material World project. How would an inventory of your possessions compare with the inventory of the Wus' possessions? Which objects would you want featured most prominently in the portrait? Which members of your family would be included? Write a set of captions for your hypothetical portrait, including a key to the picture, a list of objects in the photograph, and a set of family statistics. In lieu of an actual portrait, write a one-page description of how you would imagine composing your family portrait for the project.

2. Charles C. Mann provided the text for *Material World.* He writes: "Everywhere the Earth is habitable, it is inhabited. Homes stipple the landscape from Capetown to Nome. In each of them are mothers, fathers, and children—a billion families in total, perhaps, each full of wants and needs. It is foolish to imagine that they will not seek to fulfill them, surely immoral to try to block them from doing so. Yet satisfying their needs benignly will require enormous wisdom if we are to keep people feeling whole, to treat all fairly, and to be graceful stewards of our natural environment. Can all the people on Earth have all the things they want?" Write an essay in which you answer Mann's question, citing evidence—current projections for the supply of energy, for example—to support your argument.

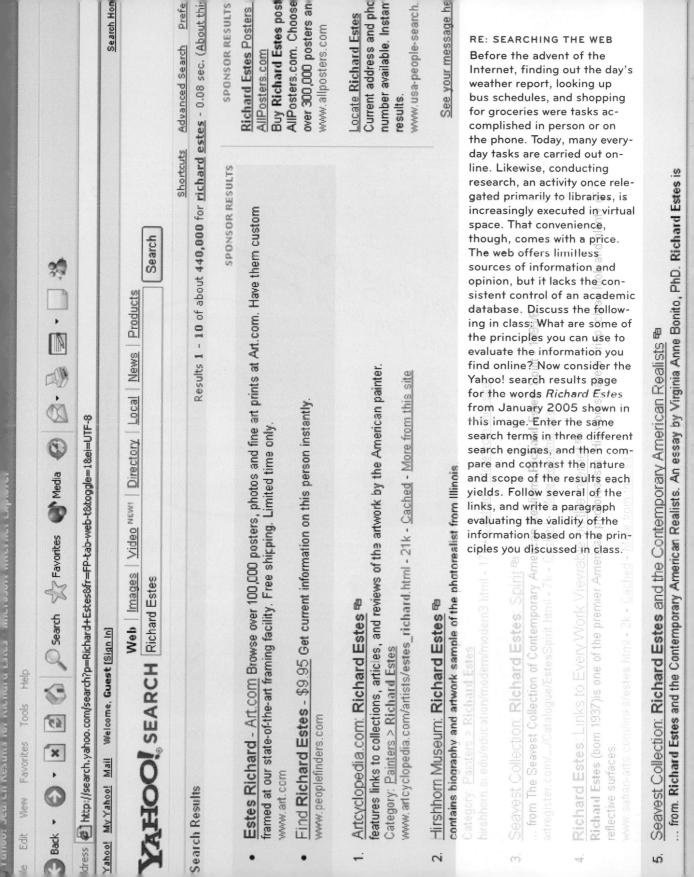

RE: SEARCHING THE WEB

Before the advent of the Internet, finding out the day's weather report, looking up bus schedules, and shopping for groceries were tasks accomplished in person or on the phone. Today, many everyday tasks are carried out online. Likewise, conducting research, an activity once relegated primarily to libraries, is increasingly executed in virtual space. That convenience, though, comes with a price. The web offers limitless sources of information and opinion, but it lacks the consistent control of an academic database. Discuss the following in class: What are some of the principles you can use to evaluate the information you find online? Now consider the Yahoo! search results page for the words *Richard Estes* from January 2005 shown in this image. Enter the same search terms in three different search engines, and then compare and contrast the nature and scope of the results each yields. Follow several of the links, and write a paragraph evaluating the validity of the information based on the principles you discussed in class.

File Edit View Favorites Tools Help

Back · · × · Search · Favorites · Media

Address: http://search.yahoo.com/search?p=Richard+Estes&fr=FP-tab-web-t&toggle=1&ei=UTF-8

Yahoo! MyYahoo! Mail Welcome, Guest [Sign In]

YAHOO! SEARCH

Web | Images | Video NEW! | Directory | Local | News | Products

Richard Estes   [Search]

Shortcuts   Advanced Search   Prefe...   Search Hom...

Search Results   Results 1 - 10 of about 440,000 for richard estes - 0.08 sec. (About thi...

1. Artcyclopedia.com: **Richard Estes**
features links to collections, articles, and reviews of the artwork by the American painter.
Category: Painters > Richard Estes
www.artcyclopedia.com/artists/estes_richard.html - 21k - Cached - More from this site

2. Hirshhorn Museum: **Richard Estes**
contains biography and artwork sample of the photorealist from Illinois.
Category: Painters > Richard Estes
hirshhorn.si.edu/education/modern/modern3.html - 17...

3. Seavest Collection: **Richard Estes** Spirit
... from The Seavest Collection of Contemporary America...
artregister.com/.../Catalogue/EstesSpirit.html - 7k - C...

4. **Richard Estes** Links to Every Work Viewable...
Richard Estes (born 1937) is one of the premier Americ...
reflective surfaces.
www.safran-arts.com/links/estes.html - 2k - Cached - More from...

5. Seavest Collection: **Richard Estes** and the Contemporary American Realists
... from **Richard Estes** and the Contemporary American Realists. An essay by Virginia Anne Bonito, PhD. **Richard Estes** is

You'll find yourself in a new world of *fun* with "P-F"! The X-Ray picture shows you just why. For here is an exclusive built-in feature that revolutionizes canvas shoe comfort! Look at all the new models...many in color, in styles to please the whole family! See them today. Remember to insist on "P-F" Canvas Shoes!

Everything you do is more fun with "P-F"

Oxfords, in all white or blue—in styles to suit the needs of children to grown ups.

The scientific foot protection that guards against flat feet, puts extra pep, spring and endurance in your legs.

1. This rigid wedge gives the bones of the foot proper orthopedic support, keeps them in their natural, normal position.

2. The sponge rubber cushion assures comfort for the sensitive area of the foot.

"P-F" means Posture Foundation

One of several sport oxfords in white or colors, for the well dressed man.

Popular athletic shoes in sand, black, brown, blue for "little" men and "big" men.

Attractive moccasin type oxfords in blue, brown, beige, white—for growing children.

"P-F" Canvas Shoes made only by B.F. Goodrich and HOOD RUBBER CO.

1940s

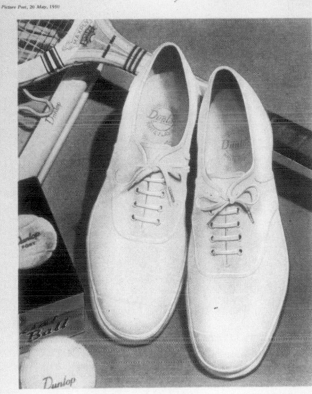

1950s

MADE FAMOUS BY WORD OF FOOT ADVERTISING.

The Nike Waffle Trainer is one of the most popular running shoes of all time.

Serious runners started wearing them years ago, for two or three good reasons.

First, the shoe has a patented Waffle sole that's designed for superior traction and cushioning of the foot when you run.

Secondly, the nylon uppers made it an extremely lightweight and comfortable shoe.

Finally, it was word of foot advertising that helped make the Nike Waffle Trainer so popular. Runners seeing other runners wearing them.

Join them.

Bring your athlete's feet to The Athlete's Foot, and tell them you want to start training on Waffles.

No one knows the athlete's foot like

The Athlete's Foot.

NIKE

272 stores...nationwide

1970s

Before Nike, people walked.

Running took off just
after we started mak-
ing running shoes.
We're still innovating;
the Air Max Light is
our most cushioned
lightweight running
shoe yet. Okay, enough
history. Go run.

1990s

2002

Tracey Baran, *Mom Ironing*, 1997

TRACEY BARAN

Tracey Baran was born in Bath, New York, in 1975. She moved to New York City in 1993 and began studying at the School of Visual Arts. Since then, Baran's photographs have been featured in museums and galleries in New York, London, and Busan, Korea.

This photograph is from a 1999 series entitled *Give and Take* that focuses on the literal and emotional landscape of Baran's childhood. When asked how she came to photograph her family life, she explained, "I was trying to figure out myself and how I reacted to certain things. I noticed my reactions were like my parents'. It's all pretty much based on my family life in upstate New York. Studying them was like studying myself. I just wanted to show the relationships between each family member and how people live and the care they give to themselves and things that are important to them."

Baran's most recent exhibition was shown at Leslie Tonkonow Artworks + Projects, a gallery in New York City in 2004.

SEEING

1. Tracey Baran's *Mom Ironing* illustrates her remarkable ability to portray ordinary activities and scenes as engaging and enduring subjects for artistic expression. What, in your view, happens to a commonplace activity such as ironing when it is captured in Baran's photograph? What do you notice about the activity presented here? Carefully examine the context within which the ironing occurs. What do you notice about the scene captured in this photograph? How would you characterize the relationship between and among the objects and people depicted in this photograph? Given what you see in this image, what is the likelihood of effective communication between the older woman and the younger woman? What details in the photograph prompt you to draw your inferences?

2. Imagine yourself in a museum viewing Baran's *Mom Ironing.* How would seeing the photograph as part of an exhibit change your understanding and appreciation of it? How would Baran's attitude influence your reading of her artistic purpose? What do you think Baran "says" in this image? On what grounds could you argue that *Mom Ironing* is a work of art? How would you defend that argument?

WRITING

1. Make a list of commonplace activities, ones that you've performed so often that you seldom think carefully about them. Choose one, and write an expository essay in which you focus your attention—and your readers'—on the details of this everyday activity or ritual. In what ways do you personalize this otherwise commonplace activity?

2. Make a list of specific similarities and differences between the scenes and relationships depicted in this photograph and in Tillie Olsen's story "I Stand Here Ironing" (page 66). After you have reread the photograph and story carefully, several times, write the first draft of an essay in which you compare and contrast the aesthetic appeal—and effectiveness—of the photograph and story.

Richard Estes, *Central Savings*, 1975 (oil on canvas)

Visualizing Composition: Close Reading

As you read each text in *Seeing & Writing*, visual or verbal, we encourage you to read closely. Doing so involves making observations about details in the text that you find engaging and memorable, and then drawing reasonable inferences from those observations. Reading closely means focusing your attention on details—that is, on specific aspects of technique, content, or style. Close reading is a part of the composition process: It is the basis for analyzing a text, for figuring out exactly why and how it works. Richard Estes uses precise detail in creating the painting *Central Savings*. The work evokes a concrete sense of a seemingly ordinary experience: walking past a storefront diner and encountering a reflection in the window of a broader scene. Here you see an example of how one student highlighted every detail she could identify in Estes's painting, along with the comments she made in the margin.

Practice reading closely. For this exercise, assume you have been asked to write an essay on how Estes evokes the senses by contrasting perception and reality in his work. Pencil in hand, examine the painting carefully a second or even a third time with your specific question in mind, marking every example you find.

1. When I first looked at this image, I couldn't tell whether it was a photograph or a painting.

2. If it was a photograph, I thought it must have been a double exposure.

3. I first noticed the countertop and the bar stools in what looks like a coffee shop or diner. I also noticed the reflection of the word *Burger* in the window of the restaurant. The counters are empty, and they seem to reflect images that seem to repeat themselves over and over.

4. Then I noticed the phrase *Central Savings* over the word *Burger* and that the phrase was reversed in the window, just like the word *Burger*.

5. Then I noticed the clock, but I couldn't tell whether it also was a reflection in the window.

6. As I looked more carefully at the image, I saw that there were outlines or shadows of people in the foreground. They appeared to be walking past the window.

7. Then I noticed the silver metal strip at the bottom of the picture, which led my eye to the silver metal border on the left of the image.

8. My attention was then drawn to the different colors in the picture—to the red countertops, the yellow colors of the buildings seen in the window, and to the dark-colored figures walking by, and, finally, to the tiny triangle of blue sky that appears between the buildings.

9. I wasn't sure it was a painting until I read the caption "oil on canvas."

Gueorgui Pinkhassov, *Pregame Prayer, Billy Ryan High School, Denton, Texas*

Gueorgui Pinkhassov, *Salat-ul-Zuhr (Noon) Prayers, Mardigian Library, University of Michigan–Dearborn*

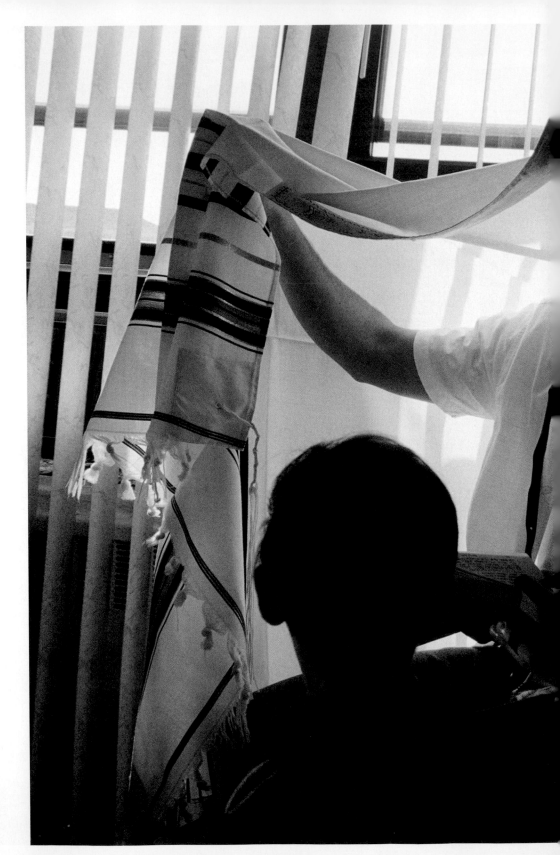

Gueorgui Pinkhassov, *Shacharit (Morning) Prayer, Kew Gardens Hills, Queens*

Gueorgui Pinkhassov, *Day of Miracles Ceremony, Land of Medicine Buddha, Soquel, California*

Gueorgui Pinkhassov, *Bedtime Prayer, The Robertson Family, Frisco, Texas*

Gueorgui Pinkhassov, *Satnam Waheguru Prayer, Minar's Taj Palace, New York*

Alfred Leslie, *Television Moon*

ALFRED LESLIE

Alfred Leslie's eye for sharp, sometimes hyperrealistic detail and his technical mastery suggest an artist steeped in the conventions of realist painting. But when Leslie first made his mark in the art world, in the late 1940s, it was as an abstract expressionist. In the 1950s he turned increasingly to narrative forms, first in film and then in his art. In fact, the stories related by many of his paintings contain a moral, in the sense that he challenges viewers to consider ethical interpretations of scenes and events. Leslie once stated he hoped to create "art like the art of David, Caravaggio, and Rubens, meant to influence the conduct of people."

Born in New York City in 1927, Leslie studied briefly at New York University and has been an independent painter since 1946. His work has been included in numerous prestigious exhibitions, and his awards include a Guggenheim Fellowship. He lives and paints in New York City.

abstract expressionist: A member of a school of painting that has little interest in representing the world realistically.

SEEING

1. Leslie's painting *Television Moon* subtly disrupts a centuries-old artistic tradition: the still life. Traditional still-life painters use simplicity and clarity to call attention to objects their audience knows well. Look closely at the painting. Where does your eye rest when you study *Television Moon*? How many objects do you see? What details do you notice about each? Look again at the television. What additional details do you notice about it? What reasonable inferences can you draw from these details and their relation to the other objects depicted?

2. In one sense, still-life paintings simply describe objects in the material world. In another, the artists who create still-life scenes often do so to interpret and comment on them. In what ways can Leslie's painting be said to interpret or serve as a commentary on contemporary American life and culture?

still life: Celebrating such ordinary objects as a bowl of fruit or a vase with flowers, still-life paintings encourage us to view familiar objects in distinct new ways.

Visit seeingandwriting.com for an interactive exercise on this selection.

WRITING

1. Using precise description, translate Leslie's *Television Moon* into a one-page verbal still life. The goal is for your readers to be able to sketch the painting on the basis of your description. (You might want to ask someone to try this after you've finished to see how close you've come.)

2. Antidrug campaigns have used an unusual version of the still life—an egg in a frying pan—to represent the danger drugs pose to our brains. Choose an object (e.g., a dollar bill, a syringe, a remote control, a mountain bike) that represents something you believe should be changed in contemporary American life. Write an essay in two parts. First, describe, either verbally or visually, how you would convey a moral message about the object through a still life. Second, discuss the effectiveness of this approach.

RESPONDING VISUALLY

Choose an ordinary object and compose a photographic still life of it. How can you use framing, lighting, and tone to create unusual angles on the mundane? Write a one-page description of your compositional choices to accompany your photograph.

TALKING PICTURES
Since the first episode aired in 1992, MTV's *Real World* has helped spark an explosion of reality television shows. Watch an episode of a current or past reality television show with the following question in mind: How real is reality TV? What aspects of real life are represented? Do some of those aspects strike you as more fiction than fact? What do you think the appeal of reality TV shows is for viewers? for advertisers? Write an essay in which you formulate answers to these questions based on a close analysis of what you've watched.

PEPÓN OSORIO

"My principal commitment as an artist is to return art to the community," says installation and video artist Pepón Osorio. Born in Santurce, Puerto Rico, in 1955, Osorio studied at the Universidad Inter-Americana in Puerto Rico; Lehman College, City University of New York; and Columbia University. From his experience as a social worker and his collaborations with avant-garde performance artist and choreographer Merián Soto, Osorio brings a social and artistic conscience to his art. The range of materials he uses to construct his installations—found objects, video, silkscreen, photography, and sound— are as rich as the experiences he draws on for inspiration.

Osorio created *Son's Bedroom* as one section of an artistic installation entitled *Badge of Honor*. (A full view of the installation is reproduced on pages 94–95.) *Son's Bedroom* is a fabricated rendition of the bedroom of a 15-year-old boy named Nelson Jr. The image on the right wall is a video screen that plays a twenty-two-minute tape of the son talking to his father, Nelson Sr.

Osorio's work has been shown in galleries and museums around the United States and Puerto Rico. He was awarded a prestigious MacArthur Fellowship in 1999 and was featured in the PBS series *art:21* in 2001. Osorio currently lives and works in Philadelphia.

found objects: Ordinary objects, originally not intended as art, that are incorporated into a work of art by the artist.

SEEING

1. Pepón Osorio has fabricated the bedroom of a teenage boy. (The boy is depicted on the video screen on the right wall of the room.) When you examine this image, what do you see first? Which objects draw your attention? What do you notice about each one? What cultural references does Osorio draw on to create this scene? What reasonable inferences can you make about this teenager's interests? Based on the details in this ordinary scene, what generalizations can you make about Osorio's style?

2. How successful has Osorio been at capturing the look of a teenage boy's bedroom? Point to specific examples to support your answer. Which aspects of Osorio's depiction of the bedroom strike you as based more on fiction or fantasy than on fact? Why? What criteria would you use to help someone understand the differences between fiction and fantasy?

style: The poet Robert Frost defined style as "the way [a person] carries himself [herself] toward his [her] ideas and deeds." In effect, style is the way in which something is said, done, performed, or expressed.

WRITING

1. Imagine yourself standing in the doorway to your bedroom at home or on campus. Compose a verbal picture of what you see as you examine the bedroom. Which aspects of the room would you want to tell others about? Which aspects would you rather not mention? Write the first draft of a descriptive essay in which you convey—in as much detail as possible—what you think someone would see in your bedroom.

2. Consider the differences between the look of your bedroom at home and that of your room on campus. Other than the size of the rooms, what differences do you notice in the ways you organize your space in the two locations? Write a comparison/contrast essay in which you discuss how these differences reflect different styles of presenting yourself at home and on campus.

Context: Osorio

Interview: Osorio

Pépon Osorio, *Badge of Honor*, 1995

Context is an essential aspect of both understanding and practicing the art of composition—whether what is being composed is an essay, a painting, a photograph, or a film. In its simplest sense, context refers to the circumstances, or the setting, within which an event occurs. Context is also the part of a text or statement that surrounds a particular word, passage, or image and helps determine its meaning. Analyzing the relationship between a text and its context— or the relationship of a part to the whole—is an effective way to appreciate and master the complexity and effectiveness of seeing clearly and writing well.

We presented the teenager's bedroom on pages 94–95 outside its original context; this image is one-half of a large work titled *Badge of Honor*, created by installa-

tion artist Pepón Osorio. The full work, shown in the photograph above, consists of the teenager's crowded bedroom and the place his father sleeps, a stark prison cell. In each of these two fabricated rooms is a video screen. The father's image appears on the screen in the cell; the son's, on the screen in the bedroom. If you were standing in front of *Badge of Honor,* you would be able to hear father and son engaged in a twenty-two-minute conversation through the wall that separates their rooms.

Does seeing the entire work change your response to *Badge of Honor*? How? Describe the visual differences between the two rooms. How does the context of each room determine what you expect to find present in—and absent from—each room? To what do you think the title of the piece refers?

especially the impact of the father's absence on the family. They challenge each other with such questions as "Can you tell time?", the father wanting to know why the son does not come home when asked to by his mother; the son wanting to know if the father realizes how long he has been away from the family while in jail. Nelson Junior talks about how much he misses weekends together, and then he declares, "I am willing to give up anything for you to be home with us. Anything." Nelson Senior asks, "If you had something special, who would you give it to?" The reply: "I would give it to mom." Likewise, the father gives the "badge of honor" to his wife: "Mommy would be the one I'd give the honor to." The father breaks down upon recognizing the intense love and admiration he has for his wife. Both acknowledge the enormous role that she plays in holding the family together, and the irreplaceable role that they all play in each other's lives, providing invaluable spiritual, emotional, and material support. But will this understanding break the cycle of the father, returning to prison? "You're in there more than you are out here with us," accuses the son.

The importance of a strong family is the paramount message of *Badge of Honor*, and it is a message visitors immediately grasped and to which they responded emotionally. No art background is required, and most visitors did not think of Osorio's work in terms of art, or at least not as their primary concern. To the contrary, the key to the work's success is its removal from an art context and its reliance on a trenchant realism that clearly and precisely presents its message. Even the video conversation between father and son, unlike that in much contemporary video art, is a straightforward dialogue that can readily be followed.

This is not to suggest that Osorio's latest work is not rife with metaphor and symbolism, for it is, or that the viewer does not recognize the fictional component of the work, for *Badge of Honor* is a masterful blend of fact and fiction. What makes the installation successful is the fact that it is filled with metaphor and symbolism that can be appreciated by a general audience. Osorio ingeniously integrates the poetical elements of the work into the literal elements, so that they have a potent emotional impact on the viewer, who may not even be aware of their existence. For example, the viewer can easily sense the dramatic physical separation of father and son in their respective rooms and their emotional desperation as they try to communicate through the shared wall that forcefully keeps them apart. Their enormous heads, projected in haunting gray halftones, have an ephemeral quality as they flicker in the low light of the installation; they are like souls floating in space, calling out to one another. In contrast to the flat images of father and son is the three-dimensional reality of the cell and bedroom, which take on a haunting stillness when the video conversation periodically stops. The boy's room, densely packed with objects, may have a dazzling visual opulence, but ultimately it is as empty and devoid of life as the father's austere cell. . . . Something is missing from both sleeping quarters—the emotional support that the video figures yearn for.

Osorio also uses metaphor to explore the tension between genders in the boy's bedroom. The artist created the space and filled it with pictures of the boy's idols: sports figures on baseball cards and karate posters that cover the walls, and images of Puerto Rican athletes who migrated to New York after World War II laminated on the two cabinets. A masculine aesthetic appears in the enormous black sound system pressed against the back wall; the rugged mountain bike with its massive chain lock; the ring studded plastic fists (actually car air-fresheners) that cover the cabinets, bed, and walls; the plethora of basketballs that are scattered about the floor and, like heraldic coats of arms, ring the walls, surrealistically mounted on outstretched plastic arms. . . .

In the midst of this otherwise masculine bedroom is the delicate note of the mother, presented metaphorically through the white satin spread embroidered with red roses covering the bed that sits in the center of the room. Her sensitive touch is also present in her emphasis on family; snapshots of the real-life family have been photo-silkscreened onto the white pillowcases. She is also present in the rose decals that ring the frame of the bed. Into these roses, the boy has screwed his plastic fists, virtually obliterating the flowers, a gesture that is a symbolic assertion of his masculinity.

Badge of Honor extends well beyond the physical installation, for it has strong social and conceptual premises that are an integral part of the work. Part of the art's social mission is the collaboration of the community, and, after its construction, its use by the community. Osorio met with Newark Museum staff, Latino social service organizations, individual social workers, support groups, public defenders and prosecutors, legal defense organizations, school groups, and individuals from the community in a series of meetings during January, February, and March 1995. He discussed the issues he wanted to raise in *Badge of Honor*, and how the Latino community would be represented by the work and thus perceived by the public. La Casa de Don Pedro, a Latino social service organi-

zation with headquarters near 33 Broadway, became his principal contact with the community. Offender Aid and Restoration became his main access to the prison system, helping him work with prison administration and meet Latino prisoners. Once *Badge of Honor* was completed, the artist held workshops in the installation with teenagers of imprisoned parents. These workshops and the meetings with organizations and the community were documented on videotape as an integral part of the artwork.

The strong conceptual premises of *Badge of Honor* extend to the fact that the work was designed to explore the relationship of the community and a museum, for *Badge of Honor*, which was commissioned by the Newark Museum, was made specifically to be installed first in a community site, and then moved to the museum, located a mile away. The artist wanted to take the museum into the community, and then lead the community to the museum. Additionally, he wanted to see how the installation would be perceived, understood, and accepted in both locations—by audiences from different interests and agendas. [10]

It should come as no surprise that Pepón Osorio has a background in sociology and as a social worker, having worked for the New York City's Human Resources Administration's Department of Special Services for Children, where he specialized in the prevention of child abuse and neglect. Like a sociologist, he studies communities, and organizations and institutions such as museums; and like a social worker, he wants to bring about change. But can *Badge of Honor* effect change? Can the installation play a role in bringing about a shift in attitude toward the family, social responsibility, art and museums, and ethnic communities?

Can *Badge of Honor* break the cycle of teenage boys following their fathers into prison? In his research, Osorio discovered that for some adolescents an imprisoned father is often literally considered a "badge of honor" that invests the youths with a special status among their peers. Which badge of honor will ultimately prevail? The mother, valiantly holding the family together, or the father, selfishly indulging in his personal needs?

But *Badge of Honor* will probably not be measured by the degree of success of its social mission. This goal is just a conceptual component to what is first and foremost a work of art. As an aesthetic vehicle, the installation is an astonishing tour de force—visually, intellectually, and emotionally. The visual riches of materials, textures, colors, and objects and the intellectual wealth of references to American, European, and Latin-American cultures as well as to past and present history result in a powerful statement about contemporary society. Despite its complexity, Osorio's message was readily understood and felt by the audience at 33 Broadway. In a comment book, which became an integral part of the exhibition, three visitors wrote:

Pepón, What can I say? The thing is that I felt so full as I looked & listened that I couldn't speak immediately. And then so much came in a rush.

Having such a work on display gives the plight of the Puerto Rican people [a] voice. I love this. We need to continue to express ourselves to ultimately understand ourselves. How can I help?

There's a lot of grief, but a lot of hope in this picture. This art—this is the real work—healing, sharing, making the bridges. Thank you. ○

JOSEPH JACOBS

Joseph Jacobs, the former curator of American art at the Newark Museum (1991–2003), now works as an independent writer, critic, and curator in New York City. His essay on Pepón Osorio's *Badge of Honor* first appeared in the museum's 1996 catalog. While at the museum, Jacobs organized many major exhibitions, including "Off Limits: Rutgers University and the Avant-Garde, 1957–1963," and "Picturing America," with work by Winslow Homer, Georgia O'Keeffe, and others in the museum's American collection. Before 1991, Jacobs served as the director of the Oklahoma City Art Museum (1989–1991), curator of modern art at the John and Mable Ringling Museum of Art (1986–1989), and director of Bucknell University's Center Gallery (1982–1986).

Jacobs's essays have appeared in numerous exhibition catalogs and anthologies, including Frank Maresca and Roger Ricco's *American Vernacular* (2002). He is currently writing the modern art chapters for a new edition of H. W. Janson's well-known *History of Art,* which will be published in 2007.

SEEING

1. After reading Jacobs's essay closely, go back and take a second look at Osorio's installation. How do the curator's words change your reading of Osorio's piece? For example, how do the excerpts from the father–son dialogue alter your understanding of the tone of the piece? How does knowing more about what it was like to experience the installation firsthand change your understanding of its purpose and message? How does learning more about Osorio's collaboration with neighborhood organizations change your understanding of the piece? To what extent do you agree with Jacobs's characterization of the use of metaphor in the installation?

2. What points of view does Jacobs offer in this essay? What points of view are absent? How would you describe the overall structure and organization of the essay? What is Jacobs's perspective in the first three paragraphs? How would you paraphrase the central points he makes in each of the subsequent paragraphs? Which arguments seem most effectively supported to you? Which do you think could use more examples or evidence?

WRITING

1. Based on your close reading of both Osorio's *Badge of Honor* and Jacobs's essay, write a one-page analysis of the title of the piece. What can *badge of honor* mean in this context? How does the title's meaning relate to the images and messages conveyed in Osorio's installation? Support your claims with specific examples.

2. "No art background is required," writes Jacobs, "and most visitors did not think of Osorio's work in terms of art, or at least not as their primary concern. . . . The key to the work's success is its removal from an art context and its reliance on a trenchant realism that clearly and precisely presents its message" (para. 5). Write an essay in which you first interpret and then agree or disagree with Jacobs's statement. Support your argument with examples from the essay and Osorio's **Badge of Honor**.

See pages 94–95.

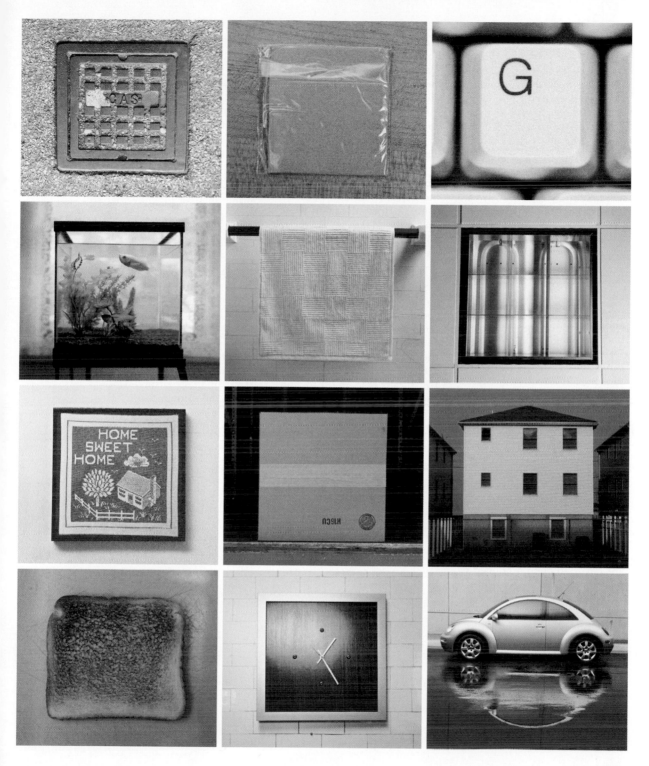

VOLKSWAGEN

The origins of the Volkswagen company, in particular the car that would become the Beetle, date back to 1930s Germany. The Reich wanted to build an affordable car for the average German citizen; it chose Ferdinand Porsche's design for the KdfWagen, a prototype of the original Beetle. (Today's Beetle, the New Beetle, was introduced in 1998). Early versions of the car, with an engine in the rear and a rounded ladybug shape, appeared around 1935, but World War II slowed its production. After the war, KdfWagen's name changed to *Volkswagen* (German for "the people's car"), and the company's production became essential to West Germany's postwar recovery. By 1955, the company had established production facilities in Western Europe, the United States, Brazil, and Canada.

During the 1960s and early 1970s, Volkswagen's "Think Small" ads were one of the most successful advertising campaigns in history, boosting sales to the highest levels. The original Beetle still holds the world record for sales, a record previously set by the Model-T Ford. More than 16 million of the cars had been produced by 1973; and by 2002, more than 21 million Beetles had been produced. Volkswagen discontinued production of the old Beetle in 2003.

SEEING

1. Make a list of each of the objects you see in the "Drivers Wanted" ad. What do they have in common? What is ordinary or extraordinary about them individually? as a group? To what extent do they appear to be drawn from similar social, cultural, or geographical contexts? What similarities and differences do you see in the way each object is presented? How would you describe the message of this ad? What concepts is it relying on to market Volkswagen cars?

2. Why do you think the designers of this ad chose to use a grid of objects? How would you describe the overall visual impact of the grid? How would you describe the placement of the car in the grid? Suppose the designers had decided on a different placement for the car—in the first block of the grid, for example, or on a row by itself. Would that change your reading of the ad?

WRITING

1. A still life captures ordinary objects. How does Volkswagen make use of still life in its "Drivers Wanted" ad? Find two other examples of still life in contemporary advertising and write an essay analyzing how advertising adapts the conventions of fine art to sell its products.

2. Choose a contemporary automobile ad in a newspaper or magazine. Write an essay in which you compare and contrast the visual and verbal strategies used in the 2004 "Drivers Wanted" ad with those used in your selection. Consider the following questions: What concepts does each ad associate with its product? What is each ad's target audience? How do you know? What verbal or visual techniques have the designers employed to help market their product?

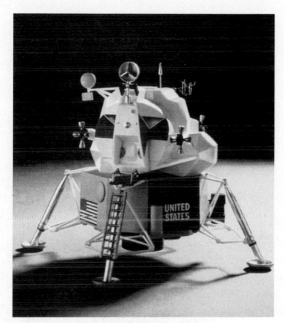

It's ugly, but it gets you there.

Volkswagen, *It's Ugly, But It Gets You There*, 1960s

Look closely at the black-and-white 1960s VW ad
"It's Ugly, But It Gets You There." How would you
compare the use of text in this ad with the words,
"Drivers Wanted" in the later ad? Write an essay
in which you interpret and then compare and contrast the taglines.

Seeing

Annie Dillard

WHEN I WAS SIX OR SEVEN YEARS OLD, GROWING up in Pittsburgh, I used to take a precious penny of my own and hide it for someone else to find. It was a curious compulsion; sadly, I've never been seized by it since. For some reason I always "hid" the penny along the same stretch of sidewalk up the street. I would cradle it at the roots of a sycamore, say, or in a hole left by a chipped-off piece of sidewalk. Then I would take a piece of chalk, and, starting at either end of the block, draw huge arrows leading up to the penny from both directions. After I learned to write I labeled the arrows: SURPRISE AHEAD or MONEY THIS WAY. I was greatly excited, during all this arrow-drawing, at the thought of the first lucky passer-by who would receive in this way, regardless of merit, a free gift from the universe. But I never lurked about. I would go straight home and not give the matter another thought, until, some months later, I would be gripped again by the impulse to hide another penny.

It is still the first week in January, and I've got great plans. I've been thinking about seeing. There are lots of things to see, unwrapped gifts and free surprises. The world is fairly studded and strewn with pennies cast broadside from a generous hand. But—and this is the point—who gets excited by a mere penny? If you follow one arrow, if you crouch motionless on a bank to watch a tremulous ripple thrill on the water and are rewarded by the sight of a muskrat kit paddling from its den, will you count that sight a chip of copper only, and go your rueful way? It is dire poverty indeed when a man is so malnourished and fatigued that he won't stoop to pick up a penny. But if you cultivate a healthy poverty and simplicity, so that finding a penny will literally make your day, then, since the world is in fact planted in pennies, you have with your poverty bought a lifetime of days. It is that simple. What you see is what you get.

I used to be able to see flying insects in the air. I'd look ahead and see, not the row of hemlocks across the road, but the air in front of it. My eyes would focus along that column of air, picking out flying insects. But I lost interest, I guess, for I dropped the habit. Now I can see birds. Probably some people can look at the grass at their feet and discover all the crawling creatures. I would like to know grasses and sedges—and care. Then my least journey into the world would be a field trip, a series of happy recognitions. Thoreau, in an expansive mood, exulted, "What a rich book might be made about buds, including, perhaps, sprouts!" It would be nice to think so. I cherish mental images I have of three perfectly happy people. One collects stones. Another—an Englishman, say—watches clouds. The third lives on a coast and collects drops of seawater which he examines microscopically and mounts. But I don't see what the specialist sees, and so I cut myself off, not only from the total picture, but from the various forms of happiness.

Unfortunately, nature is very much a now-you-see-it, now-you-don't affair. A fish flashes, then dissolves in the water before my eyes like so much salt. Deer apparently ascend bodily into heaven; the brightest oriole fades into leaves. These disappearances stun me into stillness and concentration; they say of nature that it conceals with a grand nonchalance, and they say of vision that it is a deliberate gift, the revelation of a dancer who for my eyes only flings away her seven veils. For nature does reveal as well as conceal: now-you-don't-see-it, now-you-do. For a week last September migrating red-winged blackbirds were feeding heavily down by the creek at the back of the house. One day I went out to investigate the racket; I walked up to a tree, an Osage orange, and a hundred birds flew away. They simply materialized out of the tree. I saw a tree, then a whisk of color, then a tree again. I walked closer and another hundred blackbirds took flight. Not a branch, not a twig budged: The birds were apparently weightless as well as invisible. Or, it was as if the leaves of the Osage orange had been freed from a spell in the form of red-winged blackbirds; they flew from the tree, caught my eye in the sky, and vanished. When I looked again at the tree the leaves had reassembled as if nothing had happened. Finally I walked directly to the trunk of the tree and a final hundred, the real diehards, appeared, spread, and vanished. How could so many hide in the tree without my seeing them? The Osage orange, unruffled, looked just as it had looked from the house, when three hundred red-winged blackbirds cried from its crown. I looked downstream where they flew, and they were gone. Searching, I couldn't spot one. I wandered downstream to force them to play their hand, but they'd crossed the creek and scattered. One show to a customer. These appearances catch at my throat; they are the free gifts, the bright coppers at the roots of trees.

It's all a matter of keeping my eyes open. Nature is 5 like one of those line drawings of a tree that are puzzles for children: Can you find hidden in the leaves a duck, a house, a boy, a bucket, a zebra, and a boot? Specialists can find the most incredibly well-hidden things. A book I read when I was young recommended an easy way to find caterpillars to rear: You simply find some fresh caterpillar droppings, look up, and there's your caterpillar. More recently an author advised me to set my mind at ease about those piles of cut stems on the ground in grassy fields. Field mice make them; they cut the grass down by degrees to reach the seeds at the head. It seems that when the grass is tightly packed, as in a field of ripe grain, the blade won't topple at a single cut through the stem; instead, the cut stem simply drops vertically, held in the crush of grain. The mouse severs the bottom again and again, the stem keeps dropping an inch at a time, and finally the head is low enough for the mouse to reach the seeds. Meanwhile, the mouse is positively littering the field with its little piles of cut stems into which, presumably, the author of the book is constantly stumbling.

If I can't see these minutiae, I still try to keep my eyes open. I'm always on the lookout for antlion traps in sandy soil, monarch pupae near milkweed, skipper larvae in locust leaves. These things are utterly common, and I've not seen one. I bang on hollow trees near water, but so far no flying squirrels fjords are peculiar for the spells of completely quiet weather, when there is not enough wind to blow out a match and the water is like a sheet of glass. The kayak hunter must sit in his boat without stirring a finger so as not to scare the shy seals away. . . . The sun, low in the sky, sends a glare into his eyes, and the landscape around moves into the realm of the unreal. The reflex from the mirrorlike water hypnotizes him, he seems to be unable to move, and all of a sudden it is as if he were floating in a bottomless void, sinking, sinking, and sinking. . . . Horror-stricken, he tries to stir, to cry out, but he cannot, he is completely paralyzed, he just falls and falls." Some hunters are especially cursed with this panic, and bring ruin and sometimes starvation to their families.

Sometimes here in Virginia at sunset low clouds on the southern or northern horizon are completely invisible in the lighted sky. I only know one is there because I can see its reflection in still water. The first time I discovered this mystery I looked from cloud to no-cloud in bewilderment, checking my bearings over and over, thinking maybe the ark of the covenant was just passing by south of Dead Man Mountain. Only much later did I read the explanation: Polarized light from the sky is very much weakened by reflection, but the light in clouds isn't polarized. So invisible clouds pass among visible clouds, till all slide over the mountains; so a greater light extinguishes a lesser as though it didn't exist.

In the great meteor shower of August, the Perseid, I wail all day for the shooting stars I miss. They're out there showering down, committing hara-kiri in a flame of fatal attraction, and hissing perhaps at last into the ocean. But at dawn what looks like a blue dome clamps down over me like a lid on a pot. The stars and planets could smash and I'd never know. Only a piece of ashen moon occasionally climbs up or down the inside of the dome, and our local star without surcease explodes on our heads. We have really only that one light, one source for all power, and yet we must turn away from it by universal decree. Nobody here on the planet seems aware of this

strange, powerful taboo, that we all walk about carefully averting our faces, this way and that, lest our eyes be blasted forever.

Darkness appalls and light dazzles; the scrap of visible light that doesn't hurt my eyes hurts my brain. What I see sets me swaying. Size and distance and the sudden swelling of meanings confuse me, bowl me over. I straddle the sycamore log bridge over Tinker Creek in the summer. I look at the lighted creek bottom: Snail tracks tunnel the mud in quavering curves. A crayfish jerks, but by the time I absorb what has happened, he's gone in a billowing smoke-screen of silt. I look at the water: minnows and shiners. If I'm thinking minnows, a carp will fill my brain till I scream. I look at the water's surface: skaters, bubbles, and leaves sliding down. Suddenly, my own face, reflected, startles me witless. Those snails have been tracking my face! Finally, with a shuddering wrench of the will, I see clouds, cirrus clouds. I'm dizzy, I fall in. This looking business is risky.

Once I stood on a humped rock on nearby Purgatory Mountain, watching through binoculars the great autumn hawk migration below, until I discovered that I was in danger of joining the hawks on a vertical migration of my own. I was used to binoculars, but not, apparently, to balancing on humped rocks while looking through them. I staggered. Everything advanced and receded by turns; the world was full of unexplained foreshortenings and depths. A distant huge tan object, a hawk the size of an elephant, turned out to be the browned bough of a nearby loblolly pine. I followed a sharp-shinned hawk against a featureless sky, rotating my head unawares as it flew, and when I lowered the glass a glimpse of my own looming shoulder sent me staggering. What prevents the men on Palomar from falling, voiceless and blinded, from their tiny, vaulted chairs?

I reel in confusion; I don't understand what I see. With the naked eye I can see two million light-years to the Andromeda galaxy. Often I slop some creek water in a jar and when I get home I dump it in a white china bowl. After the silt settles I return and see tracings of minute snails on the bottom, a planarian or two winding round the rim of water, roundworms shimmying frantically, and finally, when my eyes have adjusted to these dimensions, amoebae. At first the amoebae look like muscae volitantes, those curled moving spots you seem to see in your eyes when you stare at a distant wall. Then I see the amoebae as drops of water congealed, bluish, translucent, like chips of sky in the bowl. At length I choose one individual and give myself over to its idea of an evening. I see it dribble a grainy foot before it on its wet, unfathomable way. Do its unedited sense impressions include the fierce focus of my eyes? Shall I take it outside and show it Andromeda, and blow its little endoplasm? I stir the water with a finger, in case it's running out of oxygen. Maybe I should get a tropical aquarium with motorized bubblers and lights, and keep this one for a pet. Yes, it would tell its fissioned descendants, the universe is two feet by five, and if you listen closely you can hear the buzzing music of the spheres.

Oh, it's mysterious lamplit evenings, here in the galaxy, one after the other. It's one of those nights when I wander from window to window, looking for a sign. But I can't see. Terror and a beauty insoluble are a ribband of blue woven into the fringes of garments of things both great and small. No culture explains, no bivouac offers real haven or rest. But it could be that we are not seeing something. Galileo thought comets were an optical illusion. This is fertile ground: Since we are certain that they're not, we can look at what our scientists have been saying with fresh hope. What if there are *really* gleaming, castellated cities hung upside-down over the desert sand? What limpid lakes and cool date palms have our caravans always passed untried? Until, one by one, by the blindest of leaps, we light on the road to these places, we must stumble in darkness and hunger. I turn from the window. I'm blind as a bat, sensing only from every direction the echo of my own thin cries.

I chanced on a wonderful book by Marius von Senden, called *Space and Light*. When Western surgeons discovered how to perform safe cataract operations, they ranged across Europe and America operating on dozens of men and women of all ages who had been blinded by cataracts since birth. Von Senden collected accounts of such cases; the histories are fascinating. Many doctors had tested their patients' sense perceptions and ideas of space both before and after the operations. The vast majority of patients, of both sexes and all ages, had, in von Senden's opinion, no idea of space whatsoever. Form, distance, and size were so many meaningless syllables. A patient "had no idea of depth, confusing it with roundness." Before the operation a doctor would give a blind patient a cube and a sphere; the patient would tongue it or feel it with his hands, and name it correctly. After the operation the doctor would show the same objects to the patient without letting him touch them; now he had no clue whatsoever what he was seeing. One patient called lemonade "square" because it pricked on his tongue as a square shape pricked on the touch of his hands. Of another postoperative patient, the doctor writes, "I have found in her no notion of size, for example, not even within the narrow limits which she might have encompassed with the aid of touch. Thus when I asked her to show me how big her mother was, she did not stretch out her hands, but set her two index-fingers a few inches apart." Other doctors reported their patients' own statements to similar effect. "The room he was in . . . he knew to be but part of the house, yet he could not conceive that the whole house could look bigger"; "Those who are blind from birth . . . have no real conception of height or distance. A house that is a mile away is thought of as nearby, but requiring the taking of a lot of steps. . . . The elevator that whizzes him up and down gives no more sense of vertical distance than does the train of horizontal."

For the newly sighted, vision is pure sensation unencumbered by meaning: "The girl went through the experience that we all go through and forget, the moment we are born. She saw, but it did not mean anything but a lot of different kinds of brightness." Again, "I asked the patient what he could see; he answered that he saw an extensive field of light, in which everything appeared dull, confused, and in of the present. It's not that I'm observant; it's just that I talk too much. Otherwise, especially in a strange place, I'll never know what's happening. Like a blind man at the ball game, I need a radio.

When I see this way I analyze and pry. I hurl over logs and roll away stones; I study the bank a square foot at a time, probing and tilting my head. Some days when a mist covers the mountains, when the muskrats won't show and the microscope's mirror shatters, I want to climb up the blank blue dome as a man would storm the inside of a circus tent, wildly, dangling, and with a steel knife claw a rent in the top, peep, and, if I must, fall.

But there is another kind of seeing that involves a letting go. When I see this way I sway transfixed and emptied. The difference between the two ways of seeing is the difference between walking with and without a camera. When I walk with a camera I walk from shot to shot, reading the light on a calibrated meter. When I walk without a camera, my own shutter opens, and the moment's light prints on my own silver gut. When I see this second way I am above all an unscrupulous observer.

It was sunny one evening last summer at Tinker Creek; the sun was low in the sky, upstream. I was sitting on the sycamore log bridge with the sunset at my back, watching the shiners the size of minnows who were feeding over the muddy sand in skittery schools. Again and again, one fish, then another, turned for a split second across the current and flash! the sun shot out from its silver side. I couldn't watch for it. It was always just happening somewhere else, and it drew my vision just as it disappeared: flash, like a sudden dazzle of the thinnest blade, a sparking over a dun and olive ground at chance intervals from every direction. Then I noticed white specks, some sort of pale petals, small, floating from under my feet on the creek's surface, very slow and steady. So I blurred my eyes and gazed toward the brim of my hat and saw a new world. I saw the pale white circles roll up, roll up, like the world's turning, mute and

perfect, and I saw the linear flashes, gleaming silver, like stars being born at random down a rolling scroll of time. Something broke and something opened. I filled up like a new wineskin. I breathed an air like light; I saw a light like water. I was the lip of a fountain the creek filled forever; I was ether, the leaf in the zephyr; I was flesh-flake, feather, bone.

When I see this way I see truly. As Thoreau says, I [35] return to my senses. I am the man who watches the baseball game in silence in an empty stadium. I see the game purely; I'm abstracted and dazed. When it's all over and the white-suited players lope off the green field to their shadowed dugouts, I leap to my feet; I cheer and cheer.

But I can't go out and try to see this way. I'll fail, I'll go mad. All I can do is try to gag the commentator, to hush the noise of useless interior babble that keeps me from seeing just as surely as a newspaper dangled before my eyes. The effort is really a discipline requiring a lifetime of dedicated struggle; it marks the literature of saints and monks of every order East and West, under every rule and no rule, discalced and shod. The world's spiritual geniuses seem to discover universally that the mind's muddy river, this ceaseless flow of trivia and trash, cannot be dammed, and that trying to dam it is a waste of effort that might lead to madness. Instead you must allow the muddy river to flow unheeded in the dim channels of consciousness; you raise your sights; you look along it, mildly, acknowledging its presence without interest and gazing beyond it into the realm of the real where subjects and objects act and rest purely, without utterance. "Launch into the deep," says Jacques Ellul, "and you shall see."

The secret of seeing is, then, the pearl of great price. If I thought he could teach me to find it and keep it forever I would stagger barefoot across a hundred deserts after any lunatic at all. But although the pearl may be found, it may not be sought. The literature of illumination reveals this above all: Although it comes to those who wait for it, it is always, even to the most practiced and adept, a gift and a total surprise. I return from one walk knowing where the killdeer nests in the field by the creek and the hour the laurel blooms. I return from the same walk a day later scarcely knowing my own name. Litanies hum in my ears; my tongue flaps in my mouth Ailinon, alleluia! I cannot cause light; the most I can do is try to put myself in the path of its beam. It is possible, in deep space, to sail on solar wind. Light, be it particle or wave, has force: You rig a giant sail and go. The secret of seeing is to sail on solar wind. Hone and spread your spirit till you yourself are a sail, whetted, translucent, broadside to the merest puff.

When her doctor took her bandages off and led her into the garden, the girl who was no longer blind saw "the tree with the lights in it." It was for this tree I searched through the peach orchards of summer, in the forests of fall and down winter and spring for years. Then one day I was walking along Tinker Creek thinking of nothing at all and I saw the tree with the lights in it. I saw the backyard cedar where the mourning doves roost charged and transfigured, each cell buzzing with flame. I stood on the grass with the lights in it, grass that was wholly fire, utterly focused and utterly dreamed. It was less like seeing than like being for the first time seen, knocked breathless by a powerful glance. The flood of fire abated, but I'm still spending the power. Gradually the lights went out in the cedar, the colors died, the cells unflamed and disappeared. I was still ringing. I had been my whole life a bell, and never knew it until at that moment I was lifted and struck. I have since only very rarely seen the tree with the lights in it. The vision comes and goes, mostly goes, but I live for it, for the moment when the mountains open and a new light roars in spate through the crack, and the mountains slam. ○

ANNIE DILLARD

Annie Dillard was born Annie Doak in Pittsburgh in 1945. She attended Hollins College, near Roanoke, Virginia, where she studied English, theology, and creative writing; married her writing instructor, Richard Dillard; and earned a master's degree with a thesis on Henry David Thoreau and Walden Pond. Before publishing her first book, *Pilgrim at Tinker Creek* (1974), Dillard spent four seasons living near Tinker Creek in the Blue Ridge Mountains of Virginia and filled more than twenty volumes of journals with notes about her experiences and thoughts on the violence and beauty of nature, often in religious terms. Fearing that a work of theology written by a woman would not be successful, she was reluctant to publish the book. But she did, and it won the Pulitzer Prize in 1975.

In the intervening years, Dillard has published poetry, fiction, essays, memoirs, literary criticism, and autobiography, returning repeatedly to the themes of the mysteries of nature, the quest for meaning, and religious faith. *The Annie Dillard Reader,* a collection of her writing, was published in 1994.

"Seeing" is taken from *Pilgrim at Tinker Creek.* It speaks to Dillard's concern that a writer be "careful of what he reads, for that is what he will write . . . careful of what he learns, because that is what he will know."

SEEING

1. Near the end of her essay Annie Dillard observes, "Seeing is of course very much a matter of verbalization" (para. 31). Reread "Seeing" and make a list of every idiom the author uses to talk about seeing "truly." Consider, for example, the last line of paragraph 2: "What you see is what you get." Identify other idiomatic expressions, and explain how Dillard plays with the literal and figurative dimensions of each. What does she mean when she says, "This looking business is risky" (para. 18)? One of the strongest elements of Dillard's style is her use of metaphor. Identify two or three especially striking examples of metaphor in the essay, and explain the effects of each.

2. Near the end of paragraph 6, Dillard quotes the naturalist Stewart Edward White on seeing deer: "As soon as you can forget the naturally obvious and construct an artificial obvious, then you too will see deer." Dillard immediately observes, "But the artificial obvious is hard to see" (para. 7). What does "the artificial obvious" mean here? How do people construct it? Why is it "hard to see"? Later, Dillard describes another kind of seeing, "a letting go" (para. 33). What does she mean when she says, "When I see this second way I am above all an unscrupulous observer" (para. 33)?

WRITING

1. Many of us at one time or another have succumbed to the impulse to hide something and then either to lead people to it or to make it as difficult as possible for others to locate. Recall one such impulse that you had, and develop detailed notes about not only the circumstances but also the consequences of your yielding to the impulse. Draft an essay in which you recount this story and then use it as a harbinger of other, more important events or behaviors in your life.

2. Reread Larry Woiwode's "Ode to an Orange" (page 44). What do you think he would say about the nature of seeing? Using Woiwode's piece or another work in this chapter, write an essay in which you compare the author's philosophy about seeing with Dillard's—and argue that one is more compelling than the other.

Seeing Is Believing

Size matters—or so advertisers claim when they promote certain products or services. Scientists make much the same point: A photograph of a single living cell or of a distant star would be so small that it would be difficult to identify the subject without some indication of its size and scale.

Each of the texts and images on the following pages invites us to magnify our attention to discover the richness and complexity of familiar objects. Several images—from Willard Wigan's minuscule *Man v. Ant* to Harold Edgerton's *Bullet Through the Apple, 1964*, to Bryan Steiff's *terraFutura #9*—reveal how changing scale can transform the nondescript. K. C. Cole's essay **"A Matter of Scale"** provides a vocabulary and a frame of reference with which to appreciate what is extraordinary about the ordinary; and two perspectives of Chuck Close's *Self-Portrait, 2000–2001*, prove graphically that what we see depends on how closely we're looking.

THE FASCINATION OF THE MINIATURE
Steven Millhauser

Wherein lies the fascination of the miniature? Smallness alone compels no wonder. A grain of sand, an ant, a raindrop, a bottle cap, may interest or amaze the eye, but they do not arrest the attention with that peculiar intensity elicited by the miniature. They do not cast a spell. The miniature, then, must not be confused with the merely minute. For the miniature does not exist in isolation: It is by nature a smaller version of something else. The miniature, that is to say, implies a relation, a discrepancy. An object as large as a dollhouse can exert the fascination of the miniature as fully as the minutest teacup in the doll's smallest cupboard.

But why should discrepancy possess an interest? I believe the answer is this, that discrepancy of size is a form of distortion, and all forms of distortion shock us into attention: The inattentive and jaded eye, passing through a world without interest, helplessly perceives that something in the bland panorama is not as it should be. The eye is irritated into attention. It is compelled to perform an act of recognition. Perhaps for the first time since childhood, it sees. But what I have said is true of all forms of discrepancy, and not only the particular discrepancy that is the miniature. Some understanding of the spell cast by this particular discrepancy may be gained by first considering the nature of the particular discrepancy that is the gigantic. ○

From the Introduction to *A Short History of Nearly Everything*

Bill Bryson

Welcome. And congratulations. I am delighted that you could make it. Getting here wasn't easy, I know. In fact, I suspect it was a little tougher than you realize.

To begin with, for you to be here now trillions of drifting atoms had somehow to assemble in an intricate and intriguingly obliging manner to create you. It's an arrangement so specialized and particular that it has never been tried before and will only exist this once. For the next many years (we hope) these tiny particles will uncomplainingly engage in all the billions of deft, cooperative efforts necessary to keep you intact and let you experience the supremely agreeable but generally underappreciated state known as existence.

Why atoms take this trouble is a bit of a puzzle. Being you is not a gratifying experience at the atomic level. For all their devoted attention, your atoms don't actually care about you—indeed, don't even know that you are there. They don't even know that they are there. They are mindless particles, after all, and not even themselves alike. (It is a slightly arresting notion that if you were to pick yourself apart with tweezers, one atom at a time, you would produce a mound of fine atomic dust, none of which had ever been alive but all of which had once been you.) Yet somehow for the period of your existence they will answer to a single overarching impulse: to keep you you.

The bad news is that atoms are fickle and their time of devotion is fleeting—fleeting indeed. Even a long human life adds up to only about 650,000 hours. And when that modest milestone flashes past, or at some other point thereabouts, for reasons unknown your atoms will shut you down, silently disassemble, and go off to be other things. And that's it for you.

Still, you may rejoice that it happens at all. Generally speaking in the universe it doesn't, so far as we can tell. This is decidedly odd because the atoms that so liberally and congenially flock together to form living things on Earth are exactly the same atoms that decline to do it elsewhere. Whatever else it may be, at the level of chemistry life is curiously mundane: carbon, hydrogen, oxygen, and nitrogen, a little calcium, a dash of sulfur, a light dusting of other very ordinary elements—nothing you wouldn't find in any ordinary drugstore—and that's all you need. The only thing special about the atoms that make you is that they make you. That is of course the miracle of life.

Whether or not atoms make life in other corners of the universe, they make plenty else; indeed, they make everything else. Without them there would be no water or air or rocks, no stars and planets, no distant gassy clouds or swirling nebulae or any of the other things that make the universe so usefully material. Atoms are so numerous and necessary that we easily overlook that they needn't actually exist at all. There is no law that requires the universe to fill itself with small particles of matter or to produce light and gravity and the other physical properties on which our existence hinges. There needn't actually be a universe at all. For the longest time there wasn't. There were no atoms and no universe for them to float about in. There was nothing—nothing at all anywhere.

So thank goodness for atoms. But the fact that you have atoms and that they assemble in such a willing manner is only part of what got you here. To be here now, alive in the twenty-first century and smart enough to know it, you also had to be the beneficiary of an extraordinary string of biological good fortune. Survival on Earth is a surprisingly tricky business. Of the billions and billions of species of living things that have existed since the dawn of time, most—99.99 percent—are no longer around. Life on Earth, you see, is not only brief but dismayingly tenuous. It is a curious feature of our existence that we come from a planet that is very good at promoting life but even better at extinguishing it.

The average species on Earth lasts for only about four million years, so if you wish to be around for billions of years, you must be as fickle as the atoms that made you. You must be prepared to change everything about yourself—shape, size, color, species affiliation, everything—and to do so repeatedly. That's much easier said than done, because the process of change is random. To get from "protoplasmal primordial atomic globule" (as Gilbert and Sullivan put it) to sentient up-right modern human has required you to mutate new traits over and over in a precisely timely manner for an exceedingly long while. So at various periods over the last 3.8 billion years you have abhorred oxygen and then doted on it, grown fins and limbs and jaunty sails, laid eggs, flicked the air with a forked tongue, been sleek, been furry, lived underground, lived in trees, been as big as a deer and as small as a mouse, and a million things more. The tiniest deviation from any of these evolutionary shifts, and you might now be licking algae from cave walls or lolling walruslike on some stony shore or disgorging air through a blowhole in the top of your head before diving sixty feet for a mouthful of delicious sandworms.

Not only have you been lucky enough to be attached since time immemorial to a favored evolutionary line, but you have also been extremely—make that miracu-lously—fortunate in your personal ancestry. Consider the fact that for 3.8 billion years, a period of time older than the Earth's mountains and rivers and oceans, every one of your forebears on both sides has been attractive enough to find a mate, healthy enough to reproduce, and sufficiently blessed by fate and circumstances to live long enough to do so. Not one of your pertinent ancestors was squashed, devoured, drowned, starved, stranded, stuck fast, untimely wounded, or otherwise deflected from its life's quest of delivering a tiny charge of genetic material to the right partner at the right moment in order to perpetu-ate the only possible sequence of hereditary combina-tions that could result—eventually, astoundingly, and all too briefly—in you. ○

REFLECTIONS ON A MOTE OF DUST,

MAY 11, 1996

Carl Sagan

WE SUCCEEDED IN TAKING THAT PICTURE (FROM deep space), and, if you look at it, you see a dot.

That's here. That's home. That's us.

On it, everyone you ever heard of, every human being who ever lived, lived out their lives. The aggregate of all our joys and sufferings, thousands of confident religions, ideologies, and economic doctrines, every hunter and forager, every hero and coward, every creator and destroyer of civilizations, every king and peasant, every young couple in love, every hopeful child, every mother and father, every inventor and explorer, every teacher of morals, every corrupt politician, every superstar, every supreme leader, every saint and sinner in the history of our species, lived there on a mote of dust, suspended in a sunbeam.

The earth is a very small stage in a vast cosmic arena. Think of the rivers of blood spilled by all those generals and emperors so that in glory and in triumph they could become the momentary masters of a fraction of a dot. Think of the endless cruelties visited by the inhabitants of one corner of the dot on scarcely distinguishable inhabitants of some other corner of the dot. How frequent their misunderstandings, how eager they are to kill one another, how fervent their hatreds. Our posturings, our imagined self-importance, the delusion that we have some privileged position in the universe, are challenged by this point of pale light.

Our planet is a lonely speck in the great enveloping 5 cosmic dark. In our obscurity—in all this vastness—there is no hint that help will come from elsewhere to save us from ourselves. It is up to us. It's been said that astronomy is a humbling, and I might add, a character-building experience. To my mind, there is perhaps no better demonstration of the folly of human conceits than this distant image of our tiny world.

To me, it underscores our responsibility to deal more kindly and compassionately with one another and to preserve and cherish that pale blue dot, the only home we've ever known. ○

Harold Edgerton, *Bullet Through the Apple, 1964* (left); Bryan Steiff, *terraFutura #9, 2003* (right)

Looking Closer

A Matter of Scale

K. C. Cole

*How would you suspend 500,000 pounds of water in the
air with no visible means of support? (Answer: build a cloud.)*
– Bob Miller, artist

THERE IS SOMETHING MAGICALLY SEDUCTIVE about an invitation to a world where everything measures much bigger or smaller than ourselves. To contemplate the vast expanse of ocean or sky, to look at pond scum under a microscope, to imagine the intimate inner life of atoms, all cast spells that take us far beyond the realm of everyday living into exotic landscapes accessible only through the imagination. What would it be like to grow as big as a giant? As small as a bug? Alice ate a mushroom and puffed up like a Macy's Thanksgiving Day balloon, bursting out of her house; she ate some more and shrank like the Incredible Shrinking Woman, forever in fear of falling down the drain. From Stuart Little to King Kong, from *Honey, I Shrunk the Kids* to Thumbelina, the notion of changing size seems to have a powerful pull on our psyches.

There are good reasons to think a world that's different in scale will also be different in kind. More or less of something very often adds up to more than simply more or less; quantitative changes can make huge qualitative differences.

When the size of things changes radically, different laws of nature rule, time ticks according to different clocks, new worlds appear out of nowhere while old ones dissolve into invisibility. Consider the strange situation of a giant, for example. Big and strong to be sure, but size comes with distinct disadvantages. According to J. B. S. Haldane in his classic essay, "On Being the Right Size," a sixty-foot giant would break his thighbones at every step. The reason is simple geometry. Height increases only in one dimension, area in two, volume in three. If you doubled the height of a man, the cross section, or thickness, of muscle that supports him against gravity would quadruple (two times two) and his volume—and therefore weight—would increase by a factor of eight. If you made him ten times taller, his weight would be a thousand times greater, but the cross section of bones and muscles to support him would only increase by a factor of one hundred. Result: shattered bones.

To bear such weight would require stout, thick legs—think elephant or rhino. Leaping would be out of the question. Superman must have been a flea.

Fleas, of course, perform superhuman feats routinely (which is part of the science behind the now nearly extinct art of the flea circus). These puny critters can pull 160,000 times their own weight, and jump a hundred times their own height. Small creatures have so little mass compared to the area of their muscles that they seem enormously strong. While their muscles are many orders of magnitude weaker than ours, the mass they have to push around is so much smaller that it makes each ant and flea into a superbeing. Leaping over tall buildings does not pose a problem.[1]

Neither does falling. The old saying is true: The bigger they come, the harder they fall. And the smaller they come, the softer their landings. Again, the reason is geometry. If an elephant falls from a building, gravity pulls strongly on its huge mass while its comparatively small surface area offers little resistance. A mouse, on the other hand, is so small in volume (and therefore mass) that gravity has little to attract; at the same time, its relative surface area is so huge that it serves as a built-in parachute.

A mouse, writes Haldane, could be dropped from a thousand-yard-high cliff and walk away unharmed. A rat would probably suffer enough damage to be killed. A person would certainly be killed. And a horse, he tells us, "splashes."

The same relationships apply to inanimate falling objects—say, drops of water. The atmosphere is drenched with water vapor, even when we can't see it in the form of clouds. However, once a tiny particle begins to attract water molecules to its sides, things change rapidly. As the diameter of the growing droplet increases by a hundred, the surface area increases by ten thousand, and its volume a million-fold. The larger surface area reflects far more light—making the cloud visible. The enormously increased volume gives the drops the gravitational pull they need to splash down to the ground as rain.

According to cloud experts, water droplets in the air are simultaneously pulled on by electrical forces of attraction—which keep them herded together in the cloud—and gravity, which pulls them down. When the drops are small, their surface area is huge compared to volume; electrical (molecular) forces rule and the drops stay suspended in midair. Once the drops get big enough, however, gravity always wins.

Pint-size objects barely feel gravity—a force that only makes itself felt on large scales. The electrical forces that hold molecules together are trillions of times stronger. That's why even the slightest bit of electrical static in the air can make your hair stand on end.

These electrical forces would present major problems to flea-size Superman. For one thing, he'd have a hard time flying faster than a speeding bullet, because the air would be a thick soup of sticky molecules grasping him from all directions; it would be like swimming through molasses.

Flies have no problem walking on the ceiling because the molecular glue that holds their feet to the moldings is stronger than the puny weight pulling them down. The electrical pull of water, however, attracts the insects like magnets. As Haldane points out, the electrical attraction of water molecules makes going for a drink a dangerous endeavor for an insect. A bug leaning over a puddle to take a sip of water would be in the same position as a person leaning out over a cliff to pluck a berry off a bush.

Water is one of the stickiest substances around. A person coming out of the shower carries about a pound of extra weight, scarcely a burden. But a mouse coming out of the shower would have to lift its weight in water, according to Haldane. For a fly, water is as powerful as flypaper; once it gets wet, it's stuck for life. That's one reason, writes Haldane, that most insects have a long proboscis.

In fact, once you get down to bug size, almost everything is different. An ant-size person could never write a book: The keys to an ant-size typewriter

---

1. According to Exploratorium physicist Tom Humphrey, all animals jump to the same height, roughly speaking. Both fleas and humans can jump about a meter off the ground—an interesting invariant.

would stick together; so would the pages of a manuscript. An ant couldn't build a fire because the smallest possible flame is larger than its body.

Shrinking down to atom size alters reality beyond [15] recognition, opening doors into new and wholly unexpected vistas. Atom-size things do not behave like molecule-size things or human-size things. Atomic particles are ruled by the probabilistic laws of quantum mechanics. Physicists have to be very clever to lure these quantum mechanical attributes out in the open, because they simply don't exist on the scales of human instrumentation. We do not perceive that energy comes in precisely defined clumps or that clouds of electrons buzz around atoms in a permanent state of probabilistic uncertainty. These behaviors become perceptible macroscopically only in exotic situations—for example, superconductivity—a superordered state where pairs of loose electrons in a material line up like a row of Rockettes. With electrons moving in lockstep, electricity can flow through superconductors without resistance.

Scale up to molecule-size matter, and electrical forces take over; scale up further, and gravity rules. As Philip and Phylis Morrison point out in the classic *Powers of Ten,* if you stick your hand in a sugar bowl, your fingers will emerge covered with tiny grains that stick to them due to electrical forces. However, if you stick your hand into a bowl of sugar cubes, you would be very surprised if a cube stuck to your fingers—unless you purposely set out to grasp one.

We know that gravity takes over in large-scale matters because everything in the universe larger than an asteroid is round or roundish—the result of gravity pulling matter in toward a common center. Everyday objects like houses and mountains come in every old shape, but mountains can only get so high before gravity pulls them down. They can get larger on Mars because gravity is less. Large things lose their rough edges in the fight against gravity. "No such thing as a teacup the diameter of Jupiter is possible in our world," say the Morrisons. As a teacup grew to Jupiter size, its handle and sides would be pulled into the center by the planet's huge gravity until it resembled a sphere.

Add more matter still, and the squeeze of gravity ignites nuclear fires; stars exist in a continual tug-of-war between gravitational collapse and the outward pressure of nuclear fire. Over time, gravity wins again. A giant star eventually collapses into a black hole. It doesn't matter whether the star had planets orbiting its periphery or what globs of gas and dust went into making the star in the first place. Gravity is very democratic. Anything can grow up to be a black hole.

Even time ticks faster in the universe of the small. Small animals move faster, metabolize food faster (and eat more); their hearts beat faster; their life spans are short. In his book *About Time,* Paul Davis raises the interesting question: Does the life of a mouse feel shorter to a mouse than our life feels to us?

Biologist Stephen Jay Gould has answered this [20] question in the negative. "Small mammals tick fast, burn rapidly, and live for a short time; large mammals live long at a stately pace. Measured by their own internal clocks, mammals of different sizes tend to live for the same amount of time."

We all march to our own metronomes. Yet Davis suggests that all life shares the same beat because all life on Earth relies on chemical reactions—and chemical reactions take place in a sharply limited frame of time. In physicist Robert Forward's science fiction saga *Dragon's Egg,* creatures living on a neutron star are fueled by nuclear reactions; on their world, everything takes place millions of times faster. Many generations could be born and die before a minute passes on Earth.

And think how Earth would seem if we could slow our metabolism down. If our time ticked slowly enough, we could watch mountains grow and continental plates shift and come crashing together. The heavens would be bursting with supernovas, and comets would come smashing onto our shores with the regularity of shooting stars. Every day would be the Fourth of July.

An artist friend likes to imagine that if we could stand back far enough from Earth, but still see people, we would see enormous waves sweeping the globe every morning as people stood up from bed, and another huge wave of toothbrushing as people got ready to bed down for the night—one time zone after another, a tide of toothbrushing waxing and waning, following the shadow of the Sun across the land.

We miss a great deal because we perceive only things on our own scale. Exploring the invisible worlds beneath our skin can be a terrifying experience. I know because I tried it with a flexible microscope attached to a video camera on display at the Exploratorium in San Francisco. The skin on your arm reveals a dizzy landscape of nicks, creases, folds, and dewy transparent hairs the size of redwood trees—all embedded with giant boulders of dirt. Whiskers and eyelashes are disgusting—mascara dripping off like mud on a dog's tail. It is rather overwhelming to look through your own skin at blood cells coursing through capillaries. It's like looking at yourself without clothes. We forget the extent to which our view of the world is airbrushed, that we see things through a shroud of size, a blissfully out-of-focus blur.

An even more powerful microscope would reveal all the creatures that live on your face, dangling from tiny hairs or hiding out in your eyelashes. Not to mention the billions that share your bed every night and nest in your dish towels. How many bacteria can stand on the pointy end of a pin? You don't want to know.[2]

We're so hung up on our own scale of life that we miss most of life's diversity, says Berkeley microbiologist Norman Pace. "Who's in the ocean? People think of whales and seals, but 90 percent of organisms in the ocean are less than two micrometers."

In their enchanting journey *Microcosmos,* microbiologist Lynn Margulis and Dorion Sagan point out the fallacy of thinking that large beings are somehow supreme. Billions of years before creatures composed of cells with nuclei (like ourselves) appeared on Earth, simple bacteria transformed the surface of the planet and invented many high-tech processes that humans are still trying to understand—including the transformation of sunlight into energy with close to a 100 percent efficiency (green plants do it all the time). Indeed, they point out that fully 10 percent of our body weight (minus the water) consists of bacteria—most of which we couldn't live without.

Zoom in smaller than life-size, and solid tables become airy expanses of space, with an occasional nut of an atomic nucleus lost in the center, surrounded by furious clouds of electrons. As you zoom in, or out, the world looks simple, then complex, then simple again. Earth from far enough away would be a small blue dot; come in closer and you see weather patterns and ocean; closer still and humanity comes into view; closer still and it all fades away, and you're back inside the landscape of matter—mostly empty space.

So complexity, too, changes with scale. Is an egg complex? On the outside, it's a plain enough oval, like Jupiter's giant red spot. On the inside, it's white and yolk and blood vessels and DNA and squawking and pecking order and potential chocolate mousse or crème caramel.

The universe of the extremely small is so strange and rich that we can't begin to grasp it. No one said it better than Erwin Schrödinger himself:

> As our mental eye penetrates into smaller and smaller distances and shorter and shorter times, we find nature behaving so entirely differently from what we observe in visible and palpable bodies of our surroundings that no model shaped after our large-scale experiences can ever be "true." A complete satisfactory model of this type is not only practically inaccessible, but not even thinkable. Or, to be precise, we can, of course, think of it, but however we think it, it is wrong; not perhaps quite as meaningless as a "triangular circle," but more so than a "winged lion." ○

---

2. For an eye-opening view, read *The Secret House,* by David Bodanis.

Looking Closer

DIAMANTE FOR CHUCK

Jan Greenberg

Ovals
Luminous, Hot
Popping, Pulsing, Swirling
Curlicues of Color, A Kaleidoscope
Blurring, Blending, Focusing
Immense, Intense
Self

WILLARD WIGAN

Self-taught artist Willard Wigan (b. 1957) creates some of the smallest sculptures in the world, many of them nearly invisible to the naked eye. *Man v. Ant* (the ant is real) is an example of the tiny scenes he crafts on surfaces as small as the head of a pin, the eye of a needle, or a grain of sugar. His work often takes storybook or religious themes. Peering into a high-powered microscope, Wigan uses thin shards of glass to sculpt his figurines. To minimize the movement in his hands, he meditates. He works in total silence, holding his breath for up to three minutes at a stretch, and with painstaking precision in the lull between heartbeats. Wigan describes this process as "trying to pass a pin through a bubble without bursting it." His amazing skill at such detailed work has drawn the attention of microsurgeons, many of whom travel to his studio to watch him work. Wigan lives and creates in Birmingham, England.

STEVEN MILLHAUSER

Steven Millhauser (b. 1943) is the author of three volumes of short stories, one collection of novellas, and four novels, including *Martin Dressler* (1996), which won the Pulitzer Prize for Fiction in 1997. A graduate of Columbia College and Brown University, Millhauser lives in Saratoga Springs, New York, and is a professor of English at Skidmore College. "The Fascination of the Miniature" first appeared in the Summer 1983 issue of the quarterly magazine *Grand Street*.

BILL BRYSON

Born in Iowa in 1951, Bill Bryson moved to England in 1973, where he worked as a journalist for many years and wrote freelance travel articles.

Bryson's first travel book, *The Lost Continent* (1989), a humorous description of a cross-country auto trip through the back roads of America, was quite successful. It was followed by other best-selling travel books, and several books on the English language, including *Bryson's Dictionary of Troublesome Words* (2002).

The excerpt here is from *A Short History of Nearly Everything* (2003), winner of the Aventis Science Book Prize, which covers issues as diverse as the origins of the universe, relativity, and quantum theory.

CARL SAGAN

American astronomer, educator, and author Carl Sagan (1934–1996) is perhaps best known for his award-winning PBS series *Cosmos,* in which he inspired a sense of wonder and excitement about his favorite subjects: the origins of life and the search for intelligent life in the universe.

In addition to holding a twenty-five-year professorship at Cornell University, Sagan was the author of numerous scientific papers, popular articles, and books, including *The Dragons of Eden* (1977), for which he won a Pulitzer Prize in 1978, and *Pale Blue Dot: A Vision of the Human Future in Space* (1994). In the 1950s Sagan began serving as a consultant and adviser to NASA. He contributed to the Mariner, Viking, Voyager, and Galileo expeditions. "Reflections on a Mote of Dust" is an excerpt from a commencement address Sagan delivered in 1996; it was inspired by *Pale Blue Dot,* an image of the earth taken from the *Voyager 1* spacecraft.

VOYAGER 1

NASA's *Voyager 1* spacecraft was approximately 6.4 billion kilometers (4 billion miles) away when it took this photograph of the Earth on February 14, 1990. The Earth is the small speck centered in the strip of light. In the original caption NASA wrote, "In this image the Earth is a mere point of light, a crescent only 0.12 pixel in size. Our planet was caught in the center of one of the scattered light rays resulting from taking the image so close to the sun." To view other images taken by NASA expeditions, visit NASA's Planetary Photojournal web site at photojournal.jpl.nasa.gov.

HAROLD EDGERTON

 Harold Edgerton (1903–1990) developed and popularized the use of the stroboscope in photography, controlling the instrument's pulsating light to freeze precise moments on film. The technology Edgerton developed while teaching at the Massachusetts Institute of Technology found applications in countless fields of science and industry, but he may be most famous for creating artistic images like the one reproduced here of a bullet piercing an apple (1964).

BRYAN STEIFF

 The curriculum vitae on Bryan Steiff's web site (www.artnerd.net) consists of the following lowercase copy:

i am a chicago based artist
i like to make things
i am in fact an artnerd
and a photogeek
i will make you something
if you want

Steiff received his MFA in photography from Columbia College Chicago in 2004.

Steiff's art focuses largely on "constructed environments." He describes *terraFutura #9* (2003) as a series of "fabricated landscapes." In his artist's statement he writes that he constructs the landscapes "using technological materials": "These model landscapes are then photographed and printed large-scale (approximately 42 x 30 inches). Through this process of transforming everyday recognizable objects into a model for one possible future I am asking the viewer to question this view of what may come and consider its consequences. . . . By . . . making the miniature monumental the pictures speak to the impact of technology on our life and environment."

K. C. COLE

K. C. Cole has commented that her "writing career has changed gear many times." After graduating from Columbia University, she was pursuing an interest in Eastern European affairs when she "stumbled upon the Exploratorium"—a hands-on science museum in San Francisco—and soon thereafter began a career as a science and health writer. "A Matter of Scale" is one of a series of essays in *The Universe and the Teacup: The Mathematics of Truth and Beauty* (1998). In that book, Cole speaks to the relevance of mathematics to everyday life and on the ways in which math provides insight into social, political, and natural phenomena as diverse as calculating the risks of smoking to understanding election outcomes. Awarded the American Institute of Physics Award for Best Science Writer in 1995, Cole writes regularly on science for the *Los Angeles Times*.

CHUCK CLOSE

 Since the 1970s, artist Chuck Close has worked in a style known as photorealism or superrealism, which attempts to recreate in paint the aesthetic and representational experience of photography. Close paints enormous canvases of people's faces that duplicate photographic images in precise detail, such as *Self-Portrait, 2000–2001*.

Born in Monroe, Washington, in 1940, Close has lived in New York since 1967. In December 1988 he became paralyzed below his shoulders after a spinal artery suddenly collapsed, but he continues to paint colossal and powerful portraits using a brush held in his mouth.

JAN GREENBERG

Teacher, lecturer, and author of seven works of fiction and ten books on art and architecture for young readers, Jan Greenberg says her three daughters inspired her to write for a young audience. "Teenagers are the most interesting people I know," says Greenberg. "There is no other period in one's life when certain emotions—joy, sadness, or anger—seem so intense." Her most recent titles include two written with Sandra Jordan: *Action Jackson* (2002) and *Runaway Girl: The Artist Louise Bourgeois* (2003). Greenberg's poem "Diamante for Chuck" was published in *Heart to Heart* (2001), an award-winning book of poems about contemporary art. Greenberg lives in St. Louis, Missouri.

SEEING

1. "A Matter of Scale" is a masterful exercise in observing and drawing inferences from the natural world. K. C. Cole's essay stimulates and sustains our interest in the most common creatures and daily events. Reread the essay, and identify one or two paragraphs that you think are especially effective. What makes these paragraphs memorable or convincing? What techniques does Cole use to capture your attention in these paragraphs? What does Cole find "magically seductive" about observing "a world where everything measures much bigger or smaller than ourselves" (para. 1)?

2. Examine the images in this section: Wigan's sculpture of a man fighting with an ant, Edgerton's photograph of a bullet piercing an apple, Steiff's "constructed landscape," and Close's stylized self-portrait. Where does your eye linger as you look at each image? Comment on the roles that color, light, and shadow play in enhancing the effects of each image. What is your overall impression of each image? How would you describe each image to someone who has never seen it before? Write a paragraph or two about two of the images here. Swap drafts with one or more students in your class. How are your drafts different?

WRITING

1. When K. C. Cole speaks of the difference scale can make in the natural world, she declares that "quantitative changes can make huge qualitative differences" (para. 2). Then she offers compelling examples to support this assertion. Do you think a similar assertion can be made about aspects of the ordinary world? Draft an essay in which you validate or challenge the reasonableness of applying Cole's assertion to the scale of our everyday lives. Draw on your own experiences for arguments that your readers will find compelling and convincing.

2. Review the images in this section, and choose the one that interests you most. Why are you drawn to this particular image? What range of associations and metaphors does this image elicit from you? Using Bill Bryson's work as a model, draft an essay in which you use metaphor and other figurative language to describe what you imagine to be the process involved in creating the image.

2 COMING TO TERMS WITH PLACE

Richard Misrach, *12-23-97 5:09 PM*

"Where are you from?" This question invariably arises when two Americans meet for the first time, especially when traveling. "I'm from the South," "I'm from L.A.," "I'm from Cody, Wyoming"—each response conjures different cultural assumptions and associations. In fact, the meaning we attribute to these responses suggests that growing up in a particular place leaves a deep, if not indelible, mark on a person's character. As the popular saying goes, "You can take the kid out of Brooklyn, but you can't take Brooklyn out of the kid." "Place" is a fundamental component of everyday life, the "where" that locates each event and experience in our lives. Place in this sense evokes public identity, the characteristics that inform our accents, our clothes, and our behavior.

Think of a place: a town, a city, America itself. If you were asked to describe that place, what comes immediately to mind: the people? the buildings? the landscape? landmarks? a feeling? What impact have the events of September 11, 2001, had on people's awareness of "America" as a place? Americans often classify people by where they are

Richard Misrach, *3-3-98 6:25 PM*

Our sense of place is no longer limited to the physical realm. The Internet offers an electronic landscape, a virtual world in which we can frequent certain sites and form communities there. Advertisers try to convince us that we can reach any place in the real or virtual world within seconds, without leaving "the privacy of your own home."

In contemporary American culture, the centuries-old distinctions between "place" and "space" seem to be disappearing. Jerry Brown, a former governor of California and candidate for president, and now mayor of Oakland, California, drew the following distinction between "place" and "space":

> People don't live in place, they live in space. The media used to accuse me of that—living in space. But it wasn't true. Now too many people just live in their minds, not in communities. They garage themselves in their homes and live in market space. It's an alienated way for human beings to live. It's the difference between a native and an immigrant. A native lives in place, not space.

For most people, coming to terms with place is ultimately a personal matter. It can mean the

Richard Misrach, *2-21-00 4.38 PM*

Richard Misrach, *3-20-00 4:05–5:00 AM*

Richard Misrach, *4-9-00 7:49 AM*

smell of chicken roasting in the oven, the sound of traffic or a certain song, the sight of a familiar stretch of land. In many respects, place is also about relationships, both among people, and between us and our associations with a particular time and space.

The essays and images in this chapter represent an attempt to map out different ways we connect socially and culturally with others; they can help us understand how geographical location, or a sense of place, shapes our outlook on the world and who we are.

RICHARD MISRACH

This portfolio of photographs of the Golden Gate Bridge exemplifies the exquisite artistic sensibility of the celebrated American photographer Richard Misrach. Taken from the front porch of his home in the Berkeley hills, on the eastern shore of San Francisco Bay, the photographs were shot from exactly the same viewpoint but at different times of day, in every weather condition and light. They offer stunning perspectives on—and insights into—one of America's most famous structures and on the relationship of that structure to Alcatraz Island, Angel Island, the Marin Headlands, and the city of San Francisco. The sublime images transcend ordinary views of the bridge. They are, Misrach explains, "an unabashed celebration of the glorious light that is the Golden Gate." Eighty-five of these photographs of the bridge have been collected in a volume titled *Richard Misrach: Golden Gate* (2001).

Born in Los Angeles in 1949, Misrach graduated from the University of California, Berkeley, with a degree in psychology. He is the recipient of numerous fellowships and awards, including a Guggenheim Fellowship and several grants from the National Endowment for the Arts. Among his other books of photographs are *Desert Cantos* (1987), *Bravo 20: The Bombing of the American West* (1990), and *Sky Book* (2000), a photographic meditation on the desert sky.

SEEING

1. Review carefully Richard Misrach's photographs of the Golden Gate Bridge. Which photograph most engages your attention? Why? What artistic purpose(s) does the bridge seem to serve for Misrach? The word *bridge* is defined as "a structure, usually of wood, stone, brick, or iron, erected over a river or other water course, . . . to make a passageway from one bank to the other" and as "anything supported at the ends, which serves to keep some other thing from resting upon the object spanned, . . . or which forms a platform or staging over which something passes or is conveyed." After studying Misrach's photographs, what do you think the word means to him? What artistic purpose does the bridge serve for him?

2. What is present in—or absent from—Misrach's photographs that you associate with images of bridges? What details in his photographs reinforce or challenge your expectations of what a photograph of a bridge should look like? What evidence do you see in the photographs of Misrach's stance on larger issues—the relationship between people and the environment, for example?

WRITING

1. How does the image of a bridge create a sense of place? a sense of space? Choose two of Misrach's images of the Golden Gate Bridge and write the first draft of an essay in which you compare and contrast the sense of place and space each conveys.

2. Use one of Misrach's images as the basis of an argumentative essay in which you support or challenge the claim that the human struggle, the successes and failures to overcome nature, the use and abuse of nature, are readily evident in images of bridges. Please be sure to validate each of your assertions with a detailed analysis of the photograph.

EDWARD HOPPER

Edward Hopper's signature vision is expressed in virtually all his paintings—a wide array of American scenes ranging from rural landscapes and seascapes to street scenes, isolated buildings, and domestic interiors. Hopper masterfully expressed the isolation, boredom, and vacuity of modern life. Even his most colorful, luminous scenes are stripped of joy through the extreme spareness of composition and detail. His Depression-era work in particular evokes the mood of that time. However, Hopper claimed that his work expressed personal rather than national truths: "I don't think I ever tried to paint the American scene," he once said; "I'm trying to paint myself."

Born in 1882, Hopper grew up in Nyack, New York, and received his training in New York City and in Europe. He was still a young man when his work was included in the Armory Show of 1913, a New York City exhibition that featured what would become known as modernist paintings. But despite his critical success, Hopper had to work as a commercial illustrator to support himself. His career turned around when, in his forties, he married the artist Josephine Nivison (1883–1968). Through several decades of an emotionally turbulent but artistically productive relationship, Hopper created his most memorable paintings. He died in 1967.

EDWARD HIRSCH

The poet, critic, and teacher Edward Hirsch was born in 1950 in Chicago and attended Grinnell College and the University of Pennsylvania. A professor of creative writing at the University of Houston, Hirsch has published poems and reviews in *The New Yorker, The Nation,* the *New York Times Book Review,* and other leading journals. He has also published six volumes of poetry, including *Wild Gratitude* (1986), which won the National Book Critics Award, and *Lay Back the Darkness* (2003). Currently he is serving as the president of the Guggenheim Memorial Foundation; he also writes a poetry column for the *Washington Post Book World.* Hirsch has received numerous awards, including a MacArthur Foundation "genius" award and a Guggenheim Fellowship.

Hirsch edited *Transforming Vision: Writers on Art* (1994), the responses—in prose and verse—of a number of prominent writers to works on display at the Art Institute of Chicago. He argues that "the proper response to a work of visual art may well be an ode or an elegy, a meditative lyric, a lyrical meditation" because poetic descriptions of art "teach us to look and look again more closely" and "dramatize with great intensity the actual experience of encounter." The poem "Edward Hopper and the House by the Railroad (1925)" dramatizes Hirsch's own encounter with Hopper's famous painting.

SEEING

1. In *House by the Railroad,* where does Hopper direct your attention? What details do you notice about the house? its structure? its relationship to the railroad track and the sky? Where does your eye linger as you study the painting more carefully? How does each aspect of its presentation reinforce the overall effect of the painting?

2. On what features of Hopper's painting does Edward Hirsch focus in his poem? What effects does Hirsch create through personification of the house? Explain how his repetition of words, phrases, and structural elements reinforces—or detracts from—the overall impression or mood created in the poem. In what ways does Hirsch's poem change or enhance your initial reactions to Hopper's painting?

personification: Attributing human qualities to an object or an idea; often used as a poetic device.

WRITING

1. Write a page—in any form you prefer—in which you dramatize your encounter with Hopper's *House by the Railroad*. Do you agree with Hirsch that the house has the look of "someone American and gawky" (l. 38)?

2. Reread "Edward Hopper and the House by the Railroad (1925)" several times, until you feel comfortable describing and characterizing Hirsch's shifts in subject and tone. Based on your rereading of the poem, would you agree—or disagree—with the assertion that Hirsch seems more interested in Hopper the artist than in the scene he paints? How is the artist characterized in the poem? With what effects? At what point do the terms used to characterize house and artist seem to merge? What characteristics do the house and the artist share? What overall impression does Hirsch create in this comparison? Write the first draft of an essay in which you use evidence from the poem and the painting to validate your own response to the assertion that Hirsch is far more interested in Hopper as artist than in the art he has created.

Eudora Welty, *Storekeeper, 1935*

THE LITTLE STORE
Eudora Welty

TWO BLOCKS AWAY FROM THE MISSISSIPPI STATE Capitol, and on the same street with it, where our house was when I was a child growing up in Jackson, it was possible to have a little pasture behind your backyard where you could keep a Jersey cow, which we did. My mother herself milked her. A thrifty homemaker, wife, mother of three, she also did all her own cooking. And as far as I can recall, she never set foot inside a grocery store. It wasn't necessary.

For her regular needs, she stood at the telephone in our front hall and consulted with Mr. Lemly, of Lemly's Market and Grocery downtown, who took her order and sent it out on his next delivery. And since Jackson at the heart of it was still within very near reach of the open country, the blackberry lady clanged on her bucket with a quart measure at your front door in June without fail, the watermelon man rolled up to your house exactly on time for the Fourth of July, and down through the summer, the quiet of the early-morning streets was pierced by the calls of farmers driving in with their plenty. One brought his with a song, so plaintive we would sing it with him:

> "Milk, milk,
> Buttermilk,
> Snap beans—butterbeans—
> Tender okra—fresh greens . . .
> And buttermilk."

My mother considered herself pretty well prepared in her kitchen and pantry for any emergency that, in her words, might choose to present itself. But if she should, all of a sudden, need another lemon or find she was out of bread, all she had to do was call out, "Quick! Who'd like to run to the Little Store for me?"

I would.

She'd count out the change into my hand, and I 5 was away. I'll bet the nickel that would be left over that all over the country, for those of my day, the neighborhood grocery played a similar part in our growing up.

Our store had its name—it was that of the grocer who owned it, whom I'll call Mr. Sessions—but "the Little Store" is what we called it at home. It was a block down our street toward the capitol and half a block further, around the corner, toward the cemetery. I knew even the sidewalk to it as well as I knew my own skin. I'd skipped my jumping-rope up and down it, hopped its length through mazes of hopscotch, played jacks in its islands of shade, serpentined along it on my Princess bicycle, skated it backward and forward. In the twilight I had dragged my steamboat by its string (this was homemade out of every new shoebox, with candle in the bottom lighted and shining through colored tissue paper pasted over windows scissored out in the shapes of the sun, moon, and stars) across every crack of the walk without letting it bump or catch fire. I'd "played out" on that street after supper with my brothers and friends as long as "first-dark" lasted; I'd caught its lightning bugs. On the first Armistice Day (and this will set the time I'm speaking of) we made our own parade down that walk on a single velocipede—my brother pedaling, our little brother riding the handlebars, and myself standing on the back, all with arms wide, flying flags in each hand. (My father snapped that picture as we raced by. It came out blurred.)

As I set forth for the Little Store, a tune would float toward me from the house where there lived three sisters, girls in their teens, who ratted their hair over their ears, wore headbands like gladiators, and were considered to be very popular. They practiced for this in the daytime; they'd wind up the Victrola, leave the same record on they'd played before, and you'd see them bobbing past their dining-room windows while they danced with each other. Being three, they could go all day, cutting in:

"Everybody ought to know-oh
How to do the Tickle-Toe
    (how to do the Tickle-Toe)"—

They sang it and danced to it, and as I went by to the same song, I believed it.

A little further on, across the street, was the house where the principal of our grade school lived—lived on, even while we were having vacation. What if she would come out? She would halt me in my tracks— she had a very carrying and well-known voice in Jackson, where she'd taught almost everybody—saying, "Eudora Alice Welty, spell OBLIGE." OBLIGE was the word that she of course knew had kept me from making 100 on my spelling exam. She'd make me miss it again now, by boring her eyes through me from across the street. This was my vacation fantasy, one good way to scare myself on the way to the store.

Down near the corner waited the house of a little boy named Lindsey. The sidewalk here was old brick, which the roots of a giant chinaberry had humped up and tilted this way and that. On skates, you took it

fast, in a series of skittering hops, trying not to touch ground anywhere. If the chinaberries had fallen and rolled in the cracks, it was like skating through a whole shooting match of marbles. I crossed my fingers that Lindsey wouldn't be looking.

During the big flu epidemic he and I, as it happened, were being nursed through our sieges at the same time. I'd hear my father and mother murmuring to each other, at the end of a long day, "And I wonder how poor little *Lindsey* got along today?" Just as, down the street, he no doubt would have to hear his family saying, "And I wonder how is poor *Eudora* by now?" I got the idea that a choice was going to be made soon between poor little Lindsey and poor Eudora, and I came up with a funny poem. I wasn't prepared for it when my father told me it wasn't funny and my mother cried that if I couldn't be ashamed for myself, she'd have to be ashamed for me:

> There was a little boy and his name was Lindsey.
> He went to heaven with the influinzy.

He didn't, he survived it, poem and all, the same as I did. But his chinaberries could have brought me down in my skates in a flying act of contrition before his eyes, looking pretty funny myself, right in front of his house.

Setting out in this world, a child feels so indelible. He only comes to find out later that it's all the others along his way who are making themselves indelible to him.

Our Little Store rose right up from the sidewalk; standing in a street of family houses, it alone hadn't any yard in front, any tree or flowerbed. It was a plain frame building covered over with brick. Above the door, a little railed porch ran across on an upstairs level and four windows with shades were looking out. But I didn't catch on to those.

Running in out of the sun, you met what seemed total obscurity inside. There were almost tangible smells—licorice recently sucked in a child's cheek, dill-pickle brine that had leaked through a paper sack in a fresh trail across the wooden floor, ammonia-loaded ice that had been hoisted from wet croker sacks and slammed into the icebox with its sweet butter at the door, and perhaps the smell of still-untrapped mice.

Then through the motes of cracker dust, corn-meal dust, the Gold Dust of the Gold Dust Twins that the floor had been swept out with, the realities emerged. Shelves climbed to high reach all the way around, set out with not too much of any one thing but a lot of things—lard, molasses, vinegar, starch, matches, kerosene, Octagon soap (about a year's worth of octagon-shaped coupons cut out and saved brought a signet ring addressed to you in the mail. Furthermore, when the postman arrived at your door, he blew a whistle). It was up to you to remember what you came for, while your eye traveled from cans of sardines to ice cream salt to harmonicas to flypaper (over your head, batting around on a thread beneath the blades of the ceiling fan, stuck with its testimonial catch).

Its confusion may have been in the eye of its be- 15 holder. Enchantment is cast upon you by all those things you weren't supposed to have need for, it lures you close to wooden tops you'd outgrown, boy's marbles and agates in little net pouches, small rubber balls that wouldn't bounce straight, frazzly kitestring, clay bubble-pipes that would snap off in your teeth, the stiffest scissors. You could contemplate those long narrow boxes of sparklers gathering dust while you waited for it to be the Fourth of July or Christ-mas, and noisemakers in the shape of tin frogs for somebody's birthday party you hadn't been invited to yet, and see that they were all marvelous.

You might not have even looked for Mr. Sessions when he came around his store cheese (as big as a doll's house) and in front of the counter looking for you. When you'd finally asked him for, and received from him in its paper bag, whatever single thing it was that you had been sent for, the nickel that was left over was yours to spend.

Down at a child's eye level, inside those glass jars with mouths in their sides through which the grocer could run his scoop or a child's hand might be in-vited to reach for a choice, were wineballs, all-day suckers, gumdrops, peppermints. Making a row under the glass of a counter were the Tootsie Rolls, Hershey Bars, Goo-Goo Clusters, Baby Ruths. And whatever was the name of those pastilles that came stacked in a cardboard cylinder with a cardboard lid? They were thin and dry, about the size of tiddly-winks, and in the shape of twisted rosettes. A kind of chocolate dust came out with them when you shook them out in your hand. Were they chocolate? I'd say rather they were brown. They didn't taste of anything at all, unless it was wood. Their attraction was the number you got for a nickel.

Making up your mind, you circled the store around and around, around the pickle barrel, around the tower of Cracker Jack boxes; Mr. Sessions had built it for us himself on top of a packing case, like a house of cards.

If it seemed too hot for Cracker Jacks, I might get a cold drink. Mr. Sessions might have already stationed himself by the cold-drinks barrel, like a mind reader. Deep in ice water that looked black as ink, murky shapes that would come up as Coca-Colas, Orange Crushes, and various flavors of pop, were all swim-ming around together. When you gave the word, Mr. Sessions plunged his bare arm in to the elbow and fished out your choice, first try. I favored a locally bottled concoction called Lake's Celery. (What else could it be called? It was made by a Mr. Lake out of celery. It was a popular drink here for years but was not known universally, as I found out when I arrived in New York and ordered one in the Astor bar.) You drank on the premises, with feet set wide apart to miss the drip, and gave him back his bottle.

But he didn't hurry you off. A standing scales was 20 by the door, with a stack of iron weights and a brass slide on the balance arm, that would weigh you up to three hundred pounds. Mr. Sessions, whose hands were gentle and smelled of carbolic, would lift you up and set your feet on the platform, hold your loaf of bread for you, and taking his time while you stood still for him, he would make cer-tain of what you weighed today. He could even re-member what you weighed the last time, so you

EUDORA WELTY

In short stories and novels, Eudora Welty explored the frailty and strength of human character in her native Mississippi. A keen observer of behavior and social relations, she crafted fictional worlds that evoke compelling portraits of people and places. Born in Jackson in 1909, Welty published her first story in 1936. In the years following she received many awards, including a Pulitzer Prize for the novel *The Optimist's Daughter* (1972), the American Book Award for *The Collected Stories of Eudora Welty* (1980), and the National Book Critics Circle Award for her autobiographical essays in *One Writer's Beginnings* (1984). Welty died in 2001.

"The Little Store" (1975) draws on personal experience. Remembering experience, she said, helped her craft fiction out of "the *whole* fund of my feelings, my responses to the real experiences of my own life, to the relationships that formed and changed it, that I have given most of myself to."

SEEING

1. What principles of selection and order does Eudora Welty use to organize her reminiscences of running errands to the local grocery store? Reread the opening paragraphs in which she affectionately recounts some of the games she played as a child. How do these moments express her feelings toward the store? What are the effects of presenting these paragraphs before she describes the store? To which senses does she appeal in describing the Little Store? What techniques does she use to reinforce the childlike perspective of the essay? In each instance, point to specific evidence to verify your point.

2. Welty was an accomplished photographer as well as a renowned writer. (Her photographs of people and places in the South are collected in *Photographs,* 1989.) She hoped to capture "the moment in which people reveal themselves." After examining the photograph of the storekeeper, what do you think he reveals about himself? Note as many details of the photograph as you can. What, for example, do you notice about the man's stance? body language? facial expression? How does the lighting affect your impression of him? How has Welty chosen to frame her subject? What has she included in the photograph? What has she omitted?

WRITING

1. In an interview about her photography, Welty suggested that both the writer and the photographer must learn "about accuracy of the eye, about observation, and about sympathy toward what is in front of you." Consider the meaning of each of the three components of her statement, and list the ways in which you can apply them to writing and to taking photographs. Write an essay in which you explore Welty's statement about the similarities between writing and taking pictures, using her own verbal and visual takes on similar subjects to support your points.

2. When Welty observed that in her photographs, she tries to capture "the moment in which people reveal themselves," what assumptions is she making about photography and spontaneity? Draft an analytical essay in which you defend or challenge the assertion that the subject's awareness of the photographer precludes the possibility of capturing a spontaneous moment. Whichever side you argue, support your claims with evidence and anticipate— and rebut—the arguments of the other side.

I'm not very eloquent about things like this, but I think that writing and photography go together. I don't mean that they are related arts, because they're not. But the person doing it, I think, learns from both things about accuracy of the eye, about observation and about sympathy toward what is in front of you. It's about trying to see into the essence of reality. It's about honesty, or truth telling, and a way to find it in yourself, how to need it and learn from it.

I still go back to a paragraph of mine from *One Time, One Place* as the best expression I was ever able to manage about what I did or was trying to do in both fields. It's still the truth:

> I learned quickly enough when to click the shutter, but what I was becoming aware of more slowly was a story-writer's truth: The thing to wait on, to reach for, is the moment in which people reveal themselves. . . . I learned from my own pictures, one by one, and had to; for I think we are the breakers of our own hearts.

– Eudora Welty, from "Storekeeper, 1935"

Once More to the Lake

E. B. White

ONE SUMMER, ALONG ABOUT 1904, MY FATHER rented a camp on a lake in Maine and took us all there for the month of August. We all got ringworm from some kittens and had to rub Pond's Extract on our arms and legs night and morning, and my father rolled over in a canoe with all his clothes on; but outside of that the vacation was a success, and from then on none of us ever thought there was any place in the world like that lake in Maine. We returned summer after summer—always on August 1st for one month. I have since become a salt-water man, but sometimes in summer there are days when the restlessness of the tides and the fearful cold of the sea water and the incessant wind which blows across the afternoon and into the evening make me wish for the placidity of a lake in the woods. A few weeks ago this feeling got so strong I bought myself a couple of bass hooks and a spinner and returned to the lake where we used to go, for a week's fishing and to revisit old haunts.

I took along my son, who had never had any fresh water up his nose and who had seen lily pads only from train windows. On the journey over to the lake I began to wonder what it would be like. I wondered how time would have marred this unique, this holy spot—the coves and streams, the hills that the sun set behind, the camps and the paths behind the camps. I was sure that the tarred road would have found it out and I wondered in what other ways it would be desolated. It is strange how much you can remember about places like that once you allow your mind to return into the grooves which lead back. You remember one thing, and that suddenly reminds you of another thing. I guess I remembered clearest of all the early mornings, when the lake was cool and motionless, remembered how the bedroom smelled of the lumber it was made of and of the wet woods whose scent entered through the screen. The partitions in the camp were thin and did not extend clear to the top of the rooms, and as I was always the first up I would dress softly so as not to wake the others, and sneak out into the sweet outdoors and start out in the canoe, keeping close along the shore in the long shadows of the pines. I remembered being very careful never to rub my paddle against the gunwale for fear of disturbing the stillness of the cathedral.

The lake had never been what you would call a wild lake. There were cottages sprinkled around the shores, and it was in farming country although the shores of the lake were quite heavily wooded. Some of the cottages were owned by nearby farmers, and you would live at the shore and eat your meals at the farmhouse. That's what our family did. But although it wasn't wild, it was a fairly large and undisturbed lake and there were places in it which, to a child at least, seemed infinitely remote and primeval.

I was right about the tar: It led to within half a mile of the shore. But when I got back there, with my boy, and we settled into a camp near a farmhouse and into the kind of summertime I had known, I could tell that it was going to be pretty much the same as it had been before—I knew it, lying in bed the first morning, smelling the bedroom and hearing the boy sneak quietly out and go off along the shore in a boat. I began to sustain the illusion that he was I, and therefore, by simple transposition, that I was my father. This sensation persisted, kept cropping up all the time we were there. It was not an entirely new feeling, but in this setting it grew much stronger. I seemed to be living a dual existence. I would be in the middle of some simple act, I would be picking up a bait box or laying down a table fork, or I would be saying something, and suddenly it would be not I but my father who was saying the words and making the gesture. It gave me a creepy sensation.

We went fishing the first morning. I felt the same damp moss covering the worms in the bait can, and saw the dragonfly alight on the tip of my rod as it hovered a few inches from the surface of the water. It was the arrival of this fly that convinced me beyond any doubt that everything was as it always had been, that the years were a mirage and there had been no years. The small waves were the same, chucking the rowboat under the chin as we fished at anchor, and the boat was the same boat, the same color green and the ribs broken in the same places, and under the floor-boards the same freshwater leavings and débris—the dead helgramite, the wisps of moss, the rusty discarded fishhook, the dried blood from yesterday's catch. We stared silently at the tips of our rods, at the dragonflies that came and went. I lowered the tip of mine into the water, tentatively, pensively dislodging the fly, which darted two feet away, poised, darted two feet back, and came to rest again a little farther up the rod. There had been no years between the ducking of this dragonfly and the other one—the one that was part of memory. I looked at the boy, who was silently watching his fly, and it was my hands that held his rod, my eyes watching. I felt dizzy and didn't know which rod I was at the end of.

We caught two bass, hauling them in briskly as though they were mackerel, pulling them over the side of the boat in a businesslike manner without any landing net, and stunning them with a blow on the back of the head. When we got back for a swim before lunch, the lake was exactly where we had left it, the same number of inches from the dock, and there was only the merest suggestion of a breeze. This seemed an utterly enchanted sea, this lake you could leave to its own devices for a few hours and come back to, and find that it had not stirred, this constant and trustworthy body of water. In the shallows, the dark, water-soaked sticks and twigs, smooth and old, were undulating in clusters on the bottom against the clean ribbed sand, and the track of the mussel was plain. A school of minnows swam by, each minnow with its small individual shadow, doubling the attendance, so clear and sharp in the sunlight. Some of the other campers were in swimming, along the shore, one of them with a cake of soap, and the water felt thin and clear and unsubstantial. Over the years there had been this person with the cake of soap, this cultist, and here he was. There had been no years.

Up to the farmhouse to dinner through the teeming, dusty field, the road under our sneakers was only a two-track road. The middle track was missing, the one with the marks of the hooves and the splotches of dried flaky manure. There had always been three tracks to choose from in choosing which track to walk in; now the choice was narrowed down to two. For a moment I missed terribly the middle alternative. But the way led past the tennis court, and something about the way it lay there in the sun reassured me; the tape had loosened along the backline, the alleys were green with plaintains and other weeds, and the net (installed in June and removed in September) sagged in the dry noon, and the whole place steamed with midday heat and hunger and emptiness. There was a choice of pie for dessert, and one was blueberry and one was apple, and the waitresses were the same country girls, there having been no passage of time, only the illusion of it as in a dropped curtain—the waitresses were still fifteen; their hair had been washed, that was the only difference—they had been to the movies and seen the pretty girls with the clean hair.

Summertime, oh summertime, pattern of life indelible, the fade-proof lake, the woods unshatterable, the pasture with the sweetfern and the juniper forever and ever, summer without end; this was the background, and the life along the shore was the design, the cottages with their innocent and tranquil design, their tiny docks with the flagpole and the American flag floating against the white clouds in the blue sky, the little paths over the roots of the trees leading from camp to camp and the paths leading back to the outhouses and the can of lime for sprinkling, and at the souvenir counters at the store the miniature birch-bark canoes and the post cards that showed things looking a little better than they looked. This was the American family at play, escaping the city heat, wondering whether the newcomers in the camp at the head of the cove were "common" or "nice," wondering whether it was true that the people who drove up for Sunday dinner at the farmhouse were turned away because there wasn't enough chicken.

It seemed to me, as I kept remembering all this, that those times and those summers had been infinitely precious and worth saving. There had been jollity and peace and goodness. The arriving (at the beginning of August) had been so big a business in itself, at the railway station the farm wagon drawn up, the first smell of the pine-laden air, the first glimpse of the smiling farmer, and the great importance of the trunks and your father's enormous authority in such matters, and the feel of the wagon under you for the long ten-mile haul, and at the top of the last long hill catching the first view of the lake after eleven months of not seeing this cherished body of water. The shouts and cries of other campers when they saw you, and the trunks to be unpacked, to give up their rich burden. (Arriving was less exciting nowadays, when you sneaked up in your car and parked it under a tree near the camp and took out the bags and in five minutes it was all over, no fuss, no loud wonderful fuss about trunks.)

Peace and goodness and jollity. The only thing that 10 was wrong now, really, was the sound of the place, an unfamiliar nervous sound of the outboard motors. This was the note that jarred, the one thing that would sometimes break the illusion and set the years moving. In those other summertimes all motors were inboard; and when they were at a little distance, the noise they made was a sedative, an ingredient of summer sleep. They were one-cylinder and two-cylinder engines, and some were make-and-break and some were jump-spark, but they all made a sleepy sound across the lake. The one-lungers throbbed and fluttered, and the twin cylinder ones purred and purred, and that was a quiet sound too. But now the campers all had outboards. In the daytime, in the hot mornings, these motors made a petulant, irritable sound; at night, in the still evening when the afterglow lit the water, they whined about one's ears like mosquitoes. My boy loved our rented outboard, and his great desire was to achieve single-handed mastery over it, and authority, and he soon learned the trick of choking it a little (but not too much), and the adjustment of the needle valve. Watching him I would remember the things you could do with the old one-cylinder engine with the heavy flywheel, how you could have it eating out of your hand if you got really close to it spiritually. Motor boats in those days didn't have clutches, and you would make a landing by shutting off the motor at the proper time and coasting in with a dead rudder. But there was a way of reversing them, if you learned the trick, by cutting the switch and putting it on again exactly on the final dying revolution of the flywheel, so that it would kick back against compression and begin reversing. Approaching a dock in a strong following breeze, it was difficult to slow up sufficiently by the ordinary coasting method, and if a boy felt he had complete mastery over his motor, he was tempted to keep it running beyond its time and then reverse it a few feet from the dock. It took a cool nerve, because if you threw the switch a twentieth of a second too soon you could catch the flywheel when it still had speed enough to go up past center, and the boat would leap ahead, charging bull-fashion at the dock.

We had a good week at the camp. The bass were biting well and the sun shone endlessly, day after day. We would be tired at night and lie down in the accumulated heat of the little bedrooms after the long hot day and the breeze would stir almost imperceptibly outside and the smell of the swamp drift in through the rusty screens. Sleep would come easily and in the morning the red squirrel would be on the roof tapping out his gay routine. I kept remembering everything, lying in bed in the mornings—the small steamboat that had a long rounded stern like the lip of a Ubangi, and how quietly she ran on the moonlight sails, when the older boys played their mandolins and the girls sang and we ate doughnuts dipped in sugar, and how sweet the music was on the water in the shining night, and what it had felt like to think about girls then. After breakfast we would go up to the store and the things were in the same place—the minnows in a bottle, the plugs and spinners disarranged and pawed over by the youngsters from the boys' camp, the Fig Newtons and the Beeman's gum. Outside, the road was tarred and cars stood in front of the store. Inside, all was just as it had always been, except there was more Coca-Cola and not so much Moxie and root beer and birch beer and sarsaparilla. We would walk out with a bottle of pop apiece and sometimes the pop would backfire up our noses and hurt. We explored the streams, quietly, where the turtles slid off the sunny logs and dug their way into the soft bottom; and we lay on the town wharf and fed worms to the tame bass. Everywhere we went I had trouble making out which was I, the one walking at my side, the one walking in my pants.

One afternoon while we were there at that lake a thunderstorm came up. It was like the revival of an old melodrama that I had seen long ago with childish awe. The second-act climax of the drama of the electrical disturbance over a lake in America had not changed in any important respect. This was the big scene, still the big scene. The whole thing was so familiar, the first feeling of oppression and heat and a general air around camp of not wanting to go very far away. In midafternoon (it was all the same) a curious darkening of the sky, and a lull in everything that had made life tick; and then the way the boats suddenly swung the other way at their moorings with the coming of a breeze out of the new quarter, and the premonitory rumble. Then the kettle drum, then the snare, and then the bass drum and cymbals, then crackling light against the dark, and the gods grinning and licking their chops in the hills. Afterward the calm, the rain steadily rustling in the calm lake, the return of light and hope and spirits, and the campers running out in joy and relief to go swimming in the rain, their bright cries perpetuating the deathless joke about how they were getting simply drenched, and the children screaming with delight at the new sensation of bathing in the rain, and the joke about getting drenched linking the generations in a strong indestructible chain. And the comedian who waded in carrying an umbrella.

When the others went swimming my son said he was going in too. He pulled his dripping trunks from the line where they had hung all through the shower, and wrung them out. Languidly, and with no thought of going in, I watched him, his hard little body, skinny and bare, saw him wince slightly as he pulled up around his vitals the small, soggy, icy garment. As he buckled the swollen belt suddenly my groin felt the chill of death. ○

E.B. WHITE

Best known for his children's books, Elwyn Brooks White (1899–1985) was called "one of the nation's most precious literary resources" by the *New York Times*. Born in Mount Vernon, New York, White graduated from Cornell University in 1921. By 1929 he had begun writing for *The New Yorker*. There he met and married Katherine Angell, the magazine's literary editor; wrote political essays and editorials; and joined a literary circle of well-known writers that included James Thurber and Dorothy Parker.

After moving to rural Maine, White also began to write children's books. *Stuart Little* (1945), the story of a mouse, was followed in 1952 by *Charlotte's Web*, about a spider named Charlotte who befriends a pig. In 1970 White received the Laura Ingalls Wilder Medal for "his substantial and lasting contribution to literature for children."

In a *New Yorker* interview, White once described Thoreau's *Walden* as his favorite book, and he often wrote in praise of nature and rural living, as he does in "Once More to the Lake." The essay was first printed in 1941, in *Harper's*.

Over the years, White received many prestigious awards, including the Presidential Medal of Freedom, and the National Institute of Arts and Letters' Gold Medal for Essays and Criticism. He was also elected to the American Academy of Arts and Letters.

SEEING

1. When E. B. White returns to the lake as an adult, what does he find there? In what ways is the camp on the lake consistent with his childhood memories? What differences does he notice? How does the presence of his son shape his experience of revisiting "old haunts" (para. 1)? How would you characterize White's purpose in writing this essay?

2. Describe the structure of this essay. What anecdotes does White relate, in what order, and to what effect(s)? What tone and point of view does the author establish in the opening paragraphs? Now consider White's placement of the description of the thunderstorm toward the end of the piece. How does it help shape the overall arc of the piece? How does it connect to other descriptions in the essay?

RESPONDING VISUALLY

Create a visual representation of the structure of White's essay. You might draw a diagram, construct a collage, or sketch a series of events. Consider how you might visually represent the parts of the essay and how they are put together. Now write a one-page reflection on your experience of the differences between describing the essay's structure in words and representing it visually.

WRITING

1. Reread the final sentence of "Once More to the Lake." What ideas does the sentence suggest to you? How does it connect to the rest of the piece? to White's sense of experiencing the lake from both his father's perspective and his own as a boy, through his son? to the title of the essay? With these questions in mind, write a one-page interpretation of the last sentence of White's essay.

2. Let yourself "return into the grooves that lead back" (para. 2) to a place you remember from childhood. Write a descriptive essay in which you recall a childhood place through adult eyes. That is, describe how the place would strike you differently now if you were to revisit it. In your essay, draw on each of the five senses, as White does in his piece.

Kerry James Marshall,
Watts 1963, 1995

Retrospect: Camilo José Vergara's Photographs of 65 East 125th St., Harlem

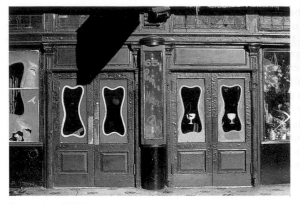

December 1977

January 1980

March 1990

September 1992

June 1997

August 2001

December 1983

November 1988

March 1994

February 1996

April 2003

February 2004

MARK PETERSON

Born (in 1955) and raised in Minneapolis, Mark Peterson began his career as a photographer while doing odd jobs for a photojournalist. "I was failing miserably as a writer," he said in a recent interview, "and thought photography would be easy. That was my first mistake in photography." After working in both Minneapolis and New York, Peterson moved to New Jersey to pursue freelance photography. His photographs, which he describes as "day in the life" reportage, have appeared in *Life, Newsweek, Fortune,* and the *New York Times Magazine.* In 1992 Peterson was awarded a W. Eugene Smith Grant for his work with revolving-door alcoholics, images produced over a twelve-year period.

Peterson's most recent projects include photographing teenagers in recovery from drug and alcohol addiction and an examination of upper-class New Yorkers and the "culture of philanthropy." Photographs from the latter project were shown at the Redux Gallery in New York City in the fall of 2004, an event that coincided with their publication in *Acts of Charity.*

The photograph here is from Peterson's series *Across the Street,* in which the photographer captures the divide between rich and poor living on and along Fifth Avenue in New York City.

SEEING

1. What exactly is the place captured by this photograph—the box? the park? the urban scene? How does the fact that someone sleeps inside the box create a sense of place? What other elements in the image mark the box as a place? How can you tell whether there is—or was—someone inside?

2. What does the photographer gain by positioning the homeless person's "place" clearly in the foreground of the image? What does he lose? Given what is visible in the picture, what changes—say, in perspective or focus—might you suggest to highlight the dramatic impact of this redefinition of *place*? What effect(s) does the photographer accentuate in the image by including the phrase "HANDLE WITH CARE"? by including the out-of-focus background of Burger King?

WRITING

1. Imagine the following scenario: The Olympic Games of 2012 are going to take place in your state. The opening ceremony is a few weeks away, and the city council is debating a resolution: that all homeless people in the city should be removed to shelters for the duration of the Games. You have been charged with advocating or challenging passage of the resolution. Write a draft of the speech you would make to the city council.

2. In a 1998 essay entitled "Distancing the Homeless," the writer and social critic Jonathan Kozol argues that the homeless are subject to many misconceptions. "A misconception . . . is not easy to uproot, particularly when it serves a useful social role. The notion that the homeless are largely psychotics who belong in institutions, rather than victims of displacements at the hands of enterprising realtors, spares us from the need to offer realistic solutions to the . . . extremes of wealth and poverty in the United States." Review the professional literature on the causes of homelessness published over the past eighteen months. Choose a still-popular misconception about homelessness—one that involves coming to terms with a sense of place—and write an argumentative essay in which you correct the mistaken or unexamined assumptions evident in this misconception.

Joel Sternfeld, *Mount Rushmore National Monument, Black Hills National Forest, South Dakota, August 1994*

"In 1868 the federal government deeded millions of acres in the Black Hills of South Dakota to the Great Sioux Nation. Nine years later, when gold was discovered in the area, Congress broke the treaty and took the land back.

"In the 1920s the state of South Dakota, eager to attract tourists, commissioned a sculptor to carve a colossal monument into Mount Rushmore. The Sioux considered the Black Hills their own sacred land.

"In 1980 the Supreme Court awarded the Sioux $17 million plus interest accrued since 1877 as compensation. The award is now valued at nearly $300 million, but the Sioux continue to refuse the money and to seek title to their land."

Portfolio: Sternfeld

Joel Sternfeld, *The Former Bryant's Grocery, Money, Mississippi, June 1994*

"In 1955 Emmett Till, a fourteen-year-old boy from Chicago, was visiting relatives near Money, Mississippi. Anxious to show new friends that he knew how to talk to white women, Till said, 'Bye, baby,' to Carolyn Bryant as he left this store.

"Three days later, Bryant's husband, Roy, and his half-brother, J. W. Milam, kidnapped, tortured, and killed Till. Milam and Bryant were found not guilty by an all-male, all-white jury. The deliberations lasted a little over an hour."

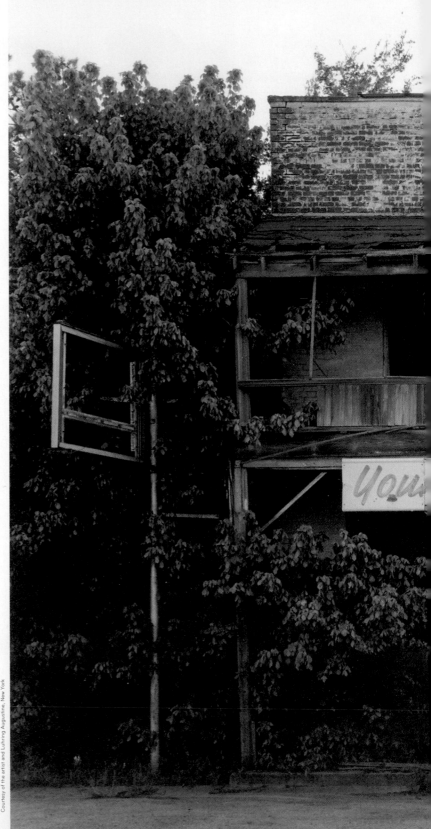

Joel Sternfeld, *Hanford
Reservation, Hanford,
Washington, August 1994*

"In 1942 the United States Army,
searching for a place to manufacture plutonium for the atomic
bomb, selected Hanford, a remote farming community in
central Washington. Fewer than
two thousand people occupied
the half-million acres around the
town. The Army took over the
land and built the world's first
large-scale nuclear reactor.
Throughout the cold war, Hanford
produced much of the raw material for America's nuclear arsenal.

"More than 440 billion gallons
of chemical and radioactive waste
were poured into the ground
at Hanford, including enough
plutonium to build two dozen
nuclear bombs. Airborne radia-
tion was deliberately released to
test the effects of iodine 131 on
the surrounding area and its
residents, who were not warned
of dangers to their health.

"Hanford's plutonium production facility was shut down in
1988. A massive cleanup effort
is underway."

Joel Sternfeld, *Metro Bus Shelter, 7th Street at E Street, Southwest, Washington, D.C., April 1995*

"Yetta M. Adams froze to death sitting upright in this bus shelter across from the Department of Housing and Urban Development in Washington, D.C., on November 29, 1993. The forty-three-year-old mother of three grown children had reportedly been turned away from a homeless shelter the night before."

JOEL STERNFELD

Joel Sternfeld's first book *American Prospects* (1987), was the culmination of eight years spent traveling across the United States to "find beauty and harmony in an increasingly uniform, technological, and disturbing America." The images in the book provide an ironic view of post-capitalist society in the tradition of Farm Security Administration photographers. (The FSA was a New Deal program to help farmers. Among the photographers who documented the conditions in rural America in the 1930s and 1940s were Carl Mydans, Walker Evans, and Dorothea Lange.)

The images here first appeared in *On This Site: Landscape in Memoriam* (1996). Sternfeld photographed fifty seemingly ordinary sites, each the scene of a tragic event. As he explains: "The landscape contains meaning, contains clues. . . . The place itself becomes very important in so many of these events. . . . Having that one bit of certainty allows you to have your emotions in a way that all of the verbiage doesn't."

Sternfeld (b. 1944) lives in New York City, and he teaches at Sarah Lawrence College. He has received two Guggenheim Fellowships, a grant from the National Endowment for the Arts, and other grants. His work has been exhibited by the Museum of Modern Art in New York City and by other major museums. In 2004 Sternfeld was awarded the Citigroup Photography Prize, one of the most prestigious of international art awards.

SEEING

1. Look at each of the photographs in this portfolio separately. What do you see first in each image? What is the range of vision—the perspective—the photographer allows us to view? Consider the structure and layout of each photograph. Comment on the effects of scale and distance. What does Sternfeld gain—and lose—by his choice of framing? What reasonable inferences can you draw from your observations of the individual images? of these photographs as a group?

2. Carefully examine the captions Sternfeld prepared to accompany his photographs. To what extent do his words increase your understanding and appreciation of the scene presented in each photograph? How would you characterize Sternfeld's tone of voice in the captions? Explain how his tone of voice compares with other elements of the photographs. Comment on Sternfeld's use of light, shade, and color to enhance the impact of these photographs. These are ordinary places. What makes them so extraordinary?

RESPONDING VISUALLY

The images in Joel Sternfeld's portfolio capture ordinary sites where extraordinary events occurred. Choose a local site that meets this criterion, photograph it, and then write a brief caption that offers the viewer a clear sense of what makes the site extraordinary. Model both your visual composition and your text composition on Sternfeld's work.

WRITING

1. One of the most prominent photographers of the Vietnam War, Nick Ut, has said that the role of photojournalism is to search for "the right moment that captures essentially the whole essence of the time and the place." How would you define *photojournalism*? Write an essay in which you define the term and apply it to one of Sternberg's photographs. Given your definition, explain how the image is—or is not—an example of photojournalism.

2. Each photograph in this series relates to a larger social issue: the land rights of Native Americans, racial violence, pollution, or homelessness. Choose one of the images and research both the place it depicts and the event Sternfeld describes in the caption. Then write the first draft of an essay in which you explain the significance of the site, elaborate on the social issue at stake, and discuss the particular point of view Sternfeld's work provides on the issue.

"Production designers create everything that audiences don't think about when they watch a movie," says Rick Carter, the mastermind behind the sets of many box office hits, including *Jurassic Park*, *Forrest Gump*, and *The Polar Express*. "Our job is to create the spirit of the place." Set designers are continually constructing representations of human places and spaces—imaginary, historical, or simply mundane, like this apartment set from *Friends*.

Choose a scene from a favorite television show or film, and write an analysis of the visual environment the set designer has created. In your analysis, consider the following questions: What types of places are used as backdrops for the narrative? What materials or techniques has the set designer used to create a sense of those places? What role do the settings play in the story?

Worried? Us?

Bill McKibben

FOR FIFTEEN YEARS NOW, SOME SMALL PERCENTAGE of the world's scientists and diplomats and activists has inhabited one of those strange dreams where the dreamer desperately needs to warn someone about something bad and imminent; but somehow, no matter how hard he shouts, the other person in the dream—standing smiling, perhaps, with his back to an oncoming train—can't hear him. This group, this small percentage, knows that the world is about to change more profoundly than at any time in the history of human civilization. And yet, so far, all they have achieved is to add another line to the long list of human problems—people think about "global warming" in the way they think about "violence on television" or "growing trade deficits," as a marginal concern to them, if a concern at all. Enlightened governments make smallish noises and negotiate smallish treaties; enlightened people look down on America for its blind piggishness. Hardly anyone, however, has fear in their guts.

Why? Because, I think, we are fatally confused about time and space. Though we know that our culture has placed our own lives on a demonic fast-forward, we imagine that the Earth must work on some other timescale. The long slow accretion of epochs—the Jurassic, the Cretaceous, the Pleistocene—lulls us into imagining that the physical world offers us an essentially stable background against which we can run our race. Humbly, we believe that the world is big and that we are small. This humility is attractive, but also historic and no longer useful. In the world as we have made it, the opposite is true. Each of us is big enough, for example, to produce our own cloud of carbon dioxide. As a result, we—our cars and our industry—have managed to raise the atmospheric level of carbon dioxide, which had been stable at 275 parts per million throughout human civilization, to about 380 parts per million, a figure that is climbing by one and a half parts per million each year. This increase began with the Industrial Revolution in the eighteenth century, and it has been accelerating ever since. The consequence, if we take a median from several respectable scientific projections, is that the world's temperature will rise by five degrees Fahrenheit (roughly two and a half degrees Celsius) over the next hundred years, to make it hotter than it has been for 400 million years. At some level, these are the only facts worth knowing about our Earth.

Fifteen years ago, it was a hypothesis. Those of us who were convinced that the Earth was warming fast were a small minority. Science was skeptical, but set to work with rigor. Between 1988 and 1995, scientists drilled deep into glaciers, took core samples from lake bottoms, counted tree rings, and, most importantly, refined elaborate computer models of the atmosphere. By 1995, the almost impossibly con-tentious world of science had seen enough. The world's most distinguished atmospheric chemists, physicists, and climatologists, who had organized themselves into a large collective called the Intergov-ernmental Panel on Climate Change, made their pro-nouncement: "The balance of evidence suggests that there is a discernible human influence on global cli-mate." In the eight years since, science has continued to further confirm and deepen these fears, while the planet itself has decided, as it were, to peer-review their work with a succession of ominously hot years (1998 was the hottest ever, with 2002 trailing by only a few hundredths of a degree). So far humanity has raised the planet's temperature by about one degree Fahrenheit, with most of that increase happening after 1970—from about fifty-nine degrees Fahren-heit, where it had been stuck since the first cities rose and the first crops grew, to about sixty degrees. Five more degrees in the offing, as I have said, but already we understand, with an almost desperate clarity, how finely balanced our world has been. One degree turns out to be a lot. In the cryosphere—the frozen por-tions of the planet's surface—glaciers are everywhere in rapid retreat (spitting out Bronze Age hunter-gatherers). The snows of Kilimanjaro are set to be-come the rocks of Kilimanjaro by 2015. Montana's Glacier National Park is predicted to lose its last glac-iers by 2030. We know how thick Arctic ice is—we know it because cold war nuclear-powered sub-marines needed the information for their voyages under the ice cap. When the data was declassified in the waning days of the Clinton administration, it emerged that Arctic ice was forty percent thinner than it had been forty years before. *Perma*frost is melting. Get it?

"Global warming" can be a misleading phrase—the temperature is only the signal that extra solar radia-tion is being trapped at the Earth's surface. That extra energy drives many things: wind speeds in-crease, a reflection of the increasing heat-driven gra-dients between low and high pressure; sea level starts to rise, less because of melting ice caps than because

warm air holds more water vapor than cold; hence evaporation increases and with it drought, and then, when the overloaded clouds finally part, deluge and flood. Some of these effects are linear. A recent study has shown that rice fertility drops by ten percent for each degree Celsius that the temperature rises above thirty degrees Celsius during the rice plant's flower-ing. At forty degrees Celsius, rice fertility drops to zero. But science has come to understand that some effects may not follow such a clear progression. To paraphrase Orwell, we may all be hot, but some will be hotter than others. If the Gulf Stream fails because of Arctic melting, some may, during some seasons, even be colder.

The success of the scientific method underlines the failure of the political method. It is clear what must happen—the rapid conversion of our energy system from fossil to renewable fuels. And it is clear that it could happen—much of the necessary technology is no longer quixotic, no longer the province of back-yard tinkerers. And it is also clear that it isn't hap-pening. Some parts of Europe have made material progress—Denmark has built great banks of wind-mills. Some parts of Euroe have made promises—the United Kingdom thinks it can cut its carbon emis-sions by sixty percent by 2050. But China and India are still building power plants and motorways, and the United States has made it utterly clear that noth-ing will change soon. When Bill Clinton was presi-dent he sat by while American civilians traded up from cars to troop-transport vehicles; George Bush has not only rejected the Kyoto treaty, he has ordered the Environmental Protection Agency to replace "global warming" with the less ominous "climate change," and issued a national energy policy that foresees ever more drilling, refining, and burning. Under it, American carbon emissions will grow an-other forty percent in the next generation.

As satisfying as it is to blame politicians, however, it will not do. Politicians will follow the path of least re-sistance. So far there has not been a movement loud or sustained enough to command political attention.

Electorates demand economic prosperity—more of it—above all things. Gandhianism, the political philosophy that restricts material need, is now only a memory even in the country of its birth. And our awareness that the world will change in every aspect, should we be so aware, is muted by the future tense, even though that future isn't far away, so near in fact that preventing global warming is a lost cause—all we can do now is to try to keep it from getting utterly out of control.

This is a failure of imagination, and in this way a literary failure. Global warming has still to produce an Orwell or a Huxley, a Verne or a Wells, a *Nineteen Eighty-Four* or a *War of the Worlds,* or in film any equivalent of *On the Beach* or *Doctor Strangelove.* It may never do so. It may be that because—fingers crossed—we have escaped our most recent fear, nuclear annihilation via the cold war, we resist being scared all over again. Fear has its uses, but fear on this scale seems to be disabling, paralyzing. Anger has its uses too, but the rage of antiglobalization demonstrators has yet to do more than alienate majorities. Shame sends a few Americans shopping for small cars, but on the whole America, now the exemplar to the world, is very nearly unshameable.

My own dominant feeling has always been sadness. In 1989, I published *The End of Nature,* the first book for a lay audience about global warming. Half of it was devoted to explaining the science, the other half to my unease. It seemed, and still seems, to me that humanity has intruded into and altered every part of the Earth (or very nearly) with our habits and economies. Thoreau once said that he could walk half an hour from his home in Concord, Massachusetts, and come to a place where no man stood from one year to the next, and "there consequently politics are not, for politics are but the cigar smoke of a man." Now that cigar smoke blows everywhere.

Paradoxically, the world also seems more lonely. Everything else exists at our sufferance. Biologists guess that the result of a rapid warming will be the greatest wave of extinction since the last asteroid crashed into the Earth. Now we are the asteroid. The notion that we live in a God-haunted world is harder to conjure up. God rebuked Job: "Were you there when I wrapped the ocean in clouds...and set its boundaries, saying, 'Here you may come but no farther. Here shall your proud waves break....Who gathers up the stormclouds, slits them and pours them out?'" Job, and everyone else until our time, had the sweet privilege of shutting up in the face of that boast—it was clearly God or gravity or some force other than us. But as of about 1990 we can answer back, because we set the sea level now, and we run the storm systems. The excretion of our economy has become the most important influence on the planet we were born into. We're what counts.

Our ultimate sadness lies in the fact that we know [10] that this is not a preordained destiny; it isn't fate. New ways of behaving, of getting and spending, can still change the future: There is, as the religious evangelist would say, still time, though not much of it, and a miraculous conversion is called for—Americans in the year 2000 produced fifteen percent more carbon dioxide than they had ten years before.

The contrast between two speeds is the key fact of our age: between the pace at which the physical world is changing and the pace at which human society is reacting to this change. In history, if it exists, we shall be praised or damned. ○

BILL MCKIBBEN

By age 26, Bill McKibben had left his job as a staff writer for *The New Yorker* and moved to the Adirondack Mountains of New York to write a book on global warming. Even before climatologists acknowledged ten years later that *The End of Nature* (1989) was prophetic, McKibben began to draw attention to overpopulation and related issues. This essay was first published in *Enough: Staying Human in an Engineered Age* (2003). In the book McKibben argues that new technologies—genetic engineering is one example—have the potential to damage human relationships, especially those between parents and children. *Enough* refers to his belief that if people's insatiable desire to control nature remains unchecked, humankind will begin to make dangerous choices of a new kind. As he said in a 1999 interview in *Conscious Choice:* "The market forces pushing convenience, individualism, and comfort are still stronger than the attraction of community, fellowship, and connection with the natural world. This is the core of the environmental crisis."

McKibben is a frequent contributor to *The New York Review of Books,* the *New York Times*, and *Outside*. His other books include: *The Age of Missing Information* (1992); *Hope, Human and Wild* (1995); *Maybe One* (1998); and *Hundred Dollar Holiday* (1998). He lives with his wife, writer Sue Halperin, and daughter in upstate New York.

SEEING

1. What does Bill McKibben mean when he says we are "fatally confused about time and space" (para. 2)? What, according to McKibben, are "the only facts worth knowing about our Earth" (para. 2)? Who or what does McKibben hold responsible for what the Intergovernmental Panel on Climate Change called the "discernible human influence on global climate" (para. 3)? What does McKibben mean when he says that the global warming movement suffers from "a failure of imagination, and in this way a literary failure" (para. 7)?

2. Why do you think McKibben wrote "Worried? Us?"? Do you think he achieves his purpose in the essay? How does he structure the piece? What specific examples and sources does he draw on to support his points? Where do you think McKibben's arguments are strongest, and which arguments do you think fall short? What additional or alternative evidence would you incorporate into a defense of his stance? a refutation of it?

WRITING

1. Visit the web site of your member of Congress, and identify his or her stance on global warming. Then draft a letter in which you explain why you agree or disagree with that position. Outline the specific measures you would like to see your representative support on the issue, and explain your rationale for your point of view.

2. McKibben argues that people suffer from the misconception "that the world is big and that we are small" (para. 2). Many of the selections in **Chapter 1's Looking Closer: Seeing Is Believing** (page 119) explore our sense of scale in relation to the natural environment. Carl Sagan, for example, argues that looking at a photograph of the Earth from space "underscores our responsibility to deal more kindly and compassionately with one another and to preserve and cherish that pale blue dot, the only home we've ever known" (page 124, para. 6). Choose one author or artist from Looking Closer: Seeing Is Believing and write an essay in which you compare his or her discussion of scale and its importance for humankind with McKibben's.

See pages 124–125.

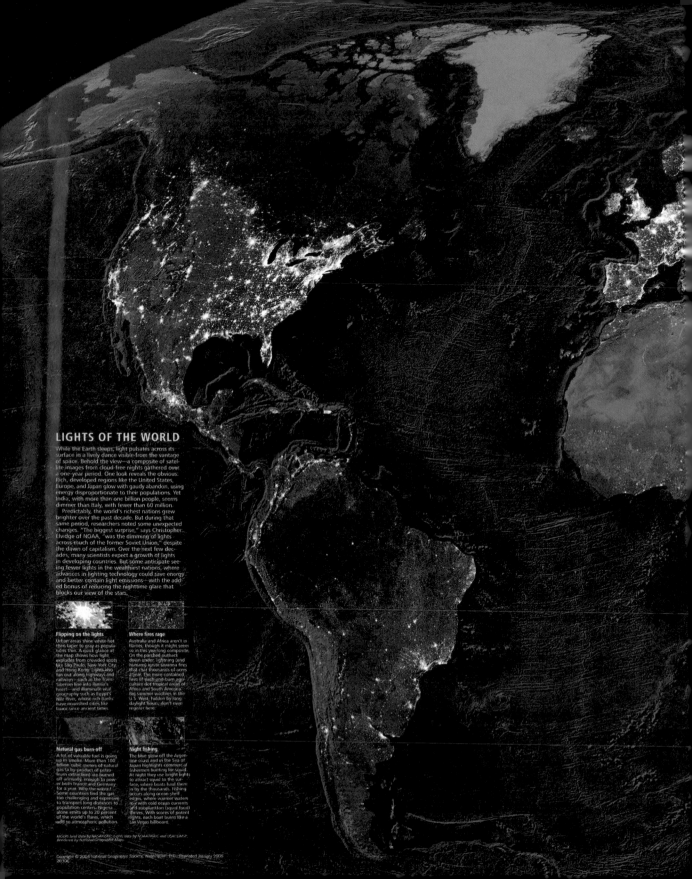

LIGHTS OF THE WORLD

While the Earth sleeps, light pulsates across its surface in a lively dance visible from the vantage of space. Behold the view—a composite of satellite images from cloud-free nights gathered over a one-year period. One look reveals the obvious: Rich, developed regions like the United States, Europe, and Japan glow with gaudy abandon, using energy disproportionate to their populations. Yet India, with more than one billion people, seems dimmer than Italy, with fewer than 60 million.

Predictably, the world's richest nations grew brighter over the past decade. But during that same period, researchers noted some unexpected changes. "The biggest surprise," says Christopher Elvidge of NOAA, "was the dimming of lights across much of the former Soviet Union," despite the dawn of capitalism. Over the next few decades, many scientists expect a growth of lights in developing countries. But some anticipate seeing fewer lights in the wealthiest nations, where advances in lighting technology could save energy and better contain light emissions—with the added bonus of reducing the nighttime glare that blocks our view of the stars.

Flipping on the lights
Urban areas shine white-hot then taper to gray as populations thin. A quick glance at the map shows how light explodes from crowded spots like São Paulo, New York City, and Hong Kong. Lights also fan out along highways and railways—such as the Trans-Siberian line into Russia's heart—and illuminate vital geography such as Egypt's Nile River, whose rich banks have nourished cities like Luxor since ancient times.

Where fires rage
Australia and Africa aren't in flames, though it might seem so in this yearlong composite. On the parched outback down under, lightning (and humans) ignite savanna fires that char thousands of acres a year. The more contained fires of slash-and-burn agriculture dot tropical areas of Africa and South America. Big summer wildfires in the U.S. West, hidden by long daylight hours, don't even register here.

Natural gas burn-off
A lot of valuable fuel is going up in smoke. More than 100 billion cubic meters of natural gas (a by-product of petroleum extraction) are burned off annually, enough to power both France and Germany for a year. Why the waste? Some countries find the gas too challenging and expensive to transport long distances to population centers. Nigeria alone emits up to 20 percent of the world's flares, which add to atmospheric pollution.

Night fishing
The blue glow off the Argentine coast and in the Sea of Japan highlights commercial fishermen hunting for squid. At night they use bright lights to attract squid to the surface, where boats haul them in by the thousands. Fishing occurs along ocean-shelf edges, where warmer waters mix with cold ocean currents and zooplankton (squid food) thrives. With scores of potent lights, each boat burns like a Las Vegas billboard.

MODIS land data by NASA/GSFC; Lights data by NOAA/NGDC and USAF/DMSP. Rendered by National Geographic Maps.

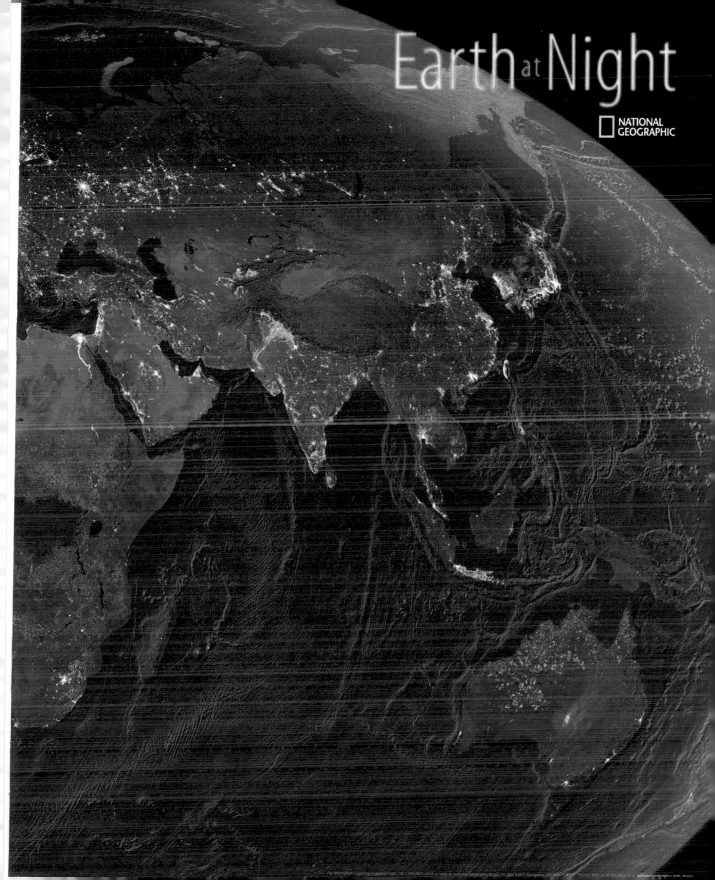

Earth at Night

NATIONAL GEOGRAPHIC

Interview: Mukherjee

You propose four key terms, or narratives, in this piece: expatriation, exile, immigration, and repatriation. How have your perspectives on these terms changed since your essay was published in 1999? What, if any, additional narratives—personal and public—have you observed?

Bharati Mukherjee My perspective on the four terms I proposed and defined in my essay "Imagining Homelands" have not changed. If anything, my conviction of their usefulness in discourses on contemporary diasporic literature and on immigrant U.S. literature has deepened. I expect the future to provide us with a larger body of English-language fiction in the narrative of repatriation. I think two distinct subnarratives of repatriation will emerge and enrich American literature.

One subnarrative will concern itself with the repossession of former "Spanish homelands" by Latino border-crossers (documented and undocumented) and their descendants, as told by the English-proficient, U.S.-born and/or U.S.-raised generation. To date, the majority of novels about the harsh experiences of Latino border-crossers that have elicited mainstream attention appear to have been written by sympathetic European-Americans. Susan Straight's *Highwire Moon* would be a good example.

The other subnarrative of repatriation will come out of the very recent phenomenon of the voluntary return to the country of one's origin by significant numbers of professionally successful, affluent, naturalized U.S. citizens in their late thirties to mid-forties and their families. This phenomenon is most evident in the South Asian–American and Chinese-American communities. The experience of repatriation is still too fresh for it to have surfaced as a body of literature. . . .

In the wake of 9/11 and the emergence of a handful of post-9/11 novels, we can speculate on a future additional subnarrative in the narrative of exile that will accommodate the experience of—and literature about—the community of "sleeper agents."

Can you describe the process of writing this essay? What were some of the most important compositional choices you made? How important were the processes of drafting and revising?

This essay was originally written as a lecture to be heard, not read. The lecture was one of five in a series on exile at the New York Public Library. The other lecturers in the series were Edward Said, Eva Hoffman, Andre Aciman, and Charles Simic. I wrote my lecture in two sittings. I needed to find a way of showing emigrants' nuanced attitudes to dislocation. "Exile" didn't accurately describe me. I am someone who has put down roots in America. I didn't begin writing my lecture until I had come up with the structure: the identification and exploration of the four large narratives within the immigrant experience. The original played to the ear. At the podium, I went off-script occasionally to illustrate arguments. When the series of lectures was published as an anthology titled *Letter of Transit,* I had to turn the lecture into a text to be read. I had to incorporate my off-the-cuff explanations and elaborations, sharpen phrases, tighten sentences, and make the punctuation more formal.

This interview was conducted via email on April 12, 2005.

Visit seeingandwriting.com for the full text of the interview.

For biographical information about Bharati Mukherjee, see page 223.

Imagining the Grand Canyon

The Grand Canyon is widely recognized as one of the scenic wonders of the world. It is also one of the most significant places in the cultural landscape of the American West, a prominent image of America's grandeur and abundance, and a symbol of its national pride. The sheer size of the canyon, its multiple shapes, its splendid range of colors, and its changing weather conditions draw millions of visitors, each seeking what Ralph Waldo Emerson called "an original relation" to the natural world.

Writers and artists have struggled to convey the wonder of the Grand Canyon and the works on the following pages document their efforts. Thomas Moran's painting ***The Chasm of the Colorado*** and Ansel Adams's photograph ***Grand Canyon National Park, from Yavapai Point, 1942*** have helped to stimulate public interest in the canyon. But the beauty of those images also has contributed to the sense of loss we can feel when a natural wonder fails to live up to its representations. Shawn Macomber addresses his disappointment with humor: For him, the Grand Canyon is simply "a hole in the ground." By inserting human figures in their images of the Grand Canyon, photographers Martin Parr and Bill Owens and artist Woody Gwyn add scale that helps us understand the vastness and the beauty of that cherished place.

Santa Fe Railroad, *Thomas Moran Sketching at Grand Canyon of Arizona*, 1909 (left):
Ansel Adams, *Grand Canyon National Park, from Yavapai Point*, 1942 (right)

Looking Closer

THE CHASM BETWEEN GRAND AND GREAT

Next to Hoover Dam, the Grand Canyon Is a Hole in the Ground

Shawn Macomber

I visited the Grand Canyon for the first time on my recent honeymoon. I didn't feel particularly small, or smaller than usual anyway. I had no sudden epiphanies. There was no reinterpeting my life's joys and sorrows as mere specks of dust in a vast universe. I also failed to come face to face with God, a feat many of my fellow travelers on the discount bus tour assured me they had easily accomplished. I suppose I must have wandered to the wrong viewing station, which is just my luck. A few weeks ago I spent five solid days at the Democratic convention and never once caught sight of Ben Affleck.

Is the Grand Canyon impressive? Well, yeah. Biggest hole I ever saw. But let's be reasonable here: It's nature's job to be impressive, isn't it? The Colorado River (conspiring with wind, rain, and gravity) has been working on that hole for more than 5 million years. It's all hypothetical, of course, but give me 5 million years and a garden trough and I'll carve you a Grand Canyon in New England. I'll make Vermont an island with relief sculptures of Howard Dean and Bernie Sanders looking out into the world and a drawbridge that goes up when those evil fast-food company execs come knocking.

Later, listening to the endless New Age meditations and ecstatic gushing of the bus driver and other tourists as we hurtled through hours of desert wasteland, I couldn't help but see myself as a bit of a killjoy. "When we're dead and gone, that canyon will still be there," one woman across the aisle said reverentially. I resisted the urge to add, "Yeah, and so will your Gatorade bottle, but I'm not going to start worshiping that." My disconnect from the others was as complete as if I had just shown up at the Indy 500 in a Prince T-shirt.

My mental self-mortification over my confessed bad attitude began to dissipate, however, as we pulled up to Hoover Dam for a quick "photo op," a stop that lasted a total of five minutes. Most people stayed on the bus, presumably to continue watching the Sandra Bullock witch flick, *Practical Magic,* on the overhead television.

So I stood looking out at this 5 massive feat of human ingenuity and wondered exactly how our priorities got so screwed up. I was facing more than 6 million tons of concrete restraining the Colorado River (something the Grand Canyon clearly cannot do) and creating Lake Mead, the largest reservoir in the United States. The Hoover Dam project was one of the only projects undertaken by the federal government to ever come in under budget and ahead of schedule. In addition to supplying water to cities up to 300 miles away, seventeen 4-million-pound generators in the dam capture 2.8 million kilowatts of electricity and send it along 2,700 miles of transmission lines to Los Angeles and other distant locales. The Hoover Dam project was a truly American effort: Every state provided supplies to the project. Ninety-six of the more than 15,000 workers involved lost their lives during the construction.

Yet all it takes is Sandra Bullock casting a computer-animated spell to reduce the attention to zero.

Perhaps in 5 million years, when whatever life-forms destined to follow us are studying the ruins of our culture, they will find value in Hoover Dam that many of us fail to ascribe to it today. When it comes down to it, the construction in the 1930s of a dam that continues to benefit millions of people to this day is without a doubt more impressive than a river wearing a channel in rock over millions of years. Hoover Dam makes a measurable, positive impact on the people in the Southwest. The Grand Canyon sells T-shirts and postcards and gives mules something to climb in and out of. I'm sure the mules would like to see us get our priorities straight as well.

Look, God isn't in the Grand Canyon—a river is. If people are searching for God or for an escape from their problems, I'd wager it's more likely to be found in the complexities and possibilities of the human mind than inside a geological structure. Now if the Grand Canyon had been a public works project, that might be another story. ○

THOMAS MORAN

 Thomas Moran (1837–1926) apprenticed with his artist brother before becoming a successful illustrator-painter in his own right. When he traveled to the Yellowstone region in 1871 as a member of a U.S. Geological Survey expedition, all he knew about the area had been gleaned from a *Scribner's Monthly* article. With frontier photographer William Henry Jackson, who became a close friend, Moran set out to document the sights. His paintings of Yellowstone and, some time later, of the Grand Canyon "helped inspire Congress to establish the National Park System in 1916." At one time *The Chasm of the Colorado* hung in the U.S. Capitol; today it is in the permanent collection of the Smithsonian American Art Museum.

SANTA FE RAILROAD

 Thomas Moran's watercolors and paintings of the American West caught the imagination of a public that dreamed of traveling there. In 1909 the Santa Fe Railroad made use of Moran in an advertisement for its "luxurious and newly-equipped" California Limited. The wilderness had become accessible in 1901, when the first Santa Fe Railroad train arrived in Grand Canyon Village. By 1905 the company had built the El Tovar Hotel; and by 1909, a depot. The close association between well-known artists and the railroad soon led to a flourishing tourist trade. Although Moran's art "would grace the pages of guidebooks published by the railroads to promote tourism to the American West," as Eleanor Harvey, a curator at the Dallas Museum of Art, observes, it also was admired by conservationists for the role it played in the creation of the National Park System.

ANSEL ADAMS

 Ansel Adams (1902–1984) first visited Yosemite as a boy. Later the legendary photographer would say that his perspective had been "colored and modulated by the great earth gesture" of the area. His love of the wilderness became both career and cause. He spent the rest of his life photographing and working to protect the natural landscape. (Adams joined the Sierra Club in 1919 and was a board member for thirty-seven years.)

In the 1940s and 1950s, with the help of three different Guggenheim Fellowships, Adams photographed the Grand Canyon and other national parks. Adams said of the Southwest, "This land is offering me a tremendous opportunity; no one has really photographed it." *Grand Canyon National Park, from Yavapai Point, 1942* reveals the technical mastery over black-and-white tonal values for which Adams is celebrated. At the time of his death, Adams's fame as a visionary photographer was secure, but he had yet to achieve many of his environmental goals.

SHAWN MACOMBER

After graduating from the University of New Hampshire in 2002, Shawn Macomber worked as a stringer for the Associated Press and then joined the staff of *The American Spectator,* a conservative newspaper in Washington, D.C. In addition to maintaining his own web site (ReturnofthePrimitive.com), Macomber writes regularly—even prolifically—for the *National Review Online, The American Enterprise Online,* and the *Union Leader.* "The Chasm between Grand and Great" appeared in the *Los Angeles Times* on August 17, 2004. The piece exemplifies Macomber: the irreverent right-wing Everyman. In an interview in 2004 in *MensNewsDaily.com,* he described his politics this way: "I'll take liberty, with all of its problems, over the nanny state any day." Self-defined as a "pro-life libertarian," he is quick to add that he means "little *l* libertarian," not the "car crash that masquerades as the official Libertarian Party."

MARTIN PARR

 Martin Parr (b. 1952) is one of the most influential photographers working today. Contributing to this English photographer's success are his skillful use of flash and bright color, and the wit with which he documents human behavior. A portfolio of his images appears in Chapter 3 (pages 239–49).

This photograph of contemporary tourists at the rim of the

Grand Canyon captures what appears to be a tour guide in Indian headdress taking a break. It reflects both Parr's humor and his keen interest in the vernacular. The image first appeared in England in 1994 in *Small World,* Parr's photographic study of the tourist industry.

Images from Parr's *Common Sense 1995–1999* series were included in *Cruel + Tender* (2003), the first major exhibition dedicated entirely to photography at the Tate Modern in London.

BILL OWENS

"The main thing in life is to live it your way" is one of photographer Bill Owens's (b. 1938) favorite quotations. For *Suburbia* (1972), an early collection, he photographed middle-class Americans living their lives their way. His neighbors in Livermore, California, proudly showed off new cars and boats and other possessions, and posed for him at Fourth of July and birthday parties. Primarily self-taught—he did study visual anthropology for a short time with a former Farm Security Administration photographer at San Francisco State—Owens follows in the social realist tradition of Walker Evans. In this color photograph, middle-class Americans engage in another middle-class ritual: milling around on a viewing platform at the Grand Canyon. Owens has received a Guggenheim Fellowship and two grants from the National Endowment for the Arts, and his photographs are in the collections of the Los Angeles County Museum of Art, the San Francisco Museum of Modern Art, and other museums in the United States and Europe. He lives and works in Hayward, California.

WOODY GWYN

When he was only 18 years old, landscape painter Woody Gwyn (born in 1944 in San Antonio, Texas) boldly requested an interview with artist Peter Hurd. With Hurd's encouragement, Gwyn bypassed college to study art at the Pennsylvania Academy of the Fine Arts in Philadelphia. For many years, Gwyn focused on the panoramic Western landscape; only in his later work has he introduced the figure. In the painting here, a form of social commentary, tiny tourist figures vie to capture the immense view of the Grand Canyon.

Gwyn's work is in the permanent collection of the Cleveland Museum of Art and other museums. He has received many honors, including a commission to paint George W. Bush's Crawford, Texas, ranch. Gwyn lives outside Santa Fe, New Mexico.

SEEING

1. Martin Parr, Bill Owens, and Woody Gwyn offer three very different representations of the Grand Canyon and the people who visit it. Look carefully at each of the images. Is the focus on the people or on the canyon itself? What relationship are you, as the audience, meant to have with the landscape and with the people in each image? Which image do you prefer and why?

2. Shawn Macomber offers an unsentimental view of seeing the Grand Canyon for the first time, on his honeymoon. Reread his essay, looking for compositional devices that enable him to debunk the importance of visiting the Grand Canyon. Then go back and study each of the images reprinted in this section. Explain how each augments—or deflates—the significance of the Grand Canyon.

WRITING

1. In the Santa Fe Railroad ad, "eminent artists" are quoted as admitting that the Grand Canyon is "the despair of the painter." To what extent do you think that a photograph can capture such a sweeping landscape better than a painting can? Using the Thomas Moran painting and the Ansel Adams photograph to support your points, write an essay in which you argue for one medium or the other as capturing the spirit of a place more effectively.

2. Reread Macomber's essay several times. Consider the specific ways in which he uses tone, irony, and understatement to reduce the iconic significance of the Grand Canyon in American culture. What other specific compositional strategies does he use to achieve his humorous and critical goals? Once you understand Macomber's strategies, choose a place that has something of the same iconic significance in your community. Write the first draft of an analytical essay in which you use humor to deflate the significance of this place.

3

CAPTURING MEMORABLE MOMENTS

Martin Parr, *Paris, 18th District*, 2000

Each generation of Americans shares memorable moments. Most Americans over age 50, for example, remember precisely where they were and what they were doing when they heard the news that President John F. Kennedy had been assassinated. No matter what our age, we have all seen the film footage of JFK and Jackie waving from their car in Dallas the second before the fatal shots were fired.

Identifying a single memorable moment for younger generations of Americans has been more difficult. Yes, there were images in the 1990s that captured the nation's attention: Rodney King being beaten, O. J. Simpson slumped across the backseat of a white Ford Bronco, the shooting of rap artist Tupac Shakur, the wreckage in a Paris tunnel that led to the death of Princess Di, Monica Lewinsky hugging President Clinton. But none of those moments seem to define today's generation.

Brian Gnatt, a student editor at the University of Michigan's *Daily* in the mid-1990s, suggested that the defining moments of his generation could be found in Hollywood rather than in the political realm:

> I . . . remember when, where, and who I was with when I saw the *Star Wars* films. To my generation, nothing we have experienced together has been as huge a phenome-

Martin Parr, *Greece, Athens, Acropolis*, 1991

non as *Star Wars*. Luke Skywalker and Han Solo are more than household names—they will be ingrained in all of our memories until the day we die.

"While my parents' generation vividly remembers where they were when JFK was shot," Gnatt explained, "my generation [has] no single event of the same caliber."

That changed September 11, 2001, when terrorists attacked the World Trade Center and the Pentagon. Young and old will never forget the horrible image of the second plane hitting the South Tower, a scene played over and over again as television commentators, like the rest of us, tried to make sense of what they had witnessed.

The events of September 11 have altered the American political and cultural landscape in profound ways. The images of that day have been etched on our national consciousness. And our perspectives on who we are—as individuals and as a nation—have been seared by our awareness of what took place that morning in New York City, in Washington, D.C., and in a field in Pennsylvania.

We can point with certainty to the moments that define us as a nation, that shape our national consciousness. A president assassinated, a plane flying

Martin Parr, *Latvia Beaches*, 1999

Martin Parr, *Italy, Venice, Piazza San Marco*, 1994

Martin Parr, *Japan, Happy Kingdom*, 1993

into a skyscraper—events so widely reported and commented on. It is far more difficult to sift through diverse and idiosyncratic personal experiences to find a single event or image that defines smaller groups of people, college students, for example. After all, every college student has experienced different rites of passage and customs: a confirmation, a bat mitzvah, becoming an Eagle Scout, a first date, a first day at a first job, winning a championship game. The moments we expect—or are expected—to remember, the events and ceremonies we feel obliged to record in our photo albums and scrapbooks, are not always those that affect the largest number of people. Often the most memorable experiences occur when we least expect them or are difficult to capture in a picture frame on a mantel: becoming blood sisters with a childhood friend; nervously finding a seat in your first college lecture class, only to find that you're in the wrong room; struggling through a complex mathematical equation and finally getting it; receiving the news that a loved one has died.

Telling stories about the most memorable moments in our lives often includes explaining *how* they have become etched in our minds. In fact, private moments, like public ones, are inextricably

Martin Parr, *Italy, Pisa, Leaning Tower*, 1990

linked to the technologies with which we record them. Most of our special occasions involve cameras; in fact, it is often the video camera at a wedding, rather than the bride and groom, that commands everyone's attention and cooperation. It almost seems as though an event has not taken place if it hasn't been photographed or videotaped. Instant replay and stop-action photography allow us to re-live, slow down, and freeze our most cherished or embarrassing moments. The success of shows like *America's Funniest Home Videos* as well as the popularity of web sites featuring a twenty-four-hour live feed from someone's living room testify to the increasing importance of the video camera in Americans' private lives.

Whether we take photographs, create scrapbooks, use home-video cameras, keep journals, describe our experiences in letters or e-mails to friends, share family stories during the holidays, or simply replay memories in our minds, we are framing our experiences—for ourselves and often for others. As those memorable events drift into the past, we often revise and embellish our stories about them. Indeed, we continually reshape the nature and tone of our stories each time we recall them.

Martin Parr, *Mexico*, 2002

The selections that follow provide an opportunity for you to practice and develop your skills of narration and revision by noticing how other writers and artists capture memorable moments. From Joe Rosenthal's dramatic photograph of marines raising the American flag at Iwo Jima to James Nachtwey's insightful reflections on the terror and loss in the wake of September 11, each selection in this chapter conveys a public or personal moment of revelation. Pay attention to the techniques and methods each artist and writer employs to tell his or her story. As you read, observe, and write about these selections, consider the range of ways in which you capture the memorable moments in your own life. How does the process of transcribing (writing, photographing, painting, videotaping, etc.) shape or change your understanding of those moments? How can you as a writer enable readers to "get inside" your own experience, to understand the details and nuances that make each particular experience memorable?

MARTIN PARR

Martin Parr was born in England in 1952. He became interested in photography at a young age, encouraged by his grandfather, amateur photographer George Parr. He spent three years studying photography at Manchester Polytechnic and then went to work on several freelance projects. His fresh eye for imagery and idiosyncratic approach to social documentary won him three awards from the Arts Council of Great Britain before he turned 30. "The best way to describe my work," says Parr, "is subjective documentary." He is known for capturing the spiritual crises of lower- and middle-class Britons, and the absurdity and mystery of tourism.

In 1994 Parr became a member of Magnum Photos, a cooperative of internationally renowned photographers. His interest in filmmaking has led to several documentaries, including *Think of England* (1999). He also applies his talents to the fashion and advertising industries: His work has been featured in campaigns for Hewlett-Packard, Absolut Vodka, and Sony. In 2002, the Barbican Art Gallery and the National Museum exhibited a retrospective of Parr's work that included some of the images shown here. Parr served as the guest artistic director for Rencontres D'Arles 2004, a festival that brings 130,000 photography enthusiasts to Provence to honor featured photographers. He is currently professor of photography at the University of Wales, Newport.

SEEING

1. Martin Parr is an unusually skillful contemporary photographer who is especially adept at capturing the subtleties and ironies of ordinary people in search of memorable moments to photograph. Which of the photographs here most effectively captures your attention? Why? Point to specific aspects of the photograph to support each point you make. Which photograph strikes you as most humorous? most ironic? most subtle?

2. Carefully examine Parr's photograph of the pink umbrella, taken on the Piazza San Marco, in Venice. Do you think the image is effective? What do you think works especially well in the photograph? What doesn't work? Explain your answers. What does Parr gain—or lose—by not creating a presence for the camera in this image? Comment on Parr's use of background in each of these photographs. In what specific ways—and with what specific effects— does he draw on the scenes that serve as a backdrop for his subjects? How do his angle of vision and his attitude toward the people and scenes he photographs contribute to the overall effect of each image?

WRITING

1. In several of the pictures here, Parr is photographing a subject who is also taking a picture. Have you ever taken a photograph of someone taking a photograph? What prompted you to take the picture? What effect were you hoping to create? How successful were you? Why? Write the first draft of a personal essay in which you describe the moment, your motivation, and what you hoped to achieve in taking the photograph. Then offer a judgment, supported by specific evidence, about whether you succeeded in achieving your goal, artistic or otherwise. If you have never taken a photograph of someone else taking a picture, then use Parr's photographs as your source and write an analytical essay about them.

2. After reviewing Parr's photographs carefully, select one that strikes you as a particularly effective statement of irony. Write the first draft of an essay in which you analyze the nature and the artistic impact of Parr's use of irony.

Joel Sternfeld, *A Young Man Gathering Shopping Carts,
Huntington, New York, July 1993*

AN ODE TO LOVED LABORS LOST
Tom Brokaw

IN THE SUMMER OF MY 15TH YEAR I WAS hired as a counselor at a Boy Scout camp in southwestern Minnesota. I was paid $100 for the two-month season and my accommodations were a tent, a Coleman lantern, and empty orange crates that doubled as end tables, bureaus, and bookcases.

More important, I was on my own, 200 miles from home, and a member of the camp royalty, the waterfront staff. We lived in a little lakeside compound, well away from the rowdiness of the weekly campers, and we supervised the most popular activities: swimming, canoeing, boating, and lifesaving techniques. I was the junior member of the team. In one tent were Dan and Mike, scholarly college students headed for Lutheran seminary and then PhDs. My tent-mate was Eldon, an equally studious high school senior who went on to Harvard, his own PhD, and a career in academia.

During the day I could hold my own in the water and in the canoes, but when darkness came, Dan, Mike, and Eldon waded into *War and Peace, Crime and Punishment,* the works of Huxley and other deep thinkers, discussing their merits and puzzling over their larger meaning. Or they would turn to theology, with the Lutherans making flanking moves on Eldon, the son of a Congregational college professor. The lively and provocative arguments would go on into the Minnesota summer night, accompanied by the soft hissing sound of the lanterns.

I sat off to the side, trying to assimilate what I could, and sensing for the first time in my young life the genuine excitement of wrestling with big ideas, and the force of intellectual curiosity.

Almost a half-century later I still remember those evenings but I also remember a fetching, slightly older girl, in a nearby town. Her father loaned me one of the family cars so I could take his daughter to a drive-in movie theater where the lessons were some distance from Russian literature or Lutheran theology. ○

JOEL STERNFELD

In his full-color portraits, photographer Joel Sternfeld links memory and place with Americans and their way of life. His photographs are timeless and yet undeniably modern. His work begins where the celebrated American photographer Walker Evans left off, and it inspires other contemporary photographers, among them Andreas Gursky.

Sternfeld is especially adept at capturing contradictions. We see this in his photograph of the bus shelter where a homeless woman died within sight of the Department of Housing and Urban Development. We see it again here: The young man gathering shopping carts could be a Calvin Klein model, but he is standing in front of the generically named Foodtown supermarket. His job calls for him to wear a shirt and tie, but the shirt is unbuttoned and the tie is loose; and his apron is hanging from his pants.

Sternfeld was born in New York City in 1944. His photographs have been exhibited at the Museum of Modern Art in New York City, the Art Institute of Chicago, and the Museum of Fine Arts in Houston. Sternfeld has received two Guggenheim Fellowships and a Prix de Rome. In 2004 he received the Citigroup Photography Prize, a prestigious international award. His books include *American Prospects* (1987, 2004), *On This Site* (1996), *Stranger Passing* (2001), and *Walking the High Line* (2002).

See page 198.

TOM BROKAW

South Dakota native Tom Brokaw (b. 1940) studied political science and worked as a radio reporter at the University of South Dakota. His journalism career began at KMTV in Omaha, Nebraska; he joined NBC News in 1966. By 1983 he was sole anchor and managing editor of *NBC Nightly News with Tom Brokaw,* a position he held until 2004. From that seat he won every major award in broadcast journalism. He also was the first American anchor to conduct an exclusive interview with Mikhail Gorbachev, the only one to report live from the Berlin Wall as it fell, and the first to report on human-rights abuses in Tibet and to interview the Dalai Lama. Today Brokaw is a media icon; but as the *New York Times* article from which the piece here comes suggests, his beginnings were humble. He is a self-made man, and much of his success and popularity can be attributed to his familiarity with the everyday American way of life.

Brokaw is also a prolific writer. In addition to numerous articles and essays, he wrote several books over the last decade, including *The Greatest Generation* (1998), the story of the men and women who came of age during World War II, and *A Long Way from Home: Growing Up in the American Heartland* (2003), a memoir. Since stepping down from *NBC Nightly News,* Brokaw has been spending more time with his family in Montana and continues to make documentaries with NBC.

SEEING

1. In his short essay, Tom Brokaw affectionately mentions several physical objects—tents, lanterns, orange crates, bureaus, and bookcases. How do the objects help frame and structure both the essay and the memories on which it is based? How do you think Brokaw's relationship to the objects has changed in the years since he was a camp counselor? Now examine Joel Sternfeld's photograph of the young man gathering shopping carts. What objects in the picture are most important? What implied presences do you sense? How do you imagine they determine the young man's relationship to his work? What do you think he might remember about them after leaving the job?

2. Look again at Sternfeld's photograph. Which aspects of the photograph are you drawn to? In what sequence? Now consider the title: *A Young Man Gathering Shopping Carts*. How do the references in the title correspond to the elements your eyes are drawn to in the photograph? What tone does the title convey? How does it influence the way you look at the photograph? If you do not feel any particular influence, what is the possible significance of that? Compose a new title for Brokaw's short essay, modeled after Sternfeld's title for the photograph. How would changing the title change your view of the essay? Suppose the title of the photograph were *An Ode to Loved Labors Lost*. How would that change your response to the image?

WRITING

1. The job Brokaw describes had benefits far beyond the small paycheck he received. What were those other benefits? Which ones do you think were most important to him? How does the tone of the piece affect your judgment? Now think of jobs you have held in which there was a discrepancy between your pay and other benefits—jobs where the pay made up for drudgery or where the pleasure of work compensated for a low salary. Write an essay about one of those jobs. Why did you take it? Why did you keep it? Why did you leave it?

2. The essay and the photograph here offer two very different views of what a teenager's job can be, and they do so through very different mediums: words versus images. Draft an essay in which you do one of the following: Using only visual details, describe a photograph that might have been taken during Brokaw's time at camp; or describe in a short essay the young man's response many years later when he comes across a copy of Sternfeld's photograph. How does changing the medium change the tone of and the information conveyed by the work? Explain your answer.

The First Thanksgiving

Sarah Vowell

When I invited my mom and dad to come to New York City to have Thanksgiving at my house, I never expected them to say yes. Not only had they never been to New York, they had never been east of the Mississippi. Nor had they ever visited me. I've always had these fantasies about being in a normal family in which the parents come to town and their adult daughter spends their entire visit daydreaming of suicide. I'm here to tell you that dreams really do come true.

I was terrified we wouldn't have enough to talk about. In the interest of harmony, there's a tacit agreement in my family; the following subjects are best avoided in any conversation longer than a minute and a half: national politics, state and local politics, any music by any person who never headlined at the Grand Ole Opry, my personal life, and their so-called god. Five whole days. When I visit them back home in Montana, conversation isn't a problem because we go to the movies every afternoon. That way, we can be together but without the burden of actually talking to each other. Tommy Lee Jones, bless his heart, does the talking for us.,

But my sister, Amy, is coming and bringing her lively seven-month-old son, Owen, along, so the cinema's not an option. Which means five days together—just us—no movies. We are heading into uncharted and possibly hostile waters, pioneers in a New World. It is Thanksgiving. The pilgrims had the *Mayflower*. I buy a gravy boat.

It's lucky that Amy's coming with Mom and Dad. Amy still lives six blocks away from them in Bozeman. She would act as interpreter and go-between among my parents and me. Like Squanto.

Amy's husband, Jay, has decided to stay home in Montana to go deer hunting with his brother. Everyone else arrives at my apartment in Chelsea. Amy and Owen are bunking with me, so I walk my parents around the corner to check them into their hotel on Twenty-third.

"Here we are," says Mom, stopping under the awning of the Chelsea Hotel. There she stands, a woman whose favorite book is called, simply, Matthew, right on the spot where the cops hauled Sid Vicious out in handcuffs after his girlfriend was found stabbed to death on their hotel room floor.

"No, Mother," I say, taking her arm and directing her down the block to the Chelsea Savoy, a hotel where they go to the trouble to clean the rooms each day.

It is around this time, oh, twenty minutes into their trip, that my dad starts making wisecracks like "Boy, kid, bet you can't wait until we're out of here." My father, a man who moved us sixteen hundred miles away from our Oklahoma relatives so he wouldn't have to see them anymore, makes a joke on average every two hours he is here about how much I'm anticipating the second they'll say good-bye. I find this charming but so disturbingly true I don't know what to say.

By halfway through the first day, I discover I needn't have worried what we would talk about, with the baby preventing us from seeing movies. When you have a baby around, the baby is the movie. We occupy an entire entertaining hour just on drool, nonnarrative drool. At this stage, baby Owen is laughing, sitting up, and able to roll over. He is the cutest, the funniest, sweetest, smartest, best-behaved baby in the world.

Then there's the sightseeing. First stop, Ellis Island. The thing 10 about going to Ellis Island is that it's a lot like going to Ellis Island. Perhaps to help you better understand the immigrant experience, they make you stand in line for the crammed ferry for an hour and a half in the windy cold. By the time we step onto the island, we are huddled masses yearning to breathe free.

Our great-grandmother Ellen passed through here on her way from Sweden. We watch a video on the health inspections given to immigrants, walk past oodles of photos of men in hats and women in shawls. Though no one says anything, I know my father and mother and sister are thinking what I'm thinking. They're thinking about when we moved away from Oklahoma to Montana, how unknown that was, how strange and lonesome. I read a letter in a display case that says, "And I never saw my mother again," and I think of my grandfather, how we just drove off, leaving him behind, waving to us in the rearview mirror. And here we are in New York, because here I am in New York, because ever since Ellen's father brought her here, every generation moves away from the one before.

It is curious that we Americans have a holiday—Thanksgiving—that's all about people who left their homes for a life of their own choosing, a life that was different from their parents' lives. And how do we celebrate it? By hanging out with our parents! It's as if on the Fourth of July we honored our independence from the British by barbecuing crumpets.

Just as Amy and I grew up and left our parents, someday Owen will necessarily grow up and ditch my sister. And, appropriately enough, it is on this weekend that Owen spends the very first night of his life away from his mother. My parents babysit while Amy and I go to a rock show. Owen lives through it, as does she, though she talks about him all night, which I guess is how it goes.

Thanksgiving morning, my parents take Owen to see the Macy's parade while Amy and I start making dinner. Let me repeat that—my mother leaves while I cook. Specifically, cornbread dressing, a dish my mother has made every Thanksgiving since before I was born. To her credit, she has not inquired about my process since she phoned to ask me if she should bring cornmeal in her suitcase. As an Okie, my mom only uses white cornmeal processed by the Shawnee Company in Muskogee. She does not even consider my cornbread to be cornbread at all because I make it with yellow cornmeal and, heresy, sugar. "You don't make cornbread," she told me, in the same deflated voice she uses to describe my hair. "You make johnnycake."

I'm standing at the cutting board chopping sage and it hits me [15] what it means that she is letting me be in charge of the dressing: I am going to die. Being in charge of the dressing means you are a grown-up for real, and being a grown-up for real means you're getting old, and getting old means you are definitely, finally, totally going to die. My mother is a grandmother and my sister is a mother and I have decided the dressing will be yellow this year, therefore, we'll all be dead someday.

"Is that enough celery?" Amy asks, pointing to a green mound on the counter. Is there ever enough celery? Do my parents have more celery in their past than they do in their future? Do I?

I have invited my friends John and David to join us for dinner, and I was a little nervous about how everyone would get along. To my delight, the meal is smooth and congenial. My friends and I talk about the West Nile virus killing birds on Long Island. My father counters with a lovely anecdote about an open copper pit in Butte that filled up with contaminated rainwater and killed 250 geese in one day. There is nothing like eating one dead bird and talking about a bunch of other dead birds to really bring people together.

The next morning, right about the time Owen starts to cry while—simultaneously—my mother jams the bathroom door and my father's on his hands and knees prying it open with a penknife, a cloud passes over me. Once or twice a day, I am enveloped inside what I like to call the Impenetrable Shield of Melancholy. This shield, it is impenetrable. Hence the name. I cannot speak. And while I can feel myself freeze up, I can't do anything about it. As my family fusses, I spend an inordinate amount of time pretending to dry my hair, the bedroom door closed, the hair dryer on full blast, pointed at nothing.

Everybody in the family goes through these little spells. I just happen to be the spooky one at this particular moment. When people ask me if I'm the black sheep of the family I always say that, no, we're all black sheep. Every few hours they're here, I look over at my dad, nervously crunching his fingers together. If he were at home for Thanksgiving, he'd be ignoring us and spending all his time in his shop. I watch him move his fingers in the air and realize he's turning some hunk of metal on an imaginary lathe.

The thing that unites us is that all four of us are homebody claustro- 20 phobes who prefer to be alone and are suspicious of other people. So the trait that binds us together as a family—preferring to keep to ourselves—makes it difficult to *be* together as a family. Paradoxically, it's at these times that I feel closest to them, that I understand them best, that I love them most. It's just surprising we ever breed.

The next day, we do the most typical thing we could possibly do as a family. We split up. I stay home cleaning, Mom goes to Macy's, Amy and Owen visit the Museum of Modern Art, and Dad tours Teddy Roosevelt's birthplace. By the time we all reconvene on Saturday evening, my ragged mother becomes so ambitious with her sightseeing that I can tell she's decided that she's never coming back. "Do you guys want to see Rockefeller Center?" I ask, and she says, "Yeah, because who knows when I'll be back again." Ditto the Empire State Building, "because who knows when I'll be back again."

If you are visiting the Empire State Building, may I offer some advice? If you are waiting in the very long line for the very last elevator and an attendant says that anyone who wants to walk up the last six flights may do so now, right away, and you are with your aging parents and a sister who is carrying a child the size of a fax machine, stay in the line for the elevator. But if you must take the stairs, go first, and do not look back; otherwise your parents will look like one of those Renaissance frescoes of Adam and Eve being expelled from the Garden of Eden, all hunched over and afraid.

So we make it to the observation deck, Brooklyn to the south of us, New Jersey to the west, places that people fled to from far away, places that people now run away from, to make another life. It's dark and cold and windy, and we're sweaty from climbing the stairs. It's really pretty though. And there we stand, side by side, sharing a thought like the family we are. My sister wishes she were home. My mom and dad wish they were home. I wish they were home too. ○

SARAH VOWELL

Sarah Vowell (b. 1969) is best known for her humorous social commentaries on NPR's *This American Life*. She also writes several columns, including one on pop culture for *Salon.com;* and her articles have appeared in *Esquire, Artforum, The Village Voice,* and other publications. This essay, "The First Thanksgiving," was published in her third book, *The Partly Cloudy Patriot* (2002), a best seller.

In an interview with *The Onion,* Vowell described both her introversion and her willingness to share personal stories in her readings and essays: "I have no . . . nervousness or fear addressing 2,000 people. But when that's over, and I'm sitting at the book-signing table having to make small talk with people one-on-one, then I can get kind of uncomfortable. The radio feels so abstract. You're basically telling a secret to a microphone. . . . Last week, I was on vacation with my sister. . . and she's telling the coffee-shop person about how I live in New York. . . . I was like, 'Can you please not broadcast my personal business to the whole coffee shop?' Then, later, I realized how hypocritical that was, because I will tell 1 million people about our Thanksgiving dinner."

Vowell was raised in Oklahoma and Montana; she currently lives in New York City.

SEEING

1. "The First Thanksgiving" offers Vowell's perspective on the patterns her family has fallen into over the years. In what ways is the Thanksgiving she describes in the essay the "first"? Is the title serious? sardonic? How does your response to the title affect your understanding of the essay? Did you finish the text with a sense that this particular Thanksgiving marks the beginning of something new? If so, why?

2. In paragraph 12, Vowell writes that Thanksgiving is "all about people who left their homes for a life of their own choosing, a life that was different from their parents' lives." To what extent do you agree with her description of the holiday? Why or why not? In the same paragraph she notes that we celebrate the decision to live a different life from our parents by spending the holiday with them. Why do you think Vowell asked her family to have Thanksgiving at her home? How would you describe her relationship with her father? her mother? her sister? Use examples from the essay to support your answers.

WRITING

1. Vowell begins her piece saying that her parents had "never been east of the Mississippi." She continues to use place names and locales throughout the essay, both to describe the places her family visits in New York City and to function as a kind of shorthand for the differences she sees between herself and her parents. Think about your own holiday geography. Are there specific places significant to your holidays, past and present? What local places, in addition to your home, figure in your celebrations? Draft an essay about a place, other than your home, that has played or continues to play an important role in your celebration of Thanksgiving or another holiday.

2. Reread Vowell's essay. What specific writing strategies does she use to elicit a humorous response from her audience? What roles do memory and tradition play in achieving that humorous effect? Write the first draft of a humorous essay in which you draw on memory and tradition in your family's Thanksgiving customs—or those of another holiday.

Fish Cheeks

Amy Tan

The Tan family—(left to right) Peter, John, me, and Daisy—in Oakland, California, the day after I was born, 1952.

1920s

1950s

1980s

Retrospect: Yearbook Photos

1930s

1940s

1960s

1970s

1990s

2000s

THIS IS EARL SANDT
Robert Olen Butler

I'VE SEEN A MAN DIE, BUT NOT LIKE THIS. THERE was silence suddenly around us when he disappeared beyond the trees, silence after terrible sounds, that hammering of his engine, the engine of his aeroplane, and the other sound, after.

He had climbed miraculously up and he had circled the field and we all took off our hats as one, the men among us. Mine as well. Hooray, we cried. My son cried out, too. Hooray. This was why we'd come to this meadow. We would peek into the future and cheer it on.

And Earl Sandt hammered overhead and down to the far edge of the pasture, defying the trees, defying the earth. The propeller of his engine spun behind him and he sat in a rattan chair, as if he was on his front porch smoking a cigar. Then he came back from the tree line, heading our way.

I reached down and touched my son on the shoulder. I had never seen an aeroplane and something was changing in me as it approached. I suppose it scared me some. I had no premonition, but I needed to touch my son at that moment. The plane came toward us and there was a stiff wind blowing—the plane bucked a little, like a nervous horse, but Earl Sandt kept him steady, kept him coming forward, and I felt us all ready to cheer again.

Then there was a movement on the wing. With 5 no particular sound. Still the engine. But there was a tearing away. If I had been Earl Sandt, if I had been sitting in that rattan chair and flying above these bared heads, I might have heard the sound and been afraid.

I lifted my camera. This had nothing to do with the thing happening on the wing. I was only vaguely aware of it in that moment. I lifted my camera and I tripped the shutter, and here was another amazing thing, it seemed to me. One man was flying above the earth, and with a tiny movement of a hand, another man had captured him.

Earl Sandt was about to die, but he was forever caught there in that box in my hand. I lowered my Kodak and for a moment the plane was before me against the sky and all I felt was a thing that I sometimes had felt as a younger man, riding up into the Alleghenys alone and there would be a turning

in the path and suddenly the trees broke apart and there was a great falling away of the land.

A falling. He fell, Earl Sandt. The aeroplane suddenly reared up on its left side, as if it wanted to turn to the right, but the nose went down and there was so little sky below, so little, and then the aeroplane tried to lift itself, briefly, but the wing was tearing away and the engine hammered loud and Earl Sandt turned sharply right again pointing to the earth and his aeroplane looped, the engine crying out, and he fell, disappearing behind a stand of pine.

There was a heavy thump beyond the trees, and I have nothing in my head to compare it to. Not a barn collapsing, not a horse going down, not the dead sugar maple, forty foot high, I had felled only yesterday in our yard. This sound was new.

And our silence followed. We all of us could not 10 take this in. He had flown, this Earl Sandt, he had raised his goggles to his eyes and stepped into his machine and he had run along the meadow and had lifted into the air, and now I looked into the empty place where he had been, only a moment before. In my head I could see once again the two great wings and the spinning of the propeller and then he was gone.

"Papa?" It was my son's voice drifting up to me from the silence.

I looked into his face.

"It's all right," I said, though I knew it was not. I could feel Matthew's bones beneath my hand, which still lay on his shoulder.

"He's gone," my son said.

I looked to the others. There was a stirring. Some 15 of the women began to cry.

"Mother of God," one man said and he moved in the direction of the pines. He was right. We had to do something now.

I let go of my son and put the camera in his hand. I turned to the place where Earl Sandt had vanished. "Stay here," I said.

We ran, perhaps a dozen of us, across the meadow grass and into the pines and I could smell burning and there was smoke up ahead and I could smell a newly familiar thing, a smell of the automobiles that had come to our town, their fuel. Then we broke into a clearing and the aeroplane was crumpled up ahead and beginning to burn.

I was behind several of the men and we were in our Sunday clothes, we had left our churches this morning and had come to see the exhibition of this wonderful thing, and now we were stripping off our coats and winding them around our hands and arms to allow us to reach into the flames, to bring Earl Sandt out. Two men were ahead of me, already bending to the tangle of canvas and wood and metal and smoke. I felt myself slow and stop.

I did not know this man. I had seen him only from afar, only briefly. He had raised his goggles and hidden his eyes and he'd had some intent in his head— to fly, of course, and he did. But he was a man, flesh and blood, and he was lying broken now, ahead of me. There were others to help him. The ones ahead, and still others now, rushing past me. I continued to hesitate, and then I turned away.

Matthew had followed me. He was standing a few yards behind, in the trees. I lifted my hand to acknowledge him, and I found it swathed in my suit coat, expecting the fire.

I moved to my son, unwrapping my arm.

"The others are helping," I said to him, so he would understand why I had turned away.

"I want to see," he said.

"No."

"Pa."

"No," I said, firm. I turned him around and we stepped out of the trees. I looked once more into the sky where Earl Sandt had been.

Matthew and I walked from the meadow and through the center of town, passing the Merchants Bank, where I had an office, where I was vice president, and we moved beneath the maples of our street, old trees, dense above us, and we were quiet, my son and I. The meadow, the open sky, all of that, was left behind. Then we reached the place along the road where I could see my house ahead.

The maple was gone from the front edge of my property, dead from blight and felled by my own hand. I looked away, not wanting to, but I felt suddenly bereft of this tree. I was sorry for its passing,

this tree. Matthew broke away from me now, began to run. I looked.

His mother was coming down the porch steps. My son ran hard to her, not calling out. She turned her face toward us, saw him approaching, sensing, I think, that something had happened.

I stopped, still separate from them. My daughter, a tall gangly girl, my sweet Naomi, emerged from the house, and for a moment they all three were before me, and the house itself, a fine house, a house we'd lived in for four years now, a solid house with its hipped roof and double-windowed dormer and its clapboard siding the color of sunlight in the brightness of noon.

My wife went down on one knee, and Matthew reached her and he threw his arms around her neck. I knew I should move forward, to explain. But what would I say? Naomi came to the two of them, put her hand on her crouching mother's shoulder. There was a seizing in my chest. I wanted to take them all three up into my arms, but instead, I stood dumbly there, watching.

Finally, Rachel's face lifted to look at me over Matthew's shoulder. I felt heavy now, rooted to this earth, as if I'd decided to take the place of the dead maple. But I made myself move. I took a step and another and there was a loosening inside me as I moved toward my family. My wife tilted her head slightly, a questioning gesture, I think. Naomi looked at me too, came around her mother, and I was glad she was drawing near, and she put her arms about me, I felt the bones in her arms pressing at my back. I held her tight.

"What was it, Daddy?"

"An accident," I said. "It was just an accident."

"Matty said he was dead, the man."

"We don't know that for sure."

"He fell?"

"Yes."

She said no more, but she needed me to hold her closer and I did. "It's all right," I said. "We're all right."

Matthew could not sleep. The house was dark and my wife and I had just extinguished the lamp, alone and undistracted at last. Then we heard his cry, wordless, and Rachel rose. I knew what it was about. As she disappeared, I looked toward the dark gape of the bedroom doorway and I gripped the sheet as if to put it aside and to rise. But I hesitated. I should not have hesitated to go to my son, but I did. For one moment and then another.

I forced myself to throw back the sheet and put my feet on the floor. I stood. I made my way across the room and down the hall, and my son's tears were fading as I approached. I stood in his doorway and his mother said to him, "It's okay, Matty. God decided he wanted an aeroplane pilot in heaven."

"Like he wanted Henry for an angel," my son said.

I turned away. I moved back down the hall and then stopped, neither here nor there. Matthew's first cousin Henry, my brother's son, had died of smallpox. My son had already encountered death. Of course he had, we had all encountered death, it was a part of our daily lives. Always, we waited for the first sneeze, the first cough, the first spot on our skin, we waited to be carried away, if not from smallpox then from influenza or scarlet fever or from diphtheria or from pneumonia or from tuberculosis. It was the way of the world. I believed in God, that he managed our lives, that he would call us when he chose to. And I was glad my son could picture his blood kin, a child of his own age, as an angel and not as a corpse in the ground.

But I stood in the middle of the hallway and I 45 dragged my forearm across my brow and I was having trouble drawing a breath.

I waited in bed, sitting propped up in the dark, sweating still.

Finally Rachel appeared in the door, quietly, pausing there in the dim light, her white nightgown glowing faintly, as if she were a ghost. I spoke to her at once, to drive that image from my mind. "Is he all right?"

"I don't know," she said, and she floated this way.

"Rachel," I said.

"Yes?" 50

She was beside the bed now. I had spoken her name without anything more to say. I just needed to say her name.

"Nothing," I said.

"What happened out there?"

"The plane crashed," I said. "These machines aren't safe."

Rachel drew back the sheet and sat beside me. 55 "Paul."

I looked toward her.

Her face was there, turned to me, featureless in the dark. She touched my hand and repeated, almost in a whisper, "What happened?"

"I don't know."

I was Earl Sandt. Sitting in my rattan chair. I looked down and the faces all turned upward and the mouths all opened to cry out but the only sound I could hear was the rush of air about me as I flew, I flew and the lift was not in my wings it was in my chest my very chest I was buoyed up and moving quickly and there was nothing around me now, not the aeroplane, not the rattan chair, only the wide bright air. I looked down again and there was only one face below and it was my own.

Mine. I woke. I sat up quickly, expecting to rise from 60 the bed and up through the ceiling and out into the night sky. But I was awake. I was sitting on my bed. Nevertheless, I lifted my eyes, and I saw the aeroplane, its broad wings, the fragile bones holding them in place, the bones stretching behind to the smaller back wings, the tail. And then suddenly the beast veered and showed me its dark underside and it dashed down.

And then the sound.

I jumped up from the bed, knocking into the bedstand.

"What is it?" Rachel cried.

"I'm all right," I said.

"Was it Matty?" 65

"It was a dream," I said.

I do not require silence at the breakfast table. We eat together each day, my wife and my son and my daughter and I. Even when my children have one leg skewed out from under the table, ready to run into the summer morning. They have their duties in this house, but the mornings are theirs. It is best to let a child feel his freedom in the morning. And they are free to speak, as well. I like to listen to the movement of my children's minds.

But this morning there was silence. A long period of silence. And their legs were under the table, in spite of it being early summer. And without urging, Matthew was eating his eggs, studiously sopping up the last bits of yolk with a piece of bread.

I had not picked up the newspaper that lay folded beside my plate. I could see, in large bold type, in the upturned quarter, the words AVIATOR KILLED. It was not uncommon for me to read the newspaper at the breakfast table, but only after we'd all had a chance to speak of the day to come.

I looked at Rachel. She was lifting her coffee cup 70 to her lips and I could see that her eyes were on Matthew. He was intent on the bread, running it around and around the plate. Naomi was looking out the kitchen door. I followed her gaze. The sun was bright. The trees quaked. A scrap of paper blew across the yard—lifting briefly into the air—and then it fell and tumbled along.

I placed my hand on the newspaper but I did not open it. I looked at my hand. It covered the words in the headline.

Finally I said, "It looks like a fine day."

Matthew lifted his face at this. "May I be excused?" he said.

"Yes."

He pushed back his chair and he rose and only now 75 was I hearing the flatness of his voice. He was a boy. This was the moment of the day that should have been relished above all others.

"Matty," my wife said. "Are you all right?"

My son had moved toward the door. He stopped now and turned to us. His two shoulders lifted slightly and fell. It was a very small gesture, really, this shrug, but it made my eyes close so as not to see it, this gesture in my son that was not the gesture of a child at all. Too late.

I opened my eyes. He was pushing through the screen door, not having spoken a word.

A Monday morning in the year of our Lord 1913. A desk in a bank. A newspaper tucked under my arm and then put away in a drawer. I sat and my hands were flat and unmoving on the top of my desk, my mahogany desk, and above me was a high window, and I have always liked the column of sky looking over me and I have liked the hush of the bank. It is not blas-

phemy to say that the hush was like that of a church. We protected the money of the people of this town, and their money was a measure of their hard work, and their hard work rightly gave them the things of this world, the things of a world changing rapidly now. The hush of the bank, and there were low voices murmuring, and I knew their words. I could hear *terrible* and I could hear *aeroplane* and I could hear *fire* and I could hear *dead*. I wanted to stand up and cry out to my tellers and my customers, Go about your business, all of you. Just go about your business.

But I did not stand. I swiveled in my chair and raised 80 my eyes to the window, to the empty morning sky. I had myself gone up into that sky. Higher even than Earl Sandt. I had stood in the air.

I had stood and looked out on a great city, on a world of business and banking, a world of making goods and buying and selling and building houses and factories and I looked out on steamships and trains and bridges and, far off, a vast sea, and I was standing within a thing as great as all of that. The Singer Building. The highest building in the world at that moment in the summer of 1909 when my host, a fellow banker, lifted his office window on the thirty-eighth floor, and I trembled like a horse before a fire. I crept forward and I felt my chest swell, I grew large with fear and happiness to look at this city, vast and multiform in its stone and marble and terra-cotta, the work of human hands.

I stepped closer still. I grew bold. The air moved on my face. An air only the clouds knew. But I was part of a race of creatures of the earth who were remaking themselves into something new. I took the last step a man could take and not fall. I pressed against the sill and I bent forward at the waist and looked across the rooftops below—rooftops that themselves were higher than any tree on earth, but far below me now—and I looked beyond the docks and masts and smokestacks, I followed the bright thread of the Hudson River to Ellis Island and the statue of Madam Liberty, her arm lifted high.

Earl Sandt, I lift my arm to you. I stand in the meadow beside my son, a blazing torch in my hand. Come here to me, guide your plane this way, fly down to this flame and land safely beside me. I look from where I sit in the rattan chair, my hands on the steering handle, I see the flame below, and my wing has not yet torn. I nudge my aeroplane gently downward, down toward the man and the boy. I will be safe.

But I am not Earl Sandt. He is dead.

I have seen men die before. My father, long ago, his lungs bricked up solid with pneumonia. A man in the Alleghenys, broken beneath a felled tree, when I was young and working in timber. And another in New York City on that day in 1909 when I went out of the Singer Building and into the streets that were dim even near noon, streets narrow and full of rushing men and the hammering of metal and the whine of wheels and the mutter of automobile engines and the clatter of a distant elevated train, and I turned to look up at the place where I'd stood, in the middle of the air, and my eyes went up and up, impossibly high, up the great bluestone and redbrick column, up to its great mansard roof and cupola and the bright sky beyond. "Step lively," a voice said, and I looked and I could not pick the speaker out of a hundred bowlered men moving all about me.

I stepped away, up the street, which was cloaked in the shadows of skyscrapers as far as I could see. I moved, and suddenly before me there was a gathering of men and some bowlers were coming off and I came up.

He was in a greatcoat in spite of the heat. He was sprawled facedown, his arms outstretched, his legs spread wide. The men about him were quiet. I thought to look up. A gray stone building loomed over us, perhaps two hundred feet high. I looked back down to the dead man. A policeman pushed past me and bent to the body.

I found myself standing beside my desk in the bank on the morning after Earl Sandt died. I could not recall the act of rising from this chair. I extended my arm, touched my hand to the corner of my desk, stiffened my fingertips, held myself up. I had to go out, I realized.

I moved to the coatrack and took my hat and I put it on my head and I stepped from my office and my secretary looked up and I said to her, "I'll be back shortly." She lifted her eyebrows ever so slightly. This was unlike me, of course. But I did not pause to explain. There was no explanation.

I stepped into the sunlight before the bank and turned toward the woods where he had gone down.

A wagon was moving toward me from the tree line as I approached. I stopped. The horse had its head lowered as if the load were heavy, but the wagon moved easily, quickly. I stepped away from it. The driver turned his face to me. A man I knew, a collector of scrap goods. He nodded, but I could not return the nod. I was leaden now in my limbs. The wagon slipped past and I glanced into the bed of it: twisted metal, charred wood, a panel of canvas. I looked sharply to the side. This whole thing was a mistake, to come here again. I thought to back away, to face toward the town, the square, the bank, the maple trees, face toward my house where I would surely live the rest of my life.

I could not. I had to press on, into the stand of pine. But I had to catch my breath first. I felt as if I'd been running a long way. I bent forward and put my hands on my knees.

Above me was the sky where Earl Sandt had spent his last moments of life. I did not look. I leaned hard onto my knees. I closed my eyes. I held tight to the steering handle and there was something terribly wrong. These wings that felt like my own limbs—I sensed them stretching out from me and lifting me up—these wings went weak and so did my limbs of flesh, I was instantly aware of the very surface of my skin, the beating of my heart. And I felt a question rise like a gasp into my throat: What was it I believed? Did I sense a God all about me in the sky? Was it he who lifted me and would take me now into his arms?

Forgive me, no.

This thing I had expected to be familiar—my own death—was all new. I fell. I fell from him. His hands receded and the trees reached up and I fell.

I could not breathe at all. I rose up from where I'd been bending and I stood straight and dragged the air into my lungs and I opened my eyes, and before me was the tree line, the pines, and beyond them was the clearing where he fell and burned, Earl Sandt. And he knew something now. Right this moment. Something that I desperately wished to know. He had been alive above me, in the sunlit air, just yesterday, and now he knew the great truth of it all.

I stepped forward, moved toward the trees. My breath had returned. Fragile. Easily taken away. But I breathed deep once, and again, and I walked into the darkness of the trees and I was filled with the smell of pine all about me and the smell of the duff beneath my feet and with other smells, not of the forest, faintly still of smoke in the air and the fuel of the aeroplane.

I pressed on, my face lowered, feeling the trees on the back of my neck, in my shoulders, in a faint wrenching upward in my chest. I've been around trees often in my life, I made a life from the forests before I became who I am, a man with a desk in a bank and a Georgian revival home and a wife and a son and a daughter and a special pew in a church where the deacons sit, and I know nothing about anything, I know only that I must press past these last few trees and into this clearing, which I do.

It is empty. It is empty. Earl Sandt's aeroplane was here and now it is gone. I move out to the center, I am surrounded by high pine, and there is something. A shapeless patch of burnt earth. I slow and stop before it. He burned here. He vanished from this life here.

I take another step. I stand precisely where he fell. For a moment I stretch out my arms, as if to fly, and they are contained within this black bareness. I hold fast to the steering column and my wings are still whole and I am racing toward those distant pines, and a thought occurs to me. I sit on the back of a horse. I am high up, above the tree line, on a slender thread of a path. Not even the smell of the pines has risen this high. I pause and I look below me. Faces turn up, their hats raised high in the air. Treetops point up to me and I have nothing inside but an enormous quiet. I find myself separated from all that I've known, from every touch every word every face, I have lifted up into the air, high on this mountain with nothing around me but the empty sky, high in the air above this meadow. And I think: This is how it feels. To be free. To be utterly alone. And my hands clench on the reins. There is only one more thing to feel, to know. My hands clench harder, wanting to slip hard to the right, to leap into that empty sky beneath me. Earl and I.

"Papa."

For a moment I do not recognize the voice.

"Papa."

It has drawn near. I look.

It is Matthew.

He stands before me. His face is smudged. His hair is tousled. His eyes are fixed hard on mine.

I want him to go away from this place, quickly. I lift my hand to him, a vague gesture, and I cannot find words. "Matty," I say, just that. I am within the circle of Earl's fire and my son is outside. I try to step to him, but I am rooted here. I look at the trees all around. And then back to my son. His face is turned up to me, waiting.

I know too much. I want him to run away now, not just from this place but from me.

"Go on home," I say.

His brow furrows very slightly.

I step from the circle, I reach out, my hand goes to him, my thumb lands gently on his brow, tries to smooth the furrow away.

He backs off.

I didn't mean to frighten him. I carry too much in these fingertips now.

But suddenly he smiles.

"Papa," he says. "Look."

His hand comes from behind his back. I don't recognize the object at first, hanging limply over his fingers.

"It's his," Matthew says.

And now I can see. Earl Sandt's goggles.

"I found it," he says.

I struggle once again to draw a breath. The moments I have yearned to share with Earl Sandt: He entered them looking through this thing in my son's hand.

But before I can think of what to do, Matthew grasps the goggles at each end and he lifts them high and the strap goes quickly over his head and the goggles slide down and are on his face and I can see his eyes for a moment, his child's eyes, the eyes of my boy, faint there and distant, and his face angles and his eyes vanish, the panes of glass go blank from the light.

And my son lifts his arms. He lifts them like wings, and he turns to his left and he begins to run, he runs swooping and lifting and falling. "Look, Papa," he cries. "Look. I'm Earl Sandt!" ○

ROBERT OLEN BUTLER

Robert Olen Butler was born in 1945 and grew up in St. Louis, Missouri. He studied theater and oral interpretation at Northwestern University and earned his master's degree in playwriting from the University of Iowa. He is the author of ten novels and three volumes of short fiction, including *A Good Scent from a Strange Mountain* (1992), stories based on his experiences during his tour of duty in Vietnam. It won the Pulitzer Prize for fiction in 1993. "This Is Earl Sandt" is from his most recent book, *Had a Good Time: Stories from American Postcards* (2004), writing inspired by Butler's collection of antique picture postcards. From those postcards—the pictures and the scant notes he found written on them—Butler fleshed out detailed American stories.

"The voices, you know, that's the thing I do," Butler has said of his niche in fiction writing. Indeed he is well known for his ability to create a distinctive voice for his characters and to root each story deeply within a character's perspective.

Butler has earned several honors, including a Guggenheim Fellowship, a grant from the National Endowment for the Arts, and a National Magazine Award. His work has appeared in several well-regarded publications, including *The New Yorker, The Atlantic, GQ,* and *The Paris Review.* He is currently the director of the Creative Writing Program at Florida State University.

SEEING

1. Consider the order in which you looked at the postcard and read the essay. How did knowing—or not knowing—the subject of the photograph influence your response to it? If you looked at the image first, how did that image change when you knew that the plane was going to crash? To what extent did that knowledge alter your focus, from plane to pilot or from pilot to plane?

2. Handwriting on the back of the postcard contains specific information: "This is Earl Sandt of Erie Pa in his Aeroplane just before it fell." It does not, despite Butler's inference, include the fate of the pilot, the name of the person who wrote the text, or the name and address of a recipient. How would knowing what actually happened to Sandt change your view of the picture? Why do you think the writer chose to include only certain information? How does the realization that the postcard was not meant to be sent change your understanding of it? For what purpose do you imagine it was intended? In what specific ways does Butler's speculation on the character of the observer match your own?

WRITING

1. In recent years, television news programs have relied increasingly on images to capture the horror of accidents. The decision to run film of victims lying on the side of a road or being extricated from the wreckage of a plane has led to charges of sensationalism and voyeurism. How do you respond to graphic images on television or in the newspaper? Did you respond differently to the picture on Butler's postcard? Why or why not? Do you think the information noted on the postcard—and what is not noted there—influenced your reaction to the image? Write the first draft of an essay in which you compare your response to the postcard with the way you usually respond to graphic images in the news.

2. In "This Is Earl Sandt," Butler removes one element of anonymity from the image: He gives us the observer, the man who took the photograph. In fact, by the end of the story, we know a great deal more about the narrator—a fictitious character—than we do about Earl Sandt. Read the story again, carefully, making a list of the "facts" Butler tells us about the pilot and about the narrator. Although we learn very little about Sandt as a person, he is an integral part of the story. Write an essay in which you explain how Butler uses Sandt both to define the narrator and to describe the narrator's response to Sandt's death.

PEOPLE WATCHING JUMPER ON HOTEL ROOF.

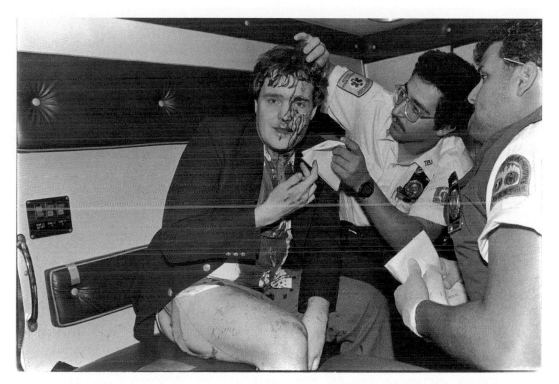

MAN COMPLAINING THAT HE WAS ATTACKED AFTER HE GAVE HIS MONEY TO ROBBERS

TAXI DRIVER EXPLAINING HOW AN ARGUEMENT WITH HIS PASSENGER CAUSED HIM TO DRIVE INTO THE RESTAURANT.

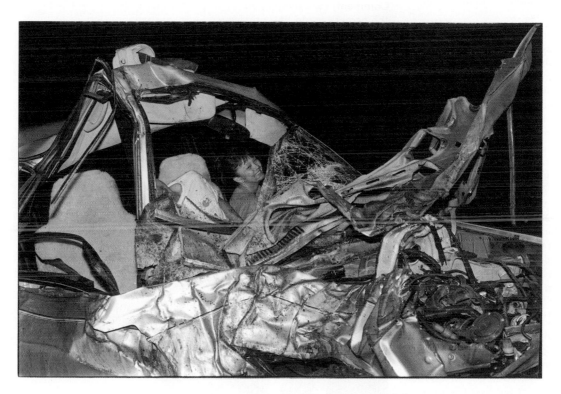

WOMAN laughing AFTER CAR WRECK.

ANDREW SAVULICH

Andrew Savulich worked as a landscape architect before turning to freelance photography and, fifteen years later, becoming a staff photographer for the *New York Daily News*. His work has been exhibited in the United States and abroad, and he has received numerous awards, including a grant from the National Endowment for the Arts.

Savulich is a master of *spot news*—spontaneous photographs of the violence and accidents, the humorous and odd events of everyday life, especially in urban areas. He explains his motivation: "We're at a point in our society where very weird things are happening in the streets, and I like taking pictures because I feel I'm recording something that's really *happening*." He thrives on the hunt: "There's a kind of adrenaline rush when you're doing this work. . . . It's all spontaneous: You have to figure things out, and you never really know what you have. That uncertainty is attractive, I think."

Savulich adds a handwritten caption below each photograph he takes, many of which are collected in *City of Chance* (2002). "I felt that the pictures needed something to describe what was happening. And I thought the easiest way would be just to write a little description on the prints themselves. And I liked the way it looked."

SEEING

1. What story does each of these photographs tell? What is especially striking and memorable about each one? What similarities or differences do you find in these four images?

2. Look carefully at each of the photographs for Andrew Savulich's artistic presence. Comment, for example, on the camera angle, the precise moment at which he chooses to take each photograph, as well as what he includes. What makes his style distinct from that of the other photographers whose work is presented in this chapter?

RESPONDING VISUALLY

Choose a photograph from this book, from your own collection, or from a magazine or newspaper. Write at least three different captions for it. Experiment with a range of styles—descriptive, sensational, or humorous, for example. How does each caption help shift the overall impact of the image? Or, to use John Berger's phrase (page 690), how does "the image illustrate the sentence"?

WRITING

1. Much of the story in each of Savulich's photographs is conveyed by its caption. Think of alternate captions for each image. Would a different caption significantly change how you read the photograph? Write a brief essay explaining why or why not.

2. Choose one of Savulich's photographs, and write a two-page journalistic account to accompany it in a newspaper. Include the sequence of events that led up to the moment depicted in the photograph, conveying the emotional aspects of the event as you do so. Base as much of your report as possible on details you see in the image, and then embellish your article with quotations, names, background information, or any other "facts" that would make your news story more compelling.

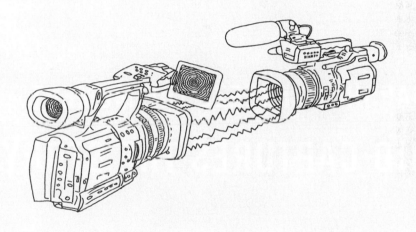

Chang / Polaris

SNAPSHOTS FREEZE THE MOMENT.

RADIO CAPTURES THE STORY.

Depend on NPR® to frame international stories with a deeper context and cultural understanding. That's because NPR reporters don't just work in other countries. They live there. With 14 international bureaus, NPR brings a richer perspective to world events by including the people and places behind them. This is more than reporting. This is bringing the world home.

To find an NPR station in your area, **visit npr.org.**

EXPERIENCE THE WORLD

National Public Radio, Snapshots Freeze the Moment. Radio Captures the Story. 2004

NATIONAL PUBLIC RADIO

National Public Radio (NPR) is a not-for-profit producer and distributor of noncommercial radio programming. Since its founding in 1970, NPR's audience has grown exponentially: from approximately 2 million listeners in the early 1980s to nearly 23 million listeners in 2005. NPR began with only 90 member stations; today it can be heard on 760 independent public radio stations. Its news programs, *Morning Edition* and *All Things Considered,* are the second and third most popular national radio programs in the United States. Among the better known NPR personalities are Terry Gross, host of *Fresh Air;* Tom and Ray Magliozzi ("Click and Clack, the Tappet Brothers"), cohosts of *Car Talk;* and Cokie Roberts, senior news analyst.

In a 2002 interview, Deborah Amos, a former NPR reporter, described NPR's audience this way: "It's a tribal thing, the public radio audience. . . . Listeners are our coauthors, our coconspirators, they engage, they imagine and participate with us. It helps to explain those 'wait in the driveway until the story is over' moments."

NPR's mission is to work in partnership with its member stations to create a more informed public, one challenged and invigorated by a deeper understanding and appreciation of events, ideas, and cultures. NPR's broadcast and print awards include more than three dozen George Foster Peabody Awards, a number of Alfred I. duPont–Columbia University Awards, and a National Medal of Arts.

SEEING

1. Photocopy the NPR advertisement. Then use a colored pencil to trace the path your eyes naturally follow through it. Draw light or heavy circles to show where you spend more time looking. Where do your eyes go first? Why? Which parts of the advertisement hold your interest longer? Why? Which parts do you only glance at? Look closely at the elements you initially overlooked. How do these details change your reading of the ad?

2. Consider the use of image and color in this advertisement. To what extent does the ad rely on the photograph to communicate its overall message? Which colors are repeated? To what effect? Which parts of the text "affect" your experience of the photograph? What relationships do you notice between the text and the image in this ad?

RESPONDING VISUALLY

Choose a journalistic medium— writing, photography, television, radio—and a news organization. Create a print ad designed to persuade your audience of the benefits of that medium and of the news outlet you've chosen. Limit your ad to one page, but use any combination of text and image that suits your message.

WRITING

1. To what extent do you find this advertisement persuasive? Does it make you want to turn to NPR for your news coverage? Why or why not? Write an analysis of the effectiveness of the advertisement. Include specific suggestions for revising the ad to target you and your friends.

2. Evaluate the claim that "snapshots freeze the moment," while "radio captures the story." How is freezing a moment different from capturing a story? What do photographs leave out, according to this ad? Do moving pictures (like movies or television) close this gap? Choose a current news story and write an essay in which you compare two different treatments of the story, one by NPR and one by another news outlet. (Visit www.npr.org for audio files of daily radio programs.) How would you characterize each news outlet's coverage of the story? In what ways is the coverage similar? different? How does each outlet inform your understanding of the event?

Front page, *Los Angeles Times,*
December 16, 2004

Front page, *New York Times,*
December 16, 2004

Front page, *USA Today,*
December 16, 2004

If radio "captures the story," how
are daily newspapers presenting
the news? Compare the front
pages of three different newspapers on the same day. How
would you describe the choices
in content, scope, tone, and overall
presentation in each? Based on
your observations, what inferences
can you draw about the principles that drive each publication's
editorial decisions?

TALKING PICTURES

"When I started in this business," remarked Tom Brokaw just before his retirement from *NBC Nightly News*, in 2004, "there were really only two planets in the evening sky: NBC and CBS. Now there are so many more choices out there. The Internet and its infinite capacity for gathering news and disseminating it has changed everything. All-news cable has changed a lot. That will affect the viewing habits of generations coming up. . . . The evening newscasts are still the big engines because of the audience they draw. When there are big events, they come to us."

Although Americans continue to turn primarily to network and local television for their news, these mainstream sources are "losing audience" according to a 2004 study by the Project for Excellence in Journalism. Visit the PEJ's web site (www.journalism.org), and read "The State of the News Media 2004: An Annual Report on American Journalism." Use the report's core areas as a starting point for formulating your own small-scale survey of how people in your community read, watch, and listen to the news. Develop a set of interview questions to determine the sources your subjects rely on for news and their overall perceptions of the news media. Interview ten subjects. Then write a report in which you present your findings, draw conclusions about the news habits of your respondents, and compare your results with those of the Project for Excellence in Journalism.

This Is Our World

Dorothy Allison

THE FIRST PAINTING I EVER SAW UP CLOSE WAS at a Baptist church when I was seven years old. It was a few weeks before my mama was to be baptized. From it, I took the notion that art should surprise and astonish, and hopefully make you think something you had not thought until you saw it. The painting was a mural of Jesus at the Jordan River done on the wall behind the baptismal font. The font itself was a remarkable creation—a swimming pool with one glass side set into the wall above and behind the pulpit so that ordinarily you could not tell the font was there, seeing only the painting of Jesus. When the tank was flooded with water, little lights along the bottom came on, and anyone who stepped down the steps seemed to be walking past Jesus himself and descending into the Jordan River. Watching baptisms in that tank was like watching movies at the drive-in, my cousins had told me. From the moment the deacon walked us around the church, I knew what my cousin had meant. I could not take my eyes off the painting or the glass-fronted tank. It looked every moment as if Jesus were about to come alive, as if he were about to step out onto the water of the river. I think the way I stared at the painting made the deacon nervous.

The deacon boasted to my mama that there was nothing like that baptismal font in the whole state of South Carolina. It had been designed, he told her, by a nephew of the minister—a boy who had gone on to build a shopping center out in New Mexico. My mama was not sure that someone who built shopping centers was the kind of person who should have been designing baptismal fonts, and she was even more uncertain about the steep steps by Jesus' left hip. She asked the man to let her practice going up and down, but he warned her it would be different once the water poured in.

"It's quite safe though," he told her. "The water will hold you up. You won't fall."

I kept my attention on the painting of Jesus. He was much larger than I was, a little bit more than life-size, but the thick layer of shellac applied to protect the image acted like a magnifying glass, making him seem larger still. It was Jesus himself that fascinated me, though. He was all rouged and pale and pouty as Elvis Presley. This was not my idea of the Son of God, but I liked it. I liked it a lot.

"Jesus looks like a girl," I told my mama.

She looked up at the painted face. A little blush appeared on her cheekbones, and she looked as if she would have smiled if the deacon were not frowning so determinedly. "It's just the eyelashes," she said. The deacon nodded. They climbed back up the stairs. I stepped over close to Jesus and put my hand on the painted robe. The painting was sweaty and cool, slightly oily under my fingers.

5

"I liked that Jesus," I told my mama as we walked out of the church. "I wish we had something like that." To her credit, Mama did not laugh.

"If you want a picture of Jesus," she said, "we'll get you one. They have them in nice frames at Sears." I sighed. That was not what I had in mind. What I wanted was a life-size, sweaty painting, one in which Jesus looked as hopeful as a young girl—something other-worldly and peculiar, but kind of wonderful at the same time. After that, every time we went to church I asked to go up to see the painting, but the baptismal font was locked tight when not in use.

The Sunday Mama was to be baptized, I watched the minister step down into that pool past the Son of God. The preacher's gown was tailored with little weights carefully sewn into the hem to keep it from rising up in the water. The water pushed up at the fabric while the weights tugged it down. Once the minister was all the way down into the tank, the robe floated up a bit so that it seemed to have a shirred ruffle all along the bottom. That was almost enough to pull my eyes away from the face of Jesus, but not quite. With the lights on in the bottom of the tank, the eyes of the painting seemed to move and shine. I tried to point it out to my sisters, but they were uninterested. All they wanted to see was mama.

Mama was to be baptized last, after three little boys, and their gowns had not had any weights attached. The white robes floated up around their necks so that their skinny boy bodies and white cotton underwear were perfectly visible to the congregation. The water that came up above the hips of the minister lapped their shoulders, and the shortest of the boys seemed panicky at the prospect of gulping water, no matter how holy. He paddled furiously to keep above the water's surface. The water started to rock violently at his struggles, sweeping the other boys off their feet. All of them pumped their knees to stay upright, and the minister, realizing how the scene must appear to the congregation below, speeded up the baptismal process, praying over and dunking the boys at high speed.

Around me the congregation shifted in their seats. My little sister slid forward off the pew, and I quickly grabbed her around the waist and barely stopped myself from laughing out loud. A titter from the back of the church indicated that other people were having the same difficulty keeping from laughing. Other people shifted irritably and glared at the noisemakers. It was clear that no matter the provocation, we were to pretend nothing funny was happening. The minister frowned more fiercely and prayed louder. My mama's friend Louise, sitting at our left, whispered a soft "Look at that," and we all looked up in awe. One of the hastily blessed boys had dog-paddled over to the glass and was staring out at us, eyes wide and his hands pressed flat to the glass. He looked as if he hoped someone would rescue him. It was too much for me. I began to giggle helplessly, and not a few of the people around me joined in. Impatiently the minister hooked the boy's robe, pulled him back, and pushed him toward the stairs.

My mama, just visible on the staircase, hesitated briefly as the sodden boy climbed up past her. Then she set her lips tightly together, and reached down and pressed her robe to her thighs. She came down the steps slowly, holding down the skirt as she did so, giving one stern glance to the two boys climbing past her up the steps, and then turning her face deliberately up to the painting of Jesus. Every move she made communicated resolution and faith, and the congregation stilled in respect. She was baptized looking up stubbornly, both hands holding down that cotton robe, while below, I fought so hard not to giggle, tears spilled down my face.

Over the pool, the face of Jesus watched solemnly with his pink, painted cheeks and thick, dark lashes. For all the absurdity of the event, his face seemed to me startlingly compassionate and wise. That face understood fidgety boys and stubborn women. It made me want the painting even more, and to this day I remember it with longing. It had the weight of art, that face. It had what I am sure art is supposed to have—the power to provoke, the authority of a heartfelt vision.

embattled heart, the child I was and the woman I have become, not Jesus at the Jordan but a woman with only her stubborn memories and passionate convictions to redeem her.

"You write such mean stories," a friend once told me. "Raped girls, brutal fathers, faithless mothers, and untrustworthy lovers—meaner than the world really is, don't you think?"

I just looked at her. Meaner than the world really is? No. I thought about showing her the box under my desk where I keep my clippings. Newspaper stories and black-and-white images—the woman who drowned her children, the man who shot first the babies in her arms and then his wife, the teenage boys who led the three-year-old away along the train track, the homeless family recovering from frostbite with their eyes glazed and indifferent while the doctor scowled over their shoulders. The world is meaner than we admit, larger and more astonishing. Strength appears in the most desperate figures, tragedy when we have no reason to expect it. Yes, some of my stories are fearful, but not as cruel as what I see in the world. I believe in redemption, just as I believe in the nobility of the despised, the dignity of the outcast, the intrinsic honor among misfits, pariahs, and queers. Artists—those of us who stand outside the city gates and look back at a society that tries to ignore us—we have an angle of vision denied to whole sectors of the sheltered and indifferent population within. It is our curse and our prize, and for everyone who will tell us our work is mean or fearful or unreal, there is another who will embrace us and say with tears in their eyes how wonderful it is to finally feel as if someone else has seen their truth and shown it in some part as it should be known.

"My story," they say. "You told my story. That is me, mine, us." And it is.

We are not the same. We are a nation of nations. Regions, social classes, economic circumstances, ethical systems, and political convictions—all separate us even as we pretend they do not. Art makes that plain. Those of us who have read the same books, eaten the same kinds of food as children, watched the same television shows, and listened to the same music, we believe ourselves part of the same nation—and we are continually startled to discover that our versions of reality do not match. If we were more the same, would we not see the same thing when we look at a painting? But what is it we see when we look at a work of art? What is it we fear will be revealed? The artist waits for us to say. It does not matter that each of us sees something slightly different. Most of us, confronted with the artist's creation, hesitate, stammer, or politely deflect the question of what it means to us. Even those of us from the same background, same region, same general economic and social class, come to "art" uncertain, suspicious, not wanting to embarrass ourselves by revealing what the work provokes in us. In fact, sometimes we are not sure. If we were to reveal what we see in each painting, sculpture, installation, or little book, we would run the risk of exposing our secret selves, what we know and what we fear we do not know, and of course incidentally what it is we truly fear. Art is the Rorschach test for all of us, the projective hologram of our secret lives. Our emotional and intellectual lives are laid bare. Do you like hologram roses? Big, bold, brightly painted canvases? Representational art? Little boxes with tiny figures posed precisely? Do you dare say what it is you like?

For those of us born into poor and working-class 40 families, these are not simple questions. For those of us who grew up hiding what our home life was like, the fear is omnipresent—particularly when that home life was scarred by physical and emotional violence. We know if we say anything about what we see in a work of art we will reveal more about ourselves than the artist. What do you see in this painting, in that one? I see a little girl, terrified, holding together the torn remnants of her clothing. I see a child, looking back at the mother for help and finding none. I see a mother, bruised and exhausted, unable to look up for help, unable to believe anyone in the world will help her. I see a man with his fists raised, hating himself but making those fists tighter all the time. I see a little girl, uncertain and angry, looking down at her own body with hatred and contempt. I see that all the time, even when no one else sees what I see. I know I am not supposed to mention what it is I see. Perhaps no one else is seeing what I see. If they are, I am pretty sure there is some cryptic covenant that requires that we will not say what we see. Even when looking at an image of a terrified child, we know that to mention why that child might be so frightened would be a breach of social etiquette. The world requires that such children not be mentioned, even when so many of us are looking directly at her.

There seems to be a tacit agreement about what it is not polite to mention, what it is not appropriate to portray. For some of us, that polite behavior is set so deeply we truly do not see what seems outside that tacit agreement. We have lost the imagination for what our real lives have been or continue to be, what happens when we go home and close the door on the outside world. Since so many would like us to never mention anything unsettling anyway, the impulse to be quiet, the impulse to deny and pretend, becomes very strong. But the artist knows all about that impulse. The artist knows that it must be resisted. Art is not meant to be polite, secret, coded, or timid. Art is the sphere in which that impulse to hide and lie is the most dangerous. In art, transgression is holy, revelation a sacrament, and pursuing one's personal truth the only sure validation.

Does it matter if our art is canonized, if we become rich and successful, lauded and admired? Does it make any difference if our pictures become popular, our books made into movies, our creations win awards? What if we are the ones who wind up going from town to town with our notebooks, our dusty boxes of prints or Xeroxed sheets of music, never acknowledged, never paid for our work? As artists, we know how easily we could become a Flannery O'Connor character, reading those journals of criticism and burying our faces in our hands, staggering under the weight of what we see that the world does not. As artists, we also know that neither worldly praise nor critical disdain will ultimately prove the worth of our work.

Some nights I think of that sweating, girlish Jesus above my mother's determined features, those hands outspread to cast benediction on those giggling uncertain boys, me in the congregation struck full of wonder and love and helpless laughter. If no one else ever wept at that image, I did. I wished the artist who painted that image knew how powerfully it touched me, that after all these years his art still lives inside me. If I can wish for anything for my art, that is what I want—to live in some child forever—and if I can demand anything of other artists, it is that they attempt as much. ○

"I know in my bones that to write well you must inhabit your creations: male, female, whatever," says Dorothy Allison, a self-described "lesbian, feminist, Southern femme partnered to a self-defined butch musician, incest survivor, . . . mother . . . working-class escapee."

Born in Greenville, South Carolina, in 1949, Allison grew up in a poor, working-class family. She says that she knew from her earliest years that she was an outsider, that she didn't fit in, but that not fitting in is one of her strengths as a writer. "Some days I think I have a unique advantage, an outsider's perspective that lets me see what others ignore." Her writing gives voice to her experience of the working-poor South, where her stepfather raped her when she was 5 years old. Her first novel, *Bastard Out of Carolina* (1992), which was a finalist for the National Book Award, is about escaping from that world. Her second novel, *Cavedweller* (1998), is about returning to it.

"As a teacher I invariably require that my students write across their own barriers," she says, "forcing young lesbians to write as middle-aged men (straight or gay) and the most fervently macho men to speak as tender girls. Climbing into a stranger's skin is the core of the writer's experience, stretching the imagination to incorporate the unimagined." This essay first appeared in the summer 1998 issue of *Doubletake* magazine.

SEEING

1. At one point in "This Is Our World," Dorothy Allison describes a magazine ad "that showed a small child high in the air dropping toward the upraised arms of a waiting figure below" (para. 29). What varying "versions of reality" (para. 39) does Allison see in this image? How does her description of each version exemplify her point that "if we were to reveal what we see in each painting, sculpture, installation, or little book, we would run the risk of exposing our secret selves" (para. 39)?

2. Allison begins her essay with memories of the first painting she "ever saw up close." At what points—and with what effects—does she refer to those memories later in the essay? When does Allison shift from personal anecdotes to more general commentary? To what extent do you think that movement is successful?

WRITING

1. "The world is meaner than we admit," Allison writes, referring to the stash of newspaper clippings she keeps under her desk (para. 37). Use a newspaper clipping of your choice—or one of the front pages we've included on page 282—to agree or disagree with Allison's assertion. Use details from your text and your knowledge of violence to support your points.

2. From the painting of Jesus she marveled at as a child, Allison writes, she "took the notion that art should surprise and astonish, and hopefully make you think something you had not thought until you saw it" (para. 1). Choose a piece of art—a visual image, an essay, or some other work—that surprised and astonished you, and use it to support or refute Allison's claim about what art should do. If you disagree with Allison, make sure you start with your own definition of the purpose of art.

http://www.alternet.org/

RSS ·

AlterNet
The Mix is the Message

START MAKING SENSE
Support independent media and get your copy now!

| Home | Archive | Columnists | Blogs | Bloggers | Multimedia | Discuss | RSS | Donate | About |

START MAKING SENSE

Search: [   ] Go

From The Wire The latest

▸ Bush says any leaker will be fired
▸ Saddam's lawyer says Baghdad too dangerous for trial
▸ FBI monitoring civil rights, anti-war groups
▸ Congress to vote on granting native Hawaiians sovereignty
▸ London Bombings Mastermind Arrested

Peek Best of the blogs

Peek: If it's perspective, debunkings, quote-refutings, or just plain tongue-lashings, here.

Full Post   Discuss | Permalink

The Evolution of Frankenfoods?
John Feffer, AlterNet

EnviroHealth: The multibillion-dollar nanotech industry wants to change what you eat at the molecular level.

To Rick, With Love
Michael Blanding, AlterNet

We, the depraved citizens of Boston, would like to thank Sen. Santorum for recognizing our city as the modern-day Gomorrah that it is, and pointing out all the ways that Boston has led to the moral decline of the nation.

Uncle Sam, Meet the Bloggers
Kelly Hearn, AlterNet

MediaCulture: An FEC commissioner's comments flame through the blogosphere, mobilizing bloggers and questioning the role of 'citizen journalists.'

RE: SEARCHING THE WEB

"Big stories change media," wrote writer and cultural critic Jon Katz on October 11, 2001, on the webzine *Slashdot*. "Radio's high-water mark was World War II, and TV news came of age after John F. Kennedy's assassination. Elvis and his death gave birth to modern mass-marketed tabloid media. Increasingly, it appears the attack on the World Trade Center and Pentagon and the shooting war that began last night [in Afghanistan] have made more distinct another evolutionary leap in information: The Net is emerging as our most serious communications medium and clearly the freest and most diverse. Conventional journalists are still obsessed with hackers and pornographers; still fuss about whether the Net is safe or factual. But increasingly, they steer readers to their web sites for more in-depth information and conversation."

To what extent do you agree with Katz's assertion? How does online news coverage differ from print, radio, and television news coverage? What, in your opinion, are the significant advantages and disadvantages of each? How have the events of September 11, 2001, altered the media? Choose a current news event, and consider its coverage in various media. Then write an essay in which you argue for or against Katz's point of view, using your news story as a case study.

The latest Rove

Earl Ofari Hutchinson:
Suzie Peña Killing Should Unite, Not Divide, Blacks and Latinos

own computer
Post by Lakshmi Chaudhry

Podcast: In an address to 700 student leaders, Bill Clinton shares his four steps to creating a progressive movement. More »

The L-Files

Censored by my

Steve McCurry, *Sharbat Gula, Pakistan, 1985*

Steve McCurry, *Sharbat Gula, Pakistan, 2002*

ART SPIEGELMAN

Art Spiegelman was born in Stockholm, Sweden, in 1948; he moved with his parents to Queens, a borough of New York City, when he was 3. His parents had hoped he would become a dentist, but by age 16, he was drawing professionally. His work has since appeared in many magazines, including *The New Yorker,* where he was a staff artist and writer from 1993 to 2003.

Spiegelman is the only person to win the Pulitzer Prize for fiction for a comic book. *Maus* (1991), a fable about the Holocaust, is based on the experiences of his parents, who survived the Nazi death camps; it portrays the Germans as cats, the Jews as mice, and the Poles as pigs. According to the *New York Times Magazine,* "It would be almost impossible to overstate the influence of *Maus* among other artists." Or among serious readers: Spiegelman's work has transformed both the nature of comics and the nature of their audience.

Spiegelman sees nothing odd about addressing weighty subjects in what has traditionally been a lightweight medium. Comics are his form of communication—the only way, he says, that he knows how to tell a story. They are also his medium for "trying to understand myself and trying to understand other things." The comic strip reproduced here is from *In the Shadow of No Towers* (2004), a collection that captures Spiegelman's horrified response to the events of September 11, 2001, and their aftermath.

SEEING

1. In the introduction to *In the Shadow of No Towers,* Spiegelman writes, "All the rage I'd suppressed after the 2000 election, all the paranoia I'd barely managed to squelch immediately after 9/11, returned with a vengeance." What visual evidence do you find of these emotions in this piece? For example, how does Spiegelman use color to show his rage? How does he use form and technique (lines, shapes, repetition) to suggest paranoia?

2. How many visual jokes can you find in the drawings? How many jokes in words? Compare the visual jokes with the verbal jokes. How do the punch lines work in each? Translate some of his visual jokes into words, and draw some of Spiegelman's verbal jokes in pictures. Are the jokes as funny in the other medium? Why or why not?

WRITING

1. Clearly Spiegelman is angry about the U.S. government's actions after September 11. Suppose he had agreed with the Bush administration's policies. What specific directions would you give to Spiegelman if he were to redraw the cartoon, panel by panel, from the perspective of someone who supports the government's response to the attacks on the World Trade Center and the Pentagon?

2. Spiegelman begins this comic strip with the sentence "Nothing like commemorating an event to help you forget it"; and he ends the piece with the words "Happy Anniversary." How do you feel about commemorating September 11? What does it mean to remember a tragic event? to commemorate it? What is the difference between the two? How should September 11 be remembered on a national level? a local level? individually? Write an essay in which you choose a forum for commemorating that day—a national memorial, a local event, a writing project, an online forum, for example—and develop a plan for your commemorative project. Your proposal should discuss the goals of your project, what you expect it to accomplish.

Interview: Spiegelman

How would you describe the content of *No Towers*?
Art Spiegelman This book is a fragment of diary. In making the book, I'm trying to work my way out. By the end of the book I'm somewhere near the end of 2002. These are really over-articulated journal entries. We're still waiting to see the denouement, especially what it means to have reduced that event to a very jingoistic and belligerent set of responses. September 11 has been so co-opted, particularly by people who wanted to lead us into war. And that became a big part of the subject matter of the strips.

As pages, they were ephemeral. They were made for newspapers and magazines that were willing to have me, mostly in my own coalition of the willing, as I've described it. And they weren't really designed to be a book.

The idea of making a book implies for me a notion of posterity. At this point, yes it's true, most books have the shelf life of yogurt, but built into the notion of a book is something that has its own small monumental qualities. To find a book out of these fragments meant making something of these strips that actually had a reason to exist together. What I was able to find was a kind of art object appropriate to the occasion: a book that looked like a tower that was both incredibly fragile and was able to get scuffed but also has that monumental quality, and a book that had a thematic discourse.

What was it?
For me, it was, what's the nature of ephemera? Here's the best I can boil it down to: When the monumental—like two 110-story towers that were meant to last as long as the Pyramids—becomes ephemeral, the ephemeral, one's daily life, the passing moment, takes on a more monumental quality. . . .

You often are quoted talking about how long it takes you to complete a page of graphic work. How many drafts of a single page will you do before you're satisfied with it?
I can't even tell you. It's just like a mush on paper until it comes together. Sometimes I'm drawing onto a computer directly, sometimes I'm drawing on paper and redrawing on the computer from there, so I can't really talk about drafts. It's just like having soft clay until it hardens. At least as much of the problem has to do with the decisions of what to represent, how to represent that, and how to reduce it down. The words in the balloons aren't particularly poetic necessarily, but it has the same problem as poetry, which is that one has to do great reduction. If I say things the way I say them in interviews, we'd have forty-page balloons. And if I tried to draw everything, you'd just have a tangled mess of a picture. The stripping down takes much longer than building up.

Just one last question: You've been photographed a lot lately wearing that peace pin upside down. You're wearing it again today. Can you explain why you wear it upside down?
I've been wearing it since September 12, or some version of it. And to me it's a little bit like a nautical convention. When a ship is at sea and it's sinking, it puts its flag upside down to indicate distress for a passing ship. So this is like a plea for peace as it sinks. It's a plea for peace against all odds.

This interview was conducted by Nina Siegel and appeared in the January 2005 issue of *The Progressive*.

IN THE SHADOW OF NO TOWERS

Art Spiegelman, cover of *In the Shadow of No Towers*, 2004

This artwork first appeared on the cover of the September 24, 2001, issue of *The New Yorker* without the box of color, title, or signature.

Ground Zero

James Nachtwey

When the attack first started, I was in my own apartment near the South Street Seaport, directly across lower Manhattan. I heard a sound that was out of the ordinary. I was far enough away so that the sound wasn't alarming, but it was definitely out of the ordinary.

When I saw the towers burning, my first reaction was to take a camera, to load it with film, go up on my roof, where I had a clear view, and photograph the first tower burning. Then I wanted to go directly to the site. I went back down and loaded my gear and went over. It was a ten-minute walk.

When I got there, people were being evacuated from both towers. In the interim, the plane had hit the second tower. Medical treatment centers were being set up on the sidewalks. It wasn't as chaotic as you might think. On the street, the people coming out initially were not seriously wounded. They were frightened, some were hurt in a minor way. I think that the real chaos was happening up inside the towers with the people who were trapped.

When the first tower fell, people ran in panic. They ran from the falling debris, girders that were falling down in an avalanche in the thick smoke and dust. Documenting a crisis situation that's clearly out of control is always very instinctual. There's no road map. No ground rules. It's all improvisations. My instinct initially, in this case, was to photograph the human situation. But once the tower fell, the people really all disappeared. They either ran away or were trapped. So my instinct then was to go to where the tower had fallen. It seemed to me absolutely unbelievable that the World Trade Center could be lying in the street, and I felt compelled to make an image of this. I made my way there through the smoke. The area was virtually deserted. It seemed like a movie set from a science-fiction film. Very apocalyptic—sunlight filtering through the dust and the destroyed wreckage of the buildings lying in the street.

As I was photographing the destruction of the first tower, the second tower fell, and I was standing right under it, literally right under it. Fortunately for me, and unfortunately for people on the west side of the building, it listed to the west. But I was still underneath this avalanche of falling debris—structural steel and aluminum siding, glass, just tons of material falling directly down onto me. I realized that I had a few seconds to find cover or else I'd be killed. I dashed into the lobby of the Millenium Hilton hotel, directly across the street from the North Tower, and I realized instantly that this hotel lobby was going to be taken out, that the debris would come flying through the plate glass and there would be no protection at all. There was no other place to turn, certainly no more time.

I saw an open elevator and dashed inside. I put my back against the wall, and about a second later the lobby was taken out. There was a construction worker who dashed inside there with me just as the debris swept through the lobby. It instantly became pitch black, just as if you were in a closet with the light out and a blindfold on. You could not see anything. It was very difficult to breathe. My nose, my mouth, my eyes were filled with ash. I had a hat on, so I put it over my face and began to breathe through it. And together, this other man and I crawled, groping,

James Nachtwey, *Crushed Car*, 2001 (facing page)

trying to find our way out. I initially thought that the building had fallen on us and that we were in a pocket, because it was so dark. We just continued to crawl, and I began to see small blinking lights, and I realized that these were the turn signals of cars that had been destroyed and the signals were still on. At that point I realized that we were in the street, although it was just as black in the street as it was in the hotel lobby, and that we would be able to find our way out.

My experiences photographing combat and being in life-threatening situations played a very important part in my being able to survive this and continue to work. It was, as I said, all instinct. I was making fast decisions with very little time to spare. And I guess that I made the right decisions, because I'm still here. I was lucky, too. I don't fold up in these situations. I've been in them enough times to somehow have developed the capacity to continue to do my job. On my way out of the smoke and ash, I was actually photographing searchers coming in. Once I got clear, I tried to clear my eyes as best I could and catch my breath. I realized I had to make my way toward what has now become known as Ground Zero. It took a while to make my way there. I spent the day there, photographing the firemen searching for people who had been trapped.

If I had been needed to help someone, I certainly would have done it, as I have many times in the past. I would have put down my camera to lend a hand, as I think anyone would have. The place was filled with firemen and rescue workers and police, and I was not needed to play that role. I realized that very clearly and therefore went about doing my job.

When I'm photographing I don't censor myself, or second-guess myself. I try to be aware of my own inner voice, my own instincts, as much as I can, and I try to follow them.

The level of dust and ash in the air was so intense that it was impossible to protect myself or my camera or my film. I've never had negatives that were so scratched and filled with marks as these. It looks like there are railroad tracks across my negatives. Every time you opened your camera back, there was no time even to dust it off, because more ash would fall in.

I worked all day until night, at which point I felt that it was time to leave. I was exhausted; I felt rather sick from all the smoke and ash that I had inhaled—not only initially, but all day long. The scene was burning and filled with acrid smoke; my lungs had burned all day long. The next day I was quite sick, almost incapacitated. Feeling dizzy, exhausted. Quite out of it.

After the buildings fell, there wasn't really any more danger, as long as you watched your footing. It wasn't as if people were shooting at us or we were being shelled or there were land mines there.

The frontline troops in this particular battle were firemen, and they put themselves in jeopardy. A lot of them lost their lives. They were frontline troops [who] didn't kill anyone; they were there to save people. That made this story very different from the wars I've covered.

The rescue workers were generally too busy to pay us [photographers] much mind. And because we weren't in the way they didn't have to pay us much mind, unless they felt like it, for whatever personal reason they might have had. The police were another matter. They instinctively try to keep us away from anything. I think that it's just the nature of the relationship, unfortunately. But there was so much chaos at the beginning that it was easy to elude the police, and once you were with the rescue workers, they didn't seem to mind at all.

I didn't see the dead. They were underneath, 15 and it wasn't clear how many were under there at that moment. I didn't witness people suffering, because they were invisible. I didn't feel it as strongly as when I witnessed people starving to death or when I've seen innocent people cut down by sniper fire. I haven't completely processed this event.

For me personally, the worst moment was when I was underneath the second tower as it fell and this tidal wave of deadly debris was about to fall on me. When I saw Ground Zero I was in a state of disbelief. It was disturbing to see this massive destruction in my own city, in my own country. I was in Grozny when it was being pulverized by Russian artillery and aircraft. I spent a couple of years in Beirut during various sieges and bombardments. But now it was literally in my own backyard, and I think one thing Americans are learning from this is that now we are a part of the world in a way we never have been before.

The first day that *Time.com* had my essay on their web site, at least 600,000 people had a look at it. To me, as a communicator, that's very gratifying. I hope publishers and editors are paying attention to this. There is power in the still image that doesn't exist in other forms. I think that there even is a necessity for it, because that many people wouldn't be looking at still pictures unless they needed to do that. I know that 600,000 people looking at a web site is small compared to a

typical TV audience, but it is [nonetheless] a sizable number of people, and the fact that people are turning to the Internet instead of television is significant. This is sort of a test case of mass appeal.

To me it's quite obvious that a tremendous crime against humanity—a barbaric act—has been perpetrated on innocent civilians. There's nothing that can justify that act.

Many years ago, I felt that I had seen too much [violence], that I didn't want to see any more tragedies in this world. But unfortunately history continues to produce tragedies, and it is very important that they be documented with compassion and in a compelling way. I feel a responsibility to continue. But believe me when I say that I would much rather these things never happen [so that] I could either photograph something entirely different or not be a photographer at all. But that's not the way the world is. ○

JAMES NACHTWEY

"The primary function of my photographs," explained James Nachtwey recently, "is to be in mass-circulation publications—during the time that the events are happening. I want them to become part of people's daily dialogue and create public awareness, public opinion, that can help bring pressure for change. That's the first and most important use of my work. A secondary use is to become an archive, entered into our collective memory, so that these events are never forgotten."

Born in Syracuse, New York, in 1948, Nachtwey has photographed violence around the world—most recently in Kosovo, Chechnya, Afghanistan, and Iraq. He has published a number of collections of photographs. He has received countless honors, including five Robert Capa Gold Medals and three International Center of Photography Infinity Awards. *War Photographer,* a documentary on his life, was nominated for an Oscar in 2001.

Despite an impressive list of photojournalism accolades, Nachtwey would like his viewers to focus on the subjects of his images rather than the photographer behind them. "I don't want people to be concerned about me. I want them to be concerned about the people in the pictures. . . . I want the first impact, and by far the most powerful impact, to be about an emotional, intellectual, and moral reaction to what is happening to these people. I want my presence to be transparent." This eyewitness photograph and essay appeared in *American Photo* 13.1.

SEEING

1. James Nachtwey is a veteran photographer who has documented wars in several parts of the world. What similarities and differences does he establish between his wartime experiences and his photographing the collapse of the World Trade Center? In paragraph 8 Nachtwey explains that "the place was filled with firemen and rescue workers and police, and I was not needed to play that role. I realized that very clearly and therefore went about doing my job." What do you think the role of a photographer should be during a time of war or in a crisis situation?

2. In paragraph 17 Nachtwey tells us that "there is power in the still image that doesn't exist in other forms. I think that there even is a necessity for it, because that many people wouldn't be looking at still pictures unless they needed to do that." Compare the power of Nachtwey's prose narrative of the events of September 11 to *Crushed Car,* one of the photographs he took that day (p. 304). This image is part of a photo essay (you can see that essay at www.time.com/photoessays/shattered). Which do you find more articulate—Nachtwey's prose or his visual essay? Why? To what extent is the power of each a reflection of its medium?

WRITING

1. The code of ethics of the National Press Photographers Association notes that "many publications and stations have conduct codes or ethics codes requiring photojournalists to report truthfully, honestly and objectively. Their codes might include statements such as 'photojournalists should at all times maintain the highest standards of ethical conduct in serving the public interest' or 'a member shall present himself, his work, his services, and his premises in such a manner as will uphold and dignify his professional status and the reputation of the station.'" Using samples from Nachtwey's photojournalism, write an expository essay in which you apply these standards to combat photography.

2. In paragraph 17, Nachtwey announces that he found it "very gratifying" to know that there were 600,000 visits to his photo essay on the *Time* web site. "The fact that people are turning to the Internet instead of television is significant. This is sort of a test case of mass appeal." Write an argumentative essay in which you support—or challenge—the assertion that the events of September 11 caused a shift in the ways we receive information and the sources of that information.

Taking Pictures

When George Eastman introduced the simple and inexpensive box camera in 1888, photography came within the reach of most Americans. Anyone could buy the preloaded Kodak #1, take one hundred exposures, and then send the camera back to Kodak to develop the film. "You press the button, we do the rest" was the slogan that enticed generations of Americans to take snapshots.

    The writers and visual artists represented on the following pages explore the ways in which pictures and picture taking have become part of American culture. Both Mike Bragg and Babbette Hines rescue old photographs: he in his *Forgotten* series, she in her collection of photo-booth images. Susan Sontag speculates about the significance of photographs in an excerpt from her now-classic essay "On Photography." Duane Hanson's *Tourists* offers an ironic view of middle-class Americans in search of a "Kodak moment." The ad "Keep the Story with a Kodak" provides a glimpse into the language and imagery that led Americans to point and shoot, while a recent Mercedes ad speaks to the relationship between the classic snapshot and material possessions. Ethan Canin builds a short story on an old photograph in "Vivian, Fort Barnwell," and N. Scott Momaday uses a photograph as an occasion for a short essay in "The Photograph." And Yutaka Sone makes and keeps the story by staging and videotaping a series of birthday parties.

Babbittry,[1] was replaced by the mystery of the group-minded Japanese tourist, newly released from his island prison by the miracle of overvalued yen, who is generally armed with two cameras, one on each hip.

Photography has become one of the principal devices for experiencing something, for giving an appearance of participation. One full-page ad shows a small group of people standing pressed together, peering out of the photograph, all but one looking stunned, excited, upset. The one who wears a different expression holds a camera to his eye; he seems self-possessed, is almost smiling. While the others are passive, clearly alarmed spectators, having a camera has transformed one person into something active, a voyeur: Only he has mastered the situation. What do these people see? We don't know. And it doesn't matter. It is an Event: something worth seeing—and therefore worth photographing. The ad copy, white letters across the dark lower third of the photograph like news coming over a teletype machine, consists of just six words: ". . . Prague . . . Woodstock . . . Vietnam . . . Sapporo . . . Londonderry . . . LEICA." Crushed hopes, youth antics, colonial wars, and winter sports are alike—are equalized by the camera. Taking photographs has set up a chronic voyeuristic relation to the world which levels the meaning of all events.

A photograph is not just the result of an encounter between an event and a photographer; picture-taking is an event in itself, and one with ever more peremptory rights—to interfere with, to invade, or to ignore whatever is going on. Our very sense of situation is now articulated by the camera's interventions. The omnipresence of cameras persuasively suggests that time consists of interesting events, events worth photographing. This, in turn, makes it easy to feel that any event, once under way, and whatever its moral character, should be allowed to complete itself—so that something else can be brought into the world, the photograph. After the event has ended, the picture will still exist, conferring on the event a kind of immortality (and importance) it would never otherwise have enjoyed. While real people are out there killing themselves or other real people, the photographer stays behind his or her camera, creating a tiny element of another world: the image-world that bids to outlast us all.

Photographing is essentially an act of nonintervention. Part of the horror of such memorable coups of contemporary photojournalism as the pictures of a Vietnamese bonze[2] reaching for the gasoline can, of a Bengali guerrilla in the act of bayoneting a trussed-up collaborator, comes from the awareness of how plausible it has become, in situations where the photographer has the choice between a photograph and a life, to choose the photograph. The person who intervenes cannot record; the person who is recording cannot intervene. Dziga Vertov's great film, *Man with a Movie Camera* (1929), gives the ideal image of the photographer as someone in perpetual movement, someone moving through a panorama of disparate events with such agility and speed that any intervention is out of the question. Hitchcock's *Rear Window* (1954) gives the complementary image: The photographer played by James Stewart has an intensified relation to one event, through his camera, precisely because he has a broken leg and is confined to a wheelchair; being temporarily immobilized prevents him from acting on what he sees, and makes it even more important to take pictures. Even if incompatible with intervention in a physical sense, using a camera is still a form of participation. Although the camera is an observation station, the act of photographing is more than passive observing. Like sexual voyeurism, it is a way of at least tacitly, often explicitly, encouraging whatever is going on to keep on happening. To take a picture is to have an interest in things as they are, in the status quo remaining unchanged (at least for as long as it takes to get a "good" picture), to be in complicity with whatever makes a subject interesting, worth photographing—including, when that is the interest, another person's pain or misfortune. ○

---

1. *Babbittry* is a crassness, a grasping for things material. The term came into use following publication of Sinclair Lewis's novel *Babbitt* (1922).

2. A *bonze* is a Buddhist monk.

PICTURE PERFECT
Babbette Hines

THERE IS SOMETHING BOTH STRANGELY FAMILIAR AND absolutely fresh in photo-booth pictures. You look at them and know that the soldiers staring into the camera with a cocky eye are off to a war fought 60 years ago, and you know that the women with their hair in finger waves, carefully coiffed, are more than likely gone. You know, and yet it doesn't matter. It is as easy to imagine their stories as it is to recall your own. If you look at them long enough, resemblances to people you know start to emerge. And if you look even longer, you begin to see yourself reflected in the faces staring back at you. . . .

It doesn't matter whether you are in a train station, on a busy street, or in the middle of an amusement park. Nor does it matter whether you have deliberately sought out the booth to record a specific moment or happened upon one unexpectedly. What matters is that you are both photographer and subject. Alone in the booth, you forgo the behaviors and attitudes expected when a camera is forced upon you. You cannot be coaxed into position; you cannot be commanded to smile. You can be sexy or goofy or tough. You can even pretend to be happier than you really are, and you get eight (or at least four) chances to do it. And if, when the picture emerges after the interminable wait, you are not pleased with the result, if it doesn't tell the story you want, there is no proof that it ever existed. . . .

In the photo-booth picture, unlike any other portrait or photograph, truth and fiction easily commingle. In a photo booth we choose the moment and the way in which we represent ourselves. We choose our truth. ○

Babbette Hines, from *Photobooth*, 2002

Looking Closer

THE PHOTOGRAPH

N. Scott Momaday

WHEN I FIRST LIVED ON THE NAVAJO RESERVATION there were no cars, except those that were government property or that belonged to the Indian Service employees. The Navajos went about in wagons and on horseback, everywhere. My father worked for the Roads Department on the Navajo reservation. I lived for those trips, for he would often take me with him. I got a sense of the country then; it was wild and unending. In rainy weather the roads became channels of running water, and sometimes a flash flood would simply wash them away altogether, and we would have to dig ourselves out of the mud or wait for the ground to freeze. And then the wagons would pass us by or, if we were lucky, some old man would unhitch his team and pull us out to firm ground.

"*Ya'at'eeh,*" the old man would say.

"*Ya'at'eeh, shicheii,*" my father would reply.

"*Hagosha' diniya?*"

"Nowhere," my father would say, "we are going 5 nowhere."

"*Aoo', atiin ayoo hastlish.*" Yes, the road is very muddy, the old man would answer, laughing, and we knew then that we were at his mercy, held fast in the groove of his humor and goodwill. My father learned to speak the Navajo language in connection with his work, and I learned something of it, too—a little. Later, after I had been away from the Navajo country for many years, I returned and studied the language formally in order to understand not only the meaning but the formation of it as well. It is a beautiful language, intricate and full of subtlety, and very difficult to learn.

There were sheep camps in the remote canyons and mountains. When we ventured out into those areas, we saw a lot of people, but they were always off by themselves, it seemed, living a life of their own, each one having an individual existence in that huge landscape. Later, when I was learning to fly an airplane, I saw the land as a hawk or an eagle sees it, immense and wild and all of a piece. Once I flew with a friend to the trading post at Low Mountain where we landed on a dirt road in the very middle of the reservation. It was like going backward in time, for Low Mountain has remained virtually undiscovered in the course of years, and there you can still see the old people coming in their wagons to get water and to trade. It is like Kayenta was in my earliest time on the reservation, so remote as to be almost legendary in the mind.

My father had a little box camera with which he liked to take photographs now and then. One day an old Navajo crone came to our house and asked to have her picture taken. She was a gnarled old woman with gray hair and fine pronounced features. She made a wonderful subject, and I have always thought very well of the photograph that my father made of her. Every day thereafter she would come to the house and ask to see the print, and every day my father had to tell her that it had not yet come back in the mail. Having photographs processed was a slow business then in that part of the world. At last the day came when the print arrived. And when the old woman came, my father presented it to her proudly. But when she took a look at it, she was deeply disturbed, and she would have nothing to do with it. She set up such a jabber, indeed, that no one could understand her, and she left in a great huff. I have often wondered that she objected so to her likeness, for it was a true likeness, as far as I could tell. It is quite possible, I think, that she had never seen her likeness before, not even in a mirror, and that the photograph was a far cry from what she imagined herself to be. Or perhaps she saw, in a way that we could not, that the photograph misrepresented her in some crucial respect, that in its dim, mechanical eye it had failed to see into her real being. ○

(top) Mike Bragg, *Beach Flower*, 2004; (bottom) Mike Bragg, *Father and Son*, 2004

Looking Closer

Keep the story with a KODAK

Today it's a picture of Grandmother reading to the children. Tomorrow it may be Bobbie playing traffic policeman or Aunt Edna at the wheel of her new car or Brother Bill back from college for the week-end or— There's always another story waiting for your Kodak.

Free at your dealer's or from us—"At Home with the Kodak," a well illustrated little book that will help in picture-making at your house.

Autographic Kodaks *$6.50 up*

Eastman Kodak Company, Rochester, N. Y., *The Kodak City*

Vivian, Fort Barnwell

Ethan Canin

I TELL MY WIFE, I'LL ALWAYS REMEMBER THIS photograph of my mother. She's out in back, hanging the blankets to dry on our backyard lines after one of our picnics, and she looks so young, the way I remember her before we moved to California. I was ten, I think. We used to have picnics out there under the water tower when my father got home from work, out in back on the grass on a set of big gray movers' blankets. My father and the man next door had built a pool from a truck tire set in concrete, and they filled it with water for my brother and me to splash in. I remember the day this picture was taken, because my mother had to hang the blankets to dry after we'd soaked them from the pool. my father was mad but she wasn't. She was never mad at us. I haven't seen that picture in years, I tell my wife. But I remember it.

And then one day, for no reason I can fathom, my wife is looking through the old cardboard-sided valise where my mother had kept her pictures, and she says, Here? Is this the one you're always talking about? And I say, Yes, I can't believe you found it. And she says, Those aren't movers' blankets, those are some kind of leaves up in the foreground.

They look like something tropical, maybe rubber leaves. She's not hanging laundry at all. I say, Wait a minute—let me see. And I laugh and say, You're right. How can that be? My whole life I've remembered that picture of her hanging those blankets after we'd soaked them. I can even remember the picnic. She says, That's funny, isn't it? I say, My mother was so beautiful.

Our own children are out back in our own yard. It's too cool here for a pool, but I've built them a swing set from redwood, and I take a look out the window at them climbing it the way I've told them not to.

And then a few minutes later my wife says, Look at this, and she hands me the picture again, turned over. On the back it says, Vivian, Fort Barnwell, 1931. That's not your mother at all, she says. That's your grandmother. I say, Let me see that. I say, My God, you're right. How could that have happened? ○

SUSAN SONTAG

From the 1960s through the 1980s, Susan Sontag was one of America's foremost intellectuals, social commentators, and provocateurs. Her essays brilliantly explained the country and its culture, especially the avant-garde. In "Notes on Camp" (1964) she accurately described the absurdity of attributes of taste; in "Against Interpretation" (1966) she limned Anglo-American fiction; in "Illness as Metaphor" (1978), which grew out of her own battle with breast cancer, she cast a fresh eye on disease, a subject that she revisited in "AIDS and Its Metaphors" (1988). Her novel *The Volcano Lover* (1992) was a best seller: "No book I ever wrote came near to selling as many copies or reaching as many readers," she said.

Sontag was born in New York City in 1933 and was raised in Tucson, Arizona, and Los Angeles. She died of leukemia in 2004.

The essay here is an excerpt from "On Photography" (2001), winner of the National Book Critics Circle Award for Criticism at the time of its initial publication in 1977. Her most recent book, *Regarding the Pain of Others* (2003), is about the photography of war.

DUANE HANSON

Sculptor Duane Hanson (1925–1996) made his mark on the art world in the 1970s with true-to-life, cast-fiberglass people. The unattractive, the elderly, the ordinary— people we overlook every day— are transformed by Hanson's sculpture into art. Dressed in real clothing and equipped with accessories, Hanson's models are shocking in their "aliveness." Notice, for example, the wrinkled skin on the man's elbow. The sculpture shown here was Hanson's first portrayal of the American tourist: he created a second in 1988.

Born in Minnesota, Hanson spent much of his life in Miami. The Whitney Museum of American Art, in New York, held a retrospective of his work in 1999, and his works continue to be exhibited today.

Visit seeingandwriting.com for an interactive exercise on this piece.

YUTAKA SONE

Yutaka Sone is a visual artist who works in a wide range of mediums. He created the whimsical videotape *Birthday Party* in 1997 for the *Skulptur Projekte* in Münster, Germany. Sone invited strangers to celebrate his birthday with him in one hundred different locations throughout the city. He videotaped the parties and then edited the footage and installed his "private" life event in a public arena, a train station. In a 1998 interview he explained how the videotape orchestrates the event: "That video is not a record of something. . . . It is edited so that the place, time, and emotion seem to delicately change. . . . I wanted to create a time that doesn't exist anywhere. Using material that everyone knows."

Sone was born in 1965 in Japan and earned a BFA and an MA in architecture there. Today he lives in Los Angeles. His work has been included in exhibitions at museums and galleries around the world.

BABBETTE HINES

"I love these tiny moments people record in their lives," Babbette Hines (b. 1968) says in a 2003 *Boston Globe* interview. "I was always drawn to these times and places that weren't mine." Hines has been collecting vintage photographs from flea markets, secondhand stores, and friends for years. She currently runs a gallery in Los Angeles called Found: Photo (www.thefoundphoto.com). Her book *Photobooth* (2002) includes more than seven hundred images of sailors, lovers, and others, spanning more than seventy-five years. Known as "self-photography," this form of vernacular photography first appeared in the late 1920s, in a time before Polaroids, when automated photo booths were placed in amusement parks and five-and-dime stores across America. Hines's collection was exhibited in 2003 at the Griffin Museum of Photography in Winchester, Massachusetts. In *Love Letters, Lost* (2005), Hines pairs salvaged love letters with photographs of couples in love.

MERCEDES-BENZ

The Mercedes-Benz company traces its genealogy back to Gottlieb Daimler and Karl Benz, who in the 1880s independently invented the first "motorized tricycle" and "horseless carriage." Both men formed companies and began to manufacture cars. In 1926, Daimler-Motoren-Gesellschaft and Benz & Cie merged, forming Daimler-Benz. The new company combined both trade names and logos, creating the Mercedes-Benz brand and the three-pointed star on its hood. In 1998, Daimler-Benz joined with Chrysler Corporation to become DaimlerChrysler.

The company has carefully crafted an image of superior engineering, quality, and service. The ad pictured here marked the launch of a campaign in the spring of 2004 that emphasized the unique loyalty between the Mercedes-Benz brand and its drivers. "What we want to do is to make the brand come alive for [people] in a way they can relate to," says Michelle Cervantez, vice president of marketing. "And we believe this campaign does that in terms of capturing what . . . is quintessentially Mercedes-Benz, . . . expressed by the passion and pride of our owners themselves."

N. SCOTT MOMADAY

N. Scott Momaday was born on a Kiowa reservation in Oklahoma in 1934. His father was Kiowa; his mother was Cherokee, French, and English. He has spent his life and his career reconstructing the story of the Kiowa tribe—its myths, its history, and, most important, its oral tradition. His first novel, *House Made of Dawn* (1968), focuses on the clash between the Native American world and the white world; it won a Pulitzer Prize. Momaday has since written essays, poetry, autobiography, and fiction, almost all of which draws on and explores the story of his people and their land. In 2004 he was named UNESCO Artist for Peace.

MIKE BRAGG

In documenting everyday scenes and objects, visual artist Mike Bragg hopes to "remind us of the importance underlying these items" and to "explore the coexisting themes of isolation and change." The images here are from Bragg's *Forgotten* series (2004), in which he "isolates" old, discarded photographs "against various surfaces that reflect the neglect and passage of time." In his statement about the series, Bragg writes: "Memories define who we are, and once forgotten, our identity and its defining moments are lost." His goal was to breathe "new life into these lost memories." *Forgotten* was selected by *Photo District News* for inclusion in its *PDN Photo Annual 2004,* a selection of the year's "most outstanding images."

Bragg lives in the Bay Area. His commercial ventures range from album covers to advertisements for Sony and Gap. One recent assignment took him to Iraq, where he documented the humanitarian efforts of medical workers.

EASTMAN KODAK

George Eastman's first "photographic outfit," which he purchased in 1875, weighed about one hundred pounds and required the use of wet glass plates and a crate of chemicals. In 1878 Eastman founded the Kodak Company with the intention of "making photography as convenient as a pencil." Roll film, handheld cameras, home movie cameras, sound-sensitive movie film, color-slide film, automated film developing, photo billboards, and digital cameras are just a few of the company's innovations. One of the largest companies in the United States, Kodak continues to pioneer new "image technologies" that affect the visual content of our daily lives.

ETHAN CANIN

Ethan Canin was born in 1960 in Ann Arbor, Michigan, and grew up in California. He studied engineering at Stanford University and then earned an MFA from the University of Iowa in 1984. Not expecting that he could earn a living from writing, he got a medical degree at Harvard in 1991. Canin's career plans changed when his first collection of short stories, *Emperor of the Air* (1988) became a critically acclaimed best seller. Since then he has published another collection of short stories and three novels, most recently *Carry Me Across the Water* (2001).

The very short story "Vivian, Fort Barnwell" appeared in the Fall 1998 issue of *Doubletake* magazine, accompanied by this editorial note: "A photograph may be seen as a window to a story, but how that story takes shape depends upon the viewer. We were curious as to how the story of this photograph would unfold in the hands of a fiction writer. Here, then, is one moment from an imagined life."

SEEING

1. Susan Sontag observes that "photography is not practiced by most people as an art. It is mainly a social rite, a defense against anxiety, and a tool of power" (para. 1). Given your own experience taking pictures, would you agree or disagree with her assertion? Now examine each of the visual images and prose selections in this section. To what extent do you think each writer and visual artist represented here would agree or disagree with Sontag? Are photographs like the ones shown by Mike Bragg merely a "defense against anxiety"? If so, anxiety about what? Does Ethan Canin's short story treat the photograph as a "tool of power"? If so, what kind of power?

2. Sontag declares that "a photograph is not just the result of an encounter between an event and a photographer; picture-taking is an event in itself, and one with ever more peremptory rights—to interfere with, to invade, or to ignore whatever is going on. Our very sense of situation is now articulated by the camera's interventions" (para. 8). Sontag seems to be saying that the camera or the act of taking pictures is more important than either the photographer or the event. Do you agree with her? Use any of the selections in this section to support your thinking.

WRITING

1. Sontag writes: "For at least a century, the wedding photograph has been as much a part of the ceremony as the prescribed verbal formulas" (para. 2). Write a comparative essay in which you compare the differences between (1) the function—and the visibility—of photography in your parents' wedding and (2) its presence and role in a wedding you attended in the past year or two. Draw inferences about the extent to which the role of photography in the more recent wedding has become analogous to what Sontag calls "prescribed verbal formulas."

2. Sontag observes that "a family's photograph album is generally about the extended family—and, often, is all that remains of it" (para. 3). How important are photographs to your sense of family? Write an essay in which you describe your extended family—grandparents, aunts, uncles, cousins—using family photographs to frame your argument.

RESPONDING VISUALLY

"No one ever poses with their toaster," or so Mercedes-Benz claims in its advertising. About what possession—or aspects of your life—are you passionate enough to pose with? Photograph, illustrate, or create a digital self-portrait in which you pose with something you are passionate about.

4 PROJECTING GENDER

4 Projecting Gender

4 projecting gender

4 Projecting Gender

From a a very early age we are taught to identify with one of the two most universally recognized icons: ♀ and ♀. Created in the early 1970s, these simple symbols for male and female have become so pervasive we take them for granted. Yet a more careful look raises important questions: How exactly do these icons communicate gender difference? What cultural assumptions are embedded in them? Why are differences in clothing such a clear indicator of gender identity and sex? How do different cultures train children to identify with—and project—gender from an early age? (See the introduction to Chapter 6, p. 499, for cross-cultural examples of these icons.) How do these representations of difference relate to larger issues of the equality of the sexes and the social construction of gender?

One hundred years ago the terms *sex* and *gender* were used interchangeably, but they mean different things today. *Sex* refers to biological structure and function, to being born with male or female genitalia. The chromosomes we inherit determine our sex. *Gender* refers to a cultural category, to the behavioral or psychological standards a society sets for masculine or feminine behavior. By definition, then, gender expectations can change with place

Robert Mapplethorpe, *Self-Portrait*, 1980

Robert Mapplethorpe, *Self-Portrait*, 1980

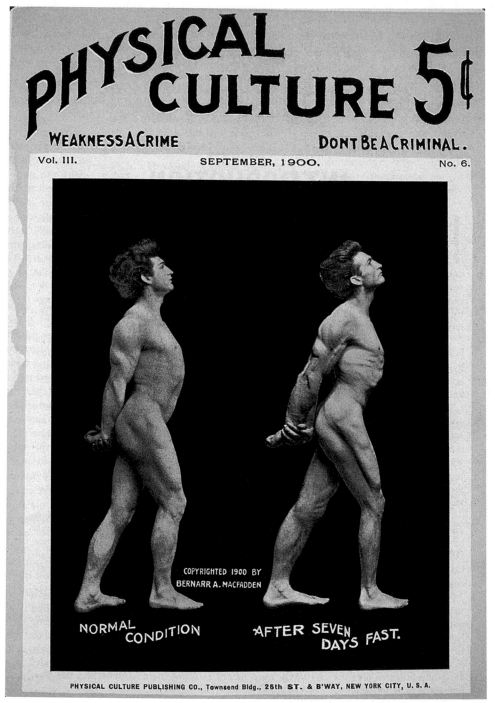

1900 (above)

1944 (right)

I Can Make YOU a New Man, Too, in Only 15 Minutes a Day!

If YOU, like Joe, have a body that others can "push around"— if you're ashamed to strip for sports or a swim—then give me just 15 minutes a day! I'll PROVE you can have a body you'll be proud of, packed with red-blooded vitality! "Dynamic Tension." That's the secret! That's how I changed myself from a spindle-shanked, scrawny weakling to winner of the title, "World's Most Perfectly Developed Man."

"Dynamic Tension" Does It!

Using "Dynamic Tension" only 15 minutes a day, in the privacy of your own room, you quickly begin to put on muscle, increase your chest measurements, broaden your back, fill out your arms and legs. Before you know it, this easy, NATURAL method will make you a finer specimen of REAL MAN-HOOD than you ever dreamed you could be! You'll be a New Man!

FREE Info Kit

Thousands of fellows have used my marvelous system. Read what my **Amazing Info Kit talks about!**

Send NOW for this **Info Kit** It tells all about "Dynamic Tension," shows you actual photos of men I've turned from puny weaklings into Atlas Champions. It tells how I can do the same for YOU. Don't put it off! Address me personally: Charles Atlas.

Charles Atlas

—actual photo of the man who holds the title, "The World's Most Perfectly Developed Man."

How Relax-A-cizor Reduces the Size of your Waistline...

Effortless exercise does it while you REST!

What happened to your waist-line? Have those belly muscles "stretched-out-of-shape"? And—you KNOW you need exercise but don't want to take the time.

NOW—there's a way! Now you can reduce the size of your abdomen and waistline . . . firm-up and tone those muscles with real exercise . . . while you REST at home! Or, do it at the office while you do your desk-work. About ½ hour a day is all the time it takes! Relax-A-cizor gives exercise WHILE YOU TAKE IT EASY!

▪ NOT A VIBRATOR ▪ NOT MAS-SAGE ▪ NOT A BICYCLE ▪ NOT A COUCH ▪ No weight loss! Relax-A-cizor does not cause or depend upon weight loss. Instead, it reduces SIZE by exercising and firming selected areas of muscles — and does this with-out effort. Doesn't make you tired; you REST while you use it. Read a book. Watch TV. Take it easy — that's the Relax-A-cizor way.

▪ This is Relax-A-cizor being used with the abdominal belt. Slip it on and, in minutes, you're ready for your exercises while you REST!

Easy to use! Compact. All you do is put a pair of Relax-A-cizor pads on the body area you want reduced in size . . . twist a dial and, presto, you're exercis-ing — *really* exercising — those muscles. Those abdominal muscles move 40 times a minute! 1200 times in a ½ hour! This concentrated, active exer-cise gives those waistline and abdomi-nal muscles that "hold-you-in" a real workout!

Why Relax-A-cizor works. Many men lack good muscle tone because they don't get enough exercise. Relax-A-cizor exercises — but, without effort — such body areas as the waistline and ab-domen 40 times a minute. This exercise firms and tones these muscles. Regular use causes these areas to reduce in size measurably to the extent these muscles lack tone because of insufficient exer-cise. And the less the muscle tone, the greater the degree of size reduction.

FOR WOMEN, TOO! Relax-A-cizor is the luxuriously effortless way to reduce the size of hips, waistline, abdomen and thighs. Relax-A-cizor beauty exercises tone and firm these muscles without a whit of work. Send coupon for free il-lustrated information.

OTHER USES, TOO! You'll use your Relax-A-cizor for restful, invigorating exercise of tense, tired muscles of shoulders, back, neck, arms and legs. Feels great!

FREE! Find out all about it. Send coupon TODAY and we'll mail your complete information and the free men's booklet "HOW TO REDUCE THE SIZE OF YOUR WAISTLINE." No cost. No obligation.

PRINCIPAL OFFICES: NEW YORK, NEW YORK, 575 Madison Ave., MU 8-4690/CHICAGO, ILL., 29 East Madison St., ST 2-5680/LOS AN-GELES, CAL., 980 N. La Cienega Bl., OL 5-8600. Available in Canada, Mexico City, Hong Kong, Manila, Milan *(foreign franchises available)*

RelaxAcizor®

Free!

Relax-A-cizor, Dept. 20-603
980 No. La Cienega Blvd.
Los Angeles, California 90054
Please mail me free information about how to reduce the size of waistline and abdomen. No cost. No obligation.
☐ MR. ☐ MRS. ☐ MISS

NAME _____
ADDRESS _____
CITY _____ STATE _____
ZIP _____ PHONE _____
☐ I am under 18. ☐ I am over 18.   20-603 707

© Relax-A-cizor 1967

ESQUIRE, JULY

1967

Let us ask you something.
And tell us the truth.

Does it
matter to you
that if you skip a day
of running,
only
one person
in the world
will ever know?
Or
is that
one person
too many?

One less excuse to skip a day: the GEL-140.™
Its substantial GEL® Cushioning System
can handle even the most mile-hungry feet.

asics

1999

375

NANCY BURSON

Well known for her work with computer-composite photographs, Nancy Burson's career combines technology and art. Born in St. Louis in 1948, Burson was trained as a painter. Soon after moving to New York City in 1968, she became interested in using computer technology to manipulate the human face. A project proposal "to simulate the aging process" led to a collaboration with MIT's Media Lab and the development of computer programs that are now used to find missing children, to identify criminal suspects, and to plan reconstructive surgery. Burson holds a patent on morphing software that applies typical patterns of aging to digitized images.

From a focus on manipulating images, Burson shifted to capturing realistic images of children and adults with startling craniofacial deformities. These were cataloged in her book *Faces* (1993).

The photographs here are untitled images from the *He/She* series. Burson explains that the androgynous images in this series are "more about the commonality of people rather than about their differences or separateness. They're meant to challenge the individual's notions of self-perception and self-acceptance by allowing viewers to see beyond superficial sexual differences to our common humanity."

Burson recently published her first text-based book, *Focus: How Your Energy Can Change the World* (2004).

SEEING

1. Carefully examine each of Nancy Burson's photographs. In your judgment, which are portraits of a man? of a woman? What evidence can you point to in each image to verify your reading? Do you find it easier to determine the subject's gender in some of these photographs than in others? Why? How do your choices compare with those of your classmates?

2. In these photographs, Burson set out to mask her subjects' gender. To that end, what artistic choices did she make? What aspects of each subject has she chosen to highlight? What does she conceal? What might these choices reveal about the ways in which we subconsciously differentiate between men and women?

WRITING

1. The *He/She* series attempts, in Burson's words, "to see beyond superficial sexual differences." Yet the images tease viewers with an implicit question: He or she? In an essay, explain why you think many people find it so important to be able to identify an individual's sex. What cultural assumptions does androgyny challenge?

2. Write an essay in which you compare and contrast Burson's portraits with Mapplethorpe's two self-portraits (pages 330–31). Setting aside the differences between a portrait and a self-portrait, what statements about gender is each of these artists making? How would you compare their artistic techniques and styles? How do these images illustrate the social construction of masculinity and femininity?

TALKING PICTURES

Critics argue that the recent success of television shows like *Will & Grace,* and *Queer Eye for the Straight Guy* signals the mainstreaming of gay culture. There is debate, however, as to whether portrayals of gay culture offer more than stereotypes.

"The original *Queer Eye* concept makes me wonder why some trafficking in stereotypes is acceptable in mainstream media and others are not," writes *Cleveland.com* columnist Michael Heaton. "If there was a show in which five black people tried to imbue a white person with 'soul,' would there be cries of racism?"

The stars of *Queer Eye for the Straight Guy* argue that they have no intention of furthering stereotypes. Fashion consultant Carson Kressley answers the charge by saying, "And one thing: Hi, it's a reality show. We're not cartoonish and we're not pretending to be supergay or superstraight or whatever. We're just being ourselves, and I'm not going to make any excuses for who I am, and I don't think any of these guys are either."

What is your take on the portrayal of gays and lesbians in contemporary TV and movies? Choose a popular show or film with an openly gay character or gay theme. To what extent do the casting, characters, and narrative reinforce stereotypes of gays or lesbians? challenge those stereotypes? Write an essay in which you argue one position or the other, citing specific examples from the show or film.

CHRIS BALLARD

Former college basketball player Chris Ballard is a staff writer for *Sports Illustrated* who covers the NBA and writes *SI.com*'s Daily Blog every Monday. He is also the author of *Hoops Nation: A Guide to America's Best Pickup Basketball,* one of *Booklist*'s "Top 10 Sports Books" in 1998. The book is the product of a seven-month trip to forty-eight states, during which Ballard and three other former college players collected information about regional styles of play, jargon, and etiquette. In the end, Ballard named New York's West Fourth Street court the best pickup court in the country.

"How to Write a Catchy Beer Ad," which first appeared in the *New York Times Magazine* in January 2003, illustrates Ballard's dynamic and detailed style. No matter the subject, from competitive eating ("That Stomach Is Going to Make You Money Someday") to extreme sports ("Cliff Hanger"), he combines vivid vignettes with sheafs of facts. Interviewed for a *Business Week* article about the growing interest in playing contact sports to make business connections, Ballard protested that the court isn't the place to curry favor: "People will respect you more if you act as an equal. They'll want to hire someone who gives 100% effort, not who says, 'Nice shot, sir.'"

SEEING

1. The success of the beer commercial Chris Ballard is writing about relied in part on its accessibility, on the illusion that the viewer is a participant. How did the ad's designers construct that accessibility? Do you think viewers were aware of the advertising agency's intent? Can you think of other ways the ad might have created the same effect?

2. According to Ballard, the final commercial was compiled from more than thirty vocal and instrumental takes. How might knowing how much editing went into making the ad both "seamless" and "spontaneous" change the way you think about the ad? Discuss how.

WRITING

1. During the creation of the "Love Songs" spot, much attention was given to what "the coveted 21- to 27-year-old male demographic" (para. 4) would both enjoy and associate with beer. Write a brief parody of the commercial, with one or two verses about things "the Holy Grail of beer advertising" would neither enjoy nor associate with beer. What do your lyrics suggest about your vision of this particular demographic?

2. How do you respond to the music producer's claim that the "Long Songs" tune is rock and roll, not a jingle (para. 1)? What distinguishes a jingle from rock and roll or any music written for a purpose other than advertising? How is all music alike? Draft an essay comparing advertising music with other forms of music.

Gender Training

We Americans—inspired by infomercials, makeovers on talk shows, ads for the hottest line of clothing—are continually reinventing ourselves. Each of us creates and expresses identities through our physical appearance and by associating ourselves with particular objects, roles, and fashion images and statements. How do you create an identity for yourself? How do you choose to present your personal style?

A crucial component of personal style is gender. Art Spiegelman, a puzzled parent in *Nature vs. Nurture,* suggests that genetics plays the larger role in defining gender. Marianne Ghantous would argue that environment does: In her *Kids Couture* experiment, younger children drew both men and women in colorful clothes and carrying purses. Katha Pollitt acknowledges that "most boys don't play with dolls," but she attributes that to the pervasive influence of the fashion industry and to other cultural pressures. The impact of those pressures on adolescents and older teens is clearly visible in Lauren Greenfield's *Ashleigh, 13* and in Brian Finke's *Untitled (Cheerleading #81)* and *Untitled (Football #75).* And the army's **"There's Something about a Soldier"** ad—by both reinforcing and subverting traditional male and female roles—tells us those pressures continue to be felt into adulthood.

Nature vs. Nurture

Art Spiegelman, *Nature vs. Nurture*, 1997 (left); Marianne Ghantous, *Kids Couture*, 2002 (right)

Looking Closer

Lauren Greenfield, *Ashleigh, 13, with Her Friend and Parents, Santa Monica,* 1997

Looking Closer

Brian Finke, *Untitled (Cheerreading #81)*, 2003 (left); Brian Finke, *Untitled (Football #75)*, 2003 (right)

Looking Closer

ART SPIEGELMAN

 Art Spiegelman was born in Sweden in 1948 and raised in New York City. He is the only person to win the Pulitzer Prize for fiction for a comic book—*Maus* (1991), a fable about the Holocaust. Spiegelman sees nothing odd about addressing weighty subjects in what traditionally has been considered a light medium. Comics are his form of communication, the only way, he says, that he knows how to tell a story. They are also his medium for "trying to understand myself and trying to understand other things." Through his work he has expanded the scope of comic drawings, almost single-handedly showing that cartoon images can hold the interest of serious readers. His latest book, *In the Shadow of No Towers* (2004), depicts his personal experience of and reaction to September 11.

MARIANNE GHANTOUS

 In an effort to go back to the drawing board, stylist Marianne Ghantous put seventeen young children to work. First she had each child draw his or her own characters. Then Ghantous offered them scaled-down cutouts of clothing and accessories from the spring/summer 2002 collections of Dior, Prada, Miu Miu, and other designers and asked the youngsters to dress their characters. The choices the children made and the outfits they put together sometimes crossed conventional gender distinctions: Male characters wore dresses and carried purses as happily as their female counterparts. The 5-year-olds blurred gender in their creations more readily than the 6- and 7-year-olds. Alison Whelan introduced the project in *Tank* magazine (2002), where the images first appeared: "For the most part, it was just another game where imagination and characters with names and lifestyles get dressed and go out to a party to play with friends."

LAUREN GREENFIELD

 After graduating from Harvard University in 1987, Lauren Greenfield launched her career with the photographic documentary *Fast Forward: Growing Up in the Shadow of Hollywood* (1997). Her disquieting images capture a wide range of young people, from Beverly Hills debutantes to Los Angeles gang members, all buying into what writer and cultural critic Richard Rodriguez calls "a dream of adolescence." From her own experience growing up in Los Angeles, Greenfield understands how that dream can become a nightmare for those who live it. She offers unremitting criticism of a culture that measures success by how closely one conforms to stereotypical images of power, wealth, and beauty.

Fast Forward, in which *Ashleigh, 13,* appears, received the Community Awareness Award from the National Press Photographers Association and the International Center of Photography Infinity Award for Young Photographers. Greenfield's photographs have appeared in *Time, Newsweek, Vanity Fair, Life,* and the *New York Times Magazine.* Her most recent book, *Girl Culture,* was published in 2002.

U.S. Army, *There's Something about a Soldier,* 1990

Looking Closer

KATHA POLLITT

Born in New York City in 1949, Katha Pollitt earned a BA from Radcliffe College in 1972. She is a widely published poet and essayist whose writing began appearing in the 1970s in such magazines as *The New Yorker* and *The Atlantic. Antarctic Traveller* (1982), a collection of Pollitt's poems, won a National Book Critics Circle Award. *Reasonable Creatures: Essays on Women and Feminism* appeared in 1994. Pollitt has received numerous honors, including a grant from the National Endowment for the Arts and a Guggenheim Fellowship. Her essays and criticism reach a wide audience through such publications as *Mother Jones,* the *New York Times, The New Yorker,* and *The Nation,* where as an associate editor she writes a regularly featured column.

Pollitt's recent book, *Subject to Debate: Sense and Dissents on Women, Politics, and Culture* (2001), is a collection of hot-topic essays written for her regular column in *The Nation.*

BRIAN FINKE

Photographer Brian Finke received a BFA from the School of Visual Arts in New York City in 1998. His work has appeared in *The New Yorker, Esquire,* the *New York Times Magazine, Time, Newsweek,* and other publications, and has been honored by the Alexia Foundation for World Peace (1998) and World Press Photo (2001). His subject matter ranges from child labor in India (a Tides Center project) to the photographs shown here of American college cheerleaders and young football players.

For *2-4-6-8: American Cheerleaders and Football Players* (2003), his first book, Finke was interested in finding the individual sensibilities behind the group image of cheerleaders and football players; in revealing how individuals differed from the group. "These teens struggle between being part of a group and defining themselves," Finke says. "I am very fortunate to be granted the kind of access to these subjects that allows me to create extremely private and personal images."

U.S. ARMY

During World War II, 150,000 women served in the army as members of the Women's Army Corps (later the Women's Auxiliary Army Corps). These women handled administrative tasks at home and overseas, freeing male soldiers for combat. In fact that was how the WAACs were recruited: Joining the corps was advertised as a way for women to serve their country by performing non-combatant duties to "free up a man" for combat.

In 2004, the army reported 200,000 women in its ranks—about 17 percent of its total force—serving in almost every capacity short of direct ground combat. Facing a shortage of combat-ready soldiers, the army is now proposing lifting the ban that prohibits women from serving on the front lines, claiming that technology has changed the nature of combat. According to a Pentagon spokesman, "There are no clearly-defined front lines anymore."

The army stepped up its recruitment efforts recently with the "Army of one" ad campaign on television and the *America's Army* video game, which is intended to simulate the army experience.

SEEING

1. How would you summarize Katha Pollitt's analysis of "why boys don't play with dolls"? What are the most compelling aspects of her argument? the least convincing? Why? Pollitt notes that "the thing the theories do most of all is tell adults that the *adult* world—in which moms and dads still play by many of the old rules even as they question and fidget and chafe against them—is the way it's supposed to be" (para. 12). What exactly is "the way it's supposed to be"?

2. How does the notion of gender training apply to Marianne Ghantous's findings? to Lauren Greenfield's 13-year-old? to Brian Finke's cheerleaders and football players? to the army ad? How does it apply to Art Spiegelman's comic strip? What sort of childhood play is the father encouraging? Imagine the comic strip with no text. What would make you assume that the child is a girl?

3. How would you characterize Spiegelman's rendering of the father in *Nature vs. Nurture*. What type of person has he drawn? What details communicate his personality? Compare Ghantous's approach in presenting her views of gender and children with Spiegelman's approach. Consider their choices of medium, the context in which each functions, and the audience.

WRITING

1. How did toys contribute to your childhood understanding of gender difference? What were your favorite toys or play activities? Would you describe them as typically male or female? Write a two-page recollection of a childhood toy or play activity that somehow informed your notions of masculinity and femininity.

2. Several authors in this book recall childhood experiences with superheroes. See, for example, Judith Ortiz Cofer's "The Story of My Body" (page 343). What superhero were you fond of as a child? How did this superhero contribute to your childhood notions of what it means to be a man or a woman? How representative is your experience of others your age? Write the first draft of an analytic essay in which you explain the nature of the appeal of superheroes.

EXAMINING

DIFFERENCE

5

Nikki S. Lee, *The Punk Project (6)*, 1997

Nikki S. Lee, *The Hispanic Project (27)*, 1998

convictions—then discrimination is about behavior—unreasonable treatment based on class or category. Racism is a structural problem, a form of discrimination based on group identity that is embedded in institutional processes of exclusion. As such, racism is a social construct, more a cause than a product of race.

The concept of race has ancient origins that emphasized the physical, linguistic, and cultural differences among groups of people. By the mid-nineteenth century, Western science and culture used the word *race* to classify people into groups on the basis of physical features as well as on the basis of mental and moral behavior. These conceptions of race depended on then-prevailing notions of heredity and superiority. In the nineteenth century the word *Negro* suggested skin color, hair texture, and other genetic characteristics, *and* inferior social status, especially in cultures where "Negroes" were marked as slaves.

Color has long provided the simplest and most convenient explanation of racial differences among people. By 1805, French comparative anatomist Georges Cuvier had divided the world into three races: white, yellow, and black. Cuvier's theory circulated for generations, not only because it told

scholar Kwame Anthony Appiah, it may well come
as "a shock to many to learn that there is a fairly
widespread consensus in the sciences of biology
and anthropology that the word 'race,' at least as
it is used in most unscientific discussions, refers
to nothing that science should recognize as real."
Appiah has also observed that scientists have
rejected not only the assertions that someone's
racial "essence" can explain, say, his or her intellectual and moral behavior but also such standard
nineteenth-century classifications as Negroid,
Caucasian, and Mongoloid. "There are simply too
many people who do not fit into any such category," Appiah explains, and "even when you
succeed in assigning someone to one of these categories . . . that implies very little about most
of their other biological characteristics." Like a
belief in ghosts, a belief in race, however inaccurate, can have serious consequences for social and
cultural life.

Despite the discrediting of so-called objective
criteria for defining race, scientific explanations—
and their representations in popular culture—linger
in both behavior and institutional practice. Racism
remains in effect a product of attitudes.

Mario Testino, *Doubles, Lima*

Mario Testino, *Shalom and Linda, Paris*

MARIO TESTINO

Born in Peru in 1954, Mario Testino is one of the world's premier fashion photographers and an integral part of the fashionable world he photographs. His dressing-room photos of supermodels reveal the private emotions behind the scenes of the fashion industry.

Testino's photographs of the late Princess Diana in the July 1997 issue of *Vanity Fair* are among his most famous, exemplifying his glamorous vision of richly saturated colors and dramatic settings. In 1998 Testino published a book of photographs, *Any Objections?,* from which the two images here are taken. In this compilation, writes artist and writer Patrick Kinmonth, "he did not choose to assemble the kind of pictures that have made him famous. . . . Instead he has selected largely unseen pictures . . . and made them into a documentary. . . . This process he describes as distinct from the business of taking fashion pictures. There his role is carefully to construct the image; here, his role is immediately to trap it as it flashes by."

Testino has also published *Mario Testino: Portraits* (2002), a collection of his celebrity and fashion photography, and *Kids* (2003), a book of children's images that benefits Sargent Cancer Care for Children, a British charity.

SEEING

1. What do you notice first about the photograph of the two men? of the two women? How would you characterize the depiction of their bodies in each photograph—the cropping, the amount of body exposed? How do the people in each photograph acknowledge the presence of the photographer? What additional points of comparison and contrast do you notice in the two photographs?

2. Testino's photograph of the two supermodels could easily be a fashion shot. Would you be surprised to find the photo of the two men in *Allure* or *Elle*? Why or why not? What is the overall effect of juxtaposing these two very different images? Does it change the way you perceive one or the other? How does reversing the order of the pictures change your perception of them?

WRITING

1. Which of Testino's photographs do you like better? Write an informal essay in two parts: In the first part, carefully describe the figures and background in each photograph, and the mood evoked by each; in the second, articulate why you respond more positively to one than to the other.

2. In the preface to his beautifully illustrated study *The Body* (1994), author and photo curator William Ewing asks: "Why is it today that the human body is at the center of so much attention? Why are magazines, newspapers, television, and advertisements saturated with images of naked, or virtually naked, bodies? Why are so many writers, artists, and photographers so profoundly concerned with the subject?" Write the first draft of a cause-and-effect essay in which you answer Ewing's question about the preoccupation with the body in contemporary American culture.

TALKING PICTURES

"It's a pretty simple joke," said comic Sacha Baron Cohen of his HBO series *Da Ali G Show*, "which is why even some kids get it." Cohen plays several different characters over the course of each episode, among them: Borat, the sex-obsessed TV show host from Kazakhstan, and Ali G, a rapper who describes himself as "easily da most respekted face on Brittish telly." "Ali G is a dumb person played smart," wrote media critic Neil Strauss, "the stereotypical white suburban would-be gangsta rapper, with a twist. With his own talk show as a forum, Ali G's hilarious interactions with his guests play off the disconnect between black and white culture, young and old, street smart and book smart, hip and square."

From the caricatures of blacks on *Amos 'n' Andy* to the portrayals of angst-ridden Jewish mothers on *Seinfeld*, racial and ethnic stereotyping has long been a staple of television and movie humor. Think about portrayals of American ethnic groups on television and in film today. To what extent are those portrayals stereotypical? Choose a character or a scene from a recent show or movie that relies on ethnic or racial identity as the source of humor. What is the nature of the stereotype? On what does the humor rely? Write an expository essay in which you discuss the relationship of humor to ethnic stereotypes.

COMING INTO THE COUNTRY
Gish Jen

IN THE OLD WORLD, THERE WAS ONE WAY OF LIFE, or 2, maybe 10. Here there are dozens, hundreds, all jammed in together, cheek by jowl, especially in the dizzying cities. Everywhere has a somewhere else just around the corner. We newish Americans leapfrog from world to world, reinventing ourselves en route. We perform our college selves, our waitress selves, our dot-com selves, our parent selves, our downtown selves, our Muslim, Greek, Hindi, South African selves. Even into the second or third generation, we speak different languages—more languages, often, than we know we know. We sport different names. I am Gish, Geesh, Jen, Lillian, Lil, Bilien, Ms. Jen, Miss Ren, Mrs. O'Connor. Or maybe we insist on one name. The filmmaker Mira Nair, for example, will be called NIGH-ear, please; she is not a depilatory product.

Of course, there are places where she does not have to insist, and places that don't get the joke, that need—that get—other jokes. It's a kind of high, switching spiels, eating Ethiopian, French, Thai, getting around. And the inventing! The moments of grand inspiration: I think I will call myself Houdini. Who could give up even the quotidian luxury of choosing, that small swell of power: To walk or to drive? The soup or the salad? The green or the blue? We bubble with pleasure. It's me. I'm taking the plane. I'll take the sofa, the chair, the whole shebang—why not?

Why not, indeed? A most American question, a question that comes to dominate our most private self-talk. In therapy-speak, we Americans like to give ourselves permission. To do what? To take care of ourselves, to express ourselves, to listen to ourselves.

We tune out the loudspeaker of duty, tune in to the whisper of desire. This is faint at first, but soon proves easily audible; indeed, irresistible. Why not go to town? Why not move away? Why not marry out? Why not? Why not? Why not?

To come to America is to be greatly disoriented for many a day. The smell of the air is wrong, the taste of the water, the strength of the sun, the rate the trees grow. The rituals are strange—the spring setting out of mulch, the summer setting out of barbecues. How willingly the men heat themselves with burgers! Nobody eats the wildlife, certainly not the bugs or leaves. And beware, beware the rules about smoking. Your skin feels tight, your body fat or thin, your children stranger than they were already. Your sensations are exhausting.

Yet one day a moment comes—often, strangely, abroad—when we find ourselves missing things. Our choice of restaurants, perhaps, or our cheap gas and good roads; or, more tellingly, our rights. To be without freedom of movement, to be without freedom of speech—these things pain everyone. But to be without our freedom of movement, without our freedom of speech is an American affliction; and in this, as in many facets of American life, possession matters. The moment we feel certain rights to be inalienable, when we feel them to be ours as our lungs are ours, so that their loss is an excision and a death, we have become American.

It's not always a happy feeling. For the more at home we become with our freedom, the more we become aware of its limits. There's much true opportunity in the land of opportunity, but between freedom in theory and freedom in practice gapes a grand canyon. As often as not, what we feel is the burn of injustice. A rise of anger, perhaps followed by a quick check on our impulse to act rashly; perhaps followed by a decision to act courageously. We gather here today to make known our grievance. For is this not America?

We wonder who we are—what does it mean to be Irish-American, Cuban-American, Armenian-American?—and are amazed to discover that others wonder, too. Indeed, nothing seems more typically American than to obsess about identity. Can so many people truly be so greatly confused? We feel very much a part of the contemporary gestalt.

Yet two or three generations later, we still may not be insiders. Recently, I heard about a basketball game starring a boy from the Cochiti pueblo in Santa Fe. The kids on his team, a friend reported, had one water bottle, which they passed around, whereas the kids on the other team each had his own. This was a heartening story, signaling the survival of a communal culture against the pressures of individualism. But did the Cochiti boy notice the other team? I couldn't help wondering. Did he feel the glass pane between himself and the mainstream, so familiar, so tangible, so bittersweet? Nobody has been here longer than we; how come our ways need protecting? Later a member of the pueblo told me that the Cochiti have started a language-immersion program for the younger generation, and that it has been a success. They are saving their language from extinction.

Hooray! The rest of us cheer. How awed we feel in the presence of tradition, of authenticity. How avidly we will surf to such sites, some of us, and what we will pay to do so! We will pay for bits of the Southwest the way we will pay handsomely, in this generation or the next, for a home. Whatever that looks like; we find ourselves longing for some combination of Martha Stewart and what we can imagine, say, of our family seat in Brazil. At any rate, we can say this much: The home of our dreams is a safe place, a still place. A communal place, to which we contribute; to which we have real ties; a place that feels more stable, perhaps, than ourselves. How American this is—to long, at day's end, for a place where we belong more, invent less; for a heartland with more heart. ○

GISH JEN

Of her early years in Scarsdale, New York, Gish Jen (b. 1956) says: "We were almost the only Asian-American family in town. People threw things at us and called us names. . . . It was only much later that I realized it had been hard." Her first novel, *Typical American* (1991), explores assimilation with wit and humor. It was a New York Times Notable Book (as were her other novels) and a finalist for the National Book Critics Circle Award.

"Coming into the Country" was first published in the *New York Times Magazine* in 2000. Here too Jen examines assimilation and American identity. Asked about diversity in an interview with Bill Moyers, she said: "It is striking to me that Americans ask themselves certain kinds of questions. And it does seem to me that by the time you ask yourself, 'Well, what does it mean to be Iranian-American, Chinese-American . . . ,' you are American 'cause it's not a question that people ask in other parts of the world."

Jen's stories have been published in *The New Yorker, The Atlantic,* and other journals. In addition to grants from the Guggenheim Foundation and other organizations, Jen received the Lannan Literary Award for Fiction in 1999. She lives in Cambridge, Massachusetts. Her latest novel, *The Love Wife,* was published in 2004.

SEEING

1. Throughout the essay Jen uses phrases such as "most American" (para. 3), "typically American" (para. 7), and "how American" (para. 9). These phrases make generalizations in a piece largely concerned with the nature and permanence of diversity. What does Jen consider "typically American"? What aspects of American life does she overlook or understate in her attempt to define a national character?

2. In paragraph 4 Jen writes that coming to America is disorienting: "The smell of the air is wrong, the taste of the water, the strength of the sun, the rate the trees grow." How does her use of natural phenomena help frame her argument? What does she gain or lose by describing culture shock in these terms?

WRITING

1. Jen notes that "between freedom in theory and freedom in practice" in America "gapes a grand canyon" (para. 6). Do you believe that's true? Write an essay in which you support or challenge Jen's claim in terms of your personal and professional goals. What is the canyon between your freedom in theory and in practice?

2. In the first paragraph Jen writes: "We perform our college selves, our waitress selves, our dot-com selves, our parent selves, our downtown selves, our Muslim, Greek, Hindi, South African selves." What audience do you think Jen is imagining for these performances? What selves do you perform? For whom? Draft an essay in which you describe one or more of your performances and audiences. Pay particular attention to how your audience influences your performance. Also consider what might happen if you assumed a particular self in an unfamiliar context.

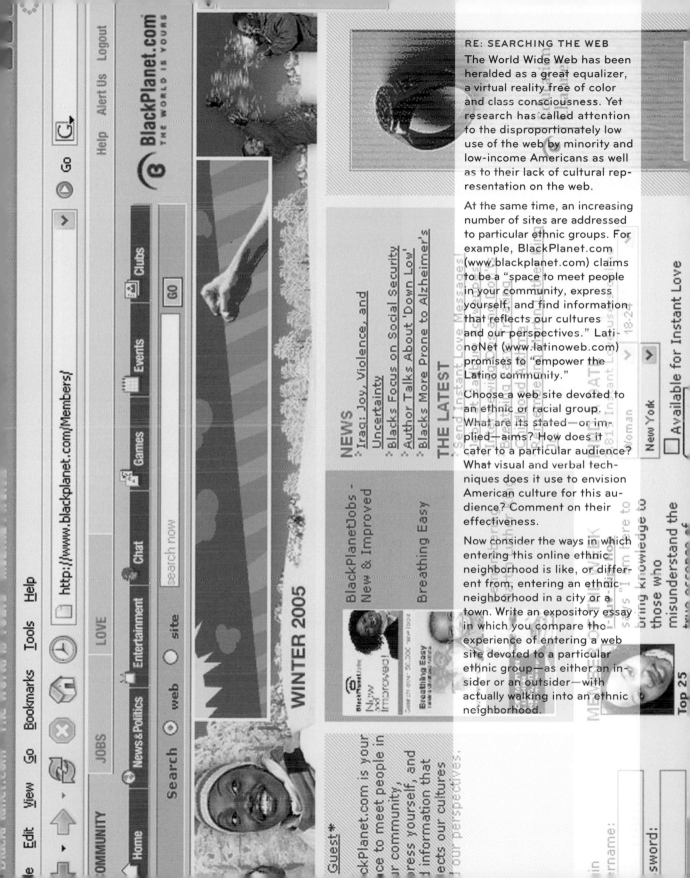

RE: SEARCHING THE WEB

The World Wide Web has been heralded as a great equalizer, a virtual reality free of color and class consciousness. Yet research has called attention to the disproportionately low use of the web by minority and low-income Americans as well as to their lack of cultural representation on the web.

At the same time, an increasing number of sites are addressed to particular ethnic groups. For example, BlackPlanet.com (www.blackplanet.com) claims to be a "space to meet people in your community, express yourself, and find information that reflects our cultures and our perspectives." LatinoNet (www.latinoweb.com) promises to "empower the Latino community."

Choose a web site devoted to an ethnic or racial group. What are its stated—or implied—aims? How does it cater to a particular audience? What visual and verbal techniques does it use to envision American culture for this audience? Comment on their effectiveness.

Now consider the ways in which entering this online ethnic neighborhood is like, or different from, entering an ethnic neighborhood in a city or a town. Write an expository essay in which you compare the experience of entering a web site devoted to a particular ethnic group—as either an insider or an outsider—with actually walking into an ethnic neighborhood.

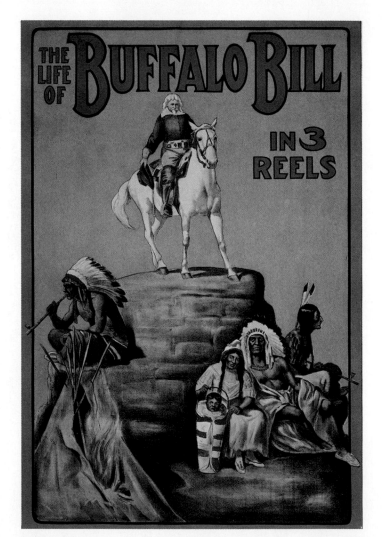

1910

1929

1990

1998

Cool Like Me

By Donnell Alexander

I'm cool like this:
I read fashion magazines like they're
   warning labels telling me what not to do.
When I was a kid, Arthur Fonzarelli
   seemed a garden-variety dork.
I got my own speed limit.
I come when I want to.   5
I maintain like an ice cube in the remote
   part of the freezer.
Cooler than a polar bear's toenails.
Cooler than the other side of the pillow.
Cool like me.
Know this while understanding that I am   10
   in essence a humble guy.

I'm the kinda nigga who's so cool that my neighbor bursts into hysterical tears whenever I ring her doorbell after dark. She is a new immigrant who has chosen to live with her two roommates in our majority-black Los Angeles neighborhood so that, I'm told, she can "learn about all American cultures." But her real experience of us is limited to the space between her Honda and her front gate; thus, much of what she has to go on is the vibe of the surroundings and the images emanating from the television set that gives her living room a minty cathode glow. As such, I'm a cop-show menace and a shoe commercial demigod—one of the rough boys from our 'hood and the living, breathing embodiment of hip-hop flava. And if I can't fulfill the prevailing stereotype, the kids en route to the nearby high school can. The woman is scared in a cool world. She smiles as I pass her way in the light of day, unloading my groceries or shlepping my infant son up the stairs. But at night, when my face is visible through the window of her door lit only by the bulb that brightens the vestibule, I, at once familiar and threatening, am just too much.

Thus being cool has its drawbacks. With cool come assumptions and fears, expectations and intrigue. My neighbor wants to live near cool, but she's not sure about cool walking past her door after dark. During the day, she sees a black man; at night what she sees in the shadow gliding across her patio is a nigga.

Once upon a time, little need existed for making the distinction between a nigga and a black—at least not in this country, the place where niggas were invented. We were just about all slaves, so we were all niggas. Then we became free on paper yet oppressed still. Today, with as many as a third of us a generation or two removed from living poor (depending on who's counting), niggadom isn't innate to every black child born. But with the poverty rate still hovering at around 30 percent, black people still got niggas in the family, even when they themselves aren't niggas. Folks who don't know niggas can watch them on TV, existing in worlds almost always removed from blacks. Grant Hill is black, Allen Iverson is a nigga. Oprah interviewing the celebrity du jour is a black woman; the woman being handcuffed on that reality TV show is a nigga.

The question of whether black people are cooler than white people is a dumb one, and one that I imagine a lot of people will find offensive. But we know what we're talking about, right? We're talking about style and spirit and the innovations that those things spawn. It's on TV; it's in the movies, sports and clothes and language and gestures and music.

See, black cool is cool as we know it. I could name names—Michael Jordan and Chris Rock and Me'shell Ndegeocello and Will Smith and bell hooks and Lil' Kim—but cool goes way back, much further than today's superstars. Their antecedents go back past blaxploitation cinema, past Ike Turner to Muddy Waters, beyond even the old jazz players and blues singers whose names you'll never know. Cool has a history and cool has a meaning. We all know cool when we see it, and now, more than at any other time in this country's history, when mainstream America looks for cool we look to black culture. Countless new developments can be called great, nifty, even keen. But, cool? That's a black thang, baby.

And I should know. My being cool is not a matter of subjectivity or season. Having lived as a nigga has made me cool. Let me explain. Cool was born when the first plantation nigga figured out how to make animal innards—massa's garbage, hog maws, and chitlins—taste good enough to eat. That inclination to make something out of nothing and then to make that something special articulated itself first in the work chants that slaves sang in the field and then in the hymns that rose out of their churches. It would later reveal itself in the music made from cast-off Civil War marching-band instruments (jazz); physical exercise turned to public spectacle (sports); and street life styling, from pimps' silky handshakes to the corner crack dealer's baggy pants.

Cool is all about trying to make a dollar out of 15 cents. It's about living on the cusp, on the periphery, diving for scraps. Essential to cool is being outside looking in. Others—Indians, immigrants, women, gays—have been "othered," but until the past 15 percent of America's history, niggas in real terms have been treated by the country's majority as, at best, subhuman and, at worst, an abomination. So in the days when they were still literally on the plantation they devised a coping strategy called cool, an elusive mellowing strategy designed to master time and space. Cool, the basic reason blacks remain in the American cultural mix, is an industry of style that everyone in the world can use. It's finding the essential soul while being essentially lost. It's the nigga metaphor. And the nigga metaphor is the genius of America.

Gradually over the course of this century, as there came to be a growing chasm of privilege between black people and niggas, the nature of cool began to shift. The romantic and now-popular image of the pasty Caucasian who hung out in a jazz club was one small subplot. Cool became a promise—the reward to any soul hardy enough to pierce the inner sanctum of black life and not only live to tell about it but also live to live for it. Slowly, watered-down versions of this very specific strain of cool became the primary means of defining American cool. But it wasn't until Elvis that cool was brought down from Olympus (or Memphis) to majority-white culture. Mass media did the rest. Next stop: high fives, chest bumps, and "Go girl!"; Air Jordans, Tupac, and low-riding pants.

White folks began to try to make the primary point of cool—recognition of the need to go with the flow—a part of their lives. But cool was only an avocational interest for them. It could never be the necessity it was for their colored co-occupants. Some worked harder at it than others. And as they came to understand coolness as being of almost elemental importance, they began obsessing on it, asking themselves, in a variety of clumsy, indirect ways: Are black people cooler than white people and, if so, why?

The answer is, of course, yes. And if you, the reader, had to ask some stupid shit like that, you're probably white. It's hard to imagine a black person even asking the question, and a nigga might not even know what you mean. Any nigga who'd ask that question certainly isn't much of one; niggas invented the shit.

Humans put cool on a pedestal because life at large is a challenge, and in that challenge we're trying to cram in as much as we can—as much fine loving, fat eating, dope sleeping, mellow walking, and substantive working as possible. We need spiritual assistance in the matter. That's where cool comes in. At its core, cool is useful. Cool gave bass to 20th-century American culture, but I think that if the culture had needed more on the high end, cool would have given that, because cool closely resembles the human spirit. It's about completing the task of living with enough spontaneity to splurge some of it on bystanders,

to share with others working through their own travails a little of your bonus life. Cool is about turning desire into deed with a surplus of ease.

Some white people are cool in their own varied ways. I married a white girl who was cooler than she ever knew. And you can't tell me Jim Jarmusch and Ron Athey and Delbert McClinton ain't smooth.

There's a gang of cool white folks, all of whom exist that way because they've found their essential selves amid the abundant and ultimately numbing media replications of the coolness vibe and the richness of real life. And there's a whole slew more of them ready to sign up if you tell 'em where. But your average wigger in the rap section of Sam Goody ain't gone nowhere; she or he hasn't necessarily learned shit about the depth and breadth of cool, about making a dollar out of 15 cents. The problem with mainstream American culture, the reason why irony's been elevated to raison d'être status and neurosis increasingly gets fetishized, is its twisted approach to cool. Most think cool is something you can put on and take off at will (like a strap-on goatee). They think it's some shit you go shopping for. And that taints cool, giving the mutant thing it becomes a de-servedly bad name. Such strains aren't even cool anymore, but an evil ersatz-cool, one that fights real cool at every turn. Advertising agencies, record-company artist-development departments, and over-art-directed bars are where ersatz-cool 20 dwells. What passes for cool to the white-guy passerby might be—is probably—just rote dupli-cation without an ounce of inspiration.

The acceptance of clone cool by so many is what makes hip-hop necessary. It's what negates the hopelessness of the postmodern sensibility at its most cynical. The hard road of getting by on metaphorical chitlins kept the sons and daughters of Africa in touch with life's essential physicality, more in touch with the world and what it takes to get over in it: People are moved, not convinced; things get done, they don't just happen. Real life doesn't allow for much fronting, as it were. And neither does hip-hop. Hip-hop allows for little de-viation between who one is and what one can ultimately represent.

Rap—the most familiar, and therefore the most 25 emblematic, example of hip-hop expression—is about the power of conveying through speech the world beyond words. Language is placed on a par with sound and, ultimately, vibes. Huston

Smith, a dope white guy, wrote: "Speech is alive—literally alive because speaking is the speaker. It's not the whole of the speaker, but it is the speaker in one of his or her living modes. This shows speech to be alive by definition. . . . It possesses in principle life's qualities, for its very nature is to change, adapt, and invent. Indissolubly contextual, speaking adapts itself to speaker, listener, and situation alike. This gives it an immediacy, range, and versatility that is, well, miraculous."

Which is why hip-hop has become the most insidiously influential music of our time. Like rock, hip-hop in its later years will have a legacy of renegade youth to look back upon fondly. But hip-hop will insist that its early marginalization be recognized as an integral part of what it comes to be. When the day comes that grandmothers are rapping and beatboxing as they might aerobicize now, and samplers and turntables are as much an accepted part of leisure time as channel surfing, niggas will be glad. Their expression will have proven ascendant.

But that day's not here yet. If white people were really cool with black cool, they'd put their stuff with our stuff more often to work shit out. I don't mean shooting hoops together in the schoolyard as much as white cultural institutions like college radio, indie film, and must-see TV. Black cool is banished to music videos, sports channels, and UPN so whites can visit us whenever they want without having us live right next door in the media mix. Most of the time, white folks really don't want to be part of black cool. They just like to see the boys do a jig every once in a while.

At the same time, everyday life in black America is not all Duke Ellington and Rakim Allah. Only a few black folks are responsible for cool. The rest copy and recycle. At the historical core of black lives in this country is a clear understanding that deviation from society's assigned limitations results in punitive sanctions: lynching, hunger, homelessness. The fear of departing from the familiar is where the inclination to make chitlins becomes a downside. It's where the shoeshine-boy reflex to grin and bear it was born. Black rebellion in America from slave days onward was never based on abstract, existentialist grounds. A bird in the hand, no matter how small, was damn near everything.

Today, when deviation from normalcy not only goes unpunished but is also damn near de-

manded to guarantee visibility in our fast-moving world, blacks remain woefully wedded to the bowed head and blinders. Instead of bowing to massa, they slavishly bow to trend and marketplace. And this creates a hemming-in of cool, an inability to control the cool one makes. By virtue of their status as undereducated bottom feeders, many niggas will never overcome this way of being. But, paradoxically, black people—who exist at a greater distance from cool than niggas—can and will. That's the perplexity of the cool impulse. As long as some black people have to live like niggas, cool, as contemporarily defined, will live on. As long as white people know what niggas are up to, cool will continue to exist, with all of its baggage passed on like, uh, luggage. The question "Are black people cooler than white people?" is not the important one. "How do I gain proximity to cool, and do I want it?" is much better. The real secret weapon of cool is that it's about synthesis. Just about every important black cultural invention of this century has been about synthesizing elements previously considered antithetical. MLK merged Eastern thought and cotton-field religious faith into the civil rights movement. Chuck Berry merged blues and country music into rock 'n' roll. Michael Jordan incorporated the old school ball of Jerry West into his black game. Talk about making a dollar out of 15 cents.

Out in the netherworld of advertising, they tell us we're all Tiger Woods. He plays the emblematic white man's game as good as anyone. Well, only one nigga on this planet gets to be that motherfucker, but we all swing the same cool, to whatever distant ends. The coolness construct might tell us otherwise, but we're all handed the same basic tools at birth, it's up to us as individuals to work on our game. Some of us have sweet strokes, and some of us press too hard, but everybody who drops outta their mama has the same capacity to take a shot. O

DONNELL ALEXANDER

Donnell Alexander was born 1967 in Sandusky, Ohio. He attended junior college in Fresno, California, and began writing for local college papers and the alternative press. Soon he was writing about hip-hop culture, sports, and entertainment for *LA Weekly* and *ESPN The Magazine*.

Throughout his career, Alexander has examined topics ranging from what suit to wear on NBA draft day to the life of security guards. As a former staff writer for *LA Weekly,* he covered that city's booming hip-hop music scene as well as the O. J. Simpson trial.

Alexander's work confronts head-on the preconceptions white Americans have of African American men. Speaking with an insider's ease, Alexander has developed a style that is at once articulate, rigorous, and highly metaphorical.

Alexander left *ESPN The Magazine* to work on his memoir, *Ghetto Celebrity: Searching for My Father in Me* (2003), about his development as a writer and the challenges he faced growing up without a father.

SEEING

1. Donnell Alexander states that "Cool has a history and cool has a meaning" (para. 15). Sketch out the history that Alexander presents for "cool." How does he define the term? According to Alexander, what is the difference between "nigga" and "black"? What does he mean when he talks of the "nigga metaphor"? Outline the logical steps Alexander takes in constructing his argument about making "hip hop necessary."

2. Consider the list with which Alexander begins this piece. What does he gain—and lose—by opening the essay in this manner? How would you characterize his tone at the beginning of the essay? Does it remain consistent throughout the piece? If not, when does it change, and with what effects? Comment on his diction as well.

WRITING

1. Alexander claims that evidence of "cool" is everywhere evident in American popular culture. "We all know cool when we see it, and now, more than at any other time in this country's history, when mainstream America looks for cool we look to black culture" (para. 15). Choose an example of cool—a musician, a celebrity, an athlete, or a style of dress, to name a few possibilities—or something that passes for cool (what Alexander calls "cool clone") in mainstream American culture. Write an essay in which you use his explanation of the relationship between black culture and cool. Explain why you think your subject is "authentic" cool or a "wanna-be."

2. Early in the essay Alexander claims he is "a cop-show menace and a shoe commercial demi-god" (para. 11). This observation underscores the impression that African Americans are usually regarded as falling within one of these two categories. Consider your own experience with media representations of African Americans. Do you agree with Alexander's claim? Can you identify well-known African Americans who transcend these categories? Where, for example, would you place someone such as Bill Cosby? In what ways does someone like Cosby satisfy Alexander's definition of cool? Write an essay in which you assess the media representations of African Americans. Who among these figures can be said to be cool, and why?

Evan Agostini, *MTV TRL with P. Diddy and B5*

Is Diddy (Sean Combs) cool by Donnell Alexander's definition? Why or why not? How uncool is it to ask this question?

Goose-loose Blues for the Melting Pot

Stanley Crouch

WE WOULD DO OURSELVES A FAVOR BY BACKING away from the rhetorical hostility that attends the issue of assimilation. Assimilation is not the destruction of one's true identity. It is not, as advocates of separatism would teach us, a matter of domination and subordination, nor the conquest of one culture by another. On the contrary, it's about the great intermingling of cultural influences that comprises the American condition: the fresh ideas brought forward in our folklore, our entertainment, our humor, our athletic contests, our workplaces, even our celebrity trials and political scandals. Only the rhetorical violence left over from the 1960s prevents us from understanding what assimilation really means and how it actually happens in America.

This isn't to pretend that we as a nation have shed all bigotry based on skin tone, or sex, or religion, or nationality, or class. But if we still have troubles, and plenty of them, that doesn't mean we haven't advanced remarkably when it comes to race and ethnicity (and it doesn't mean we aren't capable of going even further). If we examine things as they actually are, we can see that what it means to be American has never been fixed or static or impervious to outsiders; we are continually creating and re-creating our traditions. In fact, American society is now so demonstrably open to variety, and so successful at gathering in those who would join it,

that it is the international model of a free and progressively integrated nation.

When the civil rights movement began, its enemy was racism, not white people per se. But as the irrational elements of Black Power congealed, the boldly nonviolent movement began to descend to a politics based in ethnic identity, sexual identity, and sexual preference. The hysteria, sentimentality, bigotry, and fantasies of Black Power extremists were taken up by other (so-called) ethnic minorities, by women, and by homosexuals. And over time, this politics of identity corroded into a politics of hostility, to the point that many Americans confused the real enemy—hateful visions like racism, sexism, and homophobia—with the white race.

Among the effects of this shift from understanding to misunderstanding was the creation of "alienation studies" programs on campuses from one end of this nation to the other. Purportedly oppressed groups were taught that their only hope was "within their own." This separatism was often joined to a naïve internationalism rooted in the paradigm of Marxist liberation. Black Americans were supposed to see themselves as part of a Third World struggle. People of color were supposed to reassert their "true" cultures, which had allegedly been ground to dust under the heels of the whites.

Not surprisingly, in this upside-down world, as-5 similation was seen as the destruction of true identity. Why should one want to disappear into an unvaried mass when one could be part of something more vital, more "authentic"? Under no circumstances was a black American to forget that, as Malcolm X had said, "You are not an American, you are a victim of *Americanism*." One had to get back to one's true roots (which were in Africa), one's true religion (which was Islam), and one's true interests (which could never coincide with the interests of the United States). Variants of these Black Power ideas have been adopted by other ostensibly oppressed groups: Latinos, Asians, women, and homosexuals have each invented versions of the "Oreo" motif (black on the outside, white on the inside), regarding assimilation as a form of "selling out." Authenticity, according to this outlook, has become an absolute—and it is an impossible condition to achieve in a melting pot.

But the separatist alienation-studies crowd couldn't be more wrong about assimilation. For most Americans, identity has never been static. It never could be, especially in an experimental society that has forever had to create its own traditions. Indeed, even against our will, we Americans have a difficult time being provincial. The different groups that make up the nation need and attract and influence each other—even those brainwashed by alienation studies partake of the nation's shifting common culture. The notion that any group could remain separate and untouched is nothing more than a mad joke.

Decades ago, the great Constance Rourke, author of the classics *American Humor* and *The Roots of American Culture*, proposed that there are four mythic figures at the core of American culture: the Indian, the Yankee, the Frontiersman, and the Negro. Director John Ford picked up the idea from her, or at least made use of it, at the conclusion of his 1939 film *Drums along the Mohawk*, which is set during the Revolutionary War. The Indian, the Yankee, the Frontiersman, and the Negro all watch as an American flag is raised over an upstate New York fort, and they realize that its flapping colors and stars symbolize a human connection, one finalized through the death and tragedy of a war fought to make a new nation. From those four archetypes come our sense of the land, our folklore, our vision of adventure, our humor, our dance, our music, and our acknowledgment—as Ralph Ellison would add—of the importance of improvisation, of learning to absorb and invent on the spot.

Improvisation is essential to understanding these United States. It was especially necessary for a nation always faced with the unknown, forever at a frontier of some sort. The unknown was often the natural environment, as the frontier moved at first gingerly and then brutally west. The unknown frontier could also be the big city, drawing people from the countryside and teaching them breathtaking, illuminating, and destructive lessons. These encounters with the new quite often demanded invention-on-the-spot. Bringing mother wit to emergency situations is surely our national ideal, so much so that in Hollywood films the villain or the monster is often dispatched by an improvised turn, an unexpected solution, a jerry-built contraption that does the job.

As the nation expanded through immigration and other means, it became equally necessary to improvise the idea of what it means to be American. The result is that cultural improvisation has become second nature as Rourke's four archetypes have been expanded. Mexican, Asian, Irish, Italian, and Eastern European strains have become part of the national identity, affecting our cowboy culture, our cuisine, our dance, our music, our slang, our Broadway shows, our films, our popular music, and our spiritual practices. American identity is never fixed or final; we are always working toward a better and deeper recognition of how to make one out of the many. The diffuse nature of our democracy leaves us with no choice. Consequently, out of this perpetual negotiation comes a collective identity that has to be, finally, as loose as the proverbial goose.

This goose-loose identity also involved some on-10 going and usually constructive conflict—the struggle of the most high-minded Americans against the worst elements of our social past. Even when our sense of ourselves was profoundly bigoted—as far back as the three-fifths rule agreed upon by our Founding Fathers, which made black slaves less human than white men—we always had a sense of a collective American reality. And even bigotry never stopped people from making use of any part of any culture that they found enjoyable or functional. Already in 1930, when psychoanalyst Carl Jung visited the United States, he observed that white Americans walked, talked, and laughed like Negroes, something we would hardly expect if we were to look at the stereotypical ways in which black people were depicted at the time in American writing, theater, films, cartoons, and advertisements.

This cross-cultural borrowing and influence works the other way as well. As more than a few Negro Americans have found out when they went back to "the motherland," Africans look upon them—unless they are trying to hustle them for money—not as their brothers or sisters but as white people with black skins. In other words, Jung could see how much black Americans had influenced white Americans, and Africans can see how much white Americans have influenced black Americans. In the same way, European immigrants to America soon discovered that their kids were influenced by what they picked up while playing in the streets and by what was being sung and laughed about in popular entertainment. This is not the result of any melting pot that destroys distinctions; it is the expression of the mutations of choice and style that occur through our living close to each other.

Again, Ralph Ellison is important to our understanding of this messy, mixed-up way of being. Ellison knew that improvisation is essential to what we make of ourselves as Americans. He recognized that we are constantly integrating the things that we find attractive in others, whether the integration is conscious or unconscious. We all know that the American wears a top hat with an Indian feather sticking out of it, carries a banjo and a harmonica, knows how to summon the voice of the blues by applying a bathroom plunger to the bell of a trumpet or a trombone, will argue about the best Chinese restaurants, eat sushi with you one on one, turn the corner and explain the differences between the dishes on the menu at an Indian restaurant, drink plenty of tequila, get down with the martial arts, sip some vodka, recite favorite passages from the Koran, have some scotch on the rocks, show you the yarmulke worn at a friend's wedding, savor some French and Italian wine made from grapes grown in the Napa Valley, charm a snake, roll some ham and cheese up in a heated flour tortilla, tell what it was like learning to square dance or ballroom or get the pelvic twists of rhythm and blues right or how it felt in one of those sweltering Latin dance halls when the mambo got as hot as gumbo on a high boil. That's how *American* assimilation works. It's a quintessential part of our national adventure. *Our* society maintains its essential identity while new layers and nuances give greater vitality to the mix.

Perhaps the best way to understand where we are now, and what we have made of ourselves as Americans, is to look at the Kennedy era that began in 1960 when a handsome young Irishman became the first of his ethnic group to take the Oval Office. Back then, newspapers, magazines, television, and presidential conventions told us that just about anything of true importance was thought about, argued about and accomplished by white men. They ran the country, the states, the cities, the towns, the villages, the networks, the stock market, the athletic teams, the entertainment world, the universities—and they were not shy about letting you know it. It was not so much that they were arrogant; they were simply the only ones around. You did not see black people, or any other people who were not white—or any women—in the highest governmental positions in Washington, D.C., or in individual state or city government. Such people were, of course, human, but they just didn't make the cut. America walked through a blizzard of white men.

Only a lunatic would cling to the idea that the America of today is that same America of 1960. That world is as long gone as the Los Angeles through which saber-toothed tigers once strode and roared. When one turns on the television today, one sees people of every color and both sexes anchoring the local news, giving their analysis of the stock market, international politics, the entertainment industry, and whatever else might be of human concern, whether important or trivial or somewhere between those extremes. Ours is now a far more integrated society, and the aspirations of children from every group are far different now that there are flesh-and-blood human beings upon whom they can base their dreams.

I began to see how deeply things had changed when my daughter, born in 1977, was around six years old and I asked her what she intended to be when she grew up. She answered that she might be an astronaut, a Supreme Court justice, a police officer, a fireman, a doctor, or maybe a pilot. I was rather startled, to be honest, because, having been born in 1945, I had heard six-year-old girls say "a mother, a teacher, or a nurse." In the early 1950s, no rational young girl—or woman—would have thought she could become a Supreme Court justice. But when I considered what my daughter had said, I realized that the feminists had won the battle for the minds and aspirations of her generation. A black girl living in Compton, California, had absorbed, through all those vastly different television images, a sense of life and possibility that included imagining women in every significant career. Life seemed an open sky.

More than a decade and a half later, the influences that inspired my daughter to express such a broad range of career options have only intensified. Over and over, throughout the day and night, our advertisements project an integrated America. What's more, they tell us that no group of Americans is defined by the worst among them. Above us, we see that whites, Negroes, Hispanics, and Asians—whether men or women—work in every capacity, from the world of the blue collar all the way up to the business suites. We also see that every group, across all classes, has families—wives, husbands, children—and what sociologist Todd Gitlin has called "common dreams." This is profoundly important, no matter its commercial motivations. In attempting to sell products by making all Americans feel free to spend money, the brain trust of the advertising world takes every opportunity to tell us that, no matter what we look like, we are all human and have as much access to what is good as the next person. Come on in. Feel welcome. Sit down. Pull out your credit card.

Toward that end, our advertising culture is based on the assumption that normal, everyday life is integrated. We are shown that people need not be ill at ease when talking with others superficially different from themselves. Nor should they assume that any kind of human problem is color-bound. In the civil rights era of the mid-1960s, it used to be joked (playing off the stereotype that dark people smelled worse than white people) that blacks would have made it all the way into American society once a Negro could be shown in a deodorant commercial. That problem has surely gone by the boards in an era when anybody can advertise anything.

Skill, intelligence, and advice cross all racial lines. In one commercial, a white man who promises his kids that he will build a tree house for them finds himself in the lumber store getting perfect advice from a black man. In another, a black woman who wants to repaint the inside of her house buys paint from a white woman who tells her that she can't be afraid of yellow, advice she repeats both to her husband and to an Asian woman and a white man who come over to see what she has done. Insurance meant to appeal to older Americans has crosscuts of various ethnic faces. Advertisements for vans show smiling families that may or may not be white. It is not surprising to see an integrated group of women laughing and joking together or extolling the supposed virtues of brands of lipstick and facial powders and lingerie and sanitary napkins. A supervisor and his or her employees can cross the spectrum. And when chil-

In the Louima case, the sodomizing cop, Justin [30] Volpe, was identified by fellow officers, tried, and sentenced to thirty years in prison. What's more, however monstrous his actions, it turned out that Volpe may not be a racist in any way that we can ascertain: He was never accused of being a bigot by his coworkers, and he even had a black fiancée. In fact, she was often harassed by black cops for going out with him—and it's possible that this is what lit a fuse in him. Without forgiving Volpe for the unforgivable, it's worth considering: If the NYPD had offered a program to address such harassment of interracial couples, perhaps Louima would have been spared his assault.

Louima, meanwhile, admitted to having lied when he claimed his assailants yelled, "It's Giuliani time": He said he had been advised to say so to bring attention to his case. When his civil case got to court, he was awarded millions by the city, something that would never have happened in his native Haiti. And in the wake of the Diallo tragedy, the New York Police Academy has instituted an elaborate set of training procedures designed to prevent anything of the sort from happening again.

Those high-profile cases did not all come out perfectly, to say the least. Yet in no case was the truth as stark as it seemed at first. In almost every instance, both blacks and whites participated in bringing the city back from the brink—and again and again justice transcended race. Our deeply American humanity triumphed over even the most divisive kinds of violence and xenophobic murder.

These lessons from New York's recent history are even more important in the wake of the terrorist attacks of September 11, 2001. Since then, we have learned the deeper reason why the twin towers were called the World Trade Center: The three thousand people who worked and died there were of every color and both sexes, they believed in all of the major religions, and they worked in every capacity from cleaning floors to trading stocks. What we saw on September 11 was integrated America under attack—and our hearts collectively broke as the buildings went down and the clouds of dust spread. Black and white and red and yellow people helped and supported one another. Americans and immigrants on their way to becoming Americans, in their work clothes and their business suits, their police uniforms and their fire department gear—all moved together through the streets and across the Brooklyn Bridge. And at that tragic moment, in their collectivity and their willingness to suffer with and for each other, they symbolized the ability of the species to stand up to disaster as human beings. The one thing that has always been true about the nation became even more true on that unforgettable morning: Our surface differences are far less important than what we have in common and what we will ourselves to be, as men and women and Americans. ○

STANLEY CROUCH

Stanley Crouch was born in Los Angeles in 1945. He was still living there in the summer of 1965, when rioting broke out in Watts. On the West Coast, he acted in and wrote plays for community theater and then taught at the college level. He moved to New York City in 1975, where he played the drums in a jazz band for five years before becoming a staff writer for the *Village Voice*. Although he has retained an interest in both teaching and jazz, he continues to write, most notably as a Sunday columnist for the *New York Daily News*.

What he witnessed in Watts led Crouch to the black nationalist movement, but the works of Ralph Ellison and Albert Murray soon had him questioning black separatism. In "Goose-loose Blues for the Melting Pot" (published in 2004 in Tamar Jacoby's *Reinventing the Melting Pot*), he addresses one of his favorite themes: that the melting-pot metaphor is still an apt one for U.S. culture.

Crouch has published several collections of essays, including *The All-American Skin Game, or the Decay of Race* (1995) and *The Artificial White Man* (2004), and a novel, *Don't the Moon Look Lonesome?* (2000). In 1993 he received both the Jean Stein Award from the American Academy of Arts and Letters and a MacArthur Fellowship. He is writing a biography of jazz musician Charlie Parker.

SEEING

1. Crouch argues that "improvisation, . . . learning to absorb and invent on the spot" (para. 7) is a core component of the American character, fundamental to our facing and coping with the unknown. It has also played a role, he insists, in defining that character: "As the nation expanded through immigration and other means, it became equally necessary to improvise the idea of what it means to be American" (para. 9). Do you think this second function helps explain Crouch's dislike of "alienation studies"? If not, why not? Do you think there is a time frame beyond which inventiveness ceases to be improvisation?

2. Compare Crouch's list of diverse American practices with Amy Tan's description of her family's Christmas Eve dinner in "Fish Cheeks" (page 261). How do their views about assimilation differ? How are they the same? Using evidence from their work, consider each author's personal history and discuss how that history might have influenced his or her stance.

WRITING

1. Crouch writes that "our deeply American humanity triumphed over even the most divisive kinds of violence and xenophobic murder" (para. 32). Why do you think he uses the word *American* to modify *humanity* in this sentence? What is he implying about the relationship between American values and those of the rest of the world? Write a brief story in which you imagine that one of the crimes Crouch describes takes place in a foreign country. How does the change in location change your assumptions about how the incident would be reported and handled?

2. In paragraph 17 Crouch writes that it was a bitter mid-1960s joke that "blacks would have made it all the way into American society once a Negro could be shown in a deodorant commercial." Today, he claims "anybody can advertise anything." Think of a racial or ethnic group of people who could not be used to advertise a given product, or to advertise any product in a given context. (The product can be an object, a value or ideal, a political candidate or party, anything that can be promoted or sold.) Then write an essay in which you explain why.

Saira Wasim,
Pakistan

The Sept. 11 attacks not only shaped world politics—they also had a strong impact on the work of artists around the world. I wanted to portray the true feelings and basic needs of an ordinary man, one who wants peace, prosperity, and love. I took inspiration from Mughal court paintings that recorded for history the victories of the kings.

Friendship after 11 September 1 shows a new era of amity between Pakistan and the United States. It depicts President Bush embracing President Pervez Musharraf for helping him in the war against terrorism in South Asia. Beneath this, people in the two countries are celebrating the victory of peace and hope: The cow and the lion (symbols of strong and weak) are together. There is an American nation that is friendly and optimistic but has suffered from state terrorism and now wants to live in peace. And there is a Pakistani nation that is happy to be friends with this superpower, as it will open new opportunities and economic hope to a poor country. There are also the mullahs, who are oblivious about their own religion (Islam being a faith of peace and love). They are the ones who misinterpret their religion and manipulate the innocent public to commit violence in the name of jihad. They are never happy with this friendship, which is why they are portrayed as sad at this occasion.

It's time to realize that only love and friendship can save this world from all disasters.

Saira Wasim, *Friendship after 11 September 1, (2001),* from the series *Bush,* 2002
Gouache on wasli paper. Collection of Koli Banik.

Portfolio: The American Effect

Yongsuk Kang,
South Korea

After the Korean War, land on the west coast of South Korea, about 50 miles from Seoul, was set aside to be used for target practice by the United States military. Residents of these areas lost farmland and fishing grounds. Over the years they suffered other losses, too: Bombs missed their targets, causing damage to civilian areas. Despite all this, South Korea and the United States have refused to move the ranges.

The gray tones in my photographs are meant to convey distance and ambiguity. We aren't at war, but we aren't at peace, either. Traditionally, war photographs were meant to appeal to the viewer's sentimentality and to evoke emotion. My landscape photographs play a different role. They do not depict real warfare. They capture the remnants of military exercises. Though the United States is here to defend us, its exercises feel like an invasion. Without emotional intervention, I strive to expose the tragedy of contemporary South Korea. In these places, we see that the disaster of the Korean War has not yet ended.

Yongsuk Kang, *Untitled,* **from the series**
Maehyang-ri, **1999**
Gelatin silver print. Collection of the artist. Translated by Shim Chung from the Korean.

Miguel Angel Rojas,
Colombia

Among the United States' influences on Latin America, the seductive effect of American culture is well known. I remember the impact of first hearing *Rock around the Clock* by Bill Haley and the Comets when I was a child. The attraction of American cultural forms is perceptible in all levels of our reality, especially in our identity.

The art of the United States is no exception. For example, Pop Art—that rich, complex and imperturbably happy school—has prompted me to reflect on our own reality in Colombia and to examine the reciprocity of inter-regional relations. The production and trafficking of drugs like cocaine would not exist without demand. This ever-growing business has produced an underground flow of dollars, which has in turn given rise to another, more horrible trade: the trafficking of arms. What for some is merely a recreational habit, an addiction, is for others war, death, and displacement.

Bratatata is an appropriation of a Roy Lichtenstein war scene, *As I Open Fire*, that I constructed in cutouts from coca leaves. I want to make drug users and the law reflect on responsibility and on the need to find solutions to these seemingly insoluble issues.

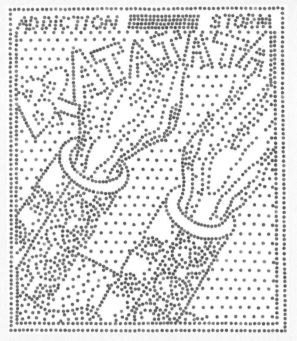

Miguel Angel Rojas, *Bratatata,* **2001 (detail)**
Coca-leaf cutouts on paper. Collection of the artist.

Andrea Robbins and Max Becher,
United States

For about 17 years, the primary focus of our work has been what we call "the transportation of place," situations in which one limited or isolated place strongly resembles another distant one. There are many reasons for these transpositions: colonialism, diaspora, war, migration, and emulation. We use our own backgrounds as starting points: One of us is German and came to the United States as a teenager (Max), the other grew up in a Jewish family in Marblehead, Mass. By locating personally familiar images in unfamiliar contexts, rather than seeking out the exotic, we hope to arrive at new meanings.

One area of particular interest to us is how American internal expansion has been sold through the figure of the gun-slinging cowboy, and how that myth has sometimes evoked unintended interpretations abroad. In Germany, for example, Karl May, the wildly popular late-19th-century novelist, helped write a German version of the Wild West in which the Indian is the protagonist. While many Americans grew up playing heroic cowboys and villainous Indians, many German children grew up playing the game with Indians as the heroes. The American cowboy myth was reinterpreted to fit local nostalgias and anxieties.

We photographed the phenomenon of Germans dressing up as Indians on weekends and at special festivals to capture what it looks like on the receiving end of an American projection. We are also asking how, in light of the Holocaust, Germans wound up identifying with the victims of American manifest destiny, rather than with its perpetrators. How could a people who waged an internal colonization within Europe less than 60 years ago, killing millions of people—Jews, Gypsies, gays, and people considered "asocial"—and banishing millions more to the four corners of the Earth, identify with native Americans, the victims of American imperialism?

Andrea Robbins and Max Becher, *Knife Thrower,* **from the series** *German Indians,* **1998**
Chromogenic color print. Collection of the artists; courtesy of Sonnabend Gallery, New York.

Alfredo Esquillo Jr., Philippines

The details of the American occupation of the Philippines were just things I had to memorize when I was in high school. They had nothing to do with my life or my future. I thought that the past was not all that important, as long as I remembered enough dates and names to get good grades in history. Little did I know how much all this would matter to me now—now that I am a visual artist trying to make sense of the ways in which Filipino society was robbed of its independence by colonial forces, and how these facts of our subjugation have been erased from our collective consciousness. History has much to say about how or what we are now: the English language, the Hollywood influence, the craze for American goods. All this has generated my urge to paint a postcolonial narrative.

MaMcKinley serves as a meditation on how American imperialism betrayed the Filipino people. The unmasking begins with an appropriation of an archival American mother and child portrait, recasting it so that the mother becomes President William McKinley, who in 1898 issued the Benevolent Assimilation Proclamation, which asserted United States control over the Philippines. The child becomes an innocent Filipino dressed in stars and stripes. However, under the hem of "Mama" McKinley's sleeves there is the hint of the barrel of a gun; her guardian hands turn into the threatening claws of an eagle.

The moral here cannot be ignored. The historical facts are bitter. Benevolent promises were made but precious lives were taken. What was the most remarkable part of the Filipino-American relationship: the handshake or the bloodshed? Especially now that terrorism has changed our lives, the past has to be reconsidered. While the painting portrays America as a colonizer with a deceiving attitude, and the Philippines as a helpless victim, it still begs for some positive result on the viewer and on society as a whole.

Alfredo Esquillo, Jr., *MaMcKinley*, 2001
Oil on canvas. Collection of Kim Atienza.

Danwen Xing,
China

Traveling between China and the United States has made me increasingly aware of the conflicts between modernity and tradition, dream and reality. These have become important themes in my work. My goal is to sketch a visual representation of 21st-century modernity. I carefully choose direct and intimate moments to portray the objects I find. The aesthetic quality of the imagery almost removes the photographed objects from their social context.

But I cannot forget that most of the e-trash I'm photographing is shipped from the United States and dumped in Guangdong Province, where people make a meager living recycling it. While we rely extensively on high-tech devices for our modern life, I was nevertheless shocked when I first confronted China's vast piles of dead and deconstructed machines, cords, wires, chips, and parts—all with the traces of America on them.

In my country, I have experienced the changes that have taken place under the influence of Western modernity. These changes, driven in large measure by the United States, have contributed to a strong and powerful push for development in China. At the same time, however, they have led to an environmental and social nightmare in remote corners of the country.

I hope by showing these photographs in New York, I can somehow bring the trash back to the United States, and bring home the fact of its existence to American audiences.

Danwen Xing, *Untitled,* **from the series** *disCONNEXION,* **2003**
Chromogenic color print. JGS, Inc., New York.

THE AMERICAN EFFECT

In June 2003, a *New York Times* article titled "How Do We Look?" previewed an exhibition at the Whitney Museum of American Art in New York City. The exhibition, which ran from July to October, was called *The American Effect.* Through the eyes of forty-seven global artists, it explored the way the world sees America.

Lawrence Rinder, curator of the exhibition, noted: "This show carries on the Whitney's longtime commitment to illuminating the times in which we live. America has a profound influence on the daily lives of the world's citizens, and the image of the United States has come to bear almost mythological weight. *The American Effect* is about the ways in which America's real and imagined effects intertwine to become a compelling source of themes, images, and ideas for artists around the world."

The Whitney Museum was founded by Gertrude Vanderbilt Whitney (1875–1942) in 1931. It collects and exhibits American art from the twentieth and twenty-first centuries. The museum's permanent collection includes more than 12,000 works and is still growing. It is the tradition of the museum to purchase art from living artists, often before they become well known, in an effort to maintain the foremost collection of American art.

SEEING

1. Consider Yongsuk Kang's claim that his images have no "emotional intervention." What kind of emotional intervention, if any, might the photograph shown here be said to have? What about the other images in this portfolio? Are these strategies reflected in the text accompanying each piece?

2. Influence can take many forms. How do the artists here define American influence in their work? in their words? For which artists is *influence* simply another word for "power"? What kinds of influence involve less power than others? How do the artists' feelings toward the United States reflect the level of power involved in America's influence in their countries? How are those feelings expressed through their art?

WRITING

1. Several of the artists here used their art to shock viewers; that is, they inserted something unexpected in their work. Were any of them successful? Did any of the works surprise you? How did you respond to those works whose artists were hoping to shock their audience? Choose a work that failed to surprise you—despite the artist's intention to shock—and then draft a brief essay explaining your reaction.

2. Each of the commentaries here was written for a specific audience—the readers of the *New York Times* op-ed page. In what ways do you think assumptions about those readers influenced what each artist was and was not willing to say about his or her work? Choose one piece of art and write a brief essay about it from the artist's(s') perspective for the artist's(s') hometown paper.

10 Questions College Officials Should Ask about Diversity

Robert Shireman

Now that the Supreme Court has upheld the use of affirmative action in college admissions, many observers are calling the ruling a victory for diversity. But issues concerning how to sustain and encourage diversity are far from settled on most campuses across America. Colleges still have to grapple with questions about the mix of students they enroll, the experiences those students have, and the academic and social progress they make.

Several years ago, the James Irvine Foundation, where I used to direct the higher-education program, decided to demand more of the 30 or so private colleges in California to which it had given grants to support diversity. Why? Progress in the enrollment of underrepresented minority students had stalled, and it was not clear whether efforts to improve the campus climate and deal with diversity in the curriculum were successful. In the early 1990s, after the first round of diversity grants, the number of minority students at those private institutions rose at a rate close to the rise in the proportion of minorities in the college-age population. But in the mid- and late 1990s, even though the elimination of affirmative action in the public sector had expanded the pool of potential private college students in the state, minority enrollment at grantee institutions barely budged and even declined on some campuses.

In response, we required colleges seeking grants to do self-assessments focused on diversity. We asked them to examine their own history and data related to diversity issues, as well as outside research, and to identify their strengths and weaknesses.

Some colleges completed impressive self-assessments on the first try, wrote proposals that focused on the key issues, and developed logical ways to assess progress. Others had an exceedingly difficult time figuring out how to evaluate their achievements and challenges. Often an institution would list the many diversity-related activities that it was engaged in: "A diversity council was formed"; "Twelve new courses were added"; "An African American admissions officer was hired"; "Student leaders participated in a racial-reconciliation workshop." We would then ask, "So what does it all add up to? How is the campus doing with regard to diversity?" In several cases, the response we got was simply a longer list of activities—just more detailed and perhaps organized differently.

Why has it been so difficult for colleges to 5 see the forest for the trees?

Foundations are part of the problem. They carry a virus called "projectosis," which causes them to look for projects to support and to ask how project A leads to outcome B—even though causation is almost always much more complicated than that. It is difficult for foundations to get out of project mode—and sometimes even more difficult for campuses because getting the money has always seemed so tied to the project.

What's more, some colleges are asking the wrong people to define the institution's diversity goals. At too many institutions, the special assistant for diversity, the development director, or a faculty member is charged with keeping foundations happy. But more often than not, those people simply don't have a broad enough view of the institution. To see the forest, they need significant guidance from above. When presidents and provosts take some responsibility for the overarching assessment and the vision for change, it makes all the difference in the world.

Even with leadership, however, it is not easy to put together a good self-assessment—especially with a diversity lens. So I'd like to suggest 10 key questions college officials should ask when evaluating their progress in diversity:

How do we define diversity? Although the Irvine Foundation was most interested in improving educational outcomes for students of color and from low-income families, we encouraged college leaders to examine diversity using a definition that makes sense for their own institutions. In many cases that will lead to an additional focus on gender, sexual orientation, religion, disability, or other factors.

In particular, colleges should analyze enroll- 10 ment and student success both by race and by "class" indicators like family income and the educational background of the parents—for several reasons. First, it can help a college determine the most effective approaches for obtaining greater diversity. For example, if an institution finds that it has a low retention rate for African American students, it should ask if such students come from lower-income families than do other students. If it turns out that low-income students of other races have similarly low retention rates, that may lead the college to look at how its financial-aid programs and other support systems help low-income students. However, if African American students have lower retention rates than other students of similar socioeconomic backgrounds, the institution might instead concentrate on improving the campus climate for black students.

Second, by focusing exclusively on race we may be feeding negative stereotypes. While achievement gaps by race are alarming, and ameliorating them must be a goal of our educational institutions, the real gaps are usually reduced when socioeconomic factors are included in the analysis. We must be more sophisticated in our thinking and consider race and class both separately and together.

Third, while not as visible as race and without the same disgraceful history, class is nonetheless an issue in America. We pretend that we are a society without class divisions because we like to think of America as a land of opportunity—a place where someone of modest means and without friends in high places can join the top tier of society through brains or brawn, and maybe a little luck. Perhaps the most important role of higher education is to make that national self-image a reality.

Why do we have this particular array of students? A college should evaluate who chooses the institution, and to whom the institution offers admission. The first part of the analysis should look at outreach: "What is the economic and ethnic profile of the high schools that we visited, the students whom we talked to, and the students who visited us?" Each institution should then compare the results to the profiles of those students who actually applied and enrolled. Although that may sound like basic enrollment management, it's amazing how often the various parts of a college can fail to work together. While one office is working furiously to redress a failure to increase the diversity of the student body, another is reaching out to the same group of predominantly white, high-income students that it always has.

Who gets financial aid? A president boasted in a newspaper about using institutional financial aid as a way to enhance his college's "reputation." He said that he gave away, for example, a $12,000 scholarship to a student who got an offer of only $2,000 from another institution. I don't know how much financial need she had, but if her major qualification was her grades, this large scholarship is questionable. Buying valedictorians in order to improve a college's reputation is like paying ringers to play on a Little League team. It is a cop-out. Instead of coaching our students to greatness, it's purchasing greatness.

However, if bringing valedictorians onto the 15 campus has an educational rather than reputational justification, then it may be a reasonable investment of some financial-aid money. As Thomas J. Kane, a researcher at the University of California at Los Angeles, points out, "Because a college's customers [students] are also contributors to their classmates' education," scholarships for talented students can be one strategy for ob-

taining a high-quality educational experience for a diverse class of students. The president who bought the valedictorian for $12,000 should be criticized for focusing on reputation rather than access and quality education. But his institution actually has a large enrollment of low-income students, and it is possible that their campus experience would benefit from a larger enrollment of less-needy, high-achieving students.

That is a good example where looking solely at a particular program or practice doesn't paint a complete enough picture. A holistic view is critical to understanding what is happening on a campus.

How successful are our students? Institutions need to ask which students are being encouraged to take leadership roles. Which undergraduates are faculty members approaching for participation in research projects? Which students are going on to graduate school?

It is also useful to look at the extent to which students of different backgrounds are concentrated in particular majors or are changing majors. During our campus visits, for example, a student told me that she had changed from economics to sociology because the latter was more supportive of diversity. We also heard complaints from students of color about faculty members who pushed them into, or away from, ethnic studies, and about counselors who encouraged them to pursue easy instead of more challenging majors. We heard of faculty members whose attitudes tended to turn off women more than men, or Latino more than non-Latino students.

Colleges should also examine who takes advantage of academic support services compared with who actually needs that support. If the data show significant gaps in achievement among groups, and that students with particular backgrounds are less likely to seek help when they need it, the campus should reach out to them.

What multicultural education are students 20 *receiving?* It is not enough to report that 30 new multicultural courses have been created or improved, and that minority students at a campus are happy with the curriculum. Colleges must be more explicit about the diversity-related content and developmental advances that they consider important and how they know their students are obtaining it.

One goal of a diversity requirement, for example, might be what Martha Nussbaum, a professor of law and ethics at the University of Chicago Law School, describes as the "capacity for critical examination of oneself and one's traditions." If that is the goal, how does the curriculum help obtain it? How does a student's own background affect his readiness for the curriculum? Which students is the curriculum reaching effectively, and which might require a different approach? Institutions should help students from various backgrounds find themselves in the curriculum, affirming their identity, but then move all students toward a common connection to humanity as a whole.

What does it feel like as a student to be here? At one campus I visited, a thoughtful student asked, "When will this be *my* campus, instead of someone else's campus that is trying to be a welcoming place for me?" In too many cases, the work that we have all done to deal with the issue of diversity has been much too shallow. Ethnic theme parties, films, and guest speakers can be important symbols, but they are a small part of what influences the campus climate.

Most important is what goes on in the classrooms—what is taught, how it is taught, and how people are treated. A professor who singles out the one Hispanic student in the classroom to provide "the Hispanic perspective" can undermine all of the other efforts to make her feel like an integral part of the campus rather than "other." It is critically important that colleges understand how the campus climate may be burdening some students more than others and not to accuse them of "causing" strife when they get the courage to raise the issues that concern them. What is needed is a more careful diagnosis of the problems, coupled with strategic interventions.

Who are our faculty leaders? Probably the most common conclusion among the colleges that the Irvine Foundation has supported has been that they need to do more to diversify their faculties. While any professor can be a role model for any student, it is difficult for students of color when there is virtually no one among the faculty members with whom they share their ethnic identity. The same has been true for women in some disciplines. Also, minority professors often bring perspectives to the curriculum that are less likely to come from other faculty members. In addition, the extent to which an institution attracts and retains faculty members of color indicates whether it has embraced diversity in more than a token way.

What are our relationships with nearby communities? Colleges generally cite the number of hours that students work in neighborhood schools, the activities that faculty members perform in the community, and the campus events to which the community members are invited. Although important, those activities help form the relationship, but they don't describe the relationship itself. How do community leaders view the college? Is the community a subject of research or an equal partner in solving problems? How would you know if the campus's relationship with various community groups was worsening?

Who is thinking about these issues on our campus? A couple years after we began requiring the self-assessments, we started asking colleges to give us a list of the people who worked on the document and a list of those who had read it. Just asking for those lists prompted institutions to do a better job involving various people throughout the institution—representatives from the faculty, student affairs, admissions, housing, community service, and sometimes even trustees and students. In many cases, the creation of the document started important conversations across various offices and constituencies.

What do we want to change, and how will we know that we have changed it? My favorite Yogi Berra quote is "You got to be very careful if you don't know where you're going, because you might not get there." Far too often, a college thinks it has made great progress but isn't able to celebrate and boast because there was no baseline and no assessment of the change. Other institutions can spend years doing the same thing and thinking it's making a difference, only to discover that it was ineffective or even damaging. The only way we will do better is if we know what we are trying to accomplish and learn from what we are doing.

In elementary and secondary education, under President Bush's No Child Left Behind program, schools are looking at how their low-income, black, and Hispanic students are performing compared with white students. They are making efforts to close those gaps and monitoring their progress. Educators on college campuses need to work at least as hard to assess student needs, intervene, monitor progress, and adjust their strategies. Only then will they be able to close achievement gaps and improve outcomes for students from all backgrounds. ○

ROBERT SHIREMAN

Robert Shireman is actively working to reform America's higher-education system to reach minority and underprivileged young men and women. In 2003 he became a senior fellow at the Aspen Institute, a global nonprofit "dedicated to fostering enlightened leadership and open-minded dialogue." He serves as the director of the Institute for College Access and Success, an independent nonprofit founded in 2004 to expand educational opportunities in America by promoting research-based programs and the responsible use of tax and charity dollars. In addition he is a visiting scholar at the University of California, Berkeley, Center for Studies in Higher Education.

During the Clinton administration, Shireman served as a senior adviser to the White House National Economic Council and was instrumental in reforming college aid, developing the America Reads and GEAR UP programs, and promoting investment in Hispanic education. In 2001 Shireman was appointed to a three-year term on the national board of the Fund for the Improvement of Postsecondary Education.

In addition to this article, which appeared in 2003 in the *Chronicle of Higher Education,* Shireman has written for the *New York Times* and the *Los Angeles Times.*

SEEING

1. Affirmative action encourages diversity in college admissions, but it leaves to the schools the responsibility for achieving and sustaining that diversity, and for defining the benefits of diversity. Based solely on the ten questions posed in this essay, what does Robert Shireman believe are the benefits of diversity? How does considering the entire text change your answer?

2. The following terms appear in Shireman's text: *African American, Latino, Hispanic, students of color.* How do these categories reinforce or undermine one another? What are the advantages—and disadvantages—of grouping students by race or ethnicity? How do you think these categories could be improved?

WRITING

1. Consider Shireman's first question: "How do we define diversity?" He notes the intersection of race and class, and argues that we should consider them "both separately and together" (para. 11). What other social categories do you think should be considered in the name of diversity? Imagine an organization or social group that is diverse in terms of both race and class but not in one of the categories you suggest. Draft an essay in which you explain the need for expanding the definition of diversity to include one or more of your suggested categories. In your work, also address any possible drawbacks of broadening the meaning of *diversity.*

2. Resistance to change is a fact of institutional life. What are the sources of that resistance in academic institutions? What aspects of colleges and universities promote change? Think of an institution—educational, economic, or political—with which you have been involved, and draft an essay about the ability or inability of that institution to pursue internal change.

Visualizing Composition: Audience

An awareness of the person—or people—for whom a text is composed is an essential ingredient of successful communication. We most often call this person "the reader." Each of us who seeks to communicate some idea to an audience needs to decide who our intended readers are, to address their needs and expectations, and to assess the effects on them of the compositional choices we make.

When we talk about the writer's need to be sensitive to an audience, we are speaking not only about the writer's ability to analyze the needs and attitudes of readers but also the ability to anticipate and therefore shape the readers' response. In effect, having a sense of audience is both a matter of the writer's adapting his or her purpose to suit the expectations of readers and a matter of the writer's knowing how to get readers to adapt themselves to his or her purpose.

Many students assume that they are writing solely to satisfy the expectations of their instructors. But writing assignments are also an opportunity to develop communication skills, to practice both accommodating the needs and expectations of actual readers and anticipating and directing the responses of implied readers. Such is the reader Nathaniel Hawthorne imagined in the preface to his novel *The Marble Faun* (1858): "that one congenial friend—more comprehensive of his purposes, more appreciative of his success, more indulgent of his short-comings, and, in all respects, closer and kinder than a brother—that all sympathizing critic, in short, whom an author never actually meets, but to whom he implicitly makes his appeal, whenever he is conscious of having done his best." As Hawthorne suggests, considering audience early in the writing process can be used heuristically to jump-start writing. Likewise, writers ought to avoid rigidity or premature closure in conceptualizing their audience, lest their ideas be stillborn.

Visa, *It's Your Life. How Do You Want to Spend It?*

Consider this advertisement for Visa credit cards. Who is the "you" being addressed? What attitudes and assumptions are embedded in the two sentences in this ad: "It's your life. How do you want to spend it?"? Write an expository essay in which you analyze the ability of the writer and designer of this ad not only to anticipate but also to manage the reader's response.

NICHOLAS D. KRISTOF

Believe It, or Not

Today marks the Roman Catholics' feast of the Assumption, honoring the moment that they believe God brought the Virgin Mary into Heaven. So here's a fact appropriate for the day: Americans are three times as likely to believe in the Virgin Birth of Jesus (83 percent) as in evolution (28 percent).

So this day is an opportunity to look at perhaps the most fundamental divide between America and the rest of the industrialized world: faith. Religion remains central to American life, and is getting more so, in a way that is true of no other industrialized country, with the possible exception of South Korea.

Americans believe, 58 percent to 40 percent, that is is necessary to believe in God to be moral. In contrast, other developed countries overwhelmingly believe that it is not necessary. In France, only 13 percent agree with the U.S. view....

The faith in the Virgin Birth reflects the way American Christianity is becoming less intellectual and more mystical over time. The percentage of Americans who believe in the Virgin Birth actually rose five points in the latest poll.

My grandfather was fairly typical of his generation: 5 A devout and active Presbyterian elder, he nonetheless believed firmly in evolution and regarded the Virgin Birth as a pious legend. Those kinds of mainline Christians are vanishing, replaced by evangelicals. Since 1960, the number of Pentecostalists has increased fourfold, while the number of Episcopalians has dropped almost in half.

The result is a gulf not only between America and the rest of the industralized world, but a growing split at home as well. One of the most poisonous divides is the one between intellectual and religious America.

Some liberals wear T-shirts declaring, "So Many Right-Wing Christians...So Few Lions." On the other side, there are attitudes like those on a Web site, dutyisours.com/gwbush.htm, explaining the 2000 election this way:

> God defeated armies of Philistines and others with confusion. Dimpled and hanging chads may also be because of God's intervention on those who were voting incorrectly. Why is GW Bush our president? It was God's choice.

The Virgin Mary is an interesting prism through which to examine America's emphasis on faith because most Biblical scholars regard the evidence for the Virgin Birth, and for Mary's assumption into Heaven (which was proclaimed as Catholic dogma only in 1950) as so shaky that it pretty much has to be a leap of faith. As the Catholic theologian Hans Kung puts it in *On Being a Christian*, the Virgin Birth is a "collection of largely uncertain, mutually contradictory, strongly legendary" narratives, an echo of virgin birth myths that were widespread in many parts of the ancient world.

Jaroslav Pelikan, the great Yale historian and theologian, says in his book *Mary through the Centuries* that the earliest references to Mary (like Mark's gospel, the first to be written, or Paul's letter to the Galatians) don't mention anything unusual about the conception of Jesus. The Gospels of Matthew and Luke do say Mary was a virgin, but internal evidence suggests that that part of Luke, in particular, may have been added later by someone else (it is written, for example, in a different kind of Greek than the rest of that gospel).

Yet despite the lack of scientific or historical evi- 10 dence, and despite the doubts of Biblical scholars, America is so pious that not only do 91 percent of Christians say they believe in the Virgin Birth, but so do an astonishing 47 percent of U.S. non-Christians.

I'm not denigrating anyone's beliefs. And I don't pretend to know why America is so much more infused with religious faith than the rest of the world. But I do think that we're in the middle of another religious Great Awakening, and that while this may bring spiritual comfort to many, it will also mean a growing polarization within our society.

But mostly, I'm troubled by the way the great intellectual traditions of Catholic and Protestant churches alike are withering, leaving the scholarly and religious worlds increasingly antagonistic. I worry partly because of the time I've spent with self-satisfied and unquestioning mullahs and imams, for the Islamic world is in crisis today in large part because of a similar drift away from a rich intellectual tradition and toward the mystical. The heart is a wonderful organ, but so is the brain. ○

NICHOLAS D. KRISTOF

Born in rural Oregon in 1959, Nicholas D. Kristof graduated Phi Beta Kappa from Harvard University and then studied law at Oxford University on a Rhodes Scholarship. After school, Kristof financed his travels all over the world by writing articles. He learned many languages, including Arabic, Chinese, and Japanese. In 1984 he joined the *New York Times,* first as an economics correspondent and then as a business correspondent based in Los Angeles, Hong Kong, Beijing, and Tokyo. In 1990 he and his wife, Sheryl WuDunn, also a *Times* reporter, won a Pulitzer Prize for their coverage of Tiananmen Square and China's democracy movement. That year they also shared the George Polk and the Overseas Press Club awards for international reporting.

In 2000 Kristof covered George W. Bush's campaign for the presidency, and he authored the chapter on Bush in *The Presidents: A Reference History* (2002; edited by Henry F. Graff). In 2001 Kristof was appointed to a special post at the *New York Times* to cover the aftermath of the September 11 attacks. Today he writes op-ed columns for the *Times* every Wednesday and Saturday. The essay here originally appeared on August 15, 2003.

Kristof and WuDunn have published two books: *China Wakes: The Struggle for the Soul of a Rising Power* (1994) and *Thunder from the East: Portrait of a Rising Asia* (2000).

SEEING

1. Kristof musters a number of statistics and anecdotes to support his assertion that "one of the most poisonous divides is the one between intellectual and religious America" (para. 6). Which do you think does a better job of supporting this statement—the statistics or the anecdotes? Why? Which of the statistics or anecdotes do you find most problematic, the least believable? Are there any you find more troubling or comforting than others?

2. Kristof acknowledges a divide between America and the rest of the world, but admits that he can't "pretend to know why America is so much more infused with religious faith than the rest of the world" (para. 11). Using Kristof's statistics, suggest several reasons why this might be so.

WRITING

1. The content of Kristof's essay clearly positions him on the side of the intellectual in the intellect-versus-religion debate; so do the form and structure of the essay. Draft an essay arguing in support of the increasing religiosity in American society. Pay particular attention to the form of your argument. To what extent are your claims in the same category as those made by Kristof? Why or why not?

2. Take a moment to look through Gueorgui Pinkhassov's portfolio of pictures in Chapter 1 (pages 74–85). Which of the images most closely corresponds to your idea of prayer? Which is the furthest from your experience? Draft an essay in which you address your feelings about the least familiar form of prayer. Do you feel in that distance one of the divides Kristof discusses? Explain your answer.

See pages 74–85.

Context: Kristof

On August 14, 2003, the day before "Believe It, or Not" appeared on the op-ed page of the *New York Times,* Nicholas D. Kristof made the following statement on the *Times* web site (nytimes.com/kristofresponds, post #142): "I want to emphasize that my point isn't to mock anyone's beliefs. As Kant noted, matters of faith cannot be proved or disproved; they belong in a separate realm. I'm simply trying to explore this gulf between the U.S. and the rest of the industrialized world, and also caution about the growing antagonism between the religious and intellectual realms."

Reprinted here are two of the Harris polls Kristof cites in the op-ed essay, a report on a Pew Research Center poll, and a geographic breakdown of religious adherents in the United States in 2000 prepared by the Association of Statisticians of American Religious Bodies. What other research on U.S. and global religious and moral beliefs can you find? Which studies do you find most helpful? Why? In what specific ways do your findings confirm or contradict what Kristof sees as a growing divide "between intellectual and religious America"?

THE HARRIS POLL #41, AUGUST 12, 1998

TABLE 1: BELIEF IN GOD AND OTHER SUPERNATURAL FORCES, PLACES, AND EVENTS

"I will read you a list of things some people believe in. Please say for each one if you believe in it, or not."

	1994 (%)	*July 1998 (%)	*All Christians (%)	All non-Christians (%)
God	95	94	99	69
Heaven	90	89	96	57
The resurrection of Christ	87	88	96	49
Survival of the soul after death	84	84	90	60
Miracles	81	86	90	66
The Virgin birth (Jesus born of Mary)	78	83	91	47
The devil	72	73	79	40
Hell	71	73	80	40
Astrology	37	37	37	37
Ghosts	36	35	34	41
Reincarnation (that you were once another person)	N/A	23	22	32

* All Adults

TABLE 2: WHERE WILL YOU GO WHEN YOU DIE?

Base: Those who believe in survival of soul after death (84%)

"When you die where do you think you will go—heaven, hell, purgatory, or somewhere else?"

	Total (%)	Yes (%)	No (%)
Heaven	76	79	48
Hell	2	1	6
Purgatory	4	5	2
Somewhere else	12	9	35
Don't know/refused	6	6	9

METHODOLOGY

This Harris Poll was conducted by telephone within the United States between July 17 and 21, among a nationwide cross section of 1,011 adults. Figures for age, sex, race, education, number of adults, and number of voice/telephone lines in the household were weighted where necessary to bring them into line with their actual proportions in the population.

In theory, with a sample of this size, one can say with 95 percent certainty that the results have a statistical precision of plus or minus 3 percentage points of what they would be if the entire adult population had been polled with complete accuracy. Unfortunately, there are several other possible sources of error in all polls or surveys that are probably more serious than theoretical calculations of sampling error. They include refusals to be interviewed (non-response), question wording and question order, interviewer bias, weighting by demographic control data, and screening (e.g., for likely voters). It is difficult or impossible to quantify the errors that may result from these factors.

These statements conform to the principles of disclosure of the National Council on Public Polls.

PEW GLOBAL ATTITUDES PROJECT, FROM "VIEWS OF A CHANGING WORLD," 2003

AGE AND SOCIAL VALUES

Just as young people are more comfortable than their elders with the pace of modern life, the two groups also hold very different views on social and religious issues. In many countries, there is a significant generation gap over homosexuality, the role of women in the workplace, and God and morality.

These differences are most pronounced on the question of whether society should accept homosexuality. In Japan, more than three-quarters of those under age 30 favor societal acceptance of homosexuality (77%); just a quarter of those age 65 and older agree (24%). In Poland, the differences are even starker. Six-in-ten Poles under age 30 believe society should accept homosexuality. The number holding that view declines among older age groups, to just 9% of those 65 and older.

Age differences also influence opinion on whether both spouses should work. Poles under the age of 30 overwhelmingly favor both spouses working (82%–18%); those age 65 and older prefer the traditional marriage (62% favor just the husband working). In the U.S., those under age 30 favor both spouses working by three-to-one (73%–24%), while older people are much more divided (53%

favor just the husband working, 42% prefer both spouses work).

In most countries, age is less of a factor in attitudes toward God and morality. In the United States, majorities in every age category say belief in God is a prerequisite for morality, though younger Americans are somewhat less likely to express this opinion than those age 65 and older (53% vs. 68%). In Canada and Western Europe, majorities in every age group hold the opposite view, though in these countries as well, younger respondents are more likely than older people to say that belief in God is not a prerequisite for morality.

But opinion in Poland on God and morality is sharply divided along generational lines. Nearly seven-in-ten of those under age 30 (68%) say it is not necessary to believe in God to be moral, while 31% disagree. Among Poles age 65 and older, those numbers are practically reversed: 64% think belief in God is necessary for morality, compared with 34% who do not. (The question on homosexuality was not asked in China, Egypt and Tanzania; the question on God and morality was not asked in China, Egypt, Jordan, Lebanon and Vietnam.)

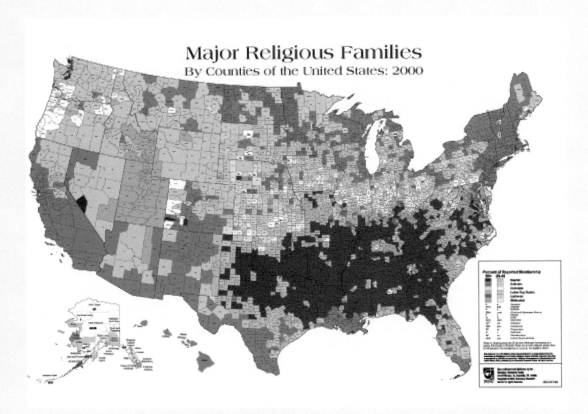

Major Religious Families

By Counties of the United States: 2000

Association of Statisticians of American Religious Bodies,
Religious Adherents as a Percentage of All Residents, 2000

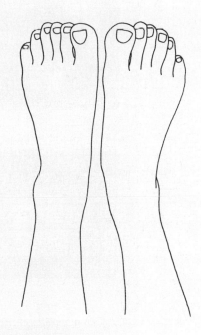

Roger Shimomura, *24 People for Whom I Have Been Mistaken*, 1999

24 People for Whom I Have Been Mistaken

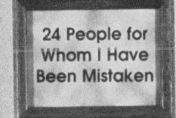

ROGER SHIMOMURA

Roger Shimomura is a sansei, the child of Japanese American parents. He was born in Seattle in 1939. After the bombing of Pearl Harbor, he and his family were forced into an internment camp. Shimomura graduated from the University of Washington with a degree in commercial design and earned an MFA from Syracuse University. Since the 1970s, he has been very successful at incorporating American pop art with traditional Japanese woodblock printing (*ukiyo-e*).

Shimomura's work often touches on his internment experience and on the xenophobia and racism he still encounters in America. Of being Japanese American he says: "My culture is not Japanese culture, it's this culture. . . . I don't live in Japan; I live in Kansas, but I don't live in Midwestern culture either; there are very few Asian Americans there. You could take it to the point where there is no culture. . . . Anyone who isn't like everyone else is seen as invasive; you live and die with that sense as a person of color in this country."

Shimomura addressed "racial insensitivity" directly in his 2003 exhibition, *Stereotypes and Admonitions,* which depicts racist incidents. The piece here, *24 People for Whom I Have Been Mistaken,* is composed of found photographs; it too reflects the challenges Shimomura has faced as a Japanese American.

SEEING

1. What do you notice about these images individually and as a group? What similarities and difference do you see? What would you describe as the characteristic shared most by those pictured? What does being mistaken for someone else mean? What social or cultural dynamics are involved?

2. Shimomura has said that "to most non-Asians in this country, the differences between the Japanese, Chinese, and other Asian people are either indistinguishable or immaterial." At first glance, which of the faces would you be most likely to mistake for one another? What particular features make them seem so alike? Which people would you be unlikely to mistake? What clues does your eye use to distinguish among the faces? Compare your answers with those of a classmate from a different race. How much does what you notice in the faces depend on your race? If your answer is "nothing," think about what led Shimomura to claim that differences among Asian people are indistinguishable to most non-Asians.

WRITING

1. Take a moment to look at each of the twenty-four images. Write one or two sentences describing the unique appearance of each of the people pictured. Then write a paragraph summarizing their common characteristics. Which task do you find more challenging? Why?

2. Whom have you been mistaken for? What about the experience made an impression on you? What has the experience revealed to you about what others assume about you? Write an essay in which you describe the experience of mistaken identity and its significance to you.

RESPONDING VISUALLY

Compose your own version of *24 People for Whom I Have Been Mistaken.* Choose photographs, clippings, or other found objects to create your own grid of images. Write a one-page artist's statement to accompany your work.

Reflecting Class

Class is the great unspoken word on most campuses in America. What you wear, what you say and how you say it, what you eat and how you eat it, where you work and what you do there, whether you watch television and what you watch on television—all are expressions of class. Class is, as Paul Fussell notes in his essay, "a touchy subject."

In its simplest sense, *class* refers to any group of plants or animals. But *class* is a complex word when it is used to refer to social distinctions. Raymond Williams noted in his classic study *Keywords: A Vocabulary of Culture and Society* (1976) that the "development of class in its modern social sense, with relatively fixed names for particular classes (lower class, middle class, upper class, working class and so on), belongs essentially to the period between 1770 and 1840, which is also the period of the Industrial Revolution and its decisive reorganization of society." From that point forward, the association of class with social and economic position became increasingly pronounced, and metaphors of mobility—the ability to move from one class to another—surfaced more often in American public discourse. The essays and images that follow offer provocative perspectives on a subject that each of us has learned how to read, reflect on, and think about—often without any formal instruction.

A Touchy Subject

Paul Fussell

ALTHOUGH MOST AMERICANS SENSE THAT THEY live within an extremely complicated system of social classes and suspect that much of what is thought and done here is prompted by considerations of status, the subject has remained murky. And always touchy. You can outrage people today simply by mentioning social class, very much the way, sipping tea among the aspidistras a century ago, you could silence a party by adverting too openly to sex. When, recently, asked what I am writing, I have answered, "A book about social class in America," people tend first to straighten their ties and sneak a glance at their cuffs to see how far fraying has advanced there. Then, a few minutes later, they silently get up and walk away. It is not just that I am feared as a class spy. It is as if I had said, "I am working on a book urging the beating to death of baby whales using the dead bodies of baby seals." Since I have been writing this book I have experienced many times the awful truth of R. H. Tawney's perception, in his book *Equality* (1931): "The word 'class' is fraught with unpleasing associations, so that to linger upon it is apt to be interpreted as the symptom of a perverted mind and a jaundiced spirit."

Especially in America, where the idea of class is notably embarrassing. In his book *Inequality in an Age of Decline* (1980), the sociologist Paul Blumberg goes so far as to call it "America's forbidden thought."

Indeed, people often blow their tops if the subject is even broached. One woman, asked by a couple of interviewers if she thought there were social classes in this country, answered: "It's the dirtiest thing I've ever head of!" And a man, asked the same question, got so angry that he blurted out, "Social class should be exterminated."

Actually, you reveal a great deal about your social class by the amount of annoyance or fury you feel when the subject is brought up. A tendency to get very anxious suggests that you are middle class and nervous about slipping down a rung or two. On the other hand, upper-class people love the topic to come up: The more attention paid to the matter the better off they seem to be. Proletarians generally don't mind discussions of the subject because they know they can do little to alter their class identity. Thus the whole class matter is likely to seem like a joke to them—the upper classes fatuous in their empty aristocratic pretentiousness, the middles loathsome in their anxious gentility. It is the middle class that is highly class-sensitive, and sometimes class-scared to death. A representative of that class left his mark on a library copy of Russell Lynes's *The Tastemakers* (1954). Next to a passage patronizing the insecure decorating taste of the middle class and satirically contrasting its artistic behavior to that of some more sophisticated classes, this offended reader scrawled, in large capitals, "BULL SHIT!" A hopelessly middle-class man (not a woman, surely?) if I ever saw one.

If you reveal your class by your outrage at the very topic, you reveal it also by the way that you define the thing that's outraging you. At the bottom, people tend to believe that class is defined by the amount of money you have. In the middle, people grant that money has something to do with it, but think education and the kind of work you do almost equally important. Nearer the top, people perceive that taste, values, ideas, style, and behavior are indispensable criteria of class, regardless of money or occupation or education. One woman interviewed by Studs Terkel for *Division Street: America* (1967) clearly revealed her class as middle both by her uneasiness about the subject's being introduced and by her instinctive recourse to occupation as the essential class criterion. "We have right on this street almost every class," she said. "But I shouldn't say class," she went on, "because we don't live in a nation of classes." Then, the occupational criterion: "But we have janitors living on the street, we have doctors, we have businessmen, CPAs."

Being told that there are no social classes in the 5 place where the interviewee lives is an old experience for sociologists. "'We don't have classes in our town' almost invariably is the first remark recorded by the investigator," reports Leonard Reissman, author of *Class in American Life* (1959). "Once that has been uttered and is out of the way, the class divisions in the town can be recorded with what seems to be an amazing degree of agreement among the good citizens of the community." The novelist John O'Hara made a whole career out of probing into this touchy subject, to which he was astonishingly sensitive. While still a boy, he was noticing that in the Pennsylvania town where he grew up, "older people do not treat others as equals."

Class distinctions in America are so complicated and subtle that foreign visitors often miss the nuances and sometimes even the existence of a class structure. So powerful is "the fable of equality," as Frances Trollope called it when she toured America in 1832, so embarrassed is the government to confront the subject—in the thousands of measurements pouring from its bureaus, social class is not officially recognized—that it's easy for visitors not to notice the way the class system works. A case in point is the experience of Walter Allen, the British novelist and literary critic. Before he came over here to teach at a college in the 1950s, he imagined that "class scarcely existed in America, except, perhaps, as divisions between ethnic groups or successive waves of immigrants." But living a while in Grand Rapids opened his eyes: There he learned of the snob power of New England and the pliability of the locals to the long-wielded moral and cultural authority of the old families.

Some Americans viewed with satisfaction the failure of the 1970s TV series *Beacon Hill,* a drama of high society modeled on the British *Upstairs, Downstairs,* comforting themselves with the belief that this venture came to grief because there is no class system here to sustain interest in it. But they were mistaken. *Beacon Hill* failed to engage American viewers because it focused on perhaps the least interesting place in the indigenous class structure, the quasi-aristocratic upper class. Such a dramatization might have done better if it had dealt with places where everyone recognizes interesting class collisions occur—the place where the upper-middle class meets the middle and resists its attempted incursions upward, or where the middle class does the same to the classes just below it.

If foreigners often fall for the official propaganda of social equality, the locals tend to know what's what, even if they feel some uneasiness talking about it. When the acute black from the South asserts of an ambitious friend that "Joe can't class with the big folks," we feel in the presence of someone who's attended to actuality. Like the carpenter who says: "I hate to say there are classes, but it's just that people are more comfortable with people of like backgrounds." His grouping of people by "like backgrounds," scientifically uncertain as it may be, is nearly as good a way as any to specify what it is that distinguishes one class from another. If you feel no need to explicate your allusions or in any way explain what you mean, you are probably talking with someone in your class. And that's true whether you're discussing the Rams and the Forty-Niners, RVs, the House (i.e., Christ Church, Oxford), Mama Leone's, the Big Board, "the Vineyard," "Baja," or the Porcellian.

In *Class: A Guide through the American Status System,* I am going to deal with some of the visible and audible signs of social class, but I stick largely with those that reflect choice. That means that I do not consider matters of race, or, except now and then, religion or politics. Race is visible, but it is not chosen. Religion and politics, while usually chosen, don't show, except for the occasional front-yard shrine or car bumper sticker. When you look at a person you don't see "Roman Catholic" or "liberal": You see "hand-painted necktie" or "crappy polyester shirt"; you hear *parameters* or *in regards to.* In attempting to make sense of indicators like these, I have been guided by perception and feel rather than by any method that could be deemed "scientific," believing with Arthur Marwick, author of *Class: Image and Reality* (1980), that "class ... is too serious a subject to leave to the social scientists."

It should be a serious subject in America especially, [10] because here we lack a convenient system of inherited titles, ranks, and honors, and each generation has to define the hierarchies all over again. The society changes faster than any other on Earth, and the American, almost uniquely, can be puzzled about where, in the society, he stands. The things that conferred class in the 1930s—white linen golf knickers, chrome cocktail shakers, vests with white piping—are, to put it mildly, unlikely to do so today. Belonging to a rapidly changing rather than a traditional society, Americans find Knowing Where You Stand harder than do most Europeans. And a yet more pressing matter, Making It, assumes crucial importance here. "How'm I doin?" Mayor Koch of New York used to bellow, and most of his audience sensed that he was, appropriately, asking the representative American question.

It seems no accident that, as the British philosopher Anthony Quinton says, "The book of etiquette in its modern form ... is largely an American product, the great names being Emily Post ... and Amy Vanderbilt." The reason is that the United States is preeminently the venue of newcomers, with a special need to place themselves advantageously and to get on briskly. "Some newcomers," says Quinton, "are geographical, that is, immigrants; others are economic, the newly rich; others again chronological, the young." All are faced with the problem inseparable from the operations of a mass society, earning respect. The comic Rodney Dangerfield, complaining that he don't get none, belongs to the same national species as that studied by John Adams, who says, as early as 1805: "The rewards ... in this life are *esteem* and *admiration* of others—the punishments are *neglect* and *contempt.* ... The desire of the esteem of others is as real a want of nature as hunger—and the neglect and contempt of the world as severe a pain as the gout or stone. ... " About the same time the Irish poet Thomas Moore, sensing the special predicament Americans were inviting with the egalitarian Constitution, described the citizens of Washington, D.C., as creatures

born to be slaves, and struggling to be lords.

Thirty years later, in *Democracy in America,* Alexis de Tocqueville put his finger precisely on the special problem of class aspiration here. "Nowhere," he wrote, "do citizens appear so insignificant as in a democratic nation." Nowhere, consequently, is there more strenuous effort to achieve—earn would probably not be the right word—significance. And still later in the nineteenth century, Walt Whitman, in *Democratic Vistas* (1871), perceived that in the United States, where the form of government promotes a condition (or at least an illusion) of uniformity among the citizens, one of the unique anxieties is going to be the constant struggle for individual self-respect based upon social approval. That is, where everybody is somebody, nobody is anybody. In a recent Louis Harris poll, "respect from others" is what 76 percent of respondents said they wanted most. Addressing prospective purchasers of a coffee table, an ad writer recently spread before them this most enticing American vision: "Create a rich, warm, sensual allusion to your own good taste that will demand respect and consideration in every setting you care to imagine."

The special hazards attending the class situation in America, where movement appears so fluid and where the prizes seem available to anyone who's lucky, are disappointment, and, following close on that, envy. Because the myth conveys the impression that you can readily earn your way upward, disillusion and bitterness are particularly strong when you find yourself trapped in a class system you've been half persuaded isn't important. When in early middle life some people discover that certain limits have been placed on their capacity to ascend socially by such apparent irrelevancies as heredity, early environment, and the social class of their immediate forebears, they go into something like despair, which, if generally secret, is no less destructive.

De Tocqueville perceived the psychic dangers. "In democratic times," he granted, "enjoyments are more intense than in the ages of aristocracy, and the numbers of those who partake in them is vastly larger." But, he added, in egalitarian atmospheres "man's hopes and desires are oftener blasted, the soul is more stricken and perturbed, and care itself more keen."

And after blasted hopes, envy. The force of sheer class envy behind vile and even criminal behavior in this country, the result in part of disillusion over the official myth of classlessness, should never be underestimated. The person who, parking his attractive car in a large city, has returned to find his windows smashed and his radio aerial snapped off will understand what I mean. Speaking in West Virginia in 1950, Senator Joseph R. McCarthy used language that leaves little doubt about what he was really getting at—not so much "Communism" as the envied upper-middle and upper classes. "It has not been the less fortunate or members of minority groups who have been selling this nation out," he said, "but rather those who have had all the benefits, the finest homes, the finest college education. . . ." Pushed far enough, class envy issues in revenge egalitarianism, which the humorist Roger Price, in *The Great Roob Revolution* (1970), distinguishes from "democracy" thus: "Democracy demands that all of its citizens begin the race even. Egalitarianism insists that they all *finish* even." Then we get the situation satirized in L. P. Hartley's novel *Facial Justice* (1960), about "the prejudice against good lucks" in a future society somewhat like ours. There, inequalities of appearance are redressed by government plastic surgeons, but the scalpel isn't used to make everyone beautiful—it's used to make everyone plain.

Despite our public embrace of political and judicial 15 equality, in individual perception and understanding—much of which we refrain from publicizing—we arrange things vertically and insist on crucial differences in value. Regardless of what we say about equality, I think everyone at some point comes to feel like the Oscar Wilde who said, "The brotherhood of man is not a mere poet's dream: it is a most depressing and humiliating reality." It's as if in our heart of hearts we don't want agglomerations but distinctions. Analysis and separation we find interesting, synthesis boring.

Although it is disinclined to designate a hierarchy of social classes, the federal government seems to admit that if in law we are all equal, in virtually all other ways we are not. Thus the eighteen grades into which it divides its civil-servant employees, from grade 1 at the bottom (messenger, etc.) up through 2 (mail clerk), 5 (secretary), 9 (chemist), to 14 (legal administrator), and finally 16, 17, and 18 (high-level administrators). In the construction business there's a social hierarchy of jobs, with "dirt work," or mere excavation, at the bottom; the making of sewers, roads, and tunnels in the middle; and work on buildings (the taller, the higher) at the top. Those who sell "executive desks" and related office furniture know that they and their clients agree on a rigid "class" hierarchy. Desks made of oak are at the bottom, and those of walnut are next. Then, moving up, mahogany is, if you like, "upper middle class," until we arrive, finally, at the apex: teak. In the army, at ladies' social functions, pouring the coffee is the prerogative of the senior officer's wife because, as the ladies all know, coffee outranks tea.

There seems no place where hierarchical status-orderings aren't discoverable. Take musical instruments. In a symphony orchestra the customary ranking of sections recognizes the difficulty and degree of subtlety of various kinds of instruments: Strings are on top, woodwinds just below, then brass, and, at the bottom, percussion. On the difficulty scale, the accordion is near the bottom, violin near the top. Another way of assigning something like "social class" to instruments is to consider the prestige of the group in which the instrument is customarily played. As the composer Edward T. Cone says, "If you play a violin, you can play in a string quartet or symphony orchestra, but not in a jazz band and certainly not in a marching band. Among woodwinds, therefore, flute, and oboe, which are primarily symphonic instruments, are 'better' than the clarinet, which can be symphonic, jazz, or band. Among brasses, the French horn ranks highest because it hasn't customarily been used in jazz. Among percussionists, tympani is high for the same reason." And (except for the bassoon) the lower the notes an instrument is designed to produce, in general the lower its class, bass instruments being generally easier to play. Thus a sousaphone is lower than a trumpet, a bass viol lower than a viola, etc. If you hear "My boy's taking lessons on the trombone," your smile will be a little harder to control than if you hear "My boy's taking lessons on the flute." On the other hand, to hear "My boy's taking lessons on the viola da gamba" is to receive a powerful signal of class, the kind attaching to antiquarianism and museum, gallery, or "educational" work. Guitars (except when played in "classical"— that is, archaic—style) are low by nature, and that is why they were so often employed as tools of intentional class degradation by young people in the 1960s and '70s. The guitar was the perfect instrument for the purpose of signaling these young people's flight from the upper-middle and middle classes, associated as it is with Gypsies, cowhands, and other personnel without inherited or often even earned money and without fixed residence.

The former Socialist and editor of the *Partisan Review* William Barrett, looking back thirty years, concludes that "the Classless Society looks more and more like a Utopian illusion. The socialist countries develop a class structure of their own," although there, he points out, the classes are very largely based on bureaucratic toadying. "Since we are bound . . . to have classes in any case, why not have them in the more organic, heterogeneous and variegated fashion" indigenous to the West? And since we have them, why not know as much as we can about them? The subject may be touchy, but it need not be murky forever. ○

JANUARY 3, 2005

The Nation

www.thenation.com

$2.95
$3.95 Canada

DOWN AND OUT IN DISCOUNT AMERICA
by LIZA FEATHERSTON

WAL★MART
MARY SUE
Our People Make The... Difference
CASH

This is affluent America.

This picture is about having everything I want.

I don't have to struggle - but I want to struggle.

I wish I could say I was interested in changing the human condition, but everything I see tells me nothing will work especially if it gets in the way of my happiness

Michael Mindel

This picture says that WE ARE a VERY Emotional & tight family, like the THREE MUSKETEERS.

Poverty sucks, but it brings us closer together. *Linda Benbo*

My dream Was to became a skool teacher.
Mrs Stone is rich.
I have talents but not opportunity.
I ~~two~~ am used to standing behind
Mrs Stone.
I have been a servant for 40 years.
Vickie Figueroa.

National Museum of the Middle Class Opens in Schaumburg, IL

SCHAUMBURG, IL—The Museum of the Middle Class, featuring historical and anthropological exhibits addressing the socioeconomic category that once existed between the upper and lower classes, opened to the public Monday.

"The splendid and intriguing middle class may be gone, but it will never be forgotten," said Harold Greeley, curator of the exhibit titled "Where the Streets Had Trees' Names." "From their weekend barbecues at homes with backyards to their outdated belief in social mobility, the middle class will forever be remembered as an important part of American history."

Museum guests expressed delight over the traditions and peculiarities of the middle class, a group once so prevalent that entire TV networks were programmed to satisfy its hunger for sitcoms.

Above: A waitress from Chicago learns what the middle class was.

"It's fascinating to think that these people once drove the same streets as we do today," said Natasha Ohman, a multimillionaire whose husband's grandfather invented the trigger-safety lock on handguns. "I enjoyed learning how the middle class lived, what their customs were, and what sorts of diversions and entertainment they enjoyed. Being part of this middle class must have been fascinating!"

During the modern industrial age, the middle class grew steadily, reaching its heyday in the 1950s, when its numbers soared into the tens of millions. According to a study commissioned by the U.S. Census Bureau, middle-class people inhabited great swaths of North America, with settlements in the Great Plains, the Rocky Mountains, the Pacific Northwest, and even the nation's urban centers.

"No one predicted the disappearance of the middle class," said Dr. Bradford Elsby, a history professor at the University of Pennsylvania. "The danger of eliminating workers' unions, which had protected the middle class from its natural predators for years, was severely underestimated. We believe that removal of the social safety net, combined with rapid political-climate changes, made life very difficult for the middle class, and eventually eradicated it altogether."

One of the 15 permanent exhibits, titled "Working for 'the Weekend,'" examines the routines of middle-class wage-earners, who labored for roughly eight hours a day, five days a week. In return, they were afforded leisure time on Saturdays and Sundays. According to many anthropologists, these "weekends" were often spent taking "day trips," eating at chain family restaurants, or watching "baseball" with the nuclear family.

"Unlike members of the lower class, middle-class people earned enough money in five days to take two days off to 'hang out,'" said Benson Watercross, who took a private jet from his home in Aspen to visit the museum. "Their adequate wages provided a level of comfort and stability, and allowed them to enjoy diversions or purchase goods, thereby briefly escaping the mundanity."

Many museum visitors found the world-view of the middle class—with its reliance on education, stable employment, and ample pensions—difficult to comprehend.

Thirty-five Booker T. Washington Junior 10 High School seventh-graders, chosen from among 5,600 students who asked to attend the school's annual field trip, visited the museum Tuesday. Rico Chavez, a 14-year-old from the inner-city Chicago school, said he was skeptical of one exhibit in particular.

"They expect us to believe this is how people lived 10 years ago?" Chavez asked. "That 'Safe, Decent Public Schools' part was total science fiction. No metal detectors, no cops or dogs, and whole classes devoted to art and music? Look, I may have flunked a couple grades, but I'm not that stupid."

Others among the 99 percent of U.S. citizens who make less than $28,000 per year shared Chavez's sense of disbelief.

"Frankly, I think they're selling us a load of baloney," said laid-off textile worker Elsie Johnson, who visited the museum Tuesday with her five asthmatic children. "They expect us to believe the *government* used to help pay for college? Come on. The funniest exhibit I saw was 'Visiting the Family Doctor.' Imagine being able to choose your own doctor and see him without a four-hour wait in the emergency room. Gimme a friggin' break!"

While some were incredulous, others described the Museum of the Middle Class as "a trip down memory lane." William Harrison, a retired social worker with middle-class heritage, said he was moved to tears by several of the exhibits.

"You wouldn't know it to look at me, but 15 my parents were middle class," Harrison said. "Even though my family fell into poverty, I cherish those roots. Seeing that section on middle-class eating habits really brought it all back: the Tuna Helper, the Capri Sun, and the cookie dough in tubes. Oh, and the 2-percent milk and reduced-cholesterol butter spread! I was thankful for the chance to rediscover my past, even if the middle class *is* gone forever."

The Museum of the Middle Class was funded primarily by the Ford Foundation, the charitable arm of the Ford automotive company, which sold cars to the middle class for nearly 100 years. ○

Above: Several members of the upper class learn how people without yachts used to pass the time.

baby phat®

by

kimora lee simmons

129 PRINCE STREET NYC

NEW YORK · LOS ANGELES · MONTREAL

BABYPHAT.COM

Cartier's
Building
CARTIER BUILDING

Bruce Gilden, *Fifth Avenue*, 1984

6

READING ICONS

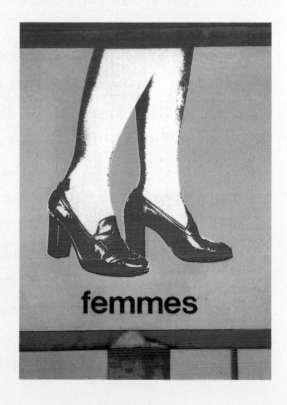

Carlos Mustienes, *Thailand*

hommes

femmes

Tom Ridgway, *France*

Open any newspaper or magazine, or simply turn on the television, and you will immediately encounter everything and everyone heralded as an icon—from blue jeans, Tupperware, the Nike swoosh, and pickup trucks, to Michael Jordan, Barbie, and Martin Luther King. Writer Russell Baker complains that the current overuse of the term *icon* has escalated to "epidemic" proportions. If we casually assign great leaders, celebrities, clothing labels, and automobiles iconic status, what has the term come to mean? And what reasonable inferences can we draw from our fascination with the term?

Perhaps the oldest association of the word is religious, the representation of a sacred figure. The word has also been used historically in natural history to refer to an illustration of a plant or animal, and in rhetoric to indicate a simile. This range in use—from the sacred and religious to the scientific and technical—has not only endured but expanded to the secular and the mundane.

At its most mundane, the word *icon* suggests a recognizable image or representation, something that stands for something else. In this sense one thing acts as a substitute or symbol for another. The signs

Neli Ruzic, *Mexico*

James Mollison, *China*

for men and women on doors to public restrooms, for example, are symbols that convey information: They tell us which door to enter. The thumbnail graphics on computer screens both communicate information about which programs are available and provide easy access to those programs.

Icon is also used to identify individuals who are the objects of attention and devotion, people who have taken on the status of an idol. Elvis Presley is a rock-and-roll icon; Michael Jordan is a basketball icon. When we say that Michael Jordan is an icon, we suggest that his image has worked its way into American culture so deeply that it now represents not only the excitement of professional basketball but also the American values of working hard, succeeding, and reaping the rewards.

Cultural commentator Aaron Betsky has described objects, people, and events as lenses through which to examine American culture. Icons, he says, are "magnets of meaning onto which we can project our memories, our hopes, and our sense of self." That may explain the proliferation of icons in contemporary society; and that "icons are all around us" may explain why the nature of icons has changed. Observes Betsky: "Part of our twentieth-century

Suse Uhman, *Morocco*

Ko Sui Lan, *Hong Kong*

Francesca Jacchia, *Hong Kong*

Rajesh Vora, *India*

Context: *American Gothic*

Americans have long been fascinated with copies, duplicates, and replicas of all sorts—counterfeits, mannequins, decoys, and, more recently, digital images, photocopies, even instant replays. Few works of American art are as celebrated—or as reproduced, imitated, and parodied—as Grant Wood's *American Gothic*. Viewing this painting might remind some of the immortal words of the legendary baseball star and hero of American folklore, Yogi Berra: "It's *déjà vu* all over again."

As Guy Davenport remarks in his analysis of Wood's *American Gothic,* this image has taken on an identity and status to which we have become "blinded by familiarity and parody" (para. 3). Like the *Mona Lisa, American Gothic* has been so often reproduced on T-shirts, postcards, and coffee mugs, as well as referenced—or alluded to—in the work of numerous painters, artists,

and writers, that it has assumed the status of an American cultural icon. Few works of American art are as celebrated . . . and less understood.

Consider, for example, Gordon Parks's photograph. What specific elements of Wood's painting does Parks repeat? With what effect(s)? How does he play off the tone and overall qualities of the painting?

Using the library and the web for research, identify other artists who have tried to reproduce the central image and distinguishing features of Wood's *American Gothic.* Then write an expository essay in which you demonstrate the extent to which Wood's image changes in the specific cultural contexts in which it is reproduced. Show how the original cultural and historical significance of the painting changes to make room for the cultural associations and meanings expressed by new generations.

Gordon Parks, *American Gothic,* 1942

She Can't Smile without You

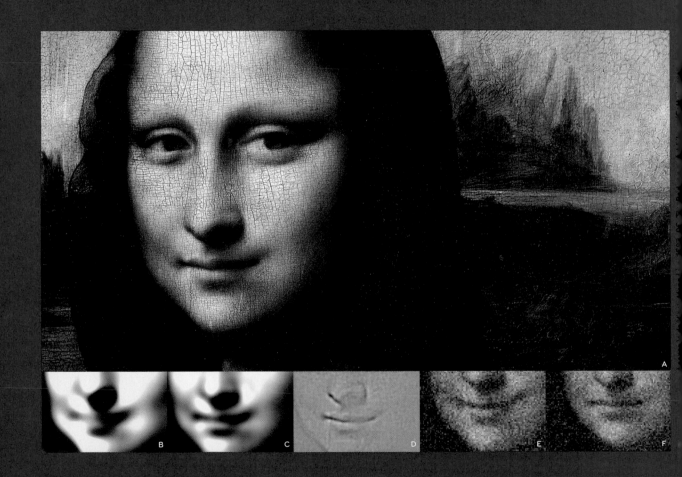

Kari Lynn Dean

The *Mona Lisa*'s half-smile is famously ambiguous. Is she grinning or grimacing? Art historians argue that her mercurial mouth is little more than Renaissance special f/x. Neuroscientists offer newer theories: It's about how your brain processes light—or how your eye perceives detail. Maybe all three explanations are right. Leonardo, as good a scientist as he was an artist, probably would have thought so.

Theory 1: Brush Strokes

Art experts credit sfumato, the brush technique da Vinci used to paint Mona's expression. From the Italian for "blended" or "smoky," *sfumato* refers to the use of featherlight strokes to apply layers of translucent color. The blended tones soften outlines, hazing the boundaries between Mona's lips and cheeks [A]. The shadows around the lips seem to pull up the corners of the mouth, suggesting a smile.

Theory 2: Fields of View

Mona's enigmatic expression may literally be in the eye of the beholder. "Look directly at her mouth—her smile disappears," says Margaret Livingstone, a Harvard neurobiologist. "Central vision does not perceive shadowy components well. Look at the eyes, seeing the mouth only with your peripheral vision, and her glorious grin becomes obvious." That's because the human eye's foveal, or central, vision is set up to best perceive detail (and is connected to a disproportionately larger chunk of the

brain's visual cortex); peripheral vision is optimized for broad visual strokes.

To illustrate the effect, Livingstone altered Mona in Photoshop. She used a Gaussian blur filter to emphasize the coarse [B] and medium [C] grains, to mimic how you'd see the painting out of the corner of your eye. Then she applied a high-pass filter to underscore the finer detail [D], isolating the dead-ahead view. The result: As detail increased, Mona's grin goes flat.

Theory 3: Mental Images

The human brain is wired to perceive emotion in facial expressions. But with millions of neurons clicking on and off, the brain is also intrinsically noisy. This neural static lends a normally imperceptible instability to what we see. And it can make Mona's face seem to flip from happy to sad, depending on what the noise distorts. The critical features: her lips and cheeks.

Researchers at San Francisco's Smith-Kettlewell Eye Research Institute tested the effect of the noise by overwriting a copy of Mona with random, computer-generated pixelation. In the images where the pixels accidentally enhanced the curvature at the corners of her mouth [E], observers saw Mona as happy. Images where the pixels got in the way of the curve, giving a straighter line [F], had the opposite effect. "It worked with a photo of my girlfriend, too," says vision scientist Leonid Kontsevich. "But she refused to have her picture published in the study."

KARI LYNN DEAN

Kari Lynn Dean is a correspondent for *Wired* magazine and a freelance writer. Her association with *Wired* began with an internship and then a job as an assistant research editor. Based in San Francisco, she writes primarily about technological advances in media and art and in politics, artificial intelligence, and environmental science. Dean's work includes a series on the 2004 recipients of MacArthur Fellowships, including Naomi Ehrich Leonard, a professor of mechanical and aerospace engineering who designs underwater robotic vehicles; Daphne Koller, a computer scientist who produces machine programs for learning; Vamsi Mootha, a biology professor and physician who identified the gene underlying a fatal metabolic disease; and James Carpenter, a designer and glass sculptor who is currently working with the architects of the new World Trade Center. Dean has also written about alternative fuels, algorithms, game-theory applications, and artificial intelligence for various publications.

In "She Can't Smile without You," first published in *Wired* in October 2004, Dean examines neurobiological explanations for Mona Lisa's smile.

SEEING

1. How do you read Mona Lisa's expression? As a grin or a grimace? How does your reading of her expression change the impact of the painting? That is, do the elements in the painting—the colors, the lighting, the shapes, the structure—come together as effectively whether she is smiling or not? Explain your answer.

2. According to the three theories Dean presents, something in the painting (brush strokes) or something in the viewer (a field of view or mental image) is responsible for how the picture looks. Which theory do you find most convincing? Why? Would *sfumato* (the brush technique) force you to see other subjects ambiguously? Why or why not? Closely follow your experience of looking at this reproduction of the picture. How well do the altered images in Dean's article capture your visual experience? Which ones work better than the others? What else might central vision and neural noise make ambiguous?

RESPONDING VISUALLY

Try to duplicate Mona Lisa's smile by painting, drawing, or simply tracing the picture. How well did your copy come out? What features were easy for you to replicate? Which ones were difficult? Now, given your own experience, do you think the painting should be judged a masterpiece? Why or why not?

WRITING

1. Some might call Mona Lisa's smile an optical illusion, an image that changes depending on how one looks at it. One of the most famous optical illusions is the duck–rabbit illusion (see facing page), a figure psychologist Joseph Jastrow first used in the late 1890s to show that perception is a function of both the image and the viewer's brain activity. How do you make yourself see one or the other image? For example, how do you go from seeing the duck to seeing the rabbit? Why can you see only one image at a time? Which image did you see when you first looked at the illusion? Write an essay in which you describe your initial response to the duck–rabbit drawing and your thoughts on why you saw one image before the other.

2. Cultural critic Joseph A. Harriss writes that "the *Mona Lisa* is in the paradoxical situation of being both the symbol of Art and the inspiration for kitsch. Artists vie to see who can do the most outrageous parody; advertising studios labor to come up with the funniest way to use the image to sell everything from aperitifs to airlines, golf clubs to strips that hold your nasal passages open." Research the history of the painting and its widespread reproduction in commercial and other popular settings. Then write an essay in which you support or refute Harriss' claim that the *Mona Lisa* is both a "symbol of Art and the inspiration for kitsch."

Joseph Jastrow, *Duck-rabbit*, 1890s

"Interestingly, children tested on Easter Sunday are more likely to see the figure as a rabbit, whereas when tested on a Sunday in October, they tend to see it as a duck." —mathworld.wolfram.com

What makes a symbol endure?

The automobile companies Karl Benz and Gottlieb Daimler founded in the late nineteenth century grew out of their individual work on the stationary gasoline engine. Benz built a three-wheeled bike around his engine; Daimler initially placed his engine in a carriage. By 1901 Benz & Cie had produced twelve hundred Velos, a lightweight two-seater, and had become "the world's leading automotive manufacturer." By contrast, Daimler-Motoren-Gesellschaft spent a number of years struggling to find its niche in the industry. Credited with the company's eventual success is Wilhelm Maybach, Daimler's longtime colleague, whose technical innovations would revolutionize carmaking. Maybach introduced the first Mercedes in December 1900, some months after Daimler died. It was developed at the urging of Emil Jellinek, a successful businessman who had begun selling DMG motor cars in Nice, France, in the late 1890s. The car was named for Jellinek's daughter.

In the economic slump following World War I, Benz & Cie and DMG were forced to merge, creating the company known as Mercedes-Benz. Having manufactured "the Car with the Star" for more than one hundred years (with temporary forays into military aircraft design), Mercedes-Benz is known for its engineering innovations and high-quality construction. Today Mercedes-Benz is a division of DaimlerChrysler AG, Europe's largest industrial manufacturer. The company sells cars in 190 countries.

(preceding pages) Mercedes-Benz, *What Makes a Symbol Endure?*, 1997

SEEING

1. Review each of the twenty-nine images depicted in this advertisement. How many can you identify immediately? Which ones do you consider to be icons? Why? What do the images have in common? In what ways do they differ? What aspects of contemporary American life do they represent? Are any significant aspects omitted? If so, identify them and explore the possible reasons for their omission.

2. Consider the copy that accompanies the ad's images. After identifying three of the icons, the writer reassures us that we can identify the images in "a split second" and that we "know exactly what they mean. Because right behind every powerful icon lies a powerful idea." What is the powerful idea behind each of the icons in the ad? What reasonable inferences about the Mercedes-Benz automobile can you draw from the "powerful ideas" the copy claims are associated with the Mercedes-Benz symbol?

WRITING

1. The advertisement says: "Our symbol has stood for all of these things for over a hundred years." Does it seem reasonable to infer that the writer equates the word *symbol* with the word *icon*? If so, why? If not, why not? How does the final line of the ad—"What makes a symbol endure?"—influence your thinking? To what extent is your response a reaction to the layout of the ad, which places this question alongside the carmaker's hood ornament? Does the text of the ad suggest a distinction between the icon (the Mercedes-Benz automobile) and the symbol (the hood ornament) chosen to represent it?

List all the meanings of icon that you can think of. Draft an essay in which you assert that *icon* and *symbol* are (or are not) terms that can be used interchangeably when talking about the images represented in contemporary culture.

2. In a 1996 article, *Investor's Business Daily* observed that "the automobile is a presence in our lives from birth until death, and the car has become a subject second only to love in our popular culture." Do you agree that the car serves as an icon for America? Write an essay in which you identify *the* American icon and explain why you've chosen it, giving specific cultural examples.

Lizzy Gardiner, 1995 Academy Awards

"I was looking for an American symbol," said Lizzy Gardiner about her choice of the American Express gold card to wear to the 1995 Academy Awards, where she accepted the Oscar for best costume design. "A Coca-Cola bottle or a Mickey Mouse would have been ridiculous, doing anything with the American flag would have been insulting, and Cadillac hubcaps were just too uncomfortable." How is the gold card an American symbol? What does it symbolize? Was was the overall effect of Gardiner's using it as the material for a dress at a Hollywood event?

Madonna Nursing the Child, c. 895

Master of the Virgin of Vysehrad, *Virgin and Child,* after 1355

Raphael, *Madonna del Granduca*, c. 1505

Lavinia Fontana, *Holy Family with Saints Margaret and Francis*, 1578

Ford Madox Brown, *Our Lady of Good Children*, 1847–1861

Fernand Léger, *Woman and Child*, 1921

Jean Cocteau, *Madonna and Child*, c. 1940s

Michael Escoffory, *A Child Is Born*, 1999

PASSING LIKENESS
Dorothea Lange's *Migrant Mother* and the Paradox of Iconicity

Sally Stein

Dorothea Lange's *Migrant Mother* is arguably the most familiar image from the Great Depression, haunting the nation and, in different ways, both the photographer and the picture's principal subject. Toward the end of her life, Lange was asked to write about her most famous photograph. She began that recollection by noting that some pictures take on a life of their own, overshadowing all the other pictures a photographer may consider to be equally, if not more important. Surely this image fits that description.[1]

Lange made the photograph at a migrant labor camp in Nipomo, California, in early March 1936, as part of her work documenting conditions of rural labor for the New Deal's Farm Security Administration (FSA). Within a few years, the FSA office used this photograph on an in-house poster to proclaim the multiple uses its growing file of government pictures served, for *Migrant Mother* had appeared in major newspapers and magazines, along with photography periodicals and museum exhibitions. In at least one installation photograph from the early 1940s, it already was being represented as worthy of special veneration and, for women, emulation. During and immediately following World War II, it seems to have been retired from active use. But it acquired new legs when its role was reprised for Edward Steichen's book and exhibition *The Family of Man* (1955), Beaumont and Nancy Newhall's book *Masters of Photography* (1958), and then Steichen's final MoMA exhibition and catalogue *The Bitter Years* (1962). As both social documentary and the populist politics of the Great Depression attracted the interest of the postwar generation coming of age in the 1960s, a wide variety of publications made frequent use of *Migrant Mother*. As a government picture in the public domain, it was readily available for minimal cost. Moreover, the picture's extensive prior usage only added to its serviceability as a shorthand emblem of both the depths of misery once widespread in this society and its heartfelt recognition by socially engaged New Dealers. Indeed, since the early 1960s, it has been reproduced so often that many call it the most widely reproduced photograph in the entire history of photographic image-making.

Celebrity, we know, attracts critics along with acolytes. It is no surprise, then, that this national icon of maternal fortitude has provoked an unending series of challenges to its documentary authenticity. As much as anyone, the photographer helped lay the groundwork for subsequent skeptics. Two years after Lange made the series that already was gaining exceptional notice, she borrowed the negative from the Washington office in order to make a fine enlargement for a traveling museum exhibition. With art on her mind, she temporarily took leave of her New Deal political senses and decided to have a corner of the negative

1. Dorothea Lange, "The Assignment I'll Never Forget." *Popular Photography* 46 (February 1960): 42.

Dorothea Lange, *Migrant Mother, Nipomo, California,* 1936. Gelatin silver print, 13½ x 10½ in. (34.3 x 26.7 cm). Oakland Museum of California, City of Oakland, the Dorothea Lange Collection, gift of Paul S. Taylor.

retouched. Since the picture had begun gaining special notice, Lange judged the intrusion of a thumb and index finger beside the tent pole to be an extraneous detail, detracting from an otherwise unified composition that was reminiscent of sacred Marian imagery. This embellishment of the picture may have led to her being fired, for one photographic historian has proposed that Lange's FSA boss, Roy Stryker, was so angered by her tampering with a government negative that he named Lange for termination when the FSA faced budget reductions at the end of the 1930s.[2]

Over time Stryker expunged this dispute from memory. In later years, he not only championed Lange's signal contribution to the file but also claimed that of all the thousands of FSA pictures *Migrant Mother* represented the apex of the documentary project.[3] But as the study of photography moved from an infancy of jubilant celebration to a more critical adolescence, others initiated their own investigations. Historian James C. Curtin questioned whether the presumed final picture was absolutely documentary; his reconstruction of the sequence of negatives she exposed in Nipomo demonstrates that Lange worked very selectively to achieve her portrait composition, in the process sacrificing any sense of location and even some family members.[4]

Feminists have brought other concerns to the reexamination of the picture. Cultural historian Wendy Kozol treated *Migrant Mother* as the quintessential example of the FSA traffic in conservative stereotypes. This modern version of the longstanding pictorial genre of mother and child, Kozol argues, chiefly served to reassure the public in the Great Depression that the most fundamental social unit—the nuclear family—was beleaguered but still strong.[5] Subsequent scholarship has extended this critique of the way *Migrant Mother* both drew upon gender conventions and in turn helped keep them in circulation, thereby perpetuating pictorial and social clichés. "Whatever reality its subject first possessed," literary historian Paula Rabinowitz declared, "has been drained away and the image become icon."[6] Some scholars contend more bluntly that study of Depression culture would benefit from shifting attention to less-celebrated pictures, preferably those depicting women engaged in wage work instead of preoccupied with domestic responsibilities.[7]

Despite these critical admonitions, not all have heeded the call to shelve this familiar photograph but instead have explored new avenues for comprehending the picture's persistent power. One lacuna in earlier discussions of *Migrant Mother* was the lack of any detailed information about the woman. Lange spent so little time making the photograph that she did not even record the name of her subject. By the time Lange died in 1965, she had come to think

2. F. Jack Hurley, *Portrait of a Decade: Roy Stryker and the Development of Documentary Photography in the Thirties* (Baton Rouge: Louisiana State University Press, 1972), pp. 142–43.

3. "To me it was 'the' picture of Farm Security," Stryker declared toward the end of his life. Quoted in Nancy Wood's introductory essay, "Portrait of Stryker," in Roy Emerson Stryker and Nancy Wood, *In This Proud Land* (Greenwich, CT: New York Graphic Society, 1973), p. 19.

4. James Curtis, "'The Contemplation of Things as They Are': Dorothea Lange and *Migrant Mother*," in James Curtis, *Mind's Eye, Mind's Truth: FSA Photography Reconsidered* (Philadelphia: Temple University Press, 1989), pp. 45–67.

5. Wendy Kozol, "Madonnas of the Fields: Photography, Gender, and 1930s Farm Relief," *Genders 2* (July 1988): 1–23.

6. Paula Rabinowitz, *They Must Be Represented: The Politics of Documentary* (London/New York: Verso, 1994), p. 87. Rabinowitz does not specify whether she means *icon* in the vernacular sense of shared cultural symbol, or in the more technical, semiotic sense of a sign that works by means of resonant likeness, or in the most traditional religious sense of an image meant for literal veneration, or some combination of these various meanings.

7. See the recent discussions of this image in Laura Hapke, *Daughters of the Great Depression: Women, Work and Fiction in the American 1930s* (Athens: University of Georgia Press, 1995), pp. 29–31; and Michael Denning, *The Cultural Front: The Laboring of American Culture in the Twentieth Century* (London/New York: Verso, 1996), pp. 137–38.

8. Bill Ganzel, *Dust Bowl Descent* (Lincoln: University of Nebraska Press, 1984), pp. 10, 30–31.

Bill Ganzel, *Florence Thompson and her daughters Norma Rydlewski (in front), Katherine McIntosh and Ruby Sprague, at Norma's house, Modesto, California*, 1979. Gelatin silver print, 11 x 14 in. (27.9 x 35.5 cm). Courtesy of the artist.

of her model as having only the generic name *Migrant Mother*. But in the 1970s, a younger generation of photographers began to revisit places and people already rendered historic by earlier documentation. In that spirit of rephotography, Nebraska-based photojournalist Bill Ganzel spent years tracking down people and locations photographed by the FSA. With the aid of a story in the *Modesto* (California) *Bee*, Ganzel located Florence Thompson and persuaded her and the same children to pose for him in 1979. The book that resulted from his wide ranging research was the first major publication to put a name to her face, yet in most other respects, the information supplied was sparse. Apparently wary of further national exposure, the family members offered only general remarks about the hard times they had survived.[8]

Ganzel's photograph offered a bit more information. For this unusual public portrait, Florence Thompson quietly displayed her own sense of style by donning white slacks and a white sleeveless top, adorned only by a Southwest-style squash blossom necklace. In itself, there is nothing conclusive about this detail; one response to the surge of Native American activism in the 1970s was the widespread fashion for silver-and-turquoise jewelry. But for Thompson it was a deliberate, if quiet, statement of identity. During the same period, this long-obscure celebrity made a point of acknowledging her Cherokee heritage in occasional interviews with news media. Thompson also volunteered that she always had resented the famed picture by Lange, and would never have allowed its being taken had she understood the way and the extent to which it would be used.[9]

But for more than a decade after her widely reported death in September 1983 and the national circulation of Ganzel's book in 1984, public information about Florence Thompson consisted largely of a proper name. Then, in the early 1990s, Geoffrey Dunn, a freelance journalist and University of California doctoral student, resolved to reconstruct her life story. Extensive interviews with surviving members of the family left him shocked by the gulf between her actual situation and the minimal details Lange had recorded. The varied details of Thompson's life that Dunn pieced together for this first biographical essay were no less stunning than his overriding conclusion of the photograph's betrayal of its immediate subject.[10]

When her path crossed that of Lange's in March 1936, Florence Owens was thirty-two years old. Born Florence Leona Christie in September 1903, she grew up in the Indian Territory of the Cherokee Nation to which both her parents claimed blood rights. Her biological father left her mother before she was born, and her mother soon married a man who did not think of himself as Indian (though his children later came to think that he may have been of part-Choctaw descent). Throughout her youth, Florence believed her mother's second husband to be her biological father. Thus, although she grew up in Indian Territory, she did not identify herself as "pure" Cherokee. In 1921, at the age of seventeen, she married Cleo Owens, a farmer's son from Missouri, and over the next decade they proceeded to have five children.

Oklahoma in the first decades of the twentieth century bore little relation to the locale envisioned in the popular World War II–era musical. The long-running Broadway show simply eradicated the Indian presence and prior claim to the land, while suggesting unlimited opportunities for all newcomers. The historical record is more dramatic. Following the white land rush at the turn of the twentieth century that had been precipitated by the forced allotment system of the federally enacted Dawes Plan, opportunities to homestead turned cutthroat: "Of the thirty million allotted acres more than twenty-seven million passed from Indians to whites by fraudulent deeds, embezzlement, and murder."[11] Florence and Cleo Owens saw no chance of farming on their own, so by the mid-twenties they opted to move west, finding work and temporary housing in the sawmill camps of California's Hill Country. By 1931, they were expecting a sixth child in northern California when Cleo Owens died of tuberculosis.

9. One such news story circulated by Associated Press appeared in the *Los Angeles Times,* Saturday, II:1 (November 18, 1978), as cited and reproduced in Martha Rosler, *Three Works* (Halifax: Press of the Nova Scotia College of Art and Design, 1981), pp. 67, 75–76.

10. Geoffrey Dunn, "Photographic License," *Santa Clara Metro* 10:47 (January 19–25, 1995): 20–24.

11. Gerald Vizenor, "Manifest Manners," in *American Indian Persistence and Resurgence,* ed. Karl Kroeber (Durham: Duke University Press, 1994), p. 233: Vizenor quotes from the extensive research of lawyer and historian Rennard Strickland's meticulous demographic research in his book *The Indians in Oklahoma* (Norman: University of Oklahoma Press, 1980), particularly chapter 2, "The Dark Winter of Settlement and Statehood," pp. 31–54.

12. I am indebted to Roger Sprague who has allowed me to read his manuscript-in-progress, "Second Trail of Tears." Excerpts from his carefully researched text can be found on his website, www.migrantgrandson.com.

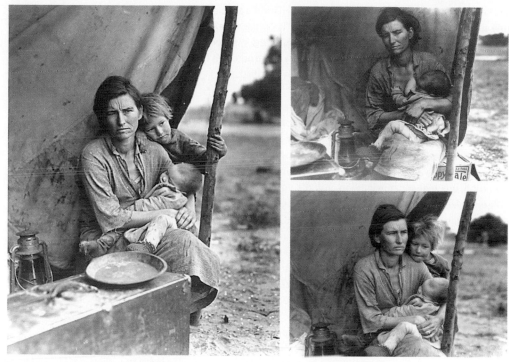

Dorothea Lange, From *Migrant Mother* series, 1936. Gelatin silver prints, dimensions vary. Library of Congress.

According to Dunn, Florence supported her family as a waitress and soon became involved with a local businessman. Florence's grandson Roger Sprague, who is currently preparing his own biography of the many generations of his grandmother's family, notes that the young widow was fiercely independent but made the mistake of obtaining county aid, which stipulated that any sexual relations with men would result in the removal of her children. When she became pregnant, she immediately left for her home state, determined to avoid any custody dispute.[12] But Oklahoma in the 1930s was devastated by drought and offered even fewer opportunities than it had in the previous decade. Florence quickly set out a second time for California.

After returning to her adopted state, Florence became involved with Jim Hill, an unemployed local man who had turned to migrant work, and with whom she had a child in 1935—the nursing infant in *Migrant Mother*. Hill had temporarily left the camp with one of Florence's sons when Lange happened upon the pea pickers' encampment and made her series of portraits. Though Hill was actually getting a radiator repaired, the photographer soon annotated the closest portrait with the detail that the family had been forced to sell the tires from their car. This factual embellishment offended the family's sense of logic as well as accuracy, since mobility was the key to even the poorest migrant's survival. Dunn's article makes no mention of when Florence married Thompson, her last name at the time of her death. But from Roger Sprague's more extensive reconstruction of his family history, I learned that the marriage followed her separation from Hill in the 1940s, and again she outlived her husband.

As Dunn makes clear, Lange was quite careless with the facts. However, this was hardly the first time a scholar has noted the liberties Lange took in her documentary practice (as well as in the facts of her own biography). Accordingly, Dunn's wholesale condemnation of the famous photographer as manipulative, condescending, colonialistic, misleading, and disingenuous made less of an impression on me than the chronicle he had sketched of *Migrant Mother*'s Native American heritage.[13] On this count, I don't think we can condemn Lange for deliberately misrepresenting or burying the information.

From all available evidence, it does not seem that Lange ever realized she had cast a Native American for the European American role of New Deal madonna. She never questioned the stranger about her ethnic identity; in fact, making such an inquiry would have risked breaking whatever current of empathy she briefly sought to establish. But if there is anything recognizably "Indian" in this striking face, Lange's misperception is more than a little curious. She prided herself on being able to distill essential truths by looking closely.[14] Moreover, she had spent a fair amount of time studying Native Americans in the Southwest. Her first husband, Maynard Dixon, was a plein-air painter who had specialized in idyllic scenes of the pristine West inhabited solely by Native Americans. It was during an early sojourn with Dixon in the Southwest that Lange began to photograph seriously outside her studio, and those efforts led to one of her first distinctive portraits. Yet, in the resulting close-cropped print of a Hopi man's face, her framing ex-

13. On Lange's radical misquotation in the case of her 1930s portrait of Nettie Featherston (*Woman of the High Plains*), long linked to the caption "If you die, you're dead—that's all," see Maren Stange, *Symbols of Ideal Life* (New York and Cambridge, England: Cambridge University Press, 1989), pp. 119–23; see also my interpretation of the photographer's logic for such counterfactual alteration in "Peculiar Grace: Dorothea Lange and the Testimony of the Body," in *Dorothea Lange: A Visual Life*, ed. Elizabeth Partridge (Washington, D.C.: Smithsonian Institution Press, 1984), pp. 81–84. On Lange's embellishment of her own educational background, see her first biography, Milton Meltzer's *Dorothea Lange: A Photographer's Life* (New York: Farrar, Straus and Giroux, 1978), p. 22.

14. Toward the end of her life she would express this idea in terms of "living the visual life," words that open the 1966 documentary film *The Closer for Me*, produced by Philip Greene and Robert Katz of KQED; transcript of the filmed interviews with the photographer in the Dorothea Lange Collection of the Oakland Museum of California.

15. On the deliberately selective practices of staging and framing by Curtis, see Christopher M. Lyman, *The Vanishing Race and Other Illusions: Photographs of Indians by Edward S. Curtis* (Washington, D.C.: Smithsonian Institution Press, 1982).

Dorothea Lange, From *Migrant Mother* series, 1936. Gelatin silver prints, dimensions vary. Library of Congress.

Dorothea Lange, Left: *Hopi Indian Man* (full frame version), 1926. Gelatin silver print. Private collection. Right: *Hopi Indian Man,* 1926. Gelatin silver print, 7¼ x 7¹¹/₁₆ in. (18.4 x 19.5 cm). Oakland Museum of California, City of Oakland, the Dorothea Lange Collection, gift of Paul S. Taylor.

cluded all conflicting cultural signs like modern, store-bought clothing. In this respect, she continued the quest to find or produce "authentic Indians," a tradition developed by a long line of artists including Dixon and photographers like Edward S. Curtis.[15] That these "authentic" stereotypes were manifestly superficial in spite of being deep-seated, proved especially true in Nipomo, California. The migrant woman who attracted Lange's attention displayed no obvious signs of "Indianness," so Lange proceeded to place her in a distinctly Euro-American scenario of hallowed Christian maternity. In turn, this iconographic context led all, including the photographer, to assume that the model was unarguably white.

Lange's mistaken assumption amplifies the generalizing tenden- [15] cies in both New Deal culture and subsequent scholarship of the period. Photography and direct observation in that era came close to enjoying the powers of a fetish, magically replete without nominal recourse to factual or reasoned discourse. Though our eyes often deceive us, the objective character of photography encourages viewers to rely on sensory appearance as the incontro- vertible bedrock of experience-based knowledge.

The photograph's history likewise exemplifies the way the New Deal was not only most concerned about "the forgotten man"—in Franklin Roosevelt's words—but equally, if less vocally, about the declining status of whites. The mass media were most inclined to focus on the plight of poor whites, and Lange's FSA boss was supremely media-oriented. On one occasion, Stryker rejected Lange's proposal to focus on the situation of blacks and the urban

"Michael Jackson," 1993

"Arnold Schwarzenegger," 1993

"Spike Lee," 1993

"Queen Elizabeth II," 1993

TIBOR KALMAN

Tibor Kalman (1949–1999) was born in Budapest. His family left Hungary in 1956 and settled in Poughkeepsie, New York. Kalman studied journalism at New York University, where he also found an outlet for his social activism. He then worked for a number of years creating signs, advertisements, and displays for the bookstore that would become Barnes & Noble.

In 1979 Kalman and his wife Maira founded M&Co, a design firm whose irreverence attracted clients ranging from the Talking Heads to New York's Museum of Modern Art. To counteract both the dishonesty and the superficiality of corporate advertising, Kalman created an offbeat, often humorous design vocabulary. It was that vocabulary that brought him to the attention of Benetton. The company wanted to launch a magazine, and it wanted Kalman to come to Rome and be its editor. In *Colors* Kalman found a platform for both his design aesthetic and his politics. Witness the images here, published in *Colors* in 1993, in an issue devoted to race, in a featured titled "What If . . ."

In 1995, artistic differences and the first symptoms of the lymphoma that would take his life four years later brought Kalman back to New York City. He began working on several projects, including *Chairman* (1998), a book about chair designer Rolf Fehlbaum, and *(un)Fashion* (2000), a study of "how real people dress," which his wife completed after Kalman died. He also worked closely with Michael Beirut and Peter Hall on *Tibor Kalman: Perverse Optimist* (1998).

SEEING

1. How did you respond to Kalman's altered images? What response does each photograph elicit from you? How does each photograph challenge your assumptions about these public figures? Which image do you find most—and least—plausible? Explain why.

2. Comment on Kalman's choices in manipulating the skin color, hair style, and eyes of each public figure. In what ways does each of these images seem more striking, more contrived, or more realistic than others you've seen of public figures? Do you find Kalman's images humorous? satiric? ironic? some combination of the three? Explain your answer. What do you think Kalman was trying to accomplish? Do you think he was successful? Why or why not?

WRITING

1. Kalman employed computer technology to manipulate the racial identity of these public figures. Imagine that you were able to assume a different racial identity. Which would you choose? Why? What would be the consequences of doing so? How might your daily life be different as a result? Write the first draft of an essay in which you imagine the impact that change would have on the spirit and substance of your daily life.

2. Choose one of the photographs and write an essay in which you explain what Kalman's manipulation of the image suggests about the role of race in that person's public life. How much does the public identity of each person portrayed here depend on his or her racial identity?

RE: SEARCHING THE WEB

Since 1998, Google has provided Internet users with a fast, simple way to search for information on the web. In 2005 the search engine boasted an index of more than 8 billion URLs. The illustrations and cartoons that adorn Google's logo on holidays and other special days have developed a cult-like following among web users. Programmer Dennis Hwang has been responsible for creating these embellished versions of the company's logo since 2000. "Mostly the art is in the letters," he explained in a 2002 interview with the *Korean Herald*. "I like to have a design that interacts with letters." Many of Hwang's illustrations, like this Ray Charles logo, integrate simple line drawings into the six letters of Google's logo. "Understandably, the *O* and the *L* are the easiest to deal with," remarked Hwang. "The *O* has become a Halloween pumpkin, a Nobel Prize medal, the Korean flag symbol, and the planet Earth. The *L* has been used as a flagpole, the Olympic flame cauldron, or a snow ski. The first *G* is the most difficult to deal with, and I don't think the *E* has gotten much action because of its location."

Visit Google's archive of holiday logos (www.google.com/holidaylogos.html), and look at the range of Hwang's designs. What symbols has Hwang used to communicate different holidays? How has he managed to reduce complex traditions into simple drawings? Which of the logos do you find most successful? Why? Choose two logos and write an essay in which you compare their compositional techniques and effectiveness.

SUPER

Chip Kidd

George Reeves in *The Adventures of Superman* television series, 1950s

Christopher Reeve in *Superman — The Movie*, 1977

I always hate it whenever Superman's outfit is referred to as a *costume*. A Superman costume is what you put on for Halloween, as a sort of imitation or homage. But the man himself? That is no costume, any more than was King Arthur's chainmail or MacArthur's fatigues. Superman's suit is a *uniform*. A uniform implies duty, mission, self-sacrifice, something official and worthy of respect.

While it has its roots in the tights worn by trapeze artists and circus tumblers—coupled with the capes of Zorro and the Scarlet Pimpernel—Superman's uniform, designed in 1937 by Jerry Siegel and Joe Shuster, is a truly unique, American creation. Its fiercely primary colors and simplified shapes invented the look of what we've known for decades as the "Superhero"—a curiously parochial, utopian being who channels the powers of the gods through the guise of your next-door neighbor. The "S" on Superman's chest is the monogram made monolithic, the family crest as modern logo.

The way the story goes, Jonathan and Martha Kent, childless, gentle farmer folk in rural Kansas, come upon a rocketship that has landed on their property. Inside they find a baby, unhurt, wrapped in red, yellow, and blue blankets. The material, as it turns out, is indestructible. So, by the way, is the child, who grows into a man, and then fashions a suit out of these miraculous swaddling clothes.

Superman's myth is so well constructed it has served us effectively in every avatar that we have required, as our needs have evolved in this century: in the Depression, the funnies; during wartime, radio; with the Cold War, television; while Vietnam festered, Broadway. And after that, perhaps most effectively, Superman became a hero of movies.

Ideally, Superman's uniform should be woven only of the varied perfections of the imagination. So the actual garments reproduced here, which were worn by two recent Supermen of the big and small screen, cannot help but disappoint. The more tattered example, worn in the 1950s by George Reeves, was made of a particularly heavy wool. Reeves really was superhuman, considering that he wore this toasty ensemble while filming under the torturously hot klieg lights of the black-and-white Superman television series.

Considerably lighter, but not necessarily sewn more skillfully, is the uniform donned by Christopher Reeve in the Superman movies of the 1970s. The disco-era Lycra fabric was more responsive to flutter-inducing wind machines and to the sculptured contours of Reeve's physique. The evolution of the uniform—from wool to Lycra, from monochrome to technicolor—suggests an increasingly immaterial incarnation of the Superman persona, pointing to a future where the uniform as a symbol and the uniform as a garment merge into the oneness of being truly super. ○

5

CHIP KIDD

Chip Kidd was born in 1964 in Reading, Pennsylvania. He graduated from Penn State with a degree in graphic design. He is best known for the hundreds of book jackets he has designed for Knopf and other publishers. Among those designs is the skeletal dinosaur that appeared on the cover of Michael Crichton's novel *Jurassic Park* (1990) and in the movie's promotions. Kidd has been a design consultant for *The Paris Review* since 1995. In 1997 he was honored by the International Center of Photography for his use of photography in graphic design; the following year he became a member of the Alliance Graphique Internationale, a professional association that "unites the world's leading graphic designers and artists."

Kidd is considered an authority on comics and pop culture. He has designed a superhero trilogy—Superman, Batman, and Wonder Woman—for Chronicle Books; and he authored and designed *Batman Collected* (1996), about Batman memorabilia, with attention to his own collection. He also has written for the *New York Times,* the *New York Observer, Entertainment Weekly,* and *Vogue* about popular culture and graphic design.

In 2001 Kidd's first novel was published: *The Cheese Monkeys: A Novel in Two Semesters.* In 2003 Yale University Press published a tribute to him and his work titled *Chip Kidd* (by Veronique Vienne). "Super" was included in a 1998 issue of *2wice* magazine on the uniform in contemporary culture. Kidd currently lives and works in New York City.

SEEING

1. Superman's uniform, writes Kidd, "is a truly unique, American creation" (para. 2). What evidence does Kidd offer to support this claim? What other aspects of Superman's uniform would you draw on to support or refute this claim? Kidd suggests several sources for Superman's uniform, including trapeze artists' tights and Zorro's cape. How do these add resonance to your understanding of the superhero's outfit? Can you suggest other influences on its design?

2. What does Kidd mean when he says that the images of Superman's uniforms shown here "cannot help but disappoint" (para. 5)? Look closely at the two images. How are they alike? different? To what extent do you agree with Kidd's interpretation of the "evolution of the uniform" (para. 6)?

RESPONDING VISUALLY

Imagine that you are a member of the production team for a film featuring a contemporary superhero. How would you dress your superhero? Draw, make a collage, or prepare a PowerPoint presentation to communicate to your team your vision of the uniform's materials and overall look and feel.

WRITING

1. Kidd is insistent that Superman's outfit is a uniform, not a costume. Think about a school uniform. How would you argue that a school uniform could be a costume, at least at times? How does wearing a uniform change behavior? Draft an essay in which you discuss the nature of uniforms and their impact on those who wear them.

2. Both this essay and Richard Woodward's "Wonder" place the hero in social context. "Superman's myth is so well constructed," writes Kidd, "it has served us effectively in every avatar that we have required, as our needs have evolved in this century" (para. 4). Think about the world today, and imagine a superhero who might meet our contemporary needs. Then write an essay in which you describe that hero and his or her uniform.

Christopher Reeve in *Superman—The Movie,* 1977

Interview: Kidd

What sets a good book cover apart from a bad book cover?
Chip Kidd Well, the boring answer is, a good book cover makes you want to pick it up. End of story. It will intrigue you enough to make you want to go to second base, as it were, with the book. The silly answer is "One with a big penis on it." It worked for me.

What would you want to avoid? What would make you say, "This will never work"?
I've been doing this long enough that to even go there is a mistake. Let's limit it to designing covers for fiction right now. That's very much a theater of the mind. Personally, I enjoy casting people in the various roles as I read along, whether it's friends or celebrities or combinations thereof. It's like when people used to have a dream on *Gilligan's Island,* and they had that trial where Gilligan was Mr. Hyde, and the skipper was the judge, and all that stuff. I do that when I'm reading books, so I want to customize the characters to the way I think they should be, or who I think they are. I used to feel like, "Okay, we're not gonna show any of the characters full-on, frontal-face. You take something away from the reader when you do that." And then at some point, inevitably—if you've been doing this for 18 years, as I have—you're going to do that. One of the things I learned while majoring in graphic design in college, that I've always taken very much to heart . . . The teacher one day drew an apple on the blackboard, and then wrote the word "apple" underneath it. He pointed to the whole thing and he said, "You should never do this." He covered up the picture and said, "You either just have the word," then covered up the word and said, "or you just have the picture. But don't do both." It's insulting to the reader, or the

viewer, or whoever. I think that's true. So what did I do on the cover for *All the Pretty Horses* by Cormac McCarthy? I showed a horse. I showed a pretty horse.

Part of a horse.
Right. But, again, there I just completely broke that rule. Yet for some reason, it works, and that's one of the covers I'm better known for.

Exceptions aside, why is that a good rule? If you're designing a cover of *Who's Irish?*, why not just show a question mark made out of shamrocks?
It's too easy. Another rule—which is breakable, as they all are—is that you discard your first idea. Many times, I've found myself going back to that first idea, thinking, "Hmm, the reason this is the first thing you thought of is that this is the best thing."

How many book covers have you done at this point?
I wish I knew. That's going to be my first question after I die. Like, "What did I eat that I didn't realize I was eating, and how many book covers did I do?" Because I don't have a comprehensive list. . . . I've been telling people 1,500 for about six years now, so that can't be accurate.

How do you avoid repeating yourself?
I don't avoid repeating myself. I rip myself off all the time. But you also have to try and constantly rethink the form. It's very important. Or everything will just get stale.

What's your process like?
It's extremely organic. The stock answer is that every book is different, or at least reasonably different, so the process is going to change from book to book, depending on what they are. Sometimes you hit it right

away, sometimes you have to do eight different things, sometimes the publisher or the author or the agent will wear you down to the point where you want it to be over with, and what you end up with is kind of a mess. You just accept it and move on. The most tiring— and yet the most rewarding—experiences are when you have to keep redoing it again and again, but what you end up with is actually the best thing. A perfect example of that is something I just did for the new David Sedaris book [*Dress Your Family in Corduroy and Denim*]. I gave three ideas, and those didn't cut it, and then I gave two more, and I heard nothing, and I started doing photo research for a different job. Luckily my design gene was secreting, and I saw an image that I thought would be perfect. It was great. Those moments are worth everything. They're some of the most pleasurable aspects of life— when you see something and the scales fall from your eyes, and it's like, "There it was the whole time. It just took until now to find it."

Do you ever worry about how your covers will age?
CK Yes, especially because of the nature of books. That's one reason why I love working in books—they are by their very nature archival. At least they're supposed to be. That very much appeals to me, and especially to the egomaniacal me that wants to live on after I've returned to the earth. So, yeah, not consciously, but subconsciously, I've got an eye for how covers will look in five years, 10 years, 15, 20. Which is maybe why I would say my design is more on the conservative side than a lot of what you see out there now. Not really in books, but in CDs and magazines and that kind of stuff. They're ephemeral. They're designed to be thrown away.

How did you decide to write your own novel? Had you written prose before?
I think I've had an eye to that ever since getting hired at Knopf right out of school. You read manuscript after manuscript, and if you have even a shred of naked ambition, like I do, you think, "Hmm, maybe I could try this." I started writing for design magazines. I wrote articles for *Print* and *Graphique* and *I.D.*, where, quite frankly, it was easy for me to get stuff published, because they knew who I was. Had I tried to do it the way normal people do it, writing for something other than a trade publication, I wouldn't have gotten very far. I could write about things like the death of phototypesetting, because I knew them and understood them from a designer's point of view. I guess I cut my teeth writing for those publications, and that got me used to figuring out how something works on a page in terms of prose and sentences and that kind of thing. Like anything else, you learn by doing.

This excerpt was taken from a longer interview conducted by Keith Phipps for the June 2, 2004, issue of *The Onion*.

Visit seeingandwriting.com for the full text of the interview.

For biographical information on Chip Kidd, see page 554.

WONDER

Richard B. Woodward

Superheroes and heroines live in a world where it's always Halloween night at Studio 54. Only in comic books does a gaudy costume or a black eye mask denote the authentic self—the true identity of a character—which ordinary street clothes halfheartedly serve to cover up and disguise.

The uniforms of comic-book warriors, unlike those of real-world soldiers or cops, celebrate freakishness rather than the collective mind-set of a group. Individuality runs rampant in the illustrated pages of pulp fiction. Clothes hug the curves of the body fantastic, both as a way to ignite sexual fires in adolescent readers and to signify a branding of the flesh. Dressing up in cape and headband is no masquerade for these characters—many of them are de facto aliens. Like a tattoo, a skin-tight outfit confirms the hero's extraordinary status as a potential savior of humankind, as well as one of its flamboyant outcasts. Wonder Woman first put on her uniform in 1942, as millions of American men and women were donning theirs. Dressed in the palette of the flag (with gold accents), she may have worn the colors of a patriot, but in her origins as an Amazon princess from Paradise Island, she was just another immigrant. Her creator at DC Comics, the bizarre William Moulton Marston (inventor of the lie detector and regular contributor to *Reader's Digest*),

supervised the fashion apparel of Princess Diana, as Wonder Woman is known in her fictive land of origin. (Diana Prince is the closet name she uses to pass as a civilian). Marston wasn't worried that a muscular female immortal would put off the traditional male comic readership. "Give them an alluring woman stronger than themselves to submit to and they'll be proud to become her willing slaves," he once proclaimed.

There are provocative—even kinky—touches throughout her wardrobe. A golden eagle stretches its wings across a red bustier that improbably features a plunging backline. The skirt, purportedly designed by her mother back in Paradise, was replaced after a few issues by a pair of stretchy star-spangled shorts that resemble a *Frederick's of Hollywood* girdle or the comics' first pair of hot pants. A golden diadem with an inset star ruby declares her royal lineage and holds back her mass of raven tresses. Red high-heel boots complete a fighting ensemble that might cause Cher to blush.

Most peculiar of all is the magic golden lasso she carries, which demands complete submission by anyone or anything it encircles. Marston enjoyed this plot device; his editor had to restrain him from overdoing bondage scenes, many with multiple prisoners. There is little doubt, however, that the rope—like Batman's hi-tech accoutrements—helped to capture her audience. Wonder Woman's 1968 redesign as a mortal career woman—without her dominatrix get-up, lasso, or superpowers—brought howls of protests from, among others, Gloria Steinem. A chastened DC Comics management quickly restored her skimpy power suit and supernatural gifts.

One of those binary figures of pop culture who can   5
be both a feminist icon worthy of a cover on *Ms.* as well as a voluptuous goddess of lust, Wonder Woman is at once pure camp and a true-blue, flag-wearing ass-kicker. Marston described her as having "all the strength of a Superman plus all the allure of a good and beautiful woman."

For more than 50 years—only Superman and Batman can boast of such a record—she has proven her crossover appeal. Like her latter-day incarnation, Xena the Warrior Princess, she has both straight male and gay female admirers who get off on her unbridled but still bodacious athleticism and her unresolved attachment to the world of men. If academia has recently focused on contemporary icons such as Madonna and Martha Stewart, then surely Wonder Woman deserves some attention. But such analysis may prove nothing more than that a lot of us are suckers for a woman in uniform. ○

RICHARD B. WOODWARD

Richard B. Woodward is a writer and a book, film, and art critic based in New York City. His articles have been published in *The Atlantic, Vanity Fair, Vogue* and the *New York Times.* His is a highly respected voice in contemporary art circles, and his essays have been featured in several art books, including *David Levinthal: Work from 1975–1996* (1997), and photographer Kevin Bubriski's book, *Pilgrimage: Looking At Ground Zero* (2002). He has been a visiting photography critic at Massachusetts College of Art, Rhode Island School of Design, and Columbia University, and was a juror in the 2005 Soho Photo National Photography Competition. He also writes often on pop culture, painting, and literature.

Woodward is also involved in filmmaking. In 1998 he co-directed *John Szarkowski: A Life in Photography,* about the photographer, critic, and curator. In 2003 he directed *Billy Collins: On the Road with the Poet Laureate,* winner of the Best Documentary Film Award at the 2004 Westchester County International Film Festival.

"Wonder" was included in a 1998 issue of *2wice* magazine on the uniform in contemporary culture.

SEEING

1. Woodward writes that superheroes' uniforms "ignite sexual fires in adolescent readers" and that "a skin-tight outfit confirms the hero's extraordinary status as a potential savior of humankind" (para. 2). He goes on to describe two very different forces that shape the final form of the uniform—the publisher and the superhero. Which aspects of Wonder Woman's uniform does Woodward attribute to the artists and writers, and which to Wonder Woman's character within the comic?

2. Both Woodward and Chip Kidd (p. 553) take their subjects quite seriously, arguing in different fashions that superheroes deserve our respect and attention. What strategies do they use to establish the significance of their subjects? How do those strategies help determine the structure and conclusions of their respective essays? Consider the ways in which mentions of family and television might be thought of as politically significant.

WRITING

1. Superheroes often are associated with values like justice, progress, and freedom. But the reaction in 1968 to the revamped Wonder Woman suggests that those values can mean very different things to different people at different times. Write an essay about Wonder Woman's relationship to freedom or to some other value that has more than one meaning.

2. Compare Woodward's opinion of Wonder Woman's uniform with Chip Kidd's thoughts about Superman's. Pay particular attention to the way Woodward frames his subject in sexual terms. Do you think the sexual emphasis comes from something innate in Wonder Woman's uniform, the fact that it is meant to be worn by a woman, or some combination of the two? Draft an essay in which you either describe Superman's uniform as overtly sexual or describe Wonder Woman's without reference to sexuality.

Wonder Woman Archives Volume 1   Lynda Carter as Wonder Woman, 1976

The Cosmic Significance of Britney Spears

Tom Perrotta

She is our most famous singing virgin, this nymphet hottie who admits she's "All about sit-ups" and has the most adorable abs in the universe to prove it. But there's more to Britney than that, isn't there? Isn't there?

Like a lot of other people, I had trouble concentrating on my work in the days after the September 11 terrorist attacks. I found it hard to focus on anything unrelated to the tragedy, hard to convince myself that what I was doing really mattered. In my case, this fairly common emotional response was exacerbated by the fact that I happened to be writing an essay about Britney Spears. The truth is, even in what now seem to have been the idyllic, clueless days preceding one of the bloodiest events in American history, I was having a certain amount of difficulty taking my subject seriously. Britney, after all, is the kind of person who can look straight into the camera, as she did in her recently televised *MTV Diary*, and tell the world, without any trace of irony, "I'm all about sit-ups."

This isn't to say she's not a likable person. I mean, what's not to like about Britney? Millions of kids think she's great, she loves her family and her totally cute world-famous boyfriend, and by all accounts she remains the sweet, God-fearing, down-to-earth southern girl she was brought up to be, miraculously unchanged by global megastardom. Plus, she looks hot in really tight pants, and you can't say that about everyone. All those sit-ups paid off, apparently.

So the question isn't whether we *like* Britney. Of course we *like* her. At least we *would* like her if we hung out with her on the patio of her $3 million dream house in the Hollywood Hills and chowed down on hot dogs and cookie-dough ice cream (her favorite foods, according to www.adoredcelebrities.com, though a recent *Rolling Stone* profile shows her snacking on steamed soybeans). The real question is: Do we need to think about Britney? Does the fact that she's currently one of the biggest pop stars in the universe, a one-name trademark on par with Oprah and Madonna, make her by definition a figure of sociological significance? Or is Britney a phenomenon of such mind-numbing simplicity that she's the pop-culture equivalent of a stealth bomber, zooming cheerfully below the radar of thoughtful analysis?

It would be easy enough to write her off as just 5 another teen idol, one in the never-ending progression of Debbies and Tiffanys the entertainment industry has been selling to American kids ever since Annette Funicello first donned her mouse ears. Then we wouldn't have to think about her at all.

On the other hand, some of the most important and revealing cultural figures of the past half century first came to our attention disguised as pop stars—think Michael Jackson, whose ghoulishly altered face tells a mythic and terrible story about race and celebrity in America. So shouldn't we consider the possibility that Britney is more than just the latest teenage wonder, the obligatory icon on this year's school lunchbox? What if she's an era-defining superstar, one of those very lucky, once-or-twice-in-a-decade figures whose job it is to tell us who we are and where we're going? Maybe she has more in common with more iconic artists like Elvis Presley or Madonna or Kurt Cobain than we ever gave her credit for. At the very least, the comparisons are instructive.

Britney and Elvis

Am I the only guy in America who doesn't lust for Britney? In a purely theoretical sense, I appreciate her aerobically engineered body and her eagerness to flash a little thong. But there's something disconcertingly childish about her persona, some willful refusal to acknowledge her own sexuality that makes it hard for me to join Bob Dole and his dog in their slack-jawed worship of this girl.

As Elvis did before her, Britney presents herself to the world as a divided personality—shy and self-effacing in private, shockingly bold in public. Unwilling or unable to acknowledge a contradiction between her avowed religious piety and her uninhibited onstage sexuality, Britney at first defended herself not by raising the flag of sexual empowerment à la Madonna but by denying any

impure intent, much as Elvis did a half century earlier. "I'm not trying to be sexy," Elvis used to claim, responding to questions about his provocatively jiggling leg. "It just automatically wiggles like that." Similarly, Britney professed bewilderment when challenged about her famously neither-here-nor-there outfits. "All I did was tie up my shirt!" she told a reporter, in reference to the sexy schoolgirl-strumpet outfit she wore in the video for ". . . Baby One More Time," which brought her to the attention of many middle-aged pedophiles. "I'm wearing a sports bra under it."

It's really not such a stretch to think of Britney and Elvis as distant celebrity cousins. They both grew up in humble circumstances in the Deep South (Elvis in Mississippi and Tennessee, Britney in Louisiana), with strong attachments to their doting mothers. Like Elvis, Britney makes a point of ritually invoking her loyalty to her small-town roots even as success calls her away from home. Elvis could have been speaking for both of them when he said, "Them people in New York and Hollywood are not going to change me none."

For Britney, being southern is a powerful per- 10 sonal identity, one she frequently mentions. "I'm from the South," she said in a recent profile, "so I'm a very open person." Her aesthetic tastes and moral values seem clearly rooted in the region: her fondness for frilly, floral-patterned furniture; her sweet disposition and unfailing good manners; the prayer diary she keeps by her bed; her public declarations of chastity until marriage; and her brief stint at Parklane Academy, a private Christian school in Mississippi.

What being southern is not for Britney—and this is where she parts company decisively with Elvis—is a musical identity. Nothing in her songs, not a single geographical reference or vocal inflection, marks her as hailing from America's richest musical region, the cradle of the blues, the home of country music, zydeco, and rockabilly. Britney's music is the musical equivalent of a big-budget Hollywood action movie; you don't need to understand English, let alone be conversant with the musical traditions of the Mississippi Delta, to enjoy the multimedia juggernaut that is Britney.

The South, of course, is far less a separate and culturally unique region in Britney's day than it was in Elvis's. By the time Britney was old enough to listen to the radio, authentic country music had pretty much been homogenized out of existence; all that was left was the high hair and cowboy hats. Until her most recent album, Britney wrote almost none of her material; her sound was created by Swedish producer Max Martin. "I'm so lucky to work with Max," she says in *Heart to Heart,* the unintentionally revealing autobiography she cowrote with her mother, Lynne. "He knows not only what will make a great song but also what I will love singing."

Elvis didn't write his own material, either, and he too was deeply indebted to a shrewd producer, Sam Phillips of Sun Records. Yet there seems to be little doubt that the 18-year-old Elvis was a musical innovator, a naive singer who somehow created a new synthesis of blues and country music, fusing the two dominant musical forms of his childhood—one black, the other white—that were constantly rubbing up against each other in the streets and on the radios in the segregated South but rarely mixing. Everyone involved in the early Sun sessions bears witness to the feeling of something totally unexpected being born, something no one had heard before, and that Elvis was the source. Elvis created himself out of the materials at hand; Britney had a musical identity imposed on her that she gratefully accepted. Britney is, and was always intended to be, a familiar and easily consumable product, appealing to a wide swath of humanity without first belonging to an actual place or community or individual consciousness. If Elvis is the particular that became universal, Britney is the universal that was never particular.

Britney and Madonna

I do believe religion and eroticism are absolutely related. And I think my original feelings of sexuality and eroticism originated in going to church.
—Madonna

I don't think I could ever look at how lucky I am now and not think that God had a hand in it.
—Britney Spears

When I first saw *Truth or Dare* in 1991, I remember feeling sorry for Madonna's brother and sisters and grateful I didn't have to contend with such a formidable sibling. I lent some of these sentiments to Tammy Warren, the Madonna-obsessed lesbian teenager in my novel *Election:* "I tried to imagine what it would be like to be a member of her family, how hard it would be to keep your spirits up, to wake up in the morning and actually believe you have a life worth living."

In *Truth or Dare,* Madonna portrays herself as an unapologetic celebrity monster—vain, self-obsessed, willing to mock and humiliate anyone who crosses her path, including her father and a childhood friend desperate for her approval. At that moment in her career, Madonna indulged her egotism without shame, daring you to deny that you would have behaved any differently in her place.

Britney poses no such challenge to her fans or the people around her. At least in her *MTV Diary,* Britney emerges as the anti-Madonna, the celebrity without an ego. She seems to want so little from her fame and fortune: She is holding off on the sex for now and is mostly indifferent to the money. Like the rest of us, she makes do with simple pleasures, seeming almost erotically disheveled after a ride on a roller coaster, deriving real satisfaction from the shot she sinks at a charity basketball game, getting choked up at her father's birthday party. She's just so pleasant and thoughtful; she wouldn't want to do or say anything that might upset anyone.

Considering their wildly different attitudes toward stardom, it's intriguing to note how often Britney refers to Madonna as a role model. Madonna successfully navigated the treacherous transition from lightweight pop singer, catering to preteen tastes and drag queens, to major artist with a loyal adult following. Over and over, Britney and her management invoke Madonna when trying to imagine a strategy for overcoming the built-in obsolescence of the teen pop star. "I admire the way Madonna always reinvents herself," Britney says in *Heart to Heart.* "I think that's one reason she's managed to stay a success for so long while other artists have fizzled out."

The superficial bond between the two performers is intensified by the fact that they occupy the same highly charged spot on the pop-culture spectrum, that narrow band where spirituality and sexuality intersect. This isn't to say they share the same attitudes about religion or sex ("I just think it's important to fuck what you want to fuck and not feel shame about it," Madonna once remarked). But simply to notice this peculiar connection between our most famous singing virgin and our most famous singing bad girl is to confront a highly revealing irony: Britney may be more conventionally devout in her personal life, but Madonna is far and away the more religiously engaged artist of the pair.

Over the years, Madonna has spoken frequently, and at times thoughtfully, about her religious upbringing, joking about her name but also connecting the Catholic concepts of sin and guilt with her own interest in sexual transgression. But even if Madonna had a different first name and never said a word about her background, the fact that she had grown up Catholic would be obvious to anyone familiar with her body of work in the '80s.

On the other hand, we know Britney is religious only because she tells us (and tells us and tells us), though to be honest, her theology seems to begin and end with gratitude toward the good Lord for making her such a big friggin' star. If we were deprived of magazine profiles and publicity materials and had access only to Britney's CDs and videos, we'd have no idea that she's a devout Baptist who attends church regularly or holds stricter ideas about sexual morality than the average pop singer. Britney specializes in featherweight love songs, her persona shifting from breathless little girl ("Dear Diary") to apologetic tease ("Oops! . . . I Did It Again"). Though a determined critic might be able to infer a desire to set sexual boundaries from some of the lyrics, her videos and live performances move strenuously in the opposite direction: They're all about breaking limits and showing midriff—from the whiff of pedophilia in ". . . Baby One More Time" to her notorious nude bodysuit at the 2000 MTV Video Music Awards.

Some observers admire Britney for this ability to simultaneously inhabit the roles of nice girl and sexpot. "I like the way that she refuses to have

any truck with virgin-or-whore stereotypes, how her Christianity sits perfectly happily alongside her breasts," wrote Julie Burchill in the *Guardian*. Others suspect her of being a hypocrite: "She and Justin Timberlake look a little close," sniffed teen actress Kirsten Dunst in a recent profile. "Maybe she is [a virgin]. I don't know." For most of us, though, Britney is simply unreadable. What does she mean when she says she's "not that innocent"? That she's lying to the public and running around behind her mama's back? That she has an elastic definition of what constitutes sexual relations, like Bill Clinton or one of those junior-high blowjob queens who've found their own ways of circumventing the virgin/whore dichotomy? Or does she mean something much more innocent than that? Your guess is as good as mine.

All I really know is that Madonna always seems deadly serious about what she's doing or saying, whereas Britney always seems as if she's kidding around. Her surprisingly lame Jungle Jane–themed performance at this year's MTV Video Music Awards is a good case in point. If Madonna performed a song called "I'm a Slave 4 U" and choreographed it with sexy multicultural dancers, vaguely Egyptian overtones, and a finale that included a huge yellow serpent, you'd immediately know that she was trying to make some kind of allegorical statement about sex, sin, and power and that these were issues she'd thought about in some sustained way and had put to the test in her private life. But when Britney does it, all you can say is, "Hey, cool, there's Britney holding a fat snake."

Britney and Cobain

When Nirvana burst onto the scene in the early '90s, they struck a lot of people as something new under the sun. And while it's true they represented a stark departure from the hair-metal poseurs then dominating the rock world, they were immediately familiar to anyone who, like me, had gone to a working-class high school in the late '70s. They were burnouts, sullen stoners who cut class, got high in the bathroom, and didn't get along with the gym teachers. That they were outcasts was part of the point—rock 'n' roll was supposed to be the music of losers, the means by which they were allowed to engineer their own redemption.

I recently spent a day switching between Britney Spears's *Heart to Heart* and *Heavier Than Heaven*, Charles R. Cross's new biography of Kurt Cobain. The effect was disorienting, like leaving a birthday party at Chuck E. Cheese to visit a friend in a mental hospital. Britney is a relentlessly upbeat and utterly inoffensive person who believes that "there's nothing . . . as good as a cold glass of iced tea on a hot summer day or the smell of fresh-cut grass in the backyard." Cobain was the kind of guy who kept a pet rat (which he accidentally stepped on and killed), named his first band Fecal Matter, and had fantasies about being raped by Chef Boyardee.

And yet, for all the vast psychic distance be- 25 tween them, Britney and Cobain are fated to be forever linked in our national consciousness as the opposing bookends of the 1990s, poster children for a schizoid decade. There's Cobain on the left, mumbling and unshaven, representing a gloomy time of war and recession. And there's Britney on the right, the official superstar of the late-'90s boom, the chipper emblem of a fat, happy country bubbling over with irrational exuberance.

Kurt Cobain's childhood prepared him well to be the spokesman for an unhappy era. A sensitive and gifted kid, he grew up in a hardscrabble logging town that was a breeding ground for dysfunction and suicide. Between the ages of 15 and 19, he lived, according to his biographer, "in ten different houses, with ten different families," at one point crashing in a cardboard box on a friend's porch. A high school dropout who worked as a janitor, dishwasher, and carpet installer, Cobain suffered from a mysterious stomach ailment that left him in chronic pain and that he later claimed to be self-medicating with his heroin habit.

Given his lifelong intimacy with pain, abandonment, and failure, it's probably not surprising that the enormous commercial success of Nirvana left Cobain feeling isolated and bewildered, at the mercy of alien forces. He responded by embracing the identity of junkie, and once he'd chosen this

path, nothing could divert him from it. He was the rare rock star who seemed genuinely uncomfortable with the idea of being rich and famous and well loved, as if it were a betrayal of who he was and where he'd come from.

Britney, of course, has no such qualms with fame—she was raised for success, in the same way that Cobain seems to have been raised for unhappiness. Her life story consists of one triumph piled on top of another, each at an absurdly young age: She wins a *Star Search* competition at 10, is picked to be a Mouseketeer at 11, signs a recording contract at 15, has a number one record at 17, and so on.

In fact, Britney and her mom are sensitive to the appearance that it's all come a little too easily. They devote a considerable amount of energy in *Heart to Heart* to establishing Britney's bona fides as an artist who has suffered for her success, but the best they can come up with is an almost comical series of incidents that barely qualify as hardships under the loosest of definitions: Most distressing was the inconvenient knee injury she incurred during a video shoot shortly after the release of her first album. Britney had to cancel several TV appearances (including one on Jay Leno!) while recuperating from arthroscopic surgery; her career was momentarily stalled. "It threw us all for a loop," Lynne Spears writes. "But this time it was her mountain to climb alone."

Music provided Kurt Cobain with a desperately 30 needed outlet for transforming pain into art. For Britney, though, therapy and self-expression are beside the point; her music serves primarily as a vehicle for advancing her career, and she talks about her craft with a cool, professional distance. "I have an amazing team of writers, musicians, and producers," she notes in her book, "and they are churning out great songs for me." As a performer, Britney resembles a young Olympic athlete more than she does an artist—she seems at times to have no inner life at all, only a burning desire to master the task at hand: "I will practice and practice a move in front of a mirror, over and over again—ten, twenty, a hundred times—until I'm happy with it." It's precisely the purity and intensity of her youthful ambition that made Britney such a potent symbol of the late '90s. The whole point of the new-economy boom was that you could be rich and powerful right now, while you were still young and good-looking—you didn't have to wait your turn to climb the corporate ladder. If you took the right risks with the right attitudes, the rewards would flow. And it worked. At least for a few years it did. By the turn of the millennium, there was no longer a distinction between youth culture and grown-up culture; youth culture was American culture, and right there at this high-achieving pinnacle of the late '90s was Britney.

The big question for Britney right now isn't whether she can make a Madonna-like transition into adult stardom but whether her moment hasn't already passed. Quite suddenly, the boom is over. The '90s are gone. Recession is knocking, and the country is at war. America has an inner life again; our demons have returned from vacation. It looks as if we may soon start casting around for someone capable of giving voice to a new mood of pain and uncertainty, and it's fair to assume that that someone's probably not going to look or sound a helluva lot like Britney. ○

TOM PERROTTA

Tom Perrotta is the author of *Bad Haircut: Stories of the Seventies* (1994), *The Wishbones* (1997), *Joe College* (2000), and *Little Children* (2004); but he may be best known for *Election: A Novel* (1997), a darkly funny story about a suburban New Jersey high school election that became a movie starring Matthew Broderick and Reese Witherspoon. All of Perrotta's stories and novels deal with the experiences of adolescence. Although his characters are sometimes exaggerated, as is the protagonist of *Election,* oftentimes they reveal how real-life teens perceive their world through pop icons like Britney Spears.

"My literary generation seems to have been defined by a group of virtuoso postmodernists in the David Foster Wallace school. I feel less affinity with those writers than I do with the realists of the previous generation. . . . I'm committed to making fiction out of 'ordinary' experience and to telling stories in a way that will make them accessible to a large audience."

Perrotta has taught expository writing at Harvard University. The *Washington Times* called him "a writer to watch," and *Newsweek* heralded him as "one of America's best-kept literary secrets." He lives in Belmont, Massachusetts. "The Cosmic Significance of Britney Spears" first appeared in the December 2001 issue of *GQ* magazine.

SEEING

1. What is the "cosmic significance" of Britney Spears? What features of an icon does she exemplify? When does Perrotta take her seriously? When does he resist taking her seriously? with what effect(s)? Are you convinced that writing an article about Britney Spears mattered "in the days after the September 11 terrorist attacks" (para. 2)? Why or why not?

2. What is the difference between *sarcasm* and *irony*? Look up both words. Once you understand the distinctions between them, reread Perrotta's article carefully to identify—and comment on—several examples of each. After you have completed this exercise, choose an example of each and convert a sarcastic example into an ironic one, and vice versa. Which is easier to transform into the other? Why?

WRITING

1. The sections of Perrotta's essay in which he compares Britney Spears to other pop stars have a simple structure. First he tells how the two stars are alike, and then he tells how they are different. Using the same structure, compare Britney Spears with another popular singer. For example, you might compare her with Faith Evans, Jennifer Lopez, or Missy Elliott; or with Billie Holiday, Bessie Smith, or Ma Rainey; or even Eminem, 50 Cent, Will Smith, or DMX.

2. According to Perrotta, Britney Spears is "a potent symbol of the late '90s" in the United States (para. 30). Find out about a young female pop star from another decade and/or another country, and write an essay in which you discuss whether or not she is a symbol of her time and nation. Choose an era or an area that you don't know much about. For example, you might compare Spears's career in North America with Shakira's career in South America. Or you could find pictures and recordings of Jenny Lind, who was an immensely popular star in England and the United States in the late nineteenth century.

Jason Mercier, *Making Faces* (portrait in makeup of Missy Elliott), 2004

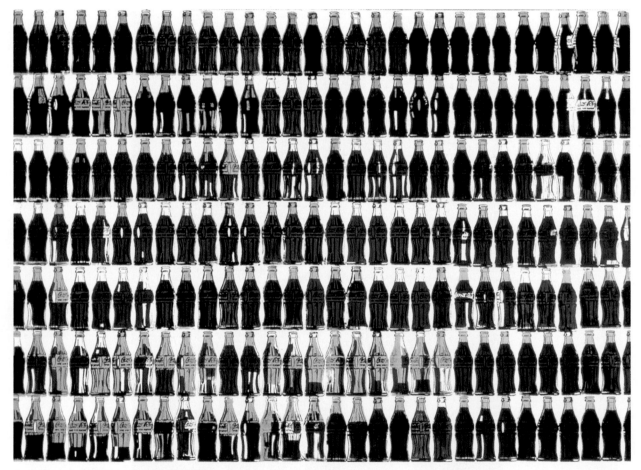

Andy Warhol, *210 Coca-Cola Bottles*, 1962

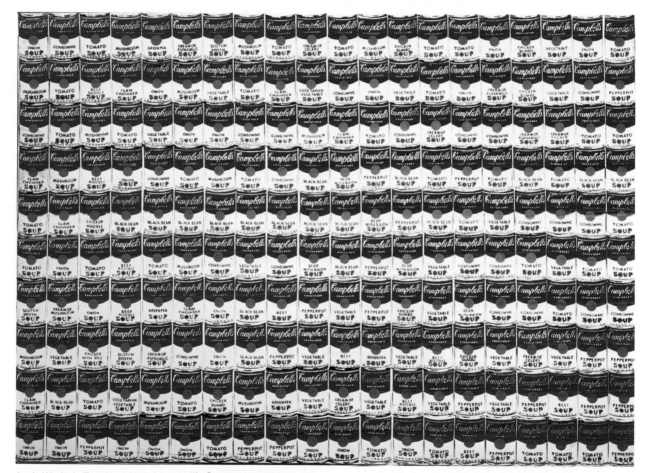

Andy Warhol, *Two Hundred Campbell's Soup Cans*, 1962

ANDY WARHOL

Born Andrew Warhola to Czech immigrant parents in Pittsburgh, Pennsylvania, the artist now known simply as "Warhol" (1928–1987) began collecting movie-star photographs and autographs as a young child. This fascination with all things glamorous helped fuel his successful career as a commercial fashion artist in New York in the 1950s.

By 1963 Warhol was at the center of the American Pop Art movement, which sought to erase the boundary between fine art and popular culture. By painting Campbell's Soup can labels on canvas and installing a sculpture of Brillo boxes, Warhol proposed an aesthetic in which the machine-made image competed with the hand-made for significance, and *image* very often was the subject itself. This was especially explicit in his paintings of Marilyn Monroe, which were based on a publicity headshot. Warhol reproduced, altered, and transformed her face into a series of brightly colored semi-abstract icons.

Warhol's studio loft in Greenwich Village became known as The Factory, a meeting place for New York's avant-garde. Here Warhol created experimental films such as *Sleep* (1963) and *Chelsea Girls* (1966). Of this work he said, "All my films are artificial, but then everything is sort of artificial. I don't know where the artificial stops and the real starts."

SEEING

1. What shared characteristics can you identify between these two Warhol paintings? What does he gain — and lose — by repeating images of the soup cans and Coca-Cola bottles? How does Warhol use color in each of these paintings? What is the overall effect of viewing these two paintings side by side?

2. What is unique about each of these paintings? What features of the advertising success of Campbell's Soup, for example, does Warhol emphasize? What role does repetition play in each painting? Please remember to point to specific aspects of each painting when formulating your response. For each painting, try to identify a distinct message that you see Warhol making — long with any cultural values you can read in these paintings as a pair.

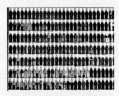

WRITING

1. Given what you have observed in these paintings, what role do you think originality and uniqueness play in Warhol's aesthetics? What cultural virtues and values seem to be privileged in his art? Draft an essay in which you discuss the relationship between the subjects and techniques of Warhol's paintings and the rise of American mass production in the decades following World War II. What role does duplication play in Warhol's painting and in that culture?

2. Compare and contrast Warhol's depiction of the soup cans or Coca-Cola bottles with another visual or verbal rendition of an ordinary object in this book. Draft an essay in which you compare and contrast the two approaches to representing an ordinary object. Please be sure to validate each of your assertions by pointing to specific evidence in the texts you choose to discuss.

The Stars and Stripes

Few symbols are as recognizable as the American flag, and few stir emotions as strong. The flag is ubiquitous. It flies on government buildings, but it also decorates front lawns, T-shirts, and bumper stickers. Americans encounter the flag not only in official ceremonies and at sports events, but in all kinds of everyday situations—in advertisements for weekend sales, on doormats, on clothing and commercial packaging—especially since September 11, 2001. Indeed, it is difficult to spend a day in this country without seeing the flag.

The Stars and Stripes evokes passionate responses—from patriotism to violence to tears—and the feelings about our right to burn this symbol are no less passionate. The **Majority Opinion** of the U.S. Supreme Court, by Justice William Brennan Jr., and the **Dissenting Opinion** by Chief Justice William Rehnquist articulate two sides of this complicated issue; and a range of images—Jesse Gordon's op-art ***What Is America?***; Matt Groening's comic strip ***Life in Hell***; an Adbusters spoof of a Tommy Hilfiger ad; and a mural from Sunnyside, Queens—suggests how central this symbol is in American life.

Looking Closer

A Piece of Cotton

Anne Fadiman

WHEN WE BOUGHT AN OLD BRICK FARMHOUSE last summer in a small New England town, the elderly couple who had lived there for many years left us a set of plastic lawn chairs, a garbage can, a tool bench, a wheelbarrow, and an American flag. On September 13, with our children's help, we raised it to half-staff. Our six-year-old son enjoyed pulling the halyard; on its way up the peeling white-painted pole, next to the big maple tree in the front yard, the flag made an interesting and satisfying sound, partway between a squeak and a ring. We'd read up on half-masting protocol, which dictates raising the flag briskly to the peak and then slowly bringing it halfway down. George said, "This flag is lowered now, but it will rise again, just as our country will." It is useful to have children around at such times: They authorize clichés that their parents deeply believe but might otherwise hesitate to voice.

Neither George nor I had ever owned a flag, not even a little one to wave on the Fourth of July. The closest George had come was the pair of stars-and-stripes bell-bottoms he had worn in the sixties (in violation of section 176d of the United States Flag Code: "The flag should never be used as wearing apparel, bedding, or drapery"). The closest I had come was the handkerchief-sized Whole Earth banner that I had affixed to the aerial of my brother's car before we drove from our home in California to college in

Massachusetts in the fall of 1970. We took the whole earth idea seriously: what a provincial notion, I remember thinking, to fly a flag that implied one was a citizen of only *part* of the earth!

If you had asked me then what it meant to be a flag owner—or, as I would have called it, a flag-waver, as if holding a flag in one's hand was inherently more ridiculous than stringing it up a pole—I would have said "Vietnam." But my answer would have been false. My disdain for the flag wasn't really political. It was social. When I burrow back into my seventeen-year-old self as thoroughly as the intervening decades allow, here's what I fear she was thinking: If you were a flag-waver, you lived in a split-level house with vinyl siding in a suburb of Omaha. You had a crew cut. Your children belonged to the 4-H Club and had a dog that, without irony—there was no irony within a five-hundred-mile radius of Omaha—they had named Fido. You read *Reader's Digest* and listened to Andy Williams. You ate tuna casserole and frozen peas for dinner, followed by lime Jell-O with little pieces of banana suspended in it. You had never traveled east of Wichita (or maybe west; I had never been to either Omaha or Wichita, and knew only that they were both somewhere in the amorphous middle of things).

"Sept. 11 made it safe for liberals to be patriots," the critic George Packer wrote recently in the *New York Times*. Like me, Packer once considered flag-waving an embarrassing display of bad taste ("senti-mental, primitive, sometimes aggressive"), though he associated it more with the working class than with the Cleavcresque middle class. Either way, it wasn't the sort of thing our families indulged in. When people like Packer and me were teenagers, we had little interest in the socioeconomic tiers that separated the upper middle class, to which we belonged, from what we might have called the "underprivileged class" (a group with which we professed heartfelt solidarity, whether or not we'd ever met any of its members). And in those days, in those circles (which pretended to be egalitarian but were in fact unthinkingly, unapologetically, unbelievably snobbish). America was itself déclassé, a simpleminded concatenation of Uncle Sam and log cabins and Smokey the Bear. I mean, really: if you wanted a stimulating dinner companion, would you pick Betsy Ross or Jean-Paul Sartre?

In March of 1918, a year after the United States entered World War I, a mob surrounded a Montana man named E. V. Starr and tried to force him to kiss an American flag. Starr refused, saying, "What is this thing anyway? Nothing but a piece of cotton with a little paint on it and some other marks in the corner there. I will not kiss that thing. It might be covered with microbes."

The previous month, Montana had enacted a flag desecration statute that became the model for the 1918 federal Sedition Act, outlawing "disloyal, profane, scurrilous, or abusive language" about the United States government or its flag. Starr was charged with sedition, fined $500, and sent to the state penitentiary for ten to twenty years of hard labor. Ruling on Starr's appeal, the federal district court judge who heard the appeal wrote:

> In the matter of his offense and sentence, obviously petitioner was more sinned against than sinning.... [The mob's] unlawful and disorderly conduct, not his just resistance, nor the trivial and innocuous retort into which they goaded him, was calculated to degrade the sacred banner and to bring it into contempt. Its members, not he, should have been punished.

Although he called the court that had sentenced Starr "stark, staring, raving mad"—no penalty that severe had ever been meted out, or would ever be meted out again, in a United States flag desecration case—the judge ruled that the state law was nonetheless constitutional and that he had no other choice than to uphold the conviction.

The unfortunate Starr's only bit of luck was that the Montana mob did not assault him, unlike the automobile workers in Lansing, Michigan, who, the same winter, after a fellow employee wiped his hands on a flag, had chopped a hole in the ice that covered the Grand River, tied a clothesline to the man's foot, and submerged him until he apologized; or the saloon patrons in Thermopolis, Wyoming, who, the previous year, had lynched a man for shouting "*Hoch lebe der Kaiser.*" (In the latter case the victim was cut down in the nick of time by the city marshal. The *Chicago Tribune* reported: "Revived with cold water, he was forced to kneel and kiss the American flag. He then was warned to get out of town. He did.")

I read about these cases—they are collected in a fascinating and disturbing book called *Desecrating the American Flag: Key Documents of the Controversy from the Civil War to 1995*, edited by Robert Justin Goldstein—while I was attending a conference in Colonial Williamsburg, the omphalos of Americana. It felt strange to underline E. V. Starr's question in a hotel room crammed with hooked rugs and embroidered samplers. What *is* this thing, anyway? I thought. Is it just a piece of cotton? Is it, as Katha Pollitt put it, explaining why she had refused her daughter's request to hang a flag in their window, a symbol of "jingoism and vengeance and war"? Or is it, as a group of New York women wrote in the dedication of a silk flag they had sewn for Union soldiers in 1861, "the emblem of all you have sworn to defend: / Of freedom and progress, with order combined, / The cause of the *Nation,* of *God,* and *Mankind*"?

After September 11, I saw for the first time that the flag—along with all its red, white, and blue collateral relations—is what a semiotician would call "polysemous": It has multiple meanings. The flag held aloft by the pair of disheveled hitchhikers who squatted next to their backpacks on Route 116, a mile from our home, meant *We will not rape or murder you.* The red, white, and blue turban worn by the Sikh umbrella vendor a friend walked past in Dupont Circle, not far from the White House, meant *Looking like someone and thinking like him are not the same thing.* The flag on the lapel of a Massachusetts attorney mentioned in our local paper—on seeing it, his opposing counsel had whispered to a colleague, "I'm so screwed, do you have a flag pin I can borrow?"— meant *I am morally superior.* The flags brandished by two cowboy-hatted singers at a country fair we attended on the day the first bombs fell on Afghanistan meant *Let's kill the bastards.* The Old Glory bandanna around the neck of the well-groomed golden retriever I saw on a trip to Manhattan meant *Even if I have a Prada bag and my dog has a pedigree, I'm still a New Yorker and I have lost something.* The flag in our front yard meant *We are sad. And we're sorry we've never done this before.*

Newspapers printed full-page color flags for flagless readers to tape on their windows. NBC put stars and stripes on its peacock. The Macdougal Street Tattoo Company in Greenwich Village gave pro bono patriotic tattoos—something new under the sun—to nearly five hundred World Trade Center rescue workers. A Pennsylvania man had a flag shaved into his buzz cut. A New York restaurant called The Tonic introduced a dessert called Stars and Stripes: white mascarpone panna cotta encircled by red and blue pomegranate- and grape-flavored stars. The design of a new 34-cent flag stamp, captioned UNITED WE STAND, was rushed through several layers of U.S. Postal Service red tape in record time so that a billion stamps could be available by November 1. The space shuttle *Endeavor* carried more than six thousand flags to the International Space Station and brought them back for distribution to the families of those killed on September 11. Our son made a flag from a leaf and a twig to mark the final days of his vegetable garden, and asked if he should fly it at half-staff.

When I visited my mother in Florida, I paused at the window of the gift shop in the Fort Myers airport. Outside, a National Guardsman with an M-16 patrolled the corridor. Inside, on a bed of gold-flecked gauze, reposed the largest collection of red, white, and blue objects I had ever seen: flags, streamers, key chains, pens, fans, T-shirts, baseball caps, figurines, coffee mugs, beer steins, shot glasses, menorahs, postcards with photographs of flags surrounded by oranges and flamingos, bumper stickers that said THESE COLORS NEVER RUN, starfish emblazoned with the words GOD BLESS AMERICA. The meaning of these objects had nothing to do with either Washington or Afghanistan; the flag was a "theme," like the "Underwater Theme" we'd chosen for our high school senior prom. ("Japan?" "Too hard to draw all those geishas." "Outer Space?" "Too much black and white." "Underwater?" "Now there's an idea.") I had recently seen a coffee-table book of flag-oriented antiques, each beautifully photographed and embellished with little air-brushed shadows, arranged on the pages like jewels in a Tiffany vitrine. *Patriotic Shield Pin Box. Uncle Sam Hat Broach. Brass and Enamel Belt Buckle. Admiral Perry Whiskey Flask. Wheatlet Trading Card.* They all looked incredibly expensive, but what they had gained in value over the years they had lost in meaning: They were no longer about patriotism in wartime, they were about being collectible. The Fort Myers gift shop window was indistinguishable from a page in that book. It was already meaningless. All it needed was a caption: "Americana—Assorted Ephemera & Folk Art, 2001."

But just because most of the flag paraphernalia was dreck didn't mean that all of it was. I was caught short by the reproduction of Edward P. Moran's flag-filled 1886 painting *Statue of Liberty Enlightening the World,* placed in the *New York Times* by the Museum of the City of New York, accompanied by a quotation from Le Corbusier: "New York is not a completed city. . . . It is a city in the process of becoming. Today it belongs to the world. Without anyone expecting it, it has became the jewel in the crown of universal cities. . . . New York is a great diamond, hard and dry, sparkling, triumphant!" Just typing those words, nearly three months later, brings on the peculiar feeling of congestion I still feel every morning when I read the *Times* obituaries and start thinking about the widow who gave birth to twins on September 15 or the woman who lost both a husband and a son. I had lived in New York for twenty-five years, twenty-two of them within walking distance of the World Trade Center. The trauma center nearest the site was the hospital where our daughter was born; Engine 24/Ladder 5, where Mayor Giuliani, covered in ash, set up his temporary command post, was our corner firehouse. I felt ashamed when I caught myself thinking of this as a neighborhood tragedy rather than a global one; it was the solipsistic fallacy of believing that the telephone pole you're closest to is taller than all the rest, just because it *looks* taller. Our Massachusetts friends said to us, "You must be so relieved to have moved!" And though we did feel relief, our feelings were complicated and contradictory. We loved New York all the more because of what had been done to it. George said it was like the upwelling of tenderness one might feel upon hearing that an old lover had been grievously injured. I knew, though it seemed like a dishonorably trivial emotion, that one of the reasons Moran and Le Corbusier affected me was homesickness.

It was good to see George watching the World Series one night. Until then, we had been unable to watch any television that did not deal with September 11. Flying above center field at Yankee Stadium was a torn flag. It was shaped like an oriflamme, the banner the kings army carried in twelfth-century France, split at one end with flying edges like two flames. The flag, which had flown somewhere inside the World Trade Center, had been found in the rubble and nearly disposed of (Flag Code section 176k: "The flag, when it is in such condition that it is no longer a fitting emblem for display, should be destroyed in a dignified way, preferably by burning"). The Port Authority intervened, and Sgt. Antonio Scannella, a police officer who had lost thirteen of his squad's eighteen members, became the flag's unoffi-

cial caretaker, saying, "You can't throw an American flag in the garbage." When Max Von Essen, the son of the New York City Fire Commissioner, sang "The Star-Spangled Banner" (the only national anthem I can think of that's specifically about a flag), my throat caught in an unfamiliar way.

Why did the lopsided flag that billowed across our television screen pull strings that had previously been unpullable? I think it moved me *because* it was damaged, like the city itself. A clean rectangle whose proportions conform precisely to the Executive Order issued in 1912 by President Taft—hoist (height) 1.0, fly (length) 1.9, hoist of union (blue field) .5385, fly of union .76, width of each stripe .0769, diameter of each star .0616—calls up less passionate associations than, for instance, the flag flown by the Sixteenth Regiment of Connecticut volunteers in the Civil War. When surrender was inevitable, the soldiers tore the flag into fragments to keep it from falling into enemy hands. A historian named F. C. Hicks wrote in 1926:

> The regiment, some five hundred strong, was sent to a prison camp where most of the men remained until the close of the war. Each piece of the colors was sacredly preserved. When a soldier died his piece was entrusted to a comrade. At the end of the war the weary prisoners returned to their homes, each bringing his bit of star or stripe with him. All these torn fragments were patched together and the regimental colors, nearly complete, are now preserved in the State House at Hartford.

To read about our nation's vexillogical history—"vexillology," the study of flags, is an excellent crossword-puzzle word that derives from the Latin *vexillum*, or banner—is to experience a series of bitter disillusionments. Betsy Ross did not design the stars and stripes; she sewed flags for the navy in the spring of 1777, but there is no evidence that the flag as we know it was conceived before June 14 of that year, when the Continental Congress, which had previously been more concerned about designing a national seal, finally got around to the flag: "RESOLVED: that the flag of the United States be made of thirteen stripes, alternate red and white; that the union be thirteen stars, white in a blue field, representing a new constellation." (Many historians now attribute the circular shape of that constellation to Francis Hopkinson, a delegate from New Jersey, though late-eighteenth-century flags show the stars disposed in a variety of arrangements, including a single vertical line and an *X*.) George Washington did not cross the Delaware with flag in hand; the Battle of Trenton was fought six months before the Flag Resolution. The flag's design did not immediately engrave itself on the memories of all who beheld it; in 1778, Benjamin Franklin and John Adams informed the King of the Two Sicilies that the stripes were "alternately red, white, and blue," and on a ceramic jug manufactured in Liverpool at about the same time, an American ship flew a flag with blue and yellow stripes. "The Star-Spangled Banner" did not immediately become the national anthem; though it was written by Francis Scott Key during the Battle of Fort McHenry in 1814 (and set to the tune of "To Anacreon in Heaven," a British drinking song celebrating a bibulous Greek poet who is said to have choked to death on a grape), it was not officially adopted until 1931.

In fact, as Scot M. Guenter explains in *The American Flag 1777–1924: Cultural Shifts from Creation to Codification,* it was not until Rebel forces fired on the flag at Fort Sumter on April 12, 1861, that the flag, which earlier had been used mainly for identifying naval and commercial vessels, was transformed into a symbol men were willing to die for. If it took the Civil War to sacralize the flag—as the historian George Henry Preble wrote in 1880, "its prose became poetry"—it took the commercialism of the ensuring decades to turn its poetry back into prose. In 1905, an antidesecration circular lamented the use of the flag in advertisements for "bicycles, bock beer, whiskey, fine cambric, bone knoll, sour mash, tar soap, American pepsin chewing gum, theatres, tobacco, Japan tea, awnings, breweries, cigars, charity balls, cuff buttons, dime museums, floor mats, fireworks, furriers, living pictures, picnic grounds, patent medicines, poolrooms, prize fights, restaurants, roof gardens, real estate agencies, sample rooms, shoe stores, soap makers, saloons, shooting galleries, tent makers, variety shows, [and] vendors of lemon acid." Tame stuff, perhaps, compared with David Bowie, his face painted red, white, and blue and a miniature vodka bottle resting on his naked clavicle (caption: "Absolut Bowie"), or with the nightmarish ads that clog the Internet ("Render this Osama Voo-Doo doll completely Pin-Laden! 6-inch doll for a Stocking Stuffer Price of $9.99! Comes with 6 red, white, and blue extra-sharp Patriot Pins").

In 1989, the School of the Art Institute of Chicago mounted an exhibit called "What Is the Proper Way to Display the American Flag?" In order to reach the leather-bound ledger in which they were asked to record their responses, viewers had to walk on a flag laid on the floor. "For days," reported the *Detroit News,* "veterans picked the flag up off the floor, folded it in the ceremonial military fashion and placed it on the shelf. Their faces were almost always stoic; one was visibly in tears at the sight of grimy footprints on the flag. Moments later, however, the flag was unfolded by supporters of the art, usually students with indignant faces, who shook out the flag like a bedsheet, and then draped it on the floor."

The same year, in a controversial case called *Texas v. Johnson,* Supreme Court Justice Anthony Kennedy explained why he had concluded, with great reluctance, that flag-burning is a form of free speech and therefore protected by the First Amendment. "Though symbols often are what we ourselves make of them," he wrote, "the flag is constant in expressing beliefs Americans share, beliefs in law and peace and that freedom which sustains the human spirit. The case here today forces recognition of the costs to which those beliefs commit us. It is poignant but fundamental that the flag protects those who hold it in contempt."

We kept our flag at half-staff longer than President Bush decreed that we should, and then, after raising it to full-staff, we continued to fly it after most of our neighbors had put theirs away. Maybe we were making up for lost time. Maybe we needed to see our flag flying in order to convince ourselves that even though protesters marching near a mosque in Bridgewater, Illinois, had waved flags and chanted "U.S.A.! U.S.A.!" we could choose another meaning in Whately, Massachusetts: the one a Chicago flag committee had in mind in 1895 when it called the Stars and Stripes "our greater self."

I had not looked closely at our flag when we raised 20 it, so I decided to take it down one day to see whether it was made of cotton or silk. It was a raw afternoon in early December; freezing rain was falling on gray patches of snow. Section 174c of the Flag Code pro-hibits display in inclement weather, but a handful of local diehards were still flying their flags rain or shine, twenty-four hours a day, so we had followed suit. The flag was sodden and looked like a shrouded bat. When I lowered it and detached the grommets from the halyard, I could see that it was made of nylon. Black letters printed on the hoist, so faded I could barely make them out, read DURA LITE. The red stitching that connected the stripes was beginning to bleed. The embroidered white stars were fraying. As I refastened the brass clip, I tried hard to keep the old, wet, shabby flag from touching the ground. ○

"freedom"
Yen, Vietnam

"money"
Frankie, Queens

"imperialism"
Aaron, New York City

"diversity"
Karine, New York City

"religious freedom"
Dhananjay, India

"plastics"
Ian, Canada

"possibility"
Raymond, St. Kitts

"choice"
Melissa, New York City

"ignorance"
Devo, Kansas City

"my adopted country"
Sister Mary, England

"needs healing"
Elijah, South Carolina

"hope"
Pat, Staten Island

"open-minded"
Isaac, Brooklyn

"jazz"
Valerie, Connecticut

"ketchup"
Constantino, Greece

"original ideas"
Charles, New York City

"business"
Adaib, Yemen

"consumerism"
Silvia, Barcelona

"fun"
Nobuhisa, Japan

"lost opportunities"
Dan, Seattle

"excess"
Katherine, Boston

"*sundar* (beautiful)"
Sharada, India

"everything"
Larry, Puerto Rico

"ahhhh!"
Jadah and Joziah, New York City

Justice William J. Brennan Jr.

AFTER PUBLICLY BURNING AN AMERICAN FLAG AS a means of political protest, Gregory Lee Johnson was convicted of desecrating a flag in violation of Texas law. This case presents the question whether his conviction is consistent with the First Amendment. We hold that it is not.

While the Republican National Convention was taking place in Dallas in 1984, respondent Johnson participated in a political demonstration dubbed the "Republican War Chest Tour." . . .

The demonstration ended in front of Dallas City Hall, where Johnson unfurled the American flag, doused it with kerosene and set it on fire. While the flag burned, the protestors chanted, "America, the red, white, and blue, we spit on you." After the demonstrators dispersed, a witness to the flag burning collected the flag's remains and buried them in his backyard. No one was physically injured or threatened with injury, though several witnesses testified that they had been seriously offended by the flag burning.

Of the approximately 100 demonstrators, Johnson alone was charged with a crime. The only criminal offense with which he was charged was the desecration of a venerated object in violation of Texas Penal Code Ann. Sec. 42.09 (a)(3) (1989) ["Desecration of a Venerated Object"]. After a trial, he was convicted, sentenced to one year in prison and fined $2,000. The Court of Appeals for the Fifth District of Texas at Dallas affirmed Johnson's conviction, but the Texas Court of Criminal Appeals reversed, holding that the State could not, consistent with the First Amendment, punish Johnson for burning the flag in these circumstances. . . .

STATE ASSERTED TWO INTERESTS

To justify Johnson's conviction for engaging in sym- 5 bolic speech, the State asserted two interests: preserving the flag as a symbol of national unity and preventing breaches of the peace. The Court of Criminal Appeals held that neither interest supported his conviction.

Acknowledging that this Court had not yet decided whether the Government may criminally sanction flag desecration in order to preserve the flag's symbolic value, the Texas court nevertheless concluded that our decision in *West Virginia Board of Education v. Barnette,* 319 U.S. 624 (1943), suggested that furthering this interest by curtailing speech was impermissible.

The First Amendment literally forbids the abridgement only of "speech," but we have long recognized that its protection does not end at the spoken or written word. . . .

Especially pertinent to this case are our decisions recognizing the communicative nature of conduct relating to flags. Attaching a peace sign to the flag, *Spence v. Washington,* 1974; saluting the flag, *Barnette,* and displaying a red flag, *Stromberg v. California* (1931), we have held, all may find shelter under the First Amendment. . . . That we have had little difficulty identifying an expressive element in conduct relating to flags should not be surprising. The very purpose of a national flag is to serve as a symbol of our country; it is, one might say, "the one visible manifestation of two hundred years of nationhood." . . .

Pregnant with expressive content, the flag as readily signifies this nation as does the combination of letters found in "America."

The Government generally has a freer hand in re- 10 stricting expressive conduct than it has in restricting the written or spoken word. . . . It may not, however, proscribe particular conduct because it has expressive elements. . . . It is, in short, not simply the verbal or nonverbal nature of the expression, but the governmental interest at stake, that helps to determine whether a restriction on that expression is valid.

The State offers two separate interests to justify this conviction: preventing breaches of the peace, and preserving the flag as a symbol of nationhood and national unity. We hold that the first interest is not implicated on this record and that the second is related to the suppression of expression. . . .

We thus conclude that the State's interest in maintaining order is not implicated on these facts. The State need not worry that our holding will disable it from preserving the peace. We do not suggest that the First Amendment forbids a state to prevent "imminent lawless action." And, in fact, Texas already has a statute specifically prohibiting breaches of the peace, Texas Penal Code Ann. Sec. 42.01 (1989), which tends to confirm that Texas need not punish this flag desecration in order to keep the peace.

If there is a bedrock principle underlying the First Amendment, it is that the Government may not prohibit the expression of an idea simply because society finds the idea itself offensive or disagreeable. . . .

We have not recognized an exception to this principle even where our flag has been involved. In *Street v. New York,* 394 U.S. 576 (1969), we held that a state may not criminally punish a person for uttering words critical of the flag. . . .

Nor may the Government, we have held, compel 15 conduct that would evince respect for the flag. . . .

We never before have held that the Government may insure that a symbol be used to express only one view of that symbol or its referents. . . . To conclude that the Government may permit designated symbols to be used to communicate only a limited set of messages would be to enter territory having no discernible or defensible boundaries.

WHICH SYMBOLS WARRANT UNIQUE STATUS?
Could the Government, on this theory, prohibit the burning of state flags? Of copies of the Presidential seal? Of the Constitution? In evaluating these choices under the First Amendment, how would we decide which symbols were sufficiently special to warrant

this unique status? To do so, we would be forced to consult our own political preferences, and impose them on the citizenry, in the very way that the First Amendment forbids us to do.

There is, moreover, no indication—either in the text of the Constitution or in our cases interpreting— that a separate juridical category exists for the American flag alone. Indeed, we would not be surprised to learn that the persons who framed our Constitution and wrote the Amendment that we now construe were not known for their reverence for the Union Jack.

The First Amendment does not guarantee that other concepts virtually sacred to our nation as a whole— such as the principle that discrimination on the basis of race is odious and destructive—will go unquestioned in the marketplace of ideas. We decline, therefore, to create for the flag an exception to the joust of principles protected by the First Amendment.

We are fortified in today's conclusion by our con- 20 viction that forbidding criminal punishment for conduct such as Johnson's will not endanger the special role played by our flag or the feelings it inspires. . . .

A REAFFIRMATION OF PRINCIPLES
We are tempted to say, in fact, that the flag's deservedly cherished place in our community will be strengthened, not weakened, by our holding today. Our decision is a reaffirmation of the principles of freedom and inclusiveness that the flag best reflects, and of the conviction that our toleration of criticism such as Johnson's is a sign and source of our strength.

The way to preserve the flag's special role is not to punish those who feel differently about these matters. It is to persuade them that they are wrong. . . .

We can imagine no more appropriate response to burning a flag than waving one's own, no better way to counter a flag-burner's message than by saluting the flag that burns, no surer means of preserving the dignity even of the flag that burned than by—as one witness here did—according its remains a respectful burial. We do not consecrate the flag by punishing its desecration, for in doing so we dilute the freedom that this cherished emblem represents. ○

ERNI ...2001... PINK SOUTH ...

Erni, Smith, and Lady Pink, *Mural*, Sunnyside, Queens, 2001

Looking Closer

DISSENTING OPINION IN *TEXAS V. JOHNSON* (1989)

Chief Justice William H. Rehnquist

IN HOLDING THIS TEXAS STATUTE UNCONSTITUtional, the Court ignores Justice Holmes's familiar aphorism that "a page of history is worth a volume of logic." For more than 200 years, the American flag has occupied a unique position as the symbol of our nation, a uniqueness that justifies a governmental prohibition against flag burning in the way respondent Johnson did here.

At the time of the American Revolution, the flag served to unify the 13 colonies at home while obtaining recognition of national sovereignty abroad. Ralph Waldo Emerson's "Concord Hymn" describes the first skirmishes of the Revolutionary War in these lines:

> By the rude bridge that arched the flood,
> Their flag to April's breeze unfurled,
> Here once the embattled farmers stood,
> And fired the shot heard round the world.

In the First and Second World Wars, thousands of our countrymen died on foreign soil fighting for the American cause. At Iwo Jima in the Second World War, United States Marines fought hand to hand against thousands of Japanese. By the time the marines reached the top of Mount Suribachi, they raised a piece of pipe upright and from one end fluttered a flag. That ascent had cost nearly 6,000 American lives....

The flag symbolizes the nation in peace as well as in war. It signifies our national presence on battleships, airplanes, military installations and public buildings from the United States Capitol to the thousands of county courthouses and city halls throughout the country....

No other American symbol has been as universally honored as the flag. In 1931 Congress declared "The Star Spangled Banner" to be our national anthem. In 1949 Congress declared June 14th to be Flag Day. In 1987 John Philip Sousa's "The Stars and Stripes Forever" was designated as the national march. Congress has also established "The Pledge of Allegiance to the Flag" and the manner of its deliverance.... All of the states now have statutes prohibiting the burning of the flag....

The result of the Texas statute is obviously to deny one in Johnson's frame of mind one of many means of "symbolic speech." Far from being a case of "one picture being worth a thousand words," flag burning is the equivalent of an inarticulate grunt or roar that, it seems fair to say, is most likely to be indulged in not to express any particular idea, but to antagonize others. . . .

The Texas statute deprived Johnson of only one rather inarticulate symbolic form of protest—a form of protest that was profoundly offensive to many—and left him with a full panoply of other symbols and every conceivable form of verbal expression to express his deep disapproval of national policy. . . .

But the Court today will have none of this. The uniquely deep awe and respect for our flag felt by virtually all of us are bundled off under the rubric of "designated symbols" that the First Amendment prohibits the Government from "establishing." But the Government has not "established" this feeling; 200 years of history have done that. The Government is simply recognizing as a fact the profound regard for the American flag created by that history when it enacts statutes prohibiting the disrespectful public burning of the flag.

The Court concludes its opinion with a regrettably patronizing civics lecture, presumably addressed to the members of both houses of Congress, the members of the 48 state legislatures that enacted prohibitions against flag burning, and the troops fighting under that flag in Vietnam who objected to its being burned: "The way to preserve the flag's special role is not to punish those who feel differently about these matters. It is to persuade them that they are wrong."

The Court's role as the final expositor of the Constitution is well established, but its role as a platonic guardian admonishing those responsible to public opinion as if they were truant school children has no similar place in our system of government. . . . 10

Even if flag burning could be considered just another species of symbolic speech under the logical application of the rules that the Court has developed in its interpretation of the First Amendment in other contexts, this case has an intangible dimension that makes those rules inapplicable.

A country's flag is a symbol of more than "nationhood and national unity." It also signifies the ideas that characterize the society that has chosen that emblem, as well as the special history that has animated the growth and power of those ideas. . . .

So it is with the American flag. It is more than a proud symbol of the courage, the determination and the gifts of nature that transformed 13 fledgling colonies into a world power. It is a symbol of freedom, of equal opportunity, of religious tolerance and of good will for other peoples who share our aspirations. . . .

The value of the flag as a symbol cannot be measured. Even so, I have no doubt that the interest in preserving that value for the future is both significant and legitimate. . . . The creation of a Federal right to post bulletin boards and graffiti on the Washington Monument might enlarge the market for free expression, but at a cost I would not pay.

Similarly, in my considered judgment, sanctioning the public desecration of the flag will tarnish its value—both for those who cherish the ideas for which it waves and for those who desire to don the robes of martyrdom by burning it. That tarnish is not justified by the trivial burden on free expression occasioned by requiring that an available, alternative mode of expression—including uttering words critical of the flag—be employed. 15

The ideas of liberty and equality have been an irresistible force in motivating leaders like Patrick Henry, Susan B. Anthony, and Abraham Lincoln, schoolteachers like Nathan Hale and Booker T. Washington, the Philippine Scouts who fought at Bataan, and the soldiers who scaled the bluff at Omaha Beach. If those ideas are worth fighting for—and our history demonstrates that they are—it cannot be true that the flag that uniquely symbolizes their power is not itself worthy of protection from unnecessary desecration. ○

Mat Groening, *Life in Hell*, 1985 (left); Adbusters, *Follow the Flock*. (right)

Looking Closer

ANNE FADIMAN

Writer Anne Fadiman was one of the founding editors of *Civilization,* a bi-monthly magazine started in 1994, and was an editor for seven years at *The American Scholar,* where "A Piece of Cotton" first appeared. The essay won a National Magazine Award in 2003.

Fadiman was born in 1953 into a literary family. Her father, Clifton Fadiman, was a well-known critic, book reviewer, and editor; her mother, Annalee Jacoby, was a correspondent for *Time* magazine and coauthor, with Theodore H. White, of *Thunder Out of China* (1946).

Anne Fadiman's work has appeared in *The New Yorker, Harper's,* and the *New York Times,* among other publications. Her first book, *The Spirit Catches You and You Fall Down* (1997), tells the story of a Hmong child and her treatment by American doctors. It won the National Book Critics Circle Award for Nonfiction. Her second book, *Ex Libris: Confessions of a Common Reader* (1998), was a best seller. In January 2005, Fadiman became the first Francis Writer in Residence at Yale.

JESSE GORDON

Jesse Gordon is a writer and filmmaker who lives in New York City. The twenty-four photographs shown here were among thirty-five that appeared in an op-art piece in the *New York Times* on July 3, 2000. The question posed to those photographed was "What is America?"

WILLIAM J. BRENNAN JR.

Justice William J. Brennan (1906–1997) was one of the most influential Supreme Court justices in the twentieth century. He served on the nation's highest court for thirty-three years, from 1956 until he retired in 1990 at the age of 84. Justice Brennan often fashioned the legal arguments that persuaded a majority of justices in difficult and controversial cases.

Texas v. Johnson is an excellent example. In 1984, while the Republican National Convention was taking place in Dallas, Gregory Lee Johnson burned an American flag as a statement of protest against the policies of the Reagan administration. He was arrested and convicted under a Texas law that made it a crime to desecrate the flag. The case reached the Supreme Court in 1989, and Justice Brennan wrote for a bare 5-to-4 majority overturning Johnson's conviction and upholding his right to burn the American flag as an exercise of his constitutionally protected freedom of speech.

MURAL, SUNNYSIDE, QUEENS

As part of the post–September 11 culture, many forms of public art emerged to express civic emotion that was evident after the attack on the World Trade Center. Three artists, who identify themselves as Erni, Smith, and Lady Pink, created a block-long mural on a wall facing the Long Island Expressway in Sunnyside, Queens. Lady Pink, who was a pioneering graffiti artist in the late 1970s, often includes the image of a large-eyed woman in her work. It is seen in this mural as a deity who watches over the firemen at Ground Zero. The artwork powerfully conveys the sense of overwhelming patriotism and unity felt by many New Yorkers at that time.

WILLIAM H. REHNQUIST

William H. Rehnquist (1924–2005) served with the Army Air Corps during World War II and then graduated from Stanford Law School in 1952. President Richard Nixon appointed him assistant attorney general in 1969. Three years later he joined the Supreme Court as an associate justice. In 1986 he was appointed chief justice by Ronald Reagan. Rehnquist died of thyroid cancer in September 2005.

For more than thirty years Chief Justice Rehnquist anchored the Court's conservative wing. In the Texas flag-burning case he voted with the minority to uphold the constitutionality of the law and wrote one of the two dissenting opinions.

MATT GROENING

America's most visible cartoonist and animator, Matt Groening (pronounced "groaning") was born in Portland, Oregon, in 1954. He worked in a sewage treatment plant, as a chauffeur, and as a ghostwriter before his *Life in Hell* comic strip (featuring two rabbits because, he says, "they are easy to draw") earned him international acclaim as a cartoonist. In 1989 Groening launched *The Simpsons* on the FOX network; it soon became the most successful animated prime-time series in television history.

ADBUSTERS

Based in Vancouver, British Columbia, Adbusters Media Foundation is a consortium of artists, writers, and activists who love to make fun of commercial America. The group's bi-monthly magazine *Adbusters*, reaches 120,000 readers who probably feel the same way its artists and writers do — that the physical, mental, and spiritual well-being of humankind is threatened by the global economy and big-brand corporations. Adbusters' mission is serious, but its articles and artwork use humor to expose the underlying messages in corporate advertising, as in this spoof of a Tommy Hilfiger ad.

SEEING

1. What do you notice about each of the images and verbal texts in this section? Explain how the American flag is represented and/or appropriated in each. Compare and contrast, for example, the way in which the flag is used in Jesse Gordon's photo essay with its use in Matt Groening's comic strip. How do the creators of these pieces use persuasion to prompt readers to take a particular course of action or to accept a particular point of view? How are their strategies similar? different?

2. In his majority opinion in *Texas v. Johnson*, Justice Brennan wrote, "Pregnant with expressive content, the flag as readily signifies this nation as does the combination of letters found in 'America'" (para. 9). In her essay, Anne Fadiman offers that the flag is "'polysemous'" (para. 9): It has multiple meanings. Many representations of and discussions about the flag in this section comment on what the flag "stands for" in American culture. Choose two of these renditions of the American flag in contemporary culture. What social and/or historical versions of America does each suggest?

WRITING

1. Since 1989, when the Supreme Court ruled that a person may not be prosecuted for burning the American flag as a peaceful political protest, the issue of whether the flag should receive special protection under the law has remained hotly debated. Write an essay in which you build an argument that the American flag should or should not be protected, and to what extent and under what circumstances. Draw on the essays, opinions, and images in these pages to support your argument.

2. The debate over the legality of flag burning involves one of the most precious rights of Americans: freedom of speech. Use the web to identify and locate source material on another recent controversy over the rights guaranteed under the First Amendment to the Constitution. Then write an expository essay in which you account for the ways in which the nature and extent of this issue are similar to—or different from—the debate over burning the American flag.

RESPONDING VISUALLY

Create your own version of Jesse Gordon's op-art piece. Photograph at least ten people holding the American flag and responding to the question "What is America?" Arrange your photographs and captions on a page, as Gordon does, or in another format of your choice—a portfolio, for example, a series of web pages, or a PowerPoint presentation.

Looking Closer

7CHAL
LENG-
ING
IM-
AGES

We chose the title "Challenging Images" for this chapter because the images and texts in this chapter provide illustrations of the different meanings of the word *challenging*. As an adjective, *challenging* suggests complexity and difficulty, and implies a need for focus and sustained attention. A challenging subject, for example, may be a topical issue (withdrawing U.S. troops from Iraq) or some perennial issue (helping to resolve the longstanding political conflict in the Middle East) that requires us to articulate and perhaps put into practice our most deeply rooted convictions and beliefs.

Challenging is also a verb form that can be said to characterize the intellectual work you have been practicing throughout *Seeing & Writing 3*. In this sense, *challenging* images requires deliberate and purposeful intellectual activity and highlights the contested nature of that thinking and writing. In effect, images challenge the mind to work differently—much in the way that a challenge is an invitation to compete, be it at a sport or in an argument.

In contemporary America, images and words challenge each other for our attention. In the competition (some would call it a battle) between images and words, images seem to be winning, or

An 80-year-old woman, one of countless civilian war victims, living in the basement of her bombed-out Chechen home. Magnum Photos

imagine

(all the people living life in peace)

Imagine a worldwide movement working to protect the dignity and rights of all people. And imagine it works. For 40 years, Amnesty International members have saved countless lives - people persecuted, imprisoned, or tortured simply for who they are or what they believe. Many more need your help. Take action. Log on. Join us.

www.amnestyusa.org

Two refugee girls at risk of joining the hundreds of thousands of child soldiers worldwide.
Photo: Peter Marlow/Magnum

Collaborate/Amnesty International, *Imagine Nothing to Kill or Die For*, 2002

imagine

(nothing to kill or die for)

Imagine a worldwide movement working to protect the dignity and rights of all people. And imagine it works.
For 40 years, Amnesty International members have saved countless lives - people persecuted, imprisoned,
or tortured simply for who they are or what they believe. Many more need your help. Take action. Log on. Join us.

...UNTIL JUSTICE ROLLS DOWN LIKE WATERS
AND RIGHTEOUSNESS LIKE A MIGHTY STREAM

MARTIN LUTHER KING JR

A young boy learns about the history of the
civil rights movement. Montgomery, Alabama.
Photo: Eli Reed/Magnum

imagine

(you may say i'm a dreamer, but i'm not the only one)

Imagine a worldwide movement working to protect the dignity and rights of all people. And imagine it works.
For 40 years, Amnesty International members have saved countless lives - people persecuted, imprisoned,
or tortured simply for who they are or what they believe. Many more need your help. Take action. Log on. Join us.

so media pundits would have us believe. Images increasingly dominate public space—on the front pages of newspapers and the covers of magazines, as well as on television, movie, and computer screens, on roadside signs, and on the sides and tops of buildings.

Images play an increasingly important role in what we know—and how we learn—about current events. In fact, more Americans get their news from TV than from newspapers, and each televised story is accompanied by a stream of moving images on the screen: the indelible images of twin towers collapsing, and sobbing parents searching for their children among the bodies of tsunami victims. The list of such enduring images grows longer each year. As media critic Neil Postman has observed, "We are now a culture whose information, ideas, and epistemology are given form by television, not by the printed word."

You have come of age at a time when images play a prominent role in determining American values and assumptions—and thus a time when questioning what we see is more important than ever before. More of us spend our leisure time, for example, visually engaged by flipping through TV channels,

watching movies, or surfing the web. Even when
we are not looking at images in the public media,
we record and sometimes even plan significant personal and private events around the photographs
and home videos they will yield.

In a similar vein, an unprecedented influx of information, data, news, and stories is pouring into
our lives at an incredible rate. Rapidly advancing
computer and digital technologies now make copy-
ing, sending, and disseminating images increasingly
speedy and accessible. Just as the invention of the
printing press facilitated the widespread distribution
of print and required people to develop verbal
literacy, today more and more people have to demonstrate another kind of literacy, a visual literacy—
the ability to read, understand, and act on the information conveyed in powerful contemporary images.

The language of constructing images has infused itself in the public consciousness. Politicians
hire consultants to perfect their public "images."
We speak of improving our "self-image." We might
even say that Americans now have become more
accustomed to looking at—and thinking about—images of things than at the things themselves. A friend
with a cell phone can take us on a virtual vacation;

a computer game has us driving a race car or piloting a spacecraft; and television daily brings war—down the street or on the other side of the globe—into our living rooms.

Differentiating between image and reality has never been easy, but the question now is whether it's even possible. Cultural commentator Neal Gabler argues that it isn't:

> Everywhere the fabricated, the inauthentic and the theatrical have gradually driven out the natural, the genuine and the spontaneous until there is no distinction between real life and stagecraft. In fact, one could argue that the theatricalization of American life is the major cultural transformation of our era. Devoured by artifice, life is a movie.

The "real" events we watch on TV are what social historian Daniel Boorstin called "pseudo-events," events that have been crafted or framed solely for media presentation . . . and audience reception. At the same time that Americans are arguably more removed from real experience, wc are nonetheless more obsessed with determining whether something is real or fake. Advertisers capitalize on the desire for authenticity: witness authentic stonewashed jeans and Coke, "The Real Thing."

RODOLF MONTIEL FLORES

IF A MILLION TREES FALL IN
AN ANCIENT FOREST, AND THIS MAN
IS NOT THERE TO HEAR THEM,
DO THEY MAKE A SOUND?

DEFENDTHEEARTH.ORG

AMNESTY INTERNATIONAL

SIERR
CLUB
FOUNDED 1892

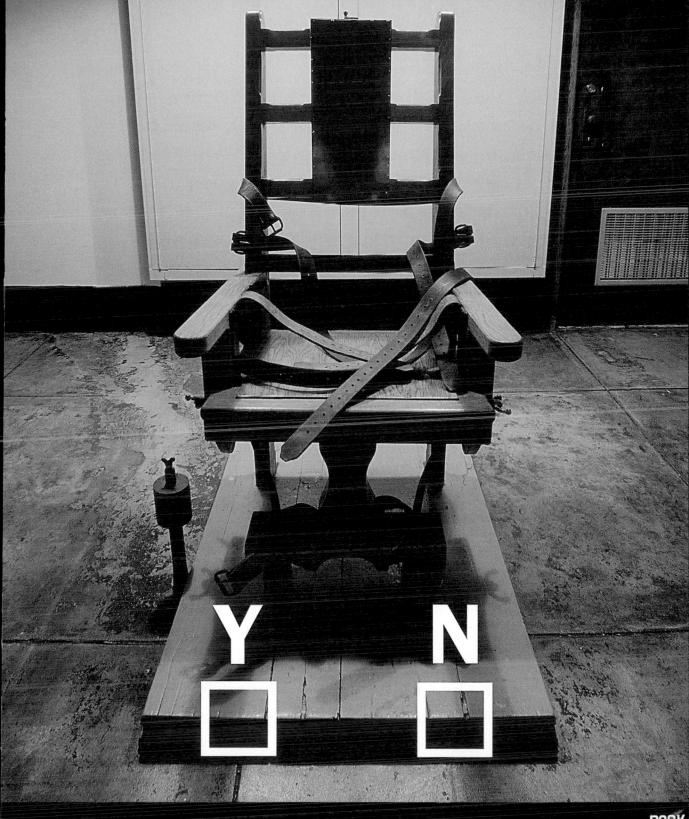

Use your voice. Make a choice.

ROCK THE VOTE

More often we accept the image as our medium of choice. One example of the way in which we're becoming accustomed to working with a representation of reality in our daily lives involves the computer. When we sit in front of a monitor, mouse in hand, navigating a program, what we're working with is a designed interface—an image, a representation of the workings of the computer. In fact, computer salespeople join cultural commentators in questioning whether computer screens will ultimately replace books as the principal format in which we read. Already book sales are decreasing, and students are demonstrating only marginal progress in reading and writing proficiency.

Meanwhile we channel surf, rapidly scanning dozens of images in a few seconds, or we click from icon to icon. How do those processes differ from reading from left to right on a page? Computers have given new meaning to the term *multitasking* for millions of workers who must shift back and forth among windows on their computer screen or simultaneously talk on the phone, type, and wait for a web page to download. How does multitasking change the way in which we can be expected to read? And how does it change the ways in which we think and write?

Today writers must think like designers, and designers must think like writers. If you're writing text for a web page, how do the visual aspects of text design—your ability to use hypertext—change the way you write as well as the content of your writing? If you are writing an article for a magazine or newspaper, how do space and design constraints affect your style and content? How would you write an article differently if you knew a photograph or illustration was going to accompany it? In more general terms, how—and to what extent—should university curricula adjust to the changing nature of reading and writing to help students become more confident and articulate readers and writers?

Some scholars have noted that rather than simply propelling us forward, rapidly advancing computer technology is also drawing on the past. Voice recognition software, for example, might allow us to return to the oral tradition of using our voices to create and record. And Scott McCloud reminds us (see page 694) that ancient civilizations have long integrated the visual and verbal in their communication systems: Think of hieroglyphics or the iconographic character sets of Chinese and Japanese languages. What consequences do you think the new "age of the image" has for writing and reading? We invite you to explore this question, and to form and revise your own judgments, as you critically read the authors and artists in this chapter.

COLLABORATE

Based in San Francisco, new breed ad agency Collaborate works across media for a wide range of clients from the retail, consumer technology, entertainment, and nonprofit sectors. Its client roster includes Amnesty International, Gore-Tex, Logitech, Franklin Templeton Investments, Rock the Vote, Seagate, and the University of California, Berkeley.

Collaborate designed and produced the campaigns in this portfolio for Amnesty International, the Sierra Club, and Rock the Vote. Referred to in the advertising industry as "cause-related" work, each leverages the power of print, online, and broadcast media to help advocate a social or political issue to specific or mass audiences.

Amnesty International launched its *Imagine* campaign in 2002 after Yoko Ono gave the organization the rights to John Lennon's song in the wake of 9/11. The vision for the campaign, according to Amnesty International, is "to engage and inspire the next generation of human rights activists." The International Right to Know Initiative, a joint project for Amnesty International and the Sierra Club, promotes the intersection of environmental and human rights. Collaborate's award-winning *Yes/No* campaign for Rock the Vote utilized multiple media to feature graphic representations of social issues like gun control, same-sex marriage, the death penalty, and abortion.

SEEING

1. The posters and advertisements for Amnesty International, the Sierra Club, and Rock the Vote were created by Collaborate, a creative communications agency based in San Francisco. What do you understand to be the overarching message of each piece in this portfolio of challenging images? How would you characterize the relationship of words to illustration in each image? To what exent—and in what specific ways—does each visual text reinforce the verbal text?

2. What similarities—and differences—do you notice in the style, graphics, verbal strategy, and overall design of these images? How would you characterize Collaborate's style? Comment on the effects of the choices Collaborate has made in typeface and type size, the position of the language in relation to the illustration, and the use of color. What cultural references and allusions does Collaborate evoke in these pieces? Which do you judge to be the most effective? Why?

WRITING

1. Think carefully about the phrase "a picture is worth a thousand words." With what experiences do you associate this expression? What patterns can you identify between and among those experiences? Are they, for example, personal experiences? more public in nature? something else? Explain your answer. Write the first draft of an essay in which you argue for or against the applicability of this phrase to the circumstances of your life.

2. Turn to Andrew Savulich's news photographs (page 274). Examine the role Savulich's descriptive titles play in establishing the impact of his photographs. How do even these brief descriptions affect your understanding of the photographs? How might you interpret Savulich's photographs if the titles were worded differently? Draft an essay in which you compare and contrast the manner and impact of combining words and images in Savulich's work and in Collaborate's.

Frank Fournier, *Omayra Sanchez, Colombia, 1985*

OMAYRA SANCHEZ

Isabel Allende

WHEN I SAW THIS PICTURE IN 1985, I THOUGHT nothing like this could ever happen to my children, but I now have a daughter who's very ill and may die. Just as Omayra agonized trapped in the mud, so is my daughter trapped in a body that doesn't function anymore. For a year I have been at her bedside and often the memory of Omayra comes to me, she has never quite left me, really. She will always be with me. She brings the same message now as she did before: of endurance and the love of life, and, ironically, the acceptance of tragedy and death. When I first saw the picture I thought, "Maybe she's asking for help." Then I thought, "No, she has not died yet. She's still alive." It reminds me of how fragile life is. She demonstrates such passion, she never begged for help, never complained.

In all these years, I've become acquainted with her and I identify with her. In some ways I am her; she's inside me, there's something between us that's very strange. She's a ghost that haunts me. I often wonder about what she feels. I don't think she's thinking, she just *feels*. Later it was discovered that when her house had crumbled, she was stuck between two pieces of wood and the bodies of her brothers. Her body *feels* the cold, the fear, the stress. She looks so uncomfortable in the mud, so much in pain. And yet, look at her hands, they're so elegant.

The wonder of photography is that it does what no words can. I think in images. I remember my life in images. The earliest memory of my life, and the only memory I have of my father, is when I was two years old. My father and I are standing on the stairs of our house in Lima, where I was born. And I can see his legs and his shoes—back then, men wore shoes in two colors, black and white. And I remember my brother, who couldn't walk yet, wearing white pants and white shoes, and then, all of a sudden, he tumbled and fell, and there was blood. I have this image of my father's trousers stained with blood.

The lessons that Omayra has taught me are about life and about death. What I have learned, what she has taught me, is very complex. Every time I go back to this photograph, new things come up. This girl is alone. No one from her family is with her. I don't know if they were all dead at that time or if they had run away. The only people with her were cameramen, photographers, and people from the Red Cross who were strangers. She died alone, and I wish I had been there to hold her, the way I hold my daughter.

Western culture forces us to ignore anything that is inexplicable or uncontrollable, like poverty, death, sickness, or failure. But this is not so in the rest of the world, where people share pain more than they share happiness, because there is *more* pain than happiness most of the time. There's nothing surprising or horrifying about dying.

In this picture Omayra is not very afraid, maybe because she has seen so much death, and she has been poor all of her life. The life expectancy in Colombia isn't very high, so she walked around hand in hand with death, as most poor people do all over the world. Only people who live in very privileged bubbles think that they're going to live forever. This girl is dead, yet we're talking about her years later. We've never met her and are living at the other end of the world, but we've been brought together because of her. She never dies, this girl. She never dies. She's born every instant. ○

FRANK FOURNIER

Frank Fournier was born in France in 1948. He attended the School of Graphic Design in Vevey, Switzerland, and moved to New York City in 1972. During his career as a commercial photographer he has covered a range of international events. His work documenting the lives of Romanian babies with AIDS was on exhibit at the Musée de l'Elysée in Switzerland in the early 1990s. And his haunting photographs of a New York devastated by the attack of September 11, 2001, have appeared in *Vanity Fair, Time* magazine, and *U.S. News & World Report.* Fournier also has contributed to Day in the Life projects in the United States, the former Soviet Union, Spain, and Canada.

The image here, of a young victim of a volcano in Colombia, was named the World Press Photo of the Year in 1985. The slow death of Omayra Sanchez was broadcast on news programs around the world. "Some thirty thousand people died," Fournier recalls. "Very few survived, some fought very hard but never made it. Among them an incredible and heroic person, a small little girl of 13, Omayra. . . . Her courage and dignity in death contrasted with the incredible cowardice of all the elected officials. . . . Anybody who saw her fight is now older and a lot more humble."

ISABEL ALLENDE

Isabel Allende was born in 1942 in Chile; she left her native country in 1975 after her uncle, President Salvador Allende, was assassinated. She worked as a journalist in Chile and then in Venezuela until 1984. Her first novel, *The House of the Spirits* (published in the United States in 1985), began as a letter to her 99-year-old grandfather. It established Allende's reputation as one of the most important contemporary Latin American authors. She has subsequently received literary awards in Latin America, Europe, and the United States. Among her other works are *The Stories of Eva Luna* (1988), *Daughter of Fortune* (1999), and *My Invented Country: A Nostalgic Journey through Chile* (2003). *Paula* (1995) is a memoir she began as a gift for her daughter. She would finish it as a memorial: Paula died in 1992.

Allende first encountered the image of Omayra Sanchez through television reports of the volcanic eruption in Colombia in 1985. Fournier's photograph of the 13-year-old left an indelible impression on her. She chose to write about it for Marvin Heiferman's book *Talking Pictures: People Speak about the Pictures That Speak to Them* (1994), in which seventy "people of our era—some famous, some not—speak out about the singular image that speaks to them."

SEEING

1. "The wonder of photography," Allende writes, "is that it does what no words can" (para. 3). In what ways has the image of a young girl Allende never met "spoken" to her since she first saw it?

2. What aspects of the photograph strike you the most? Consider how Fournier framed Omayra Sanchez in the photograph. What has he chosen to reveal about his subject? What has he left out? To what aspects of Fournier's photograph does Allende draw our attention? What details do you notice that Allende does not mention?

WRITING

1. In "Richard Billingham" (page 618), Nick Hornby writes that the "immediacy" of photography "seems to expose people in a way that writing never can. . . . Prose mediates and transforms, creates a distance even while trying to tell you things about a character's innermost soul. It's only writing, in other words, whereas photography is real life." The plight of Omayra Sanchez deeply affected both Frank Fournier and Isabel Allende. Which representation of Omayra moves you more—the photograph or the essay? Does reading one make the other more powerful? Write a page comparing the impact of the essay with that of the image.

2. Twentieth-century technology has made it possible to broadcast the most personal and private moments to global audiences. Television, magazines, and the web allow us to visit a family's living room after they've successfully delivered sextuplets, or witness a stranger's turmoil in the wake of a disaster, without ever leaving home. Choose a published photograph or image of a memorable moment that made a profound impression on you. Write an essay that, like Allende's, describes both your first impression of the image and what it means to you today.

Interview: Fournier

Can you tell the story of how you came to take this photograph?
Frank Fournier It was on a Wednesday night that the Nevado del Ruiz volcano blew up. . . .

At 10:30 P.M., when villagers in and around Armero heard that there had been a small eruption, they all got scared and started to panic. There was a soccer game on television that night that everyone was watching. The electricity went out and everyone panicked. They knew that the volcano had done something and they went to church to pray. At around 11:15, about 45 minutes later, the first lava and water and stones started to reach Armero. In a very short amount of time, it wiped out the town and kept going. There was chaos, of course. I think the total was between 28 and 32,000 people killed.

These deaths could have been prevented. The church was involved, the military was involved, and the politicians were all involved. What was so frustrating was that none of them took the fundamental responsibility to protect the people. People were expecting some kind of leadership, but it never came. Knowing that there was going to be an eruption, an evacuation plan should have already been in place. . . .

When we arrived, Omayra was by herself because other villagers and rescue people were trying to take care of someone else a little further away. By then, the Colombian government had simply declared the entire area a "national cemetery." This was revolting to us, that in twenty-four hours the government would decide that this was a national cemetery, period. It cleared the government from further rescue attempts and allowed them to spray chalk over the entire area. (This is usually done to avoid the spread of disease and bacteria.)

. . . When I reached [Omayra], it was about 6:30 in the morning. I tried talking to her. She was confused about what had happened. She could remember that she had been in her house and that she had been to church, but after that, she could not remember a thing.

According to local people, Omayra was now about a mile away from her house. She had been pushed along with much debris against a hill on the edge of town. Among the debris was a lot of corrugated metal, along with sections of homes and parts belonging to coffee warehouses. Not only was she stuck, trapped from the waist down by a huge amount of weight that was putting pressure on her legs, but according to a villager who was at her side, she had also been perforated at the hips.

When I reached Omayra, she had already been trapped there for the three days. Initially she had been stuck there with her aunt, who died attached to her. When the aunt died Omayra almost drowned with her. Many people tried to help Omayra. Phone calls were placed to rescue teams operating in the area. Medical equipment and personnel were badly needed, but none arrived.

My experience in these situations is that you need highly trained technicians and medical people to take care of a person in that kind of situation. When you have so much pressure on a leg, you have to run [an] IV with some kind of inflating device to maintain pressure on it, because if you release the pressure right away, toxic chemicals that form by a lack of circulation will spread through the body. You can kill a person this way. There had been big debates in Mexico a month before. People were pulled out of an earthquake very fast. They were alive and then two hours later they died from blood toxins. Other people were pulled out very slowly, and the survival rates were much higher.

So even if medical help had arrived in time, it would have been very challenging to save Omayra. I knew that at the time. When I saw her, I knew she was going to die, and I knew that there was no way out for her. I have a bit of a medical background. When I was younger, I studied medicine for four years, so I knew there was little chance.

I was devastated by what I was seeing, and by my inability to help her. You have to be pretty strong to face this kind of situation. To be so weak and unable to help is incredibly demanding and frustrating. I must say, I had been in difficult situations before, but my religious, ethical, and moral values were definitely going through an earthquake of their own. I was unable to help and save this person.

She was incredibly loving. She was twelve-and-a-half years old, very gentle and very sweet. She talked about where she came from. She saw that I was a foreigner and she even tried a couple of words in English with me. She even said: "Can you please help me get out of here? I don't want to be late for school; it starts at eight-thirty."

. . . Many people's first reaction to Omayra's photograph is to ask: Why didn't he help her? This reaction does not anger me. In a certain way, when people are mad at me or at the situation, I understand that reaction. I think it's healthy in some ways. Photography is not television; it's different. In a sense it can be more powerful. In general, people seem to remember photographs better than video. Nobody blames what the television shows. TV crews were interviewing Omayra like a sport person after an event . . . How was it? How do you feel? What's going on? Did you talk to your mother? Do you know that your father is dead? That kind of thing. And so when they saw the photograph, somehow they got mad at the photographer.

Why do you think that is?
I can't say why, I just know it's like that. People can take more time to look at a photograph. It's a more private kind of experience than television. With television, you have the sound; there is a distance between you and the screen. You may be watching the news as you prepare the evening meal. I think the photographic memory, and the connection to hold a magazine and look at it, makes it a little more physical and maybe helps people to connect better. One can take time—or not—to travel into the photograph and get details. You have time for emotions to develop; in television you have twenty seconds. . . .

The point is that Omayra reached many, many people. About a year after the eruption, the Colombian Ambassador to the Netherlands informed me that an enormous sum of money had reached Colombia to aide all of those who had survived and been displaced by the eruption. He also informed me that everybody in Colombia and in other parts of the world knew of Omayra. In a way, she and many other victims helped to create a real evacuation plan for the future. Local villagers were trained to flee to higher ground for safety. That is why I thought it was so important to report the death of Omayra. I wanted to be sure that survivors were helped and that people would never have to face a needless death.

This interview was conducted on April 21, 2005.

Visit seeingandwriting.com for the full text of the interview.

For biographical information about Frank Fournier, see page 614.

Richard Billingham

Nick Hornby

However enthusiastic you felt about Charles Saatchi's traveling exhibition *Sensation,* much of it was unlikely to detain you for long. I don't mean that in any pejorative sense, or at least, I don't think I do: Presumably there are critics who would argue that any successful work of art should provoke at least a break in a gallery visitor's stride, and that therefore works such as Sarah Lucas's *Au naturel* (the one with the dirty mattress, and his'n'hers melons, bucket, banana, and oranges) are comprehensive failures. You see it coming, as it were, from the other side of the room; you snort—with existential and aesthetic despair, if you are Brian Sewell, or with amusement, if you are a normal person—and you move on. I don't have a problem with that. For a few seconds I loved *Au naturel,* which means that I loved it more than I have loved other works that demanded much more of me and turned out not to repay the effort.

Even if they do nothing else—although actually they do plenty else—the photographs of Richard Billingham do detain you. You might not want to be detained; you might think, when you see his pictures of his battered, bewildered, distressed, and alcoholic father

Raymond, and of Elizabeth, his enormous, tattooed mother, that you'd rather wander off and look at something funnier, or more beautiful, or less real (and despite the proliferation of blood and pudenda and intestines elsewhere in *Sensation,* nobody could describe the show as sober). But you can't. Wandering off is simply not an option, not if you have any curiosity at all: There is too much to think about, too much going on, too much narrative.

The first thing to think about is the rights and wrongs of these pictures, because anyone who has ever had parents of any kind, let alone parents like Billingham's, would wonder whether it were possible to justify snapping their moments of distress and plastering them all over the walls of the Royal Academy. You could argue that Billingham is unfortunate that he is a photographer: The immediacy of his medium seems to expose people in a way that writing never can. Tobias Woolf, Mary Karr, Blake Morrison, Tim Lott, and Katherine Harrison, among many others, have all displayed and analyzed their parents' crises and failings in recent years, but prose mediates and transforms, creates a distance even while trying to tell you things about a character's innermost soul. It's only writing, in other words, whereas photography is real life. But of course that is one of the tricks Billingham plays on you, because part of his art is to strip distances away, to convince you that this is life unmediated—an artistic device in itself.

Spend enough time with these pictures and eventually you realize that their complexity and empathy answers any of the questions you might ask of them and their creator: There's nothing exploitative going on here. Empathy is not to be confused with sentimentality, however: Whatever else it is, Billingham's work is not sentimental. One of the most striking photographs in the *Sensation* exhibition shows Raymond sitting on the floor by the lavatory, his eyes cast down so that he seems to be in a state of philosophical and weary self-acceptance. His fly is undone, the soles of his sneakers are facing the lens; the toilet seat is broken, and some indistinct bodily waste—puke? blood?—is trickling down the outside of the bowl. It was never going to be a pretty picture, but Billingham's pitiless, neutral gaze doesn't overweigh it, and consequently it is allowed to take its place in the ongoing narrative of his parents' life together.

It takes some talent, and some nerve, to be able to do this, and it is Billingham's impeccable judgment that impresses one first of all. It would have been easy for the artist to let these pictures become self-pitying—what sort of childhood and young adulthood is possible in this domestic climate?—but they are not: There is too much tolerance. Nor are they angry, hectoring, or loud. Even the pictures depicting violence, a violence born, presumably, out of alcohol and despair, don't succeed in turning the collection into a campaign about this or a plea to the government for that.

It is hard to be definitive about how Billingham pulls this off, but his insistence on giving Raymond and Elizabeth, his two leads, equal attention is certainly wise, because then these

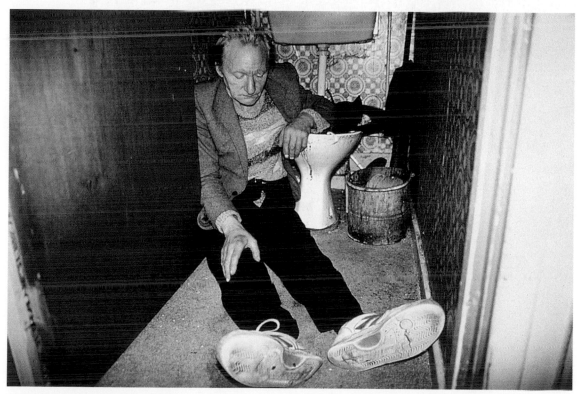

Richard Billingham, *Untitled*, 1994

Richard Billingham, *Untitled*, 1995

pictures become the portrait of a marriage as much as an analysis of social despair or urban alienation, and the artist is at pains to show that this marriage has its moments of calm domesticity and evidently peaceable companionship, as well as all the other stuff. Elizabeth sitting over a jigsaw (a brilliantly realized shot, this, with the jigsaw pieces, Elizabeth's floral print dress, and her tattoos coming together in an orchestrated riot of synthetic color); Raymond and Elizabeth sitting watching TV on the sofa, a roast dinner on their laps, gravy down their fronts, the family pets in between them; even the spectacular shot of Ray hurling the cat violently through the air is a strangely matter-of-fact, life-goes-on moment. Given their context, these photos are rich and strange.

But there is blood on the walls in this household, and Billingham shows it to us—quite literally, in the case of one photograph, which depicts a thin claret trickle apparently emerging from one of those cutesy mass-produced

portraits of a mannequin that you used to be able to buy in Boots. There is more action here than one might expect to find in a selection of family snapshots: Three of the pictures in Billingham's *Sensation* selection deal with violence or its immediate aftermath, and the changes of clothes alert you to the fact that this is not a sequence, but simply part of an ongoing domestic pattern. That Billingham was able to take the pictures at all is a clear indication that physical abuse is an organic part of the day; Raymond and Elizabeth would, presumably, have preferred their spats to take place away from their son's lens, but in the end were unable to stop themselves.

There is an inherent and perverse fascination, of course, in seeing grown people knock lumps off each other, and the fascination in this case is intensified by Elizabeth's obviously immense physical power. In one picture the couple are resting after what must have been a particularly vehement disagreement. Elizabeth has a

Richard Billingham, *Untitled*, 1995

Open Arms

I wait for it with open arms, reaching for it with all my strength.
It's running its craziness—
I can't keep up with it.
It's the tornado you see but can't get hold of.

Take me take me with you.   5
I am waiting also to be known.

Sandra Reyes, 16
International Studies Academy

Ghetto Haiku

A yuppie bumps
into me on the bus

                hardly notices.

A moment later

           whispers "excuse me"   5
when he brushes shoulders
with a well dressed man holding the paper.

The bus ride teaches me more than you think
I think more than you teach me.

Antonio Caceres, 21
WritersCorps intern

Dear God

Dear God put me under ya wing
I'm tired of life, hustlin'
sellin' dope to the fiends.

I wonder,
if I robbed or killed, would you   5
forgive my sins
and if it
was my time to go
would you let me in?

See thugs cry too, and when   10
the Lead hits,
we die too.

Dear God keep an angel
over my head
for when I fall.   15

I wonder is this life
that I'm going through?

Cecil T., 17
Log Cabin Ranch

Hidden Scars

Born to a land of battle fields
lost lives, grief and pain.
Forced to be exposed to violence
and destruction at a very young age.
Weapons of mass corruption   5
handled by men in every direction.
Living in a time zone
where everything in eye sight
was nothing but war.
I was mentally free   10
but physically enslaved
by having to live in poverty.
Like a lion hungry for food
with nothing to feed on
but the misery I lived through.   15
Life was a struggle
had to be hard and go for the kill in
order to survive.
Still I dream of murder.
As images hit   20
I feel his death like it
was at my side.
Leaving one war to come to another.
How many more do I have to live through
to conquer?   25
But still I stand
as a restless soldier
in these nights of rage.
While the devil stays at my side.

Irving S., 15
Log Cabin Ranch

Himalaya

I am the green of your eyes
and the red tiny tomatoes
filled with the water of sadness.

I am the snow bear
skating on a frozen lake,   5
and the Himalaya
shrinking day after day,
and everyone knows why.

It's hard to say my name.
That's why people call me my nickname, Abdul.   10

I am the soccer ball who never
betrayed its team and offered them
the World Cup.

I am a young male red apple
feeding humanity,   15
an African of Moroccan blood,
fishing for the fourth language.

I am a giant cactus all alone
in the center of the ocean
protecting myself from the noise.   20

I am the end of the week
at school, the day of my favorite food,
couscous on the moon.

I am the blood of the Red Sea,
calm and warm.   25

I am glad I was born.
If I wasn't born, I wouldn't see
this wonderful life I am having now.

Abdessalam Mansori, 15
Mission High School

WRITERSCORPS

The poems and images in this portfolio were created by five young people who participated in WritersCorps in the spring of 2005. WritersCorps, a project of the San Francisco Arts Commission, places professional writers in community settings to teach creative writing to youth. According to the organization, "Since its inception in 1994, the program has helped over 12,000 young people from neighborhoods throughout San Francisco improve their literacy and increase their desire to learn."

Sandra Reyes, Antonio Caceres, Cecil T., Irving S., and Abdessalam Mansori were taught by photographer and writer Katharine Gin. "The students began by writing poems about themselves, their lives, or the issues they cared about," explains Gin. "Once they reached a point of satisfaction and clarity with each poem, I asked them to imagine and then compose a visual image to accompany it. All of the students started by taking digital photographs; some chose to work with Photoshop, a graphics-editing software, to enhance or alter their compositions. The experience of creating images often inspired students to write entirely new poems, thus resulting in a cyclical exchange between text and images." These images and poems are included in Gin's collection of student work in *Where Were You: Poetry and Images from WritersCorps* (2005).

SEEING

1. Examine each of the images and poems in this portfolio. Consider them first as individual pieces and then as a group. Which works do you find most compelling individually? Why? What observations can you make about the works as a group? How would you summarize the topics and perspectives of these works? If you were to present these poems and images in a museum or gallery, what would you title the exhibit?

2. Consider the relationships between each image and the related poem. Do some of the images seem more closely tied to the poems than others? Why? How does the relationship between image and poem increase the impact of each pair?

WRITING

1. Imagine that you are a magazine editor interested in publishing one of the poems in this collection. Choose a poem and then find another image to include with it. What sort of image did you choose? Why? How does the image complement the poem? Is it illustrative? Does it provide contrast? Something else? Write a one-page memo to the magazine's editor-in-chief explaining why you think the magazine should print the additional image with the student's poem and image.

2. Create your own image–poem pair. Begin by writing a poem about yourself or a subject about which you are passionate. Then create an image—a photograph, an illustration, a collage—to accompany your poem.

TALKING PICTURES

When movie-goers watched the characters in *ET: The Extra-Terrestrial* (1982) munching on Reese's Pieces, the candy's sales shot up by 65 percent and the brand became a household name. Since then, the nature of product placements on television and in film has become more and more sophisticated. As one media critic put it, "Nowadays, the movie and TV industries are molding products, logos, and slogans into the very building blocks of popular culture—often without audiences realizing it." *American Idol* judges drink Coke, for example, and *Survivor* contestants use materials from Home Depot. According to a 2005 report by PQ Media, a media research firm, "the value of television product placements soared 46.4% to $1.87 billion in 2004, and grew at a compound annual rate of 21.5% from 1999 to 2004."

Watch a few hours of prime-time TV or a feature-length film. How many brand-name products can you identify? How often is each product shown? Which kinds of products seem to be displayed more often than others? Do you notice a relationship between the type of product placement and the targeted audience? Explain your answer. To what extent would you characterize these product placements as "successful"? Why or why not? Write an expository essay in which you identify and analyze the nature of the product placements in a specific TV show or film.

James Rosenquist, *Professional Courtesy*, 1996

JAMES ROSENQUIST

Pop artist James Rosenquist (b. 1933) first gained notoriety in the early 1960s, with *President Elect,* in which he took John F. Kennedy's face from a campaign poster and layered it with the images of "half a Chevrolet and a piece of stale cake"—what the artist later described as Kennedy's campaign "promise." In 1965 he completed the 86-foot-wide picture *F-111,* which was shown worldwide and is still considered to be his signature work. This brightly colored panorama features images of an angel food cake, a tire, lightbulbs, a blond girl sitting under a hair dryer, a nuclear explosion, an umbrella, and tinned spaghetti, all pasted across the length of a fighter plane.

In the introduction to his book *Target Practice,* from which the painting shown here is taken, Rosenquist wrote, "I want to illustrate the stark look and confrontation of a handgun. . . . Young people are confused by the way guns are depicted in the movies and on television. It shows the hero being shot, getting up, brushing himself off, and then going on to act in another movie—becoming an even bigger star. The reality of being shot is really death forever and a big flame usually comes out of a real gun. These paintings are intended to be nondecorative and oblique. I hope they question the idea of who really is the target."

A retrospective of Rosenquist's work was shown at the Guggenheim Museum from October 2003 to February 2004.

SEEING

1. How would you characterize the overall effect of this painting? Where are your eyes drawn? Why? Rosenquist's painting measures 4 feet by 4 feet. What does this considerably reduced reproduction gain or lose by virtue of its size when compared with the original? What kinds of shapes, colors, and details become more or less important as the image becomes larger or smaller? Why? How does reducing the size of the painting change its impact on the viewer? Which aspects of the painting would you need to change to make the smaller image have the same impact as the original?

2. Rosenquist characterizes the series of paintings that includes *Professional Courtesy* in the following terms: "These paintings are intended to be nondecorative and oblique." What does he mean by these words, especially in this context? Under the headings "Nondecorative" and "Oblique," list specific elements in the painting that would justify the use of each adjective. Consider, for example, color, shape, style, and the relationships between and among these elements.

Visit seeingandwriting.com for an interactive exercise based on *Professional Courtesy.*

WRITING

1. A commonplace saying is that "every picture tells a story." What story does Rosenquist's painting tell? Imagine that the painting is a photograph. Write the first draft of a narrative that tells the story of how the picture came to be. Make your story as realistic as possible, and account for such obvious elements as the two guns, the two hands, and the red background, as well as less obvious aspects of it: the shadows, the position of the photographer, and so on.

2. In everyday language, *professional courtesy* is a service offered to someone who works in the same field. In what ways does the painting play with this meaning? How do the historical meanings of the words connect with the meaning of the painting? For example, the word *professional* comes from the word *profess,* which is made up of the Greek prefix *pro-* (which indicated motion from a source to a target) and *phatos* (which can be translated as "claim" or "statement"). A professional is like a gun: A gun shoots bullets: a professional produces expert statements. Write an expository essay in which you account for how the two sets of meaning (historical and current) work together to enrich the painting's message and significance.

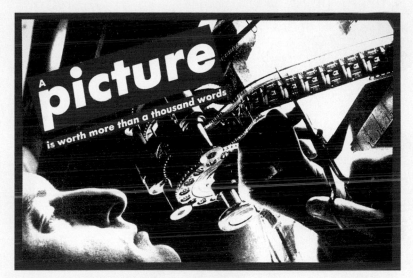

Barbara Kruger, *Untitled*, 1992

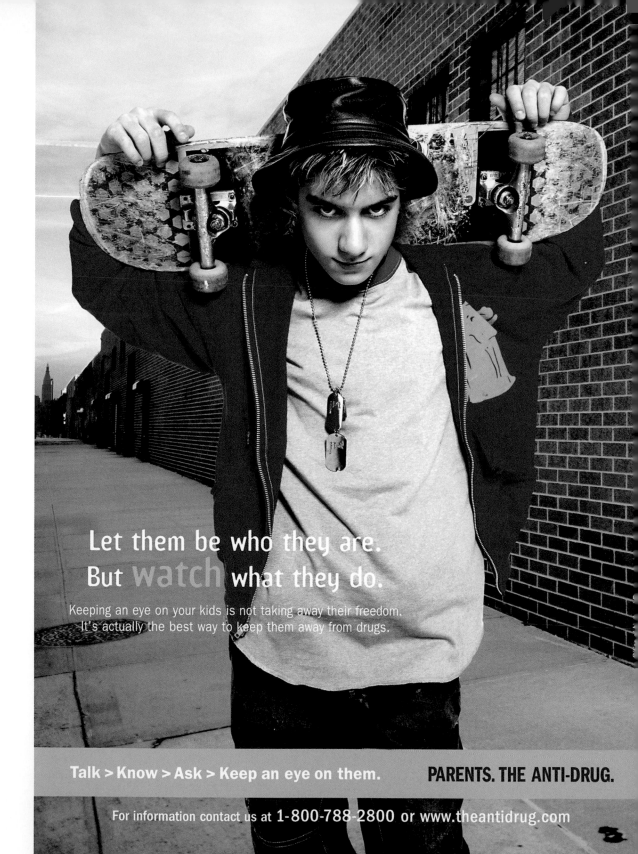

Let them be who they are.
But watch what they do.

Keeping an eye on your kids is not taking away their freedom.
It's actually the best way to keep them away from drugs.

Talk > Know > Ask > Keep an eye on them.   PARENTS. THE ANTI-DRUG.

For information contact us at 1-800-788-2800 or www.theantidrug.com

OFFICE OF NATIONAL DRUG CONTROL POLICY

The White House Office of National Drug Control Policy (ONDCP) is an agency within the Executive Office of the President. The ONDCP was born out of the Anti-Drug Abuse Act of 1988. Its mission is "to establish policies, priorities, and objectives for the country's drug control program . . . to reduce illicit drug use, manufacturing, and trafficking, drug-related crime and violence, and drug-related health consequences." The director of ONDCP, also known as the nation's "Drug Czar," oversees national anti-drug programs, a budget, and guidelines for cooperation among federal, state, and local entities.

To reduce drug use among teenagers, the ONDCP, through the National Youth Anti-Drug Media Campaign, relies heavily on public service announcements on television and radio and on print ads. (Links to a gallery of TV, radio, and print ads in a number of languages can be found at www.mediacampaign.org.) The ad shown here is part of the "Parents. The Anti-Drug" campaign, which was formulated by the George W. Bush administration. The message: Parent-to-child communication is the key to keeping kids off drugs.

SEEING

1. This advertisement presents the seemingly contradictory idea that surveillance is compatible with individual freedom. How does the picture work to make this idea seem reasonable? Why would the parents of this boy agree that keeping an eye on him is still letting him be himself? What is there about the boy in the picture that lets the viewer know he needs someone to watch him? What details indicate that the boy might be in danger of becoming a drug user?

2. Compare the use of colors in the picture to the use of colors in the text. For example, consider orange. Why is the word *watch* the same color as the logo on the boy's jacket and the highlight band around "Talk > Know > Ask > . . . "? In other words, how does the use of that particular color tie those particular elements together? Also, look at the contrast between the bright colors of the boy's shirt and jacket and the gray of the street. How does this contrast contribute to the advertisement's message?

WRITING

1. Imagine that you're this boy's parent. Write an essay in which you describe how you would go about watching him. Create a detailed surveillance schedule that includes as many ways of monitoring him as you can imagine, from tapping his phone to paying informers. How might thinking of your child as someone you need to keep an eye on change your relationship with the child for the better? for the worse?

2. What are the laws governing children's rights to privacy? What kinds of things can be done without a child's permission? What kinds of things cannot be done? How do the laws change as the child grows into a teenager? Which laws do you think are justified? Search the Internet for information on children's rights to privacy. (One good source is the Electronic Privacy Information Center, a public interest research center. EPIC maintains a web site at epic.org.) Then write the first draft of an argumentative essay in which you advocate for specific changes in the current law.

Office of National Drug Control Policy, Tommy

Context: Partnership for a Drug-Free America

Perhaps no other public service announcement is more famous than the television spot created and sponsored by the Partnership for a Drug-Free America in 1987. Directed by Joe Pytka, this advertisement has achieved iconic status within the advertising industry. The advertisement features contrasting images of the brain—in a normal state and on drugs. "This is your brain," a confident voice announces over the image of a brain at rest. As we watch an egg being fried in a pan, the voiceover solemnly intones: "This is your brain on drugs."

In 2001 the Partnership issued an updated version of the spot titled *Frying Pan*. The new advertisement features actor Rachael Leigh Cook destroying an entire kitchen with a frying pan—a demonstration of the effects of heroin addiction on users, their families, and their friends.

This historical context informs the anti-drug ad reprinted on page 636. As you ex-amine this ad, identify the approaches the agency has taken toward communicating its message to a new generation of young people. How—and to what extent—have its core message, rhetorical strategies, techniques, and methods changed over the past two decades?

The Office of National Drug Control Policy maintains a comprehensive web site (www.mediacampaign.org) where you can view and study its latest anti-drug spots and print ads. Choose two different ads from this site and then write an expository essay in which you compare and contrast the message, the rhetorical strategies, and the techniques used in them. To what specific audience (age, socioeconomic group, ethnic group) is each advertisement addressed? Which do you feel is more successful? Why? (You might consider, for example, comparing and contrasting an ad targeted toward caregivers with one addressed to teenagers.)

Partnership for a Drug-Free America, *This Is Your Brain on Drugs*, 1987

150TH ANNIVERSARY: 1851–2001

The Assignment Is to Get the Story, but the Image Can Rise to Art

Michael Kimmelman

On the days just after, we paused, many of us, to look at the photographs of the events that had seemed to rush by on the streets and on our televisions. We woke up, hoping it wasn't true, to check with the newspapers whose still images of the smoking towers and fleeing people confirmed what had happened. They gave us a chance, which we reluctantly needed, to grasp the unimaginable by stopping time, as still images do. Instead of the same endless video loop of jets going into the World Trade Center towers that we had watched on Sept. 11, until it had almost become a blur, we saw details:

We saw the tiny figure of a man standing on the edge of a gaping hole that looked like a broken-tooth grimace, where the first plane had just crashed into the north tower, an inferno behind him, nowhere to go, one arm raised. (To shade his eyes? To signal for help?) We saw the photograph by Shannon Stapleton, of Reuters, of five dust-covered rescue workers carrying out the Rev. Mychal F. Judge, a Fire Department chaplain, who had just died in a rain of debris while ministering to victims when the towers collapsed, a modern-day Pietà. And we saw the photograph by Richard Drew of the Associated Press, maybe the most excruciat-

ing and indelible of all the images that ran in the *Times*, of a man tumbling headfirst from the north tower.

We saw these photographs, and since then, even against our will, we have not been able to forget them. They may or may not be the most horrific images of any atrocities we have seen, but they can seem as if they are the most horrific at this moment because these are our buildings and our streets and our families and our lives. In their immediate aftermath, it is impossible to imagine the photographs ever fading from anybody's memory or losing their national symbolism.

BEAUTY, PERHAPS, BUT RARELY ART

The magnitude of that event enhanced the urgency of the photographs, but it did not automatically raise their status. In photojournalism the balance isn't easily tipped from the utilitarian picture, which delivers information quickly, efficiently, even deeply affectingly, to a work of art, which delivers more than information. It is rarely just a question of the scale of the recorded subject or the intention of the photographer. All photojournalists hope their best pictures are good enough to be considered art, but most of the time they don't succeed. They can't.

The task of conveying news, an honorable and complicated job, generally relegates the picture, like the event it records, to ephemera. The picture may be complete and even beautiful in its way. It may go so far as to shape history and therefore endure, like Eddie Adams's unforgettable photograph of the South Vietnamese [general] shooting a Vietcong prisoner. But the picture does not transcend its event, which is where the art comes in.

This transcendence entails a novel composition, an expression, the echo of some previous images we have seen, maybe in museums or books, which are stored in

our memories as archetypes and symbols, so that the photograph, by conscious or unconscious association and special variation, is elevated from the specific to the universal.

Often this is just a fluke of fate, a result of an accident, serendipity. Or rather it is the serendipity of good photographers who by nature seem to have the uncanny instinct to be in the right spot at the right moment.

It wasn't many years ago that readers scanning photographs in the *New York Times* over breakfast could expect a lean diet of single-column black-and-white head shots accompanying the news. The Gray Lady was gray back then, and it wasn't just that she hadn't made the leap yet to color (almost a century after color photography's invention, but who's counting).

Now, the world having rapidly changed, this newspaper, like most newspapers, has gradually changed with it. In the age of the Internet and television, papers including the *Times* have had to think differently. The reading public is more accustomed to looking at pictures, which doesn't just mean that it is more comfortable getting information from them. It means that people are smarter about how pictures work: The belief that facts were whatever appeared through a viewfinder seems quaint in our digital age. So a more visually shrewd populace expects a more visually sophisticated menu of the day's events over its coffee and toast.

This proliferation of competing images and the acuteness of public attention to visual culture permit fresh latitudes (within the bounds of truth). Look at the front page of Aug. 3, 2001, the 51,834th number of the *Times*, an average day before Sept. 11, and you will see two photographs. One, above the fold, is a fairly straightforward spot-news shot of Radislav Krstic, a Bosnian Serb general, on crutches, in The Hague, where he was found guilty of genocide. Below is a picture by Ruth Fremson of the *Times*, apropos of nothing much except summertime: It shows a boy, arms out, face heavenward, standing before a wall of electric fans that belong to an artwork at the P.S. 1 Contemporary Art Center in Queens.

The weather photograph is one of the oldest journalistic clichés, but here it is turned into something akin to the famous Cartier-Bresson image, a surreal masterpiece of a Spanish boy, eyes skyward, arms out, as if in ecstasy. Cartier-Bresson excluded from his picture the ball the boy had tossed and was waiting to catch. One ordinary truth yielded to a deeper one about joy and transcendence. That is how art works. Now look at the two photographs on the front page. Which sticks in your mind?

Notwithstanding its formerly gray reputation, the *Times* has published hundreds of memorable pictures, documenting not just history but the history of photomechanical reproduction, from the first photographs ever published in the newspaper—credit-card-size head shots of Stephen A. Douglas and John Bell on Sept. 6, 1896—through what must be the most memorable photographs ever taken: stills from the video transmissions of the Apollo 11 moon landing, published on July 21, 1969. By then, most readers had already seen these pictures on television, the newly dominant medium.

In between was the photograph that Richard E. Byrd claimed to be the first aerial shot of the North Pole, transmitted via radio from London to New York. It appeared under a banner headline with the lead article on the front page of May 29, 1926, and not once, not twice, but three times it was stated in the headline and subheadings that the photograph, which is hard to make out, had been radioed from London. This was as much a technological marvel, and thus news, as the fact

that Byrd had taken a picture near the pole from an airplane.

But none of those historic photographs are art. The *Times* published plenty of artful photographs, too: Ernest Sisto's vertiginous view from atop the Empire State Building looking down at the wreckage made by a bomber that had crashed into the 78th and 79th floors (published July 29, 1945), a memorable image, even considering what happened to the twin towers; Gilles Peress's sprinting rioters in Belfast on May 5, 1981, the day Bobby Sands died after a hunger strike; Sebastião Salgado's series of firefighters and oil workers in Kuwait (June 9, 1991); and Meyer Liebowitz's Weegee-like picture of the dead Umberto Anastasia in the barbershop of the Park Sheraton Hotel after his gangland-style rub-out—although when the photograph appeared on Oct. 26, 1957, the body was cropped out in keeping with a policy of weighing the gory content of such photographs against their importance as news (an equation that has been altered somewhat with color printing).

Some of Dorothea Lange's classic Depression-era photographs of migrant families in California also appeared in the newspaper, including one of a mother holding two children beside a makeshift shelter made of canvas sheets roughly stretched between a beat-up car and a tent—an image doubly interesting today because if you look at the *Times*'s original copy, you see that it was touched up, with the faces drawn in to make them reproduce more clearly. Nobody thought much about airbrushing in the days before digital technology. Paradoxically, tinkering, now that it is so easy to do, is not done, because everyone is more sensitive to its ramifications.

Two photographs, both unconnected to Sept. 11, and therefore perhaps a little easier to see clearly, sum up the current state

of the art of photojournalism. One, by Stephen Crowley of the *Times*, is from the last presidential campaign and appeared on Jan. 22, 2000: Gov. George W. Bush is shown behind the lunch counter in a drugstore in Grinnell, Iowa, pretending to wait on customers for the benefit of news cameras, which you see beyond the counter. In the foreground a woman looks peevishly away, toward something out of the picture. The image bespeaks artifice and alienation—but wittily, turning a mundane event into a symbol of modern American political life.

The other photograph, by Alan Chin, on assignment for the *Times*, shows mourners around the dead body of Ali Paqarizi, a 19-year-old Albanian killed by a Serb booby trap. It depicts not Paqarizi's formal military funeral, but what happened that day in his family's living room, where his mother, surrounded by grieving women, cried over her son's corpse. The picture captures not the public display of political defiance, but its root: the private despair that is the outcome of war.

The formal geometry of this image, with the semicircle of mourners, is locked in place by the horizontal body of the dead man in his striped shroud and by the vertical axis of his mother's foreshortened arm, his impassive mask set against her explicit grief. As a document of human expression it achieves what good art achieves on a basic level. The purpose of a newspaper photograph, after all, is to amplify a story in ways that words can't. This picture, which appeared on Oct. 29, 1998, with an article about the funeral of a young man in a town in Serbia that most readers have never heard of, speaks for itself insofar as it articulates the larger meaning of the conflict in the Balkans and, most important, of suffering generally. It is proof not only that art imitates life but that life, when captured in the most profound news photograph, is art. ○

MICHAEL KIMMELMAN

Michael Kimmelman is chief art critic for the *New York Times;* he also is curious about how artists view art. This curiosity led him to invite prominent artists—among them Cindy Sherman and Lucian Freud—to various museums to wander through the galleries and talk about the exhibits. The result was Kimmelman's book *Portraits: Talking with Artists at the Met, the Modern, the Louvre, and Elsewhere* (1998). In its pages artists from Balthus to Chuck Close share their thoughts on the art in famous museums. Kimmelman's *The Accidental Masterpiece: On the Art of Life and Vice-Versa* was published in 2005.

The essay here appeared in the *New York Times* in November 2001, just two months after the terrorist attack on the World Trade Center. The images of September 11 led Kimmelman to think about photojournalism as art—the documentation of "human expression" that can make a new photograph something more than reportage. Kimmelman's willingness to expand the traditional boundaries of art is not surprising. In an earlier piece he noted: "I refuse to bow to the enormous pressure in America to accept the old Puritan idea that art is a therapeutic occupation, and that if it is not somehow good for us then it isn't really good art. I think that on some level art is profoundly a frivolous thing and also completely indispensable."

Kimmelman is also an accomplished pianist. He was a finalist in the first Van Cliburn International Piano Competition for Outstanding Amateurs, held in 1999.

SEEING

1. What does Michael Kimmelman see in "art" photographs that he doesn't see in other photographs? Make a list of all the things that an art photograph should do and be, according to the article. How would you rank the items on the list? Which characteristics do you think are not necessary to a working definition of a photograph as art? Which characteristics would you judge to be essential? Explain why.

2. Find a passage in which Kimmelman describes an art photograph and one in which he talks about a photograph that he doesn't think is art. How does his language change from one to the other? What kinds of words does he use when he describes art photographs? What about the nature of his sentences? Do they become less artistic when he's writing about photographs he does not consider art? Are they more artistic when he writes about art photographs?

WRITING

1. Pick a photograph in this book that you think qualifies as an art photograph, whether or not Kimmelman would agree with you. Then draft a letter to Kimmelman explaining why you think the picture is art. Be sure to respond to the points he makes in his article.

2. Kimmelman argues that Eddie Adams's photograph of a South Vietnamese officer shooting a Vietcong prisoner is "unforgettable," but that "the picture does not transcend its event" (para. 5). Use an Internet search engine to locate a copy of Adams's photograph and compare it with another photograph from the Vietnam War that you feel does transcend the event. Write an expository essay in which you explain why the other photograph transcends the chronological limitations of the war whereas that of the execution does not. Pay special attention to the compositional details and the structural aspects of each picture. Other than the subject matter, what makes one picture art and the other reportage?

Visualizing Composition: Point of View

Whether we are responding to what someone else has written or are generating our own prose, the question of point of view has always been at the center of effective reading and writing: From whose "eye" do we see the story being told or the points being made in an argument? This fundamental question leads to two other aspects of point of view that deserve special attention from readers and writers:

1. What is the *perspective* from which a story is told or a line of reasoning is developed?

2. What particular *bias* is immediately evident—or eventually surfaces—in that perspective?

Most of us can recall the moments in our high school English class when our teacher first directed our attention to thinking about how narrative is structured in works of fiction. Many of us still carry a useful distinction when responding to reading fiction: An author writes a story; someone else—a narrator—tells the story.

On the surface, determining a writer's point of view seems relatively simple: Pay attention to the writer's use of pronouns. Personal narrative is distinguished by the writer's "I"—be it an autobiographical essay (like Judith Ortiz Cofer's "The Story of My Body" on page 343) or a work of literary fiction, like Mark Twain's *Huckleberry Finn* or J. D. Salinger's *Catcher in the Rye*. In these two classic novels, a character narrates the story from a distinctive first-person point of view. But not all first-person narrators are the central figure in the narrative. Consider, for example, Marlow in Joseph Conrad's novels *The Heart of Darkness* and *Lord Jim*.

Other writers rely on third-person narration to tell their story: "she said," "he did," "they decided," and the like. This point of view usually is limited to the perspective of a single character and can involve exploring the mind of that character. A more encompassing perspective is called *omniscient point of view:* The author creates a narrator who stands, almost godlike, outside the people and events being described, and "sees" all. The narrator not only can observe and describe the action but also can see into the minds of the characters and account for what motivates them.

As you think about point of view in your own writing, you should also consider how your perspective has a particular built-in bias. We are using *bias* here to signal the preference(s) or inclination(s) that surface in writing, especially ones that inhibit impartial judgment. As you read and revise your drafts, attending to the bias of your point of view can be one of the most effective means of strengthening your credibility and increasing the impact of your writing. The basic compositional purpose of point of view is simple enough: Establish a clear and consistent point of view, and attend to the prejudices built into it.

Carefully examine the advertisements reprinted here. What points of view can you identify in the exchange between the bottle of vodka and the tomato? and the orange? What perspective and bias are evident in the point of view from which each character speaks? Prepare the first draft of what you envision as the next ad in this sequence, one in which you use playful banter to convince your audience that buying Wolf-schmidt's vodka will improve their social lives.

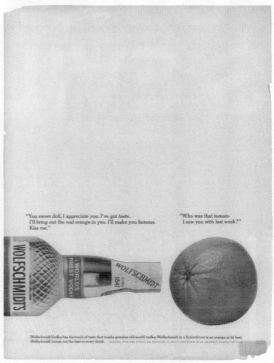

Wolfschmidt's Vodka, 1961

POWERPOINT IS EVIL

Power Corrupts.
PowerPoint Corrupts Absolutely.

Edward Tufte

Imagine a widely used and expensive prescription drug that promised to make us beautiful but didn't. Instead the drug had frequent, serious side effects: It induced stupidity, turned everyone into bores, wasted time, and degraded the quality and credibility of communication. These side effects would rightly lead to a worldwide product recall.

Yet slideware—computer programs for presentations—is everywhere: in corporate America, in government bureaucracies, even in our schools. Several hundred million copies of Microsoft PowerPoint are churning out trillions of slides each year. Slideware may help speakers outline their talks, but convenience for the speaker can be punishing to both content and audience. The standard PowerPoint presentation elevates format over content, betraying an attitude of commercialism that turns everything into a sales pitch.

Of course, data-driven meetings are nothing new. Years before today's slideware, presentations at companies such as IBM and in the military used bullet lists shown by overhead projectors. But the format has become ubiquitous under PowerPoint, which was created in 1984 and later acquired by Microsoft. PowerPoint's pushy style seeks to set up a speaker's dominance over the audience. The speaker, after all, is making power points with bullets to followers. Could any metaphor be

GOOD

Estimates of relative survival rates, by cancer site[12]

	% survival rates and their standard errors			
	5 year	10 year	15 year	20 year
Prostate	98.8 0.4	95.2 0.9	87.1 1.7	81.1 3.0
Thyroid	96.0 0.8	95.8 1.2	94.0 1.6	95.4 2.1
Testis	94.7 1.1	94.0 1.3	91.1 1.8	88.2 2.3
Melanomas	89.0 0.8	86.7 1.1	83.5 1.5	82.8 1.9
Breast	86.4 0.4	78.3 0.6	71.3 0.7	65.0 1.0
Hodgkin's disease	85.1 1.7	79.8 2.0	73.8 2.4	67.1 2.8
Corpus uteri, uterus	84.3 1.0	83.2 1.3	80.8 1.7	79.2 2.0
Urinary, bladder	82.1 1.0	76.2 1.4	70.3 1.9	67.9 2.4
Cervix, uteri	70.5 1.6	64.1 1.8	62.8 2.1	60.0 2.4

A traditional table: rich, informative, clear

BAD

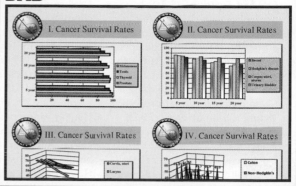

PowerPoint chartjunk: smarmy, chaotic, incoherent

worse? Voicemail menu systems? Billboards? Television? Stalin?

Particularly disturbing is the adoption of the Power-Point cognitive style in our schools. Rather than learning to write a report using sentences, children are being taught how to formulate client pitches and infomercials. Elementary school PowerPoint exercises (as seen in teacher guides and in student work posted on the Internet) typically consist of 10 to 20 words and a piece of clip art on each slide in a presentation of three to six slides—a total of perhaps 80 words (15 seconds of silent reading) for a week of work. Students would be better off if the schools simply closed down on those days and everyone went to the Exploratorium or wrote an illustrated essay explaining something.

In a business setting, a PowerPoint slide typically shows 40 words, which is about eight seconds' worth of silent reading material. With so little information per slide, many, many slides are needed. Audiences consequently endure a relentless sequentiality, one damn slide after another. When information is stacked in time, it is difficult to understand context and evaluate relationships. Visual reasoning usually works more effectively when relevant information is shown side by side. Often, the more intense the detail, the greater the

clarity and understanding. This is especially so for statistical data, where the fundamental analytical act is to make comparisons.

Consider an important and intriguing table of survival rates for those with cancer relative to those without cancer for the same time period. Some 196 numbers and 57 words describe survival rates and their standard errors for 24 cancers.

Applying the PowerPoint templates to this nice, straightforward table yields an analytical disaster. The data explodes into six separate chaotic slides, consuming 2.9 times the area of the table. Everything is wrong with these smarmy, incoherent graphs: the encoded legends, the meaningless color, the logotype branding. They are uncomparative, indifferent to content and evidence, and so data-starved as to be almost pointless. Chartjunk is a clear sign of statistical stupidity. Poking a finger into the eye of thought, these data graphics would turn into a nasty travesty if used for a serious purpose, such as helping cancer patients assess their survival chances. To sell a product that messes up data with such systematic intensity, Microsoft abandons any pretense of statistical integrity and reasoning.

Presentations largely stand or fall on the quality, relevance, and integrity of the content. If your numbers are boring, then you've got the wrong numbers. If your words or images are not on point, making them dance in color won't make them relevant. Audience boredom is usually a content failure, not a decoration failure.

At a minimum, a presentation format should do no harm. Yet the PowerPoint style routinely disrupts, dominates, and trivializes content. Thus PowerPoint presentations too often resemble a school play—very loud, very slow, and very simple.

The practical conclusions are clear. PowerPoint is a competent slide manager and projector. But rather than supplementing a presentation, it has become a substitute for it. Such misuse ignores the most important rule of speaking: Respect your audience.

Tufte satirizes the totalitarian impact of presentation slideware.

EDWARD TUFTE

Edward Tufte (b. 1940) is a professor emeritus at Yale University, where he has taught statistics, information design, and political science. He is the author of several books, including *The Visual Display of Quantitative Information* (1983), *Visual Explanations* (1997), *Data Analysis for Politics and Policy* (1997), and *Beautiful Evidence* (2005). His self-published books have received more than forty awards for content and design, and *Utne Reader* named Tufte one of its 1995 Visionaries, one hundred "people who could change your life."

Describing the field of information design, he said, "My discovery is that the same basic design strategies have occurred again and again, in widely different fields and throughout the . . . centuries— text–figure integration of the scientific notebook, small multiples, various kinds of data compression. . . . There is some kind of universality, almost like Chomskian grammar. . . producing this commonality of five or six solutions. My contribution is to identify those solutions, give them names and explain why they work. . . . Plainly, all of our nonsymbolic information, and some of our symbolic information, is coming via [the visual] channel. . . . Especially in data-rich sciences like meteorology or nuclear physics, which generate tremendous amounts of information, the only way you can think about it is to see it."

"PowerPoint Is Evil" was published in *Wired* magazine in September 2003.

SEEING

1. What do you make of Tufte's claim in paragraph 9 that "the PowerPoint style routinely disrupts, dominates, and trivializes content"? What visual elements make up PowerPoint's style? How do those elements disrupt content? Usually elements that dominate our attention—color, shape, and animation, for example—interest us. How does PowerPoint manage to dominate attention and bore at the same time? What does Tufte mean by "trivializes content"?

2. What specific examples does Tufte use to support his claim that "PowerPoint is evil"? Do you agree with him? Why or why not? What additional examples would you offer to support or refute his claim? Consider Tufte's comparison of the "good" and "bad" presentations of cancer survival rates. What differences does he point out? What similarities and differences do you notice?

RESPONDING VISUALLY

Choose an essay or report you have authored— this semester or in the past—and create a PowerPoint version of it. Then write an essay in which you compare and contrast the two versions of your piece. To what extent does the presentation medium alter the content of your piece? Which version do you find more compelling? more informative? more effective? Why?

WRITING

1. "PowerPoint shows you how to make a powerful impression on your audience," or so Microsoft's Teacher's Guide to PowerPoint promises. Tufte and other critics argue that it has the opposite effect. "Rather than supplementing a presentation," writes Tufte, PowerPoint, "has become a substitute for it. Such misuse ignores the most important rule of speaking: Respect your audience" (para. 10). Write an essay in which you explore the assumptions and rationale behind each of these statements. What sorts of presentation topics and techniques engage an audience? What advice for engaging an audience would you give to your classmates?

2. "Tufte is correct in that most talks are horrible and most PowerPoint slides are bad—but that's not PowerPoint's fault," said author Donald A. Norman in a 2004 interview in *Presentations* magazine. "Most writing is awful, too, but I don't go railing against pencils or chalk." What benefits and uses of PowerPoint do you think Tufte ignores in this piece? Write an essay in which you argue in favor of PowerPoint as a presentation tool.

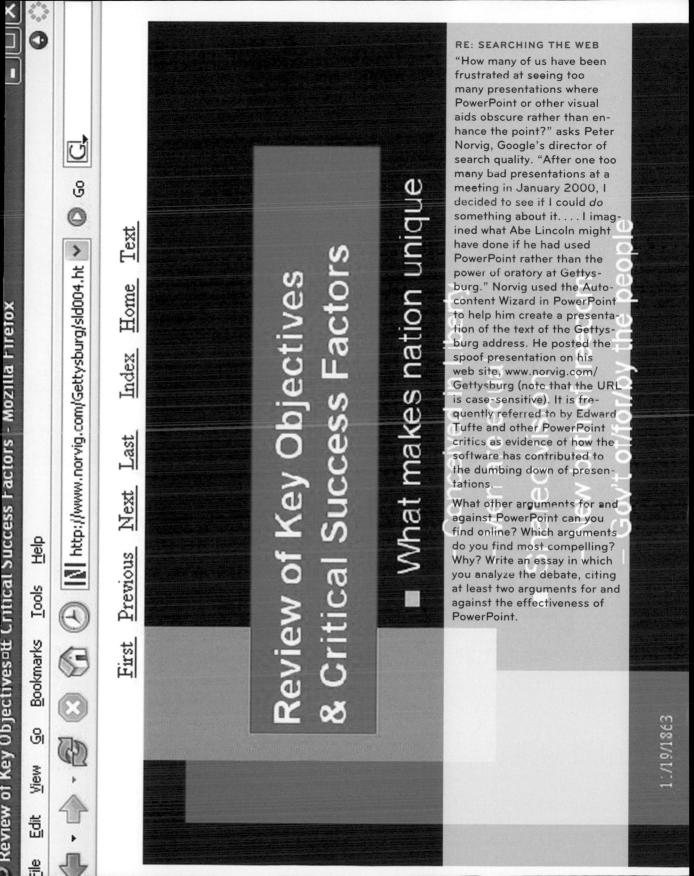

RE: SEARCHING THE WEB

"How many of us have been frustrated at seeing too many presentations where PowerPoint or other visual aids obscure rather than enhance the point?" asks Peter Norvig, Google's director of search quality. "After one too many bad presentations at a meeting in January 2000, I decided to see if I could *do* something about it. . . . I imagined what Abe Lincoln might have done if he had used PowerPoint rather than the power of oratory at Gettysburg." Norvig used the Autocontent Wizard in PowerPoint to help him create a presentation of the text of the Gettysburg address. He posted the spoof presentation on his web site, www.norvig.com/Gettysburg (note that the URL is case-sensitive). It is frequently referred to by Edward Tufte and other PowerPoint critics as evidence of how the software has contributed to the dumbing down of presentations.

What other arguments for and against PowerPoint can you find online? Which arguments do you find most compelling? Why? Write an essay in which you analyze the debate, citing at least two arguments for and against the effectiveness of PowerPoint.

THE CIVIL WAR

Alexander Gardner, *Home of a Rebel Sharpshooter, Gettysburg, July, 1863*

The Men of the 308th, the "Lost Battalion," April 28, 1919

WORLD WAR II

Robert Capa, *Omaha Beach*, June 6, 1944

Greenhouse Dog, 1951

THE VIETNAM WAR

Nick Ut, *Children Fleeing a Napalm Strike, Vietnam*, June 8, 1972

Jean-Marc Bouju, *Iraqi Man at a Regroupment Center for POWs, Najaf, Iraq, March 31, 2003*

Regarding the Pain of Others

Susan Sontag

OFTEN SOMETHING LOOKS, OR IS FELT TO LOOK, "better" in a photograph. Indeed, it is one of the functions of photography to improve the normal appearance of things. (Hence, one is always disappointed by a photograph that is not flattering.) Beautifying is one classic operation of the camera, and it tends to bleach out a moral response to what is shown. Uglifying, showing something at its worst, is a more modern function: didactic, it invites an active response. For photographs to accuse, and possibly to alter conduct, they must shock.

An example: A few years ago, the public health authorities in Canada, where it had been estimated that smoking kills 45,000 people a year, decided to supplement the warning printed on every pack of cigarettes with a shock photograph—of cancerous lungs, or a stroke-clotted brain, or a damaged heart, or a bloody mouth in acute periodontal distress. A pack with such a picture accompanying the warning about the deleterious effects of smoking would be 60 times more likely to inspire smokers to quit, a research study had somehow calculated, than a pack with only the verbal warning.

Let's assume this is true. Still one might wonder, for how long? Does shock have term limits? Right now the smokers of Canada are recoiling in disgust, if they do look at these pictures. Will those smoking five years from now still be upset? Shock can become familiar. Shock can wear off. Even if it doesn't, one can *not* look. People have means to defend themselves against what is upsetting—in this instance, unpleasant information for those wishing to continue to smoke. This seems normal, that is, adaptive. As one can become habituated to horror in real life, one can become habituated to the horror of certain images.

Yet there are cases where repeated exposure to what shocks, saddens, appalls does not use up a full-hearted response. Habituation is not automatic, for images (portable, insertable) obey different rules than real life. Representations of the Crucifixion do not become banal to believers, if they really are believers. This is even more true of staged representa-

tions. Performances of *Chushingura,* probably the best-known narrative in all of Japanese culture, can be counted on to make a Japanese audience sob when Lord Asano admires the beauty of the cherry blossoms on his way to where he must commit seppuku—sob each time, no matter how often they have followed the story (as a Kabuki or Bunraku play, as a film); the ta'ziyah drama of the betrayal and murder of Imam Hussayn does not cease to bring an Iranian audience to tears no matter how many times they have seen the martyrdom enacted. On the contrary. They weep, in part, because they have seen it many times. People want to weep. Pathos, in the form of a narrative, does not wear out.

But do people want to be horrified? Probably not. 5 Still, there are pictures whose power does not abate, in part because one cannot look at them often. Pictures of the ruin of faces that will always testify to a great iniquity survived, at a cost: the faces of horribly disfigured First World War veterans who survived the inferno of the trenches; the faces melted and thickened with scar tissue of survivors of the American atomic bombs dropped on Hiroshima and Nagasaki; the faces cleft by machete blows of Tutsi survivors of the genocidal rampage launched by the Hutus in Rwanda—is it correct to say that people get *used to these?*

Indeed, the very notion of atrocity, of war crime, is associated with the expectation of photographic evidence. Such evidence is, usually, of something posthumous: the remains, as it were—the mounds of skulls in Pol Pot's Cambodia, the mass graves in Guatemala and El Salvador, Bosnia and Kosovo. And this posthumous reality is often the keenest of summations. As Hannah Arendt pointed out soon after the end of the Second World War, all the photographs and newsreels of the concentration camps are misleading because they show the camps at the moment the Allied troops marched in. What makes the images unbearable—the piles of corpses, the skeletal survivors—was not at all typical for the camps, which, when they were functioning, exterminated their inmates systematically (by gas, not starvation and illness), then immediately cremated them. And photographs echo photographs: It was inevitable that the photographs of emaciated Bosnian prisoners at Omarska, the Serb death camp created in northern Bosnia in 1992, would recall memories of the photographs taken in the Nazi death camps in 1945.

Photographs of atrocity illustrate as well as corroborate. Bypassing disputes about exactly how many were killed (numbers are often inflated at first), the photograph gives the indelible sample. The illustrative function of photographs leaves opinions, prejudices, fantasies, misinformation untouched. The information that many fewer Palestinians died in the assault on Jenin than had been claimed by Palestinian officials (as the Israelis had said all along) made much less impact than the pictures of the razed center of the refugee camp. And, of course, atrocities that are not secured in our minds by well-known photographic images, or of which we simply have had very few images—the total extermination of the Herero people in Namibia decreed by the German colonial administration in 1904; the Japanese onslaught in China, notably the massacre of nearly 400,000 and the rape of 80,000 Chinese in December 1937, the so-called Rape of Nanking; the rape of some 130,000 women and girls (10,000 of whom committed suicide) by victorious Soviet soldiers unleashed by their commanding officers in Berlin in 1945—seem more remote. These are memories that few have cared to claim.

The familiarity of certain photographs builds our sense of the present and immediate past. Photographs lay down routes of reference, and serve as totems of causes: Sentiment is more likely to crystalize around a photograph than around a verbal slogan. And photographs help construct—and revise—our sense of a more distant past, with the posthumous shocks engineered by the circulation of hitherto unknown photographs. Photographs that everyone recognizes are now a constituent part of what a society chooses to think about, or declares that it has chosen to think about. It calls these ideas "memories," and

that is, over the long run, a fiction. Strictly speaking, there is no such thing as collective memory—part of the same family of spurious notions as collective guilt. But there is collective instruction.

All memory is individual, unreproducible—it dies with each person. What is called collective memory is not a remembering but a stipulating: that *this* is important, and this is the story of how it happened, with the pictures that lock the story in our minds. Ideologies create substantiating archives of images, representative images, which encapsulate common ideas of significance and trigger predictable thoughts, feelings. Poster-ready photographs—the mushroom cloud of an A-bomb test, Martin Luther King, Jr., speaking at the Lincoln Memorial in Washington, D.C., the astronaut on the moon—are the visual equivalent of sound bites. They commemorate, in no less blunt fashion than postage stamps, Important Historical Moments; indeed, the triumphalist ones (the picture of the A-bomb excepted) become postage stamps. Fortunately, there is no one signature picture of the Nazi death camps.

As art has been redefined during a century of 10 modernism as whatever is destined to be enshrined in some kind of museum, so it is now the destiny of many photographic troves to be exhibited and preserved in museum-like institutions. Among such archives of horror, the photographs of genocide have undergone the greatest institutional development. The point of creating public repositories for these and other relics is to ensure that the crimes they depict will continue to figure in people's consciousness. This is called remembering, but in fact it is a good deal more than that.

The memory museum in its current proliferation is a product of a way of thinking about, and mourning, the destruction of European Jewry in the 1930s and 1940s, which came to institutional fruition in Yad Vashem in Jerusalem, the Holocaust Memorial Museum in Washington, D.C., and the Jewish Museum in Berlin. Photographs and other memorabilia of the Shoah have been committed to a perpetual recirculation, to ensure that what they show will be remembered. Photographs of the suffering and martyrdom of a people are more than reminders of death, of failure, of victimization. They invoke the miracle of survival. To aim at the perpetuation of memories means, inevitably, that one has undertaken the task of continually renewing, of creating, memories—aided, above all, by the impress of iconic photographs. People want to be able to visit—and refresh—their memories. Now many victim peoples want a memory museum, a temple that houses a comprehensive, chronologically organized, illustrated narrative of their sufferings. Armenians, for example, have long been clamoring for a museum in Washington to institutionalize the memory of the genocide of Armenian people by the Ottoman Turks. But why is there not already, in the nation's capital, which happens to be a city whose population is overwhelmingly African American, a Museum of the History of Slavery? Indeed, there is no Museum of the History of Slavery—the whole story, starting with the slave trade in Africa itself, not just selected parts, such as the Underground Railroad—anywhere in the United States. This, it seems, is a memory judged too dangerous to social stability to activate and to create. The Holocaust Memorial Museum and the future Armenian Genocide Museum and Memorial are about events that didn't happen in America, so the memory-work doesn't risk rousing an embittered domestic population against authority. To have a museum chronicling the great crime that was African slavery in the United States of America would be to acknowledge that the evil was *here.* Americans prefer to picture the evil that was *there,* and from which the United States—a unique nation, one without any certifiably wicked leaders throughout its entire history—is exempt. That this country, like every other country, has its tragic past does not sit well with the founding, and still all-powerful, belief in American exceptionalism. The national consensus on American history as a history of progress is a new setting for distressing photographs—one that focuses our attention on wrongs, both here and elsewhere, for which America sees itself as the solution or cure. ○

SUSAN SONTAG

One of America's leading social commentators, Susan Sontag (1933–2004) was hailed as a brilliant critic and provocative thinker. Raised in Arizona and California, she studied at a number of universities, among them the University of Chicago, Harvard, and Oxford. Her formal schooling finished, she soon began writing essays for *The New Yorker, The New York Review of Books,* and other magazines. Beginning in 1964 with "Notes on Camp," a brilliant essay on the avant-garde, her work was both widely discussed and well received. She published two groundbreaking collections of essays on culture and politics in the 1960s: *Against Interpretation* (1966) and *Styles of Radical Will* (1969). Over the next several decades she continued to explore a wide range of cultural phenomena, from illness to art. In later years she published work in other genres, including a best-selling historical novel, *The Volcano Lover* (1992). This piece is taken from *Regarding the Pain of Others* (2003), a book on war imagery in which the author decried the birth of a "culture of spectatorship," arguing that it "neutralized the moral force of photographs of atrocities." Sontag's many honors and awards included membership in the American Academy of Arts and Sciences, a MacArthur Fellowship, and a National Book Award.

A selection from one of Sontag's best-known works, *On Photography* (1977), can be found on pages 310–12.

SEEING

1. Sontag's essay is dense with provocative statements and questions about the cultural functions and meanings of photography. Create an outline of her essay in which you title and then paraphrase each of her core arguments. List the examples she uses to support each assertion. To what extent do you agree with each of her points?

2. Review your outline and imagine that you are going to elaborate on each of Sontag's points in an essay. Find at least one additional image—from this book or another source—that refutes or supports each argument. Cite the source of each image and note how you would use it.

RESPONDING VISUALLY

"Photographs lay down routes of reference, and serve as totems of causes," writes Sontag; "Sentiment is more likely to crystalize around a photograph than around a verbal slogan." (para. 8) Choose a cause you believe in and create an image to serve as its totem. You might take a photograph, draw a picture, or make a collage. Using an image, what is the minimum number of words you need to clearly communicate—and to generate sympathy for—your cause? Now create another version of your piece using only words. Did you find it necessary to add words? Which version do you and your classmates find more compelling? Why?

WRITING

1. What does Sontag mean when she writes in paragraph 6 that, "photographs echo photographs: It was inevitable that the photographs of emaciated Bosnian prisoners at Omarska, the Serb death camp created in northern Bosnia in 1992, would recall memories of the photographs taken in Nazi death camps in 1945"? Begin by conducting Internet searches for *Omarska* and *Nazi death camps.* Then look for examples of other photographs that "echo" each other. Write an expository essay in which you explain Sontag's statement by analyzing two additional sets of photographs that echo each other.

2. Sontag writes that "the Holocaust Memorial Museum and the future Armenian Genocide Museum and Memorial are about events that didn't happen in America, so the memory-work runs no risk of rousing an embittered domestic population against authority. To have a museum chronicling the great crime that was African slavery in the United States of America would be to acknowledge that the evil was there" (paras. 12–13). To what extent do you agree with Sontag's statement? Imagine that your town or city is considering a proposal for a museum of the history of slavery. Write an argumentative essay in which you argue for or against the proposal. Should the history of slavery be commemorated in a "memory museum"? Why or why not?

The Ethics of Representation

Looking Closer

Is seeing really believing? Photographs may never have been the documents of truth that they initially were assumed to be, and now the accessibility of digital technology has made it possible for even home-computer users to alter the look of a holiday portrait. Doctoring family snapshots may seem benign, but what are the ethics of enhancing or altering news photographs?

As Mitchell Stephens describes in **"Expanding the Language of Photographs,"** magazines and advertisers have a history of enhancing and manipulating photographs. George Hunt's photograph is evidence that photo-doctoring has long been a staple of government propaganda. The selections that follow remind us that the debate over tampering with photography remains as heated as ever. See, for example, the hoax photo created from Lance Cheung's and Charles Maxwell's images, Kelly K. Spors's **"Where All School Photos Are Above Average,"** and Carla Marinucci's account of how a political group spliced separate photographs of John Kerry and Jane Fonda from different occasions to create the impression that they appeared together at the same antiwar rally. In **"Ethics in the Age of Digital Photography,"** John Long underscores how easily—and frequently—the manipulation of images can occur at a time when digital imagery is widely available and understood by the general public.

EXPANDING THE LANGUAGE OF PHOTOGRAPHS
Mitchell Stephens

A PHOTO ON THE FRONT PAGE OF *NEW YORK Newsday* on Feb. 16, 1994, showed two well-known Olympic ice skaters, Tonya Harding and Nancy Kerrigan, practicing together. By the standards of the tabloid war then raging in New York City (a war *New York Newsday* would not survive), this shot of Harding and the fellow skater she had been accused of plotting to assault did not seem particularly incendiary. But there was something extraordinary about this photograph: The scene it depicted had not yet taken place. Harding and Kerrigan, as the paper admitted in the caption, had not in fact practiced together. A computer had stitched together two separate images to make it appear as if they already had.

Newsday was certainly not the first publication to have taken advantage of techniques that allow for the digital manipulation of photographs. In 1982, for example, a *National Geographic* computer had nudged two pyramids closer together so that they might more comfortably fit the magazine's cover. In July 1992, *Texas Monthly* had used a computer to place the head of then-Gov. Ann Richards on top of the body of a model riding a Harley-Davidson motorcycle. But you had to be an expert on pyramids to

figure out what *National Geographic* had done, and you had to miss a fairly broad joke to take umbrage with *Texas Monthly*. *New York Newsday*'s editors had fiddled with photos featuring two of the most talked-about individuals of the day, and they weren't joking. The results of their efforts were clearly visible on newsstands all over Manhattan.

Defenders of journalism's accuracy and reliability quickly grabbed their lances and mounted their steeds: "A composite photograph is not the truth," Stephen D. Isaacs, then acting dean of the Columbia Graduate School of Journalism, thundered. "It is a lie and, therefore, a great danger to the standards and integrity of what we do." The dean of the S. I. Newhouse School of Public Communication at Syracuse University, David M. Rubin, concluded that "*New York Newsday* has taken leave of its ethical moorings."

This front-page photo in a major daily seemed to announce that craven journalists had found a powerful new way to debase themselves: computer reworkings of photographs.

Others of us, however, heard a different announcement on that winter day in 1994: *Newsday*'s rather ordinary-looking attempt to further exploit an unpleasant, mostly unimportant story, we believed, was an early indication that news images might finally be coming of age.

To understand the significance of *New York Newsday*'s digital manipulation of this photograph, it is first necessary to acknowledge all the other ways photographs are manipulated. Photographers choose angles, making sure, for example, that the crowd of reporters isn't in the shot. They use filters, adjust contrast, and vary depth of field. They frame and crop, and routinely transform reds, blues, and yellows into blacks, grays, and whites. Aren't these distortions of sorts?

It is also necessary to acknowledge the ways in which we manipulate language. Words are routinely arranged so that they describe events that are not currently occurring, as in the sentence: "Nancy Kerrigan and Tonya Harding will practice together." Words are even deployed in tenses that describe events that likely will not or definitely will not occur: "She might have won the gold medal." And words frequently speak of one thing as if it were another: Despite its proximity to New York harbor, *New York Newsday* did not literally possess "ethical moorings." Deans Isaacs and Rubin, for all their devotion to journalistic integrity, probably did not grab lances or mount steeds. In their efforts to approach the truth, words regularly depart from the literal truth.

In fact, words have gained much of their strength through speculation, negation, hypothesizing, and metaphor—through what, by Dean Isaacs's definition, might qualify as lies. In the first century and a half of their existence, photographic images, on the other hand, have been held back by their inability to speak of what will be, what might be, and what won't be; their inability to present something as if it were something else. "Pictures," the theorist Sol Worth wrote dismissively in 1975, "cannot depict conditionals, counter-factuals, negatives, or past future tenses." Well, now they can. Alert observers of journalism learned that on Feb. 16, 1994.

The above-board computer manipulation of photographs will give responsible journalists—those

with their ethical moorings intact—a powerful new tool. Sometimes the results will be fanciful: an image of Bill Clinton and Newt Gingrich arm wrestling, perhaps. Sometimes such computer-altered photographs will be instructive: They might picture, for example, how that plane should have landed. Such reworked photos will allow us to peek, however hazily, into the future: showing not just how Harding and Kerrigan might look together on the ice but how that new building might change the neighborhood. They will also allow us to peek into the past: portraying, with photographic realism (not, as in TV reenactments, with clumsy actors), how a crime might have been committed. The idea should be to clarify, not to pretend.

For news photographs will not come of age by hoodwinking those who look at them. That must be emphasized. Before digital editing and digital photography, harried photographers occasionally rearranged backgrounds or restaged scenes; adept photo editors, armed with a thick black pencil, occasionally added hair where there was too little or subtracted a chin where there were too many. Computers make such attempts to deceive much easier but no more conscionable. There is no doubt that they have been used for such purposes already. *Time* magazine's surreptitious digital darkening of O. J. Simpson's face on its cover later in 1994 may qualify as an example. But *New York Newsday*'s Harding–Kerrigan photo was labeled as a "composite." "Tomorrow, they'll really take to the ice together" the paper explained on that front page, though not in as large type as we journalism professors would have liked.

Here is a standard journalism deans might more reasonably champion: Digitally manipulated photographs must not be used as a tool for deceiving. They must be labeled, clearly, as what they are. (Let's take a hard line on this, initially at least: no lightening of a shadow, no blurring of an inconvenient background without some sort of acknowledgment.) But the potential these photographs offer as a tool for communicating honestly must not be suppressed.

With the aid of computers, photographic images will be able to show us much more than just what might present itself at any one time to a well-situated lens, as words tell us about much more than just what is, at any one time, literally the case. And computers will be able to work this magic on moving as well as still photographic images, on television news video as well as newspaper and magazine photographs.

None of this should be that hard to imagine. The computer-produced graphics that increasingly illustrate print and television news stories have been perpetrating clever and effective reimaginings of reality for many years now: politicians' faces matched with piles of dollar bills, the affected states jumping out of maps, items flying in and out of shopping carts. And all this has been happening without attracting the ire of the defenders of journalism's integrity.

The notion that news photographs themselves—ot just cartoon-like graphics—are subject to these new types of alteration will take some getting used to. The labels will have to be very clear, their type very large—particularly at the start. For we have been in the habit of accepting photography as what one of its inventors, William Henry Fox Talbot, called "the pencil of nature." That was always something of a misperception. Now, if we are to take advantage of the great promise of digital technology, we'll have to wise up.

For computers are going to expand our control 15 over this pencil dramatically. Journalists will have unprecedented ability to shape the meanings their photographs, not just their sentences, can communicate. Their pictures will approach issues from many new directions. The language of photojournalism will grow. And that is good news for those who struggle to report with images. ○

Where All School Photos Are Above Average

*Digital Retouching Hits
a Staple of Childhood,
Erasing Braces and Acne*

KELLY K. SPORS

If only all adolescent traumas were so easy to airbrush away.

In perhaps the most effective assault yet on teenage scourges like acne and braces, school photographers are increasingly turning to the latest digital technology to remove them. The digital retouching runs less than $10 for a basic task like removing a pimple, to $60 and up for more intricate work such as importing a set of eyes from a different picture. Not surprisingly, kids and their parents are gladly paying the extra money.

School photographers are doing their part to make the world a more perfect place to ward off rivals who have been making major inroads into the portrait business. In recent years, studios that specialize in school portraits have lost significant sales to discounters like Wal-Mart Stores and Sears Roebuck that offer lower prices, according to Photo Marketing Association, a trade group. In addition, higher-end studios that offer advanced photo-retouching services are increasingly popular among image-conscious seniors. Today only about 35% of high-school seniors use the school-appointed photographer for yearbook pictures, down from about 55% in 1995.

As a result, studios that do the bulk of their work in schools are finally undertaking the expensive switch to digital cameras. That enables them to give their subjects a complete makeover in a matter of minutes with a personal computer and Photoshop software. Fixing crooked teeth and half-closed eyes has emerged as a key battleground in the hotly competitive school-picture business, which generated $1 billion in revenues in 2001, the most recent figures available.

When her daughter Carmen started eighth grade this fall at Johnson Middle School in Melbourne, Fla., Irene Torres paid an extra $8 for retouching, figuring that just meant eliminating any dust specks or stray hairs. But when the pictures came back, not only had the dust been removed—so had some acne on her daughter's nose. "It's just like she had a clear face," she says.

The changes go well beyond pimple removal. Consider the vexing blinking problem. "They'll have a pose and they love the expression, but their eyes are closed," says Neal Millsaps, a photographer in Winston-Salem, N.C. To fix it, he takes a pair of eyes from another photo and pastes them in. "That happens quite a bit."

While other professional photographers started using digital cameras a few years back, many school studios continued to cling to old-fashioned film photography. Last year only about 3% of school photos were taken digitally, according to the Photo Marketing Association. Many of the largest national studios, such as Minnesota-based Life-Touch, stick mostly to film because of the enormous costs of replacing their cameras and equipment.

Photographers argue that retouching isn't just about creating pictures with fewer imperfections. For kids who are particularly

High-school senior Nicole Benson paid $40 to get her school portrait retouched. "I look a lot better without braces," she says.

self-conscious—not a small group—getting rid of braces or other embarrassments can be an esteem-booster.

The services are most popular among middle- and high-school students, says Dean Stewart, the school photographer in Melbourne, Fla., who started offering the retouching service last year. For $8 on a standard photo package, he will eliminate anything from red eye to acne. Between 5% and 10% of students ask for it, he says.

On senior portraits, which usually put students in an assortment of poses, locations and outfits, retouching can get more elaborate. Studios usually charge $40 or more an hour, and can make things like tattoos disappear.

Digital retouching is taking off at studios like Events to Go, in Cape Canaveral, Fla. Since most school photos are taken right after summer break, parents want to get tan lines and bug bites zapped from their children's portraits. The studio charges $7 to $10, and can usually wipe out imperfections in a matter of minutes. A few weeks ago, one mother asked to digitally repair a decayed tooth in her third-grade son's photo by replacing it with a shiny white one.

Arik Hoek, who runs a studio in Houston that digitally alters photos for professional photographers, says he's now getting about 5% of his business from school photos, mostly senior portraits. Some parents have asked that a snake tattoo be removed from their daughter's neck or shoulder. "Someone who is pretty heavy might want to get that large double chin removed," Mr. Hoek adds.

One of the most popular requests: getting rid of clunky metal braces. Nicole Benson, a 17-year-old senior in Melbourne, Fla., had her braces erased from her senior portrait last summer. Her braces will come off in the spring, so she wants to be remembered for the smile she'll have at graduation. "I think I look a lot better without braces," she says. "People can't even tell" they were airbrushed out.

But it's not just the kids who are eager to look better. Al Scotti of Events to Go says that school principals also see a chance to improve their own image. "A lot of them want to get rid of the dark lines under their eyes," says Mr. Scotti. "Especially since their photos are hung in the front office." ○

Looking Closer

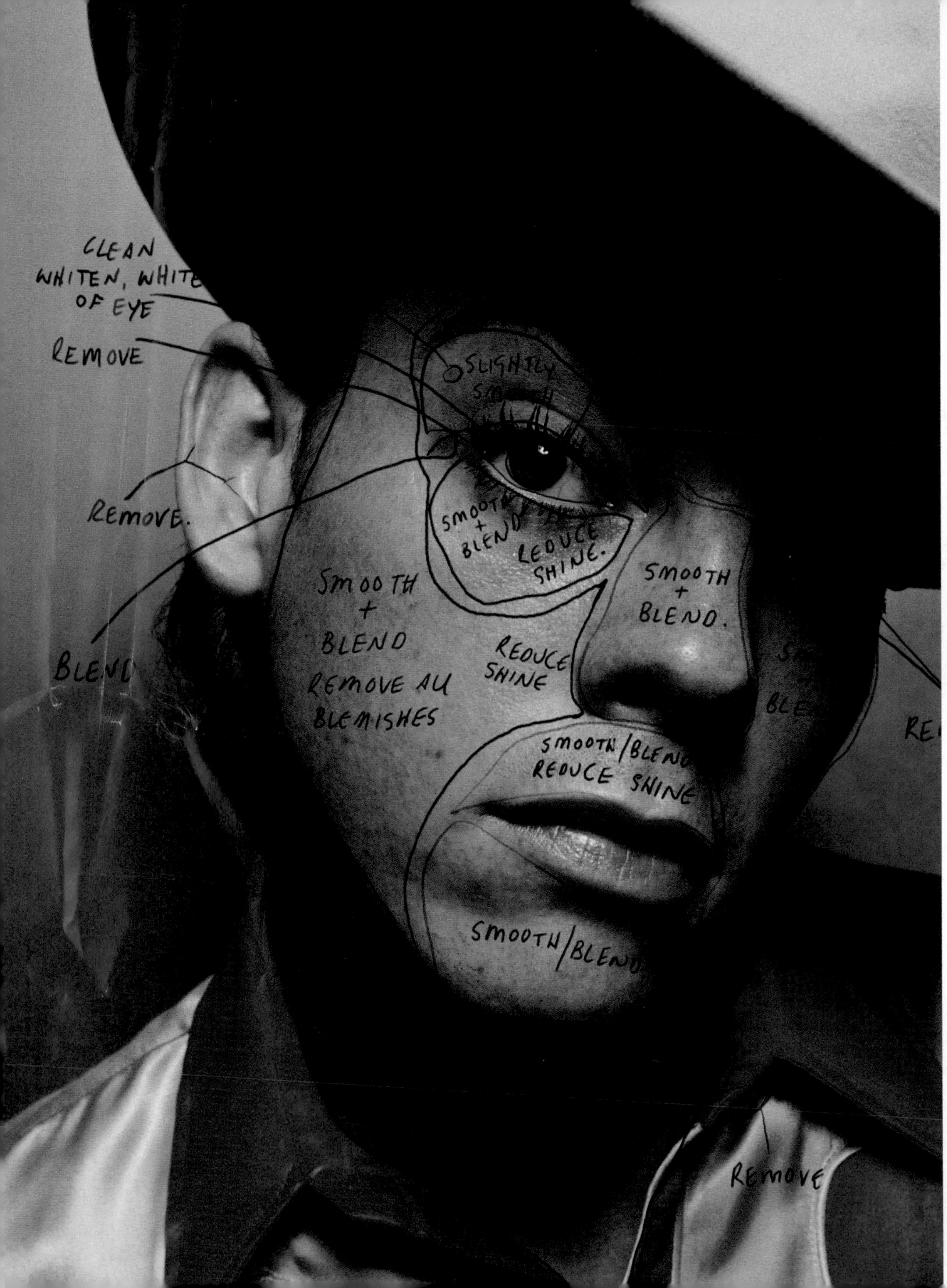
CLEAN
WHITEN, WHITE
OF EYE
REMOVE
SLIGHTLY
REMOVE.
SMOOTH + BLEND
REDUCE SHINE.
SMOOTH + BLEND
REMOVE ALL BLEMISHES
REDUCE SHINE
SMOOTH + BLEND.
BLEND
SMOOTH/BLEND
REDUCE SHINE
SMOOTH/BLEND
REMOVE

Rankin, *Bashful*

Looking Closer

Ethics in the Age of Digital Photography

John Long

Two disclaimers need to be stated before we begin:

1. My purpose is not to give answers. My purpose is to provide you with a vocabulary so you can discuss the ethical issues that may arise when using computers to process photographs. I also want to present the principles I have found helpful when trying to make decisions of an ethical nature. I do not expect everyone to agree with me. I want you to think about the issues and arrive at your own conclusions in a logical and reasoned manner.

2. The advent of computers and digital photography has not created the need for a whole new set of ethical standards. We are not dealing with something brand new. We merely have a new way of processing images, and the same principles that have guided us in traditional photojournalism should be the principles that guide us in the use of the computers. This fact makes dealing with computer-related ethics far less daunting than if we had to begin from square one.

We have many problems in journalism today that threaten our profession and in fact threaten the Constitution of our country. Photo ops, lack of access to news events, rock show contracts, yellow tape, and bean counters are just a few. Everyone has a spin; everyone wants to control the news media. We are under attack from all sides.

One of the major problems we face as photojournalists is the fact that the public is losing faith in us. Our readers and viewers no longer believe everything they see. All images are called into question because the computer has proved that images are malleable, changeable, fluid. In movies, advertisements, TV shows, magazines, we are constantly exposed to images created or changed by computers. As William J. Mitchell points out in his book *The Reconfigured Eye, Visual Truth in the Post-Photographic Era* we are experiencing a paradigm shift in how we define the nature of a photograph. The photograph is no longer a fixed image; it has become a watery mix of moveable pixels, and this is changing how we perceive what a photograph is. The bottom line is that documentary photojournalism is the last vestige of the real photography.

Journalists have only one thing to offer the public and that is CREDIBILITY. This is the first vocabulary word I want you to remember, and the most important. Without credibility we have nothing. We might as well go sell widgets door to door since without the trust of the public we cannot exist as a profession.

Our credibility is damaged every time a reputable news organization is caught lying to the public, and one of the most blatant and widely recognized cases was the computer enhancement of the *Time* magazine cover photo of O. J. Simpson. *Time* took the mug shot of Simpson when he was arrested and changed it before using it on their cover. They would not have been caught if *Newsweek* had not used the same photo on their cover photo just as it had come from the police. The two covers showed up on the newsstands next to each other, and the public could see something was wrong.

Time darkened the handout photo, creating a five o'clock shadow and a more sinister look. They darkened the top of the photo and made the police lineup numbers smaller. They decided Simpson was guilty so they made him look guilty. (There are two issues here: One is a question of photographic ethics and the other is a question of racial insensitivity by *Time* in deciding that blacker means guiltier. The black community raised this issue when the story broke, and [it] needs to be the subject of another article. My concern is with the issue of photographic ethics.)

In an editorial the next week, *Time*'s managing editor wrote, "The harshness of the mug shot—the merciless bright light, the stubble on Simpson's face, the cold specificity of the picture—had been subtly smoothed and shaped into an icon of tragedy." In other words, they changed the photo from what it was (a document) into what they wanted it to be. *Time* was making an editorial statement, not reporting the news. They presented what looked like a real photograph and it turned out not to be real; the public felt deceived, and rightly so. By doing this, *Time* damaged their credibility and the credibility of all journalists.

In order to have a rational, logical discussion of ethics, a distinction needs to be drawn between ethics and taste. *Ethics* refers to issues of deception, or lying. *Taste* refers to issues involving blood, sex, violence, and other aspects of life we do not want to see in our morning paper as we eat breakfast. Not everyone defines *taste–ethics* this way, but I find it useful. Issues of taste can cause a few subscription cancellations and letters to the editor, but they tend to evaporate in a few days. Ethics violations damage credibility, and the effects can last for years. Once you damage your credibility, it is next to impossible to get it back.

The photo of the dead American soldier being dragged through the streets of Mogadishu raises issues of taste, not issues of ethics. This photo is a fair and accurate representation of what happened in Somalia that day. (I hesitate to use the word *truthful*. Truth is a loaded concept, open to personal interpretation. What is true for one person may not be true for another. I prefer to use the terms *fair* and *accurate*. These terms are more precise, though not completely without debate over their meaning.)

If we are to use this photo, a photo that is ethically correct but definitely of questionable taste (no one wants to see dead American soldiers in the newspaper), we need to have a compelling reason. Earlier I mentioned I would give you some principles that I find useful, and this is the first: If the public needs the information in the photo in order to make informed choices for society, then we must run the photo. We cannot make informed choices for our society unless we have access to fair and accurate information. A free society is based on this right. It is codified in our country as the First Amendment. We have to know what is happening in our towns, in our country, in our world, in order to make decisions that affect us as a society. The First Amendment does not belong to the press; it belongs to the American people. It guarantees all of us the right to the fair and accurate information we need to be responsible citizens.

We needed to see the dead soldier in the streets so we could make an informed choice as a country as to the correctness of our being in Somalia. Words can tell us the facts, but photos hit us in the gut. They give us the real meaning, the deep and emotional impact of what was happening, much better than words can. As a society we decided that we needed to leave that country.

I feel bad for the family of the soldier, but sometimes the needs of the many outweigh the needs of the few, or the one. In our country, we have the right to our privacy (usually the Sixth Amendment is cited) but we also have to live together and act collectively. This need is addressed by the First Amendment: "Congress shall make no law respecting an establishment of religion, or prohibiting the free exercise thereof; or abridging the freedom of speech or of the press; or the right of the people peaceably to assemble, and to petition the government for a redress of grievances."

Honest photographs can have an ethical dimension when it concerns the personal ethics of the photographer. Did the photographer violate some ethical standard in the process of making the picture?

For example, take the very famous photo of the young child dying in Sudan while a vulture stands behind her, waiting. It was taken by Kevin Carter, who won a Pulitzer Prize for the photo (a photo that raised a lot of money for the relief agencies). He was criticized for not helping the child; he replied there were relief workers there to do that. After receiving his Pulitzer, Kevin Carter returned to Africa and committed suicide. He had a lot of problems in his life but, with the timing of the sequence of events, I cannot help thinking there is a correlation between his photographing the child and his suicide.

This is the kind of choice all journalists will face 15 sometime in [their] career; maybe not in the extreme situation that Carter faced, but in some way, we all will be faced with choices of helping or photographing. Someday we will be at a fire or a car accident and we will be called upon to put the camera down and help. It is a good idea to think about these issues in advance because when the hour comes, it will come suddenly and we will be asked to make a choice quickly.

Here is the principle that works for me. It is not a popular one and it is one that many journalists disagree with, but it allows me to sleep at night. If you have placed yourself in the position where you can help, you are morally obligated to help. I do not ask you to agree with me. I just want you to think about this and be prepared: At what point do you put the camera down and help? At what point does your humanity become more important than your journalism?

It is time to get back to the theme of this report— the ethics involved with the use of computers to process images.

I like the *Weekly World News*. It provides a constant source of photos for these discussions about ethics. One of the more famous front pages shows a space alien shaking hands with President Clinton. It is a wonderful photo, guaranteed to make the career of any photographer who manages to get an exclusive shot of this event.

We can laugh at this photo, and I have no real problem with the *Weekly World News* running such digitally created photos because of the context of where this photo is running. This is the second of the vocabulary words I want to give you: CONTEXT. Where the photo runs makes all the difference in the world. If this same photo ran on the front page of the *New York Times,* it would damage the credibility of the *Times.* In the context of *Weekly World News,* it cannot damage their credibility because that newspaper does not have any credibility to begin with (it seems we need to create a new set of terms when we can refer to the *Weekly World News* and the *New York Times* both as newspapers).

Context becomes a problem when we find digitally 20 altered photos in reputable publications, and there have been many. For example, the cover of *Texas Monthly* once ran a photo of then Governor Ann Richards astride a Harley-Davidson motorcycle. It came out that the only part of the photo that was Ann Richards was her head. The body on the motorcycle belonged to a model, and the head of the governor was electronically attached to the model.

On the credit page in very small type, the editors claimed they explained what they had done and that this disclosure exonerated them. They wrote:

Cover photograph by Jim Myers
Styling by Karen Eubank
Accessories courtesy of Rancho Loco, Dallas; boots courtesy of Boot Town, Dallas; motorcycle and leather jacket courtesy of Harley-Davidson, Dallas; leather pants by Patricia Wolfe
Stock photograph (head shot) by Kevin Vandivier / Texastock

In the first place this was buried on the bottom of a page very few people look at, in a type size few over 40 can read, and was worded in a way as to be incomprehensible.

Secondly, my feeling is that no amount of captioning can forgive a visual lie. In the context of news, if a photo looks real, it better be real. This photo looked real, but it was a fake. We have an obligation to history to leave behind us a collection of real photographs. This photo of Ann Richards entered into the public domain, and on the day she lost her re-election bid, AP ran the photo on the wire for its clients. AP had to run a mandatory kill when they were informed it was not a real photo.

Janet Cooke was a reporter at the *Washington Post* who won a Pulitzer Prize in 1981 for a story she wrote about an 8-year old heroin addict named Jimmy. The prize was taken back and she was fired when it was discovered that she made up the story. Can you imagine if the *Post* put a disclaimer in italics at the end of the story when it first ran, that said something along these lines: "We know this exact kid does not exist, but we also know this kind of thing does happen and so we created this one composite kid to personalize the story. Even though Jimmy does not exist, you can believe everything else we wrote." The *Post* would have been the laughing stock of the industry, and yet this is what *Texas Monthly* is doing by captioning away a visual lie. You have to have the same respect for the visual image as you have for the written word. You do not lie with words, nor should you lie with photographs.

In one of the early Digital Conferences, the Reverend Don Doll, S.J., pointed out that there are degrees of changes that can be done electronically to a photograph. There are technical changes that deal only with the aspects of photography that make the photo more readable, such as a little dodging and burning, global color correction, and contrast control. These are all part of the grammar of photography, just as there is a grammar associated with words (sentence structure, capital letters, paragraphs) that maked it possible to read a story, so there is a grammar of photography that allows us to read a photograph. These changes (like their darkroom counterparts) are neither ethical nor unethical—they are merely technical.

Changes to content can be Accidental or Essential 25 (this is an old Aristotelian distinction)—Essential changes change the meaning of the photograph, and Accidental changes change useless details but do not change the real meaning. Some changes are obviously more important than others. Accidental changes are not as important as Essential changes, but both kinds are still changes.

If you had a photograph of a bride and groom and removed the groom, this would constitute an Essential change because it would change the meaning of the photograph. (In fact, there are companies that will provide this service if you get a divorce. I guess the wedding book would end up looking like the bride got all dressed up and married herself.)

In the two photos of the ladies on the parade float,[1] the photo on the left has a set of wires running behind the ladies. In the photo on the right, the lines have been removed. It takes only a few seconds with the cloning tool in Photoshop to remove these lines. Removing the lines is an Accidental change, a change of meaningless details. If we had changed the flag to a Confederate flag, or removed a couple of the ladies, this would have changed the meaning of the photo and it would have been an Essential change. But if we

---

[1] For reasons of space and copyright, we are unable to reproduce these two photos.

just remove the lines, what is the big deal? Who is harmed? As far as I am concerned, we are all harmed by any lie, big or small.

I do not think the public cares if it is a little lie or a big lie. As far as they are concerned, once the shutter has been tripped and the MOMENT has been captured on film, in the context of news, we no longer have the right to change the content of the photo in any way. Any change to a news photo—any violation of that MOMENT—is a lie. Big or small, any lie damages your credibility.

The reason I get so adamant when I discuss this issue is that the documentary photograph is a very powerful thing, and its power is based on the fact that it is real. The real photograph gives us a window on history; it allows us to be present at the great events of our times and the past. It gets its power from the fact that it represents exactly what the photographer saw through the medium of photography. The raw reality it depicts, the verisimilitude makes the documentary photo come alive. Look at the photo of Robert Kennedy dying on the floor of the hotel in California; look at the works of David Douglas Duncan or the other great war photographers; look at the photo of Martin Luther King martyred on the balcony of a motel in Memphis. The power of these photographs comes from the fact they are real moments in time captured as they happened, unchanged. To change any detail in any of these photographs diminishes their power and turns them into lies. They would no longer be what the photographer saw but what someone else wanted the scene to be. The integrity of the Moment would be destroyed in favor of the editorial concept being foisted, as is the case in the O. J. Simpson *Time* cover.

There have been many cases of digital manipulation over the past 20 years or so, the first of note being the famous pyramids cover of *National Geographic* in 1982. *National Geographic* had a horizontal photo of the pyramids in Egypt and wanted to make a vertical cover from it. They put the photo in a computer and squeezed the pyramids together—a difficult task in real life but an easy task for the

computer. They referred to it as the "retroactive repositioning of the photographer" (one of the great euphemisms of our age), saying that if the photographer had been a little to one side or the other, this is what he would have gotten. The photographer was not 10 feet to the right and he did not get the photo they wanted, so they created a visual lie. They damaged their credibility, and (as I said before) taste issues have a short life span, ethics issues do not go away. Here we are almost 20 year later, and we are still talking about what *Geographic* did.

Sports Illustrated recently produced a special edition for Connecticut on the UConn national championship basketball season. In one photo, they showed a star player, Ricky Moore, going up for a layup with another player, Kevin Freeman, in the frame. They also used the same photo on the cover of the regular edition of the magazine, cropped tighter but with Kevin Freeman removed. I guess he cluttered up the cover, so he was expendable.

The point I want to make here is that if *Sports Illustrated* had not used the same photo twice, they would not have been caught. The computer allows for seamless changes that are impossible to see, and if you shoot with an electronic camera, you do not even have film to act as a referent. How many times has *Sports Illustrated* or *Time* or *Newsweek* or any of a long list of newspapers and magazines changed a photo and we the reading public not known about it? This is the Pandora's box of the computer age.

It is not just in the computer that photographers and editors can lie. We can lie by setting up photos or by being willing partners to photo ops. These things are as big, if not bigger, threats to our profession as the computers. The *L. A. Times* ran a photo of a fireman dousing his head with water from a swimming pool as a house burned in the background. In doing preparations for contest entries, they discovered that the photographer had said to the fireman something along the lines of, "You know what would make a good photo? If you went over by the pool and poured water on your head." The photo was a setup.

It was withdrawn from competition, and the photographer was disciplined severely.

This is as much a lie as what can be done in Photoshop. Neither is acceptable.

"A Day in the Life" series of books has a long history of manipulated covers. In *A Day in the Life of California,* for example, the photo was shot on a gray day as a horizontal. The hand came from another frame; the surfboard was moved closer to the surfer's head, and the sky was made blue to match his eyes. They had about 30,000 images to pick from and could not find one that looked like California to them, so they had to create an image—an image of what they wanted California to look like.

The list can go on for pages: *Newsweek* straightened the teeth of Bobbi McCaughey, the mother of the septuplets; *Newsday* ran a photo supposedly showing Nancy Kerrigan and Tonya Harding skating together a day before the event really happened; *People* ran a photo of famous breast cancer survivors made from five separate negatives; the *St. Louis Post Dispatch* removed a Coke can from a photo of their Pulitzer Prize winner. This just scratches the surface.

How many cases have not become known? The cumulative effect is the gradual erosion of the credibility of [the] entire profession, and I am not sure we can win this war. We are being bombarded from all sides, from movies, television, advertisements, the Internet, with images that are not real, that are created in computers, and documentary photojournalism is the victim.

We may be in a death struggle, but the end is worth fighting for. Real photos can change the hearts and minds of the people. Real photographs can change how we view war and how we view our society. Vietnam is a prime example. Two photos sum up that war: the Nick Ut photo of the girl burned by napalm running naked down the street and the Eddie Adams photo of the man being executed on the streets of Saigon. These photos changed how we perceived that war. They are powerful, and they get their power from the fact that they are real Moments captured for all time on film.

No one has the right to change these photos or the content of any documentary photo. It is our obligation to history to make sure this does not happen. ○

DOCTORED KERRY PHOTO BRINGS ANGER, THREAT OF SUIT Software, Net make it easy to warp reality

Carla Marinucci

The photographer who snapped John Kerry attending a 1971 anti-war rally says he and his photo agency intend to track down—and possibly sue—whoever doctored and circulated a photo that made it appear that the then 27-year-old Vietnam veteran was appearing alongside actress Jane Fonda.

Ken Light, now a UC Berkeley professor of journalism ethics, says he photographed Kerry at an anti-war rally in Mineola, N.Y., on June 13, 1971. The decorated Vietnam veteran was preparing to give a speech at the rally—but Fonda was never at the event.

Light's photo gained prominence when someone took it and merged the shot of the now Democratic presidential frontrunner with another separate photo of Fonda—one taken by photographer Owen Franken as the actress spoke to a 1972 rally in Miami Beach, Fla.

The fabricated Kerry–Fonda photo was circulated with an identifying logo of the Associated Press and became the subject of talk show fodder after it was placed on many web sites as evidence of Kerry's "anti-American" activities after his war service.

Light said this week that the use— 5 and misuse—of his copyrighted photo might result in legal action.

"(We're) doing everything possible to track down who it was and bring them to justice," said Light, who said the Associated Press also intended to examine the issue of who would use the agency's copyright for fraudulent purposes.

A spokesman for Light's photo agency, Corbis, said its photographers' work and copyrights are treated seriously.

The agency will "investigate this matter and take appropriate action as necessary," the spokesman said.

Light, who teaches at the journalism school at UC Berkeley, said he regularly instructed his students on matters of law and photo ethics. But ironically, this year, "I've become the lesson," he said, referring to how easy it has become to produce sophisticated and potentially damaging photos via computer.

"With modern technology, anybody can do it," he said of the doctored photo 10 of Kerry, now a 60-year-old, four-term Massachusetts senator. "Someone has

Fonda Speaks To Vietnam Veterans At Anti-War Rally

An image of Jane Fonda from 1972, right, was added to a photo of John Kerry at an anti-war rally in Mineola, N.Y., in 1971, above, to produce the doctored picture above.

to be really motivated and understand what they're doing."

Still, "it's one thing to (create) an image and another to try to make it look like it came right from a newspaper," Light said. The addition of the Associated Press logo suggested that whoever fabricated the photo was "definitely more than someone having fun. . . . People just see it, and it creates this impression that it really happened."

Light said he was outraged by his almost 33-year-old photo's popping into the news and becoming the subject of such Internet chatter.

"I was completely shocked and a little disappointed there would be this type of fakery in a political campaign," he said.

"You become very concerned for democracy when you realize people are so angry, they're desperately trying to find anything to tilt the direction of what people are thinking," he said. ○

Lance Cheung, *Members of the 129th Rescue Squadron, Moffitt Federal Airfield, CA, 2001*

Charles Maxwell, *Breaching Great White Shark*, South Africa

"THE Photo of the Year," 2001 (hoax photograph)
"and you think your [sic] having a bad day at work!! Although this looks like a picture taken from a Hollywood movie, it is in fact a real photo, taken near the South African coast during a military exercise by the British Navy. It has been nominated by National Geographic as 'THE photo of the year'."

MITCHELL STEPHENS

Mitchell Stephens (b. 1949) teaches journalism and mass communications at New York University. An acclaimed commentator on both the history and the practice of journalism, he has written on the topic for newspapers and has also published several journalism textbooks. His general-interest publications include *A History of News* (1996, rev. ed.) and *The Rise of the Image, the Fall of the Word* (1998). In the latter work he challenges the belief that "visual" information is eroding the intelligence of the news audience, arguing instead that future viewers will become as adept at reading the subtleties of moving pictures and images as they now are at understanding the nuances of language.

Stephens recently spent a year traveling abroad, reporting on globalization for NPR's *On the Media.*

GEORGE HUNT

Anthropologist Franz Boas and photographer George Hunt were members of a late-nineteenth-century expedition to study and record indigenous cultures of the North Pacific, which were facing increasing westernization. While cameras provided an ideal tool for capturing daily life and cultural practices, the still-cumbersome technology created ample opportunities for staging or manipulating "authentic" culture. This photograph, featured in an American Museum of Natural History exhibition, shows Boas (left) and Hunt (right) preparing a backdrop for a photograph of a cedar bark weaving by a Kwakiutl woman.

KELLY K. SPORS

Kelly Spors is a staff reporter for the *Wall Street Journal,* where this article first appeared on December 16, 2003. Spors writes frequently on a range of financial and consumer's rights issues, especially pocketbook issues—among them credit card debt, 401(k) rollovers, school loans, property taxes, mortgages, and buying products online. For example, in an August 1, 2004, article, "Paying the Same . . . but Getting Less," Spors educated consumers about product downsizing, describing it as "a common inflation-fighting move by food and consumer-product makers" and then explored the possibility that it constitutes a deceptive advertising practice. In "Where All School Photos Are above Average," Spors notes that the cost of digital retouching is dropping, making it more affordable to more consumers. Retouching is consequently a new consumer option, one that may change the image, quality, and cost of school photographs in years to come.

RANKIN

British-born John Rankin Waddell (b. 1966) has earned an international reputation for his fashion and portrait photography. He began his career in Europe in the early 1990s and has since published several books of his work, including *CeleBritation* (2000), a collection of his celebrity portraits; *Breeding* (2000), which challenges perceptions of gender and beauty with stunning images of androgynous models; and *Works in Progress 2: Girls on Top* (2003), a celebration of female form and sexuality.

In 1991, he co-founded the British fashion magazine *Dazed & Confused,* to capture what the magazine describes as the "unprecedented explosion of young creative talent in British fashion, music, art, and photography." From that venture sprang Dazed Books, to publish hip, edgy fashion and photography titles. Rankin also has shot advertising campaigns for numerous products and directed *Perfect,* a short film on domestic abuse (2003).

"The world he portrays is a 'fake,'" wrote critic Von Jochen Siemens. "Rankin makes his pictures by drawing on the tensions and contradictions and glamour that lie between faked and authentic reality. For example his photos of faces and heads painted with instructions of what is to be touched up and where. You could almost call it an act of piracy against the fake world of advertising photography—everybody can see how big a lie beauty really is."

JOHN LONG

John Long was president of the National Press Photographers Association (1989–1990) and currently chairs its Ethics/ Standards Committee. The essay here was written in 1999. Long feels strongly that certain principles must guide photojournalists: "Each day when you step out onto the street, remember that you have been granted a sacred trust to be truthful. You have the responsibility to produce only honest images. You have no right to set up pictures; you have no right to stage the news; you have no right to distort the facts. Your fellow citizens trust you. If you destroy the credibility of your work, *even in small ways,* it destroys the credibility of your newspaper or TV station in the eyes of the people you are covering." Today Long is a photojournalist for the *Hartford Courant.*

CARLA MARINUCCI

Carla Marinucci is a political writer for the *San Francisco Chronicle,* where she was also an investigative and business reporter for many years. Marinucci has won more than twenty awards for journalism, including the John Jacobs Award (with Lance Williams) for daily news coverage of the California gubernatorial race in 2002. The article here first appeared in the *Chronicle* on February 20, 2004.

Marinucci often investigates areas of possible ethical conflict. For example, in a January 16, 2005, *Chronicle* article, she reported on California Governor Arnold Schwarzenegger's executive editorship of two bodybuilding magazines. She wrote: "Sheldon Rampton, research director for the Center for Media and Democracy in Washington, D.C., which studies media and ethics issues, said Schwarzenegger might increasingly be 'crossing a lot of boundaries between self-promotion and the financial interests of his long-time sponsors.'"

HOAX PHOTOGRAPH

This photograph, purportedly *National Geographic*'s "photo of the year," began circulating on the Internet in August 2001. By August 2002, its staff overwhelmed with inquiries, the magazine official declared the image a hoax. (You can read an updated statement at news. nationalgeographic.com). The photograph is a composite of a U.S. Air Force photograph of an HH-60G Pave Hawk helicopter taken by Lance Cheung near San Francisco's Golden Gate Bridge and a photograph of a breaching great white shark taken by South African photographer Charles Maxwell. "I'd like to make contact with the person who did this," said Maxwell, "not to get him or her into trouble, but because it's a lot of fun and it is a good job. However, I must make clear that I would not like to see this happen to one of my photographs again. It is wrong to take images from a web site without permission."

Looking Closer

SEEING

1. In "Expanding the Language of Photographs," Mitchell Stephens draws a distinction between *Time*'s manipulation of O. J. Simpson's image and *Newsday*'s composite image of Harding and Kerrigan. The former, Stephens argues, is unethical; the latter is not. To what extent do you agree with Stephens? What are the ethics involved in each case? What was manipulated in each instance, and how? Did the editors act ethically in each instance? Why or why not? In your view, is an image used as cover art subject to the same standards as a news photograph?

2. Here is what one critic said after the Kerrigan–Harding photo was printed: "Different standards applied to photographic and textual evidence [indicate] that photographs have a lower status in the editorial hierarchy. Whereas *Time*'s editors would presumably never consider rewriting a quotation from O. J. Simpson, attempting to say it better for him, they evidently felt fewer qualms about altering the police photograph in order to lift . . . 'a common police mug shot to the level of art, with no sacrifice to the truth.'" Do you agree with this distinction? with its implications?

WRITING

1. Stephens argues that manipulating photographs is not unlike choosing words in journalism, that words are shaped and edited. Compare and contrast a news photo and a written report of the same event. How is the event framed visually? verbally? What did the photographer and writer/editor choose to include? to omit? How would you compare the overall point of view and tone of the photograph with the same aspects of the verbal description? Draft an essay in which you argue for—or against—the assertion that visual and verbal material are held to the same standards of evidence in journalism.

2. Draft an argumentative essay in which you agree or disagree with Stephens's proposed standard for labeling manipulated news photos: "Digitally manipulated photographs must not be used as a tool for deceiving. They must be labeled, clearly, as what they are. (Let's take a hard line on this, initially at least: no lightening of a shadow, no blurring of an inconvenient background without some sort of acknowledgment.)" (para. 11).

APPENDIX A
ON THE THEORY AND PRACTICE OF SEEING

As visual images have become increasingly integrated into our lives, the call to define the term *visual literacy* has grown louder. What does it mean to be visually literate? How exactly do we see? How should we train ourselves to see clearly and read images analytically? How do images affect us? How are images different from or similar to words? How are visual images the products of their cultural contexts? Scholars and cultural commentators in the fields of art history, science, social history, design, and literary and cultural studies have responded to these questions in dozens of studies.

Appendix A presents two fundamental theoretical works: the first essay in John Berger's *Ways of Seeing*, and the sixth chapter (entitled "Show and Tell") in Scott McCloud's *Understanding Comics: The Invisible Art*.

Of his book *Ways of Seeing,* John Berger writes in a note to the reader, "The form of the book has as much to do with our purpose as the arguments contained within it." The same might be said of Scott McCloud's illustrated "essay."

Each of these selections uses text and images to present theories on both *how we see* and *how visual images have been seen* throughout history. You are encouraged to use these texts to re-examine any of the visual and verbal selections presented in *Seeing & Writing 3*.

JOHN BERGER

JOHN BERGER

John Berger was born in 1926 in London, where he attended Central School of Art and Chelsea School of art. Known primarily as an art critic and social historian, Berger is also a distinguished novelist, artist, poet, essayist, Marxist critic, screenwriter, translator, and actor. He has published more than eight works of fiction and fifteen works of nonfiction, along with numerous articles and screenplays, during a remarkably prolific career. His novel *G: A Novel* won the Booker Prize in 1972.

Berger began his career as an artist and drawing teacher. While exhibiting his work at local galleries in London, he also wrote art criticism for British journals. Beginning with *Permanent Red: Essays in Seeing* (1960), Berger focused his criticism on the broad issues of seeing as a social and historical act. He introduced a mixed-media approach—combining poetry, photography, essays, and criticism—to the field of art criticism in books such as *Ways of Seeing* (1972), *About Looking* (1980), and *Another Way of Telling* (1982). His most recent work is *Here Is Where We Meet: A Fiction* (2005), a collection of semi-autobiographical vignettes. Berger currently lives and works in a small French village.

The selection printed here is the first essay in *Ways of Seeing*, which was based on a BBC television series.

WAYS OF SEEING

John Berger

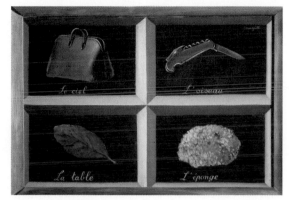

The Key of Dreams by Magritte (1898–1967).

SEEING COMES BEFORE WORDS. THE CHILD LOOKS and recognizes before it can speak.

But there is also another sense in which seeing comes before words. It is seeing which establishes our place in the surrounding world; we explain that world with words, but words can never undo the fact that we are surrounded by it. The relation between what we see and what we know is never settled. Each evening we *see* the sun set. We *know* that the earth is turning away from it. Yet the knowledge, the explanation, never quite fits the sight. The Surrealist painter Magritte commented on this always-present gap between words and seeing in a painting called *The Key of Dreams*.

The way we see things is affected by what we know or what we believe. In the Middle Ages when men believed in the physical existence of Hell the sight of fire must have meant something different from what it means today. Nevertheless their idea of Hell owed a lot to the sight of fire consuming and the ashes remaining—as well as to their experience of the pain of burns.

When in love, the sight of the beloved has a completeness which no words and no embrace can match: a completeness which only the act of making love can temporarily accommodate.

Yet this seeing which comes before words, and can never be quite covered by them, is not a question of 5

mechanically reacting to stimuli. (It can only be thought of in this way if one isolates the small part of the process which concerns the eye's retina.) We only see what we look at. To look is an act of choice. As a result of this act, what we see is brought within our reach—though not necessarily within arm's reach. To touch something is to situate oneself in relation to it. (Close your eyes, move round the room and notice how the faculty of touch is like a static, limited form of sight.) We never look at just one thing; we are always looking at the relation between things and ourselves. Our vision is continually active, continually moving, continually holding things in a circle around itself, constituting what is present to us as we are.

Soon after we can see, we are aware that we can also be seen. The eye of the other combines with our own eye to make it fully credible that we are part of the visible world.

If we accept that we can see that hill over there, we propose that from that hill we can be seen. The reciprocal nature of vision is more fundamental than that of spoken dialogue. And often dialogue is an attempt to verbalize this—an attempt to explain how, either metaphorically or literally, "you see things," and an attempt to discover how "he sees things."

In the sense in which we use the word in this book, all images are manmade [see below]. An image is a

sight which has been recreated or reproduced. It is an appearance, or a set of appearances, which has been detached from the place and time in which it first made its appearance and preserved—for a few moments or a few centuries. Every image embodies a way of seeing. Even a photograph. For photographs are not, as is often assumed, a mechanical record. Every time we look at a photograph, we are aware, however slightly, of the photographer selecting that sight from an infinity of other possible sights. This is true even in the most casual family snapshot. The photographer's way of seeing is reflected in his choice of subject. The painter's way of seeing is reconstituted by the marks he makes on the canvas or paper. Yet, although every image embodies a way of seeing, our perception or appreciation of an image depends also upon our own way of seeing. (It may be, for example, that Sheila is one figure among twenty; but for our own reasons she is the one we have eyes for.)

Images were first made to conjure up the appearance of something that was absent. Gradually it became evident that an image could outlast what it represented; it then showed how something or somebody had once looked—and thus by implication how the subject had once been seen by other people. Later still the specific vision of the image-maker was also recognized as part of the record. An image became a record of how X had seen Y. This was the result of an increasing consciousness of individuality, accompanying an increasing awareness of history. It would be rash to try to date this last development precisely. But certainly in Europe such consciousness has existed since the beginning of the Renaissance.

No other kind of relic or text from the past can offer such a direct testimony about the world which surrounded other people at other times. In this respect images are more precise and richer than literature. To say this is not to deny the expressive or imaginative quality of art, treating it as mere documentary evidence; the more imaginative the work, the more profoundly it allows us to share the artist's experience of the visible.

Yet when an image is presented as a work of art, the way people look at it is affected by a whole series of learnt assumptions about art. Assumptions concerning:

Beauty
Truth
Genius
Civilization
Form
Status
Taste, etc.

Many of these assumptions no longer accord with the world as it is. (The world-as-it-is is more than pure objective fact, it includes consciousness.) Out of touch with the present, these assumptions obscure the past. They mystify rather than clarify. The past is never there waiting to be discovered, to be recognized for exactly what it is. History always constitutes the relation between a present and its past. Consequently fear of the

Regents of the Old Men's Alms House by Hals (1580–1666).

Regentesses of the Old Men's Alms House by Hals (1580–1666).

present leads to mystification of the past. The past is not for living in; it is a well of conclusions from which we draw in order to act. Cultural mystification of the past entails a double loss. Works of art are made unnecessarily remote. And the past offers us fewer conclusions to complete in action.

When we "see" a landscape, we situate ourselves in it. If we "saw" the art of the past, we would situate ourselves in history. When we are prevented from seeing it, we are being deprived of the history which belongs to us. Who benefits from this deprivation? In the end, the art of the past is being mystified because a privileged minority is striving to invent a history which can retrospectively justify the role of the ruling classes, and such a justification can no longer make sense in modern terms. And so, inevitably, it mystifies.

Let us consider a typical example of such mystification. A two-volume study was recently published on Frans Hals.[1] It is the authoritative work to date on this painter. As a book of specialized art history it is no better and no worse than the average.

The last two great paintings by Frans Hals portray the Governors and the Governesses of an Alms House for old paupers in the Dutch seventeenth-century city of Haarlem. They were officially commissioned portraits. Hals, an old man of over eighty, was destitute. Most of his life he had been in debt. During the winter of 1664, the year he began painting these pictures, he obtained three loads of peat on public charity, otherwise he would have frozen to death. Those who now sat for him were administrators of such public charity.

The author records these facts and then explicitly [15] says that it would be incorrect to read into the paintings any criticism of the sitters. There is no evidence, he says, that Hals painted them in a spirit of bitterness. The author considers them, however, remarkable works of art and explains why. Here he writes of the Regentesses:

> Each woman speaks to us of the human condition with equal importance. Each woman stands out with equal

clarity against the *enormous* dark surface, yet they are linked by a firm rhythmical arrangement and the subdued diagonal pattern formed by their heads and hands. Subtle modulations of the *deep,* glowing blacks contribute to the *harmonious fusion* of the whole and form an *unforgettable contrast* with the *powerful* whites and vivid flesh tones where the detached strokes reach *a peak of breadth and strength.* [Berger's italics]

The compositional unity of a painting contributes fundamentally to the power of its image. It is reasonable to consider a painting's composition. But here the composition is written about as though it were in itself the emotional charge of the painting. Terms like *harmonious fusion, unforgettable contrast,* reaching *a peak of breadth and strength* transfer the emotion provoked by the image from the plane of lived experience, to that of disinterested "art appreciation." All conflict disappears. One is left with the unchanging "human condition," and the painting considered as a marvellously made object.

Very little is known about Hals or the Regents who commissioned him. It is not possible to produce circumstantial evidence to establish what their relations were. But there is the evidence of the paintings themselves: the evidence of a group of men and a group of women as seen by another man, the painter. Study this evidence and judge for yourself.

1. Seymour Slive, *Frans Hals* (Phaidon, London).

The art historian fears such direct judgement:

> As in so many other pictures by Hals, the penetrating characterizations almost seduce us into believing that we know the personality traits and even the habits of the men and women portrayed.

What is this "seduction" he writes of? It is nothing less than the paintings working upon us. They work upon us because we accept the way Hals saw his sitters. We do not accept this innocently. We accept it in so far as it corresponds to our own observation of people, gestures, faces, institutions. This is possible because we still live in a society of comparable social relations and moral values. And it is precisely this which gives the paintings their psychological and social urgency. It is this—not the painter's skill as a "seducer"—which convinces us that we *can* know the people portrayed.

The author continues:

> In the case of some critics the seduction has been a total success. It has, for example, been asserted that the Regent in the tipped slouch hat, which hardly covers any of his long, lank hair, and whose curiously set eyes do not focus, was shown in a drunken state. [below]

This, he suggests, is a libel. He argues that it was a fashion at that time to wear hats on the side of the head. He cites medical opinion to prove that the Regent's expression could well be the result of a facial

paralysis. He insists that the painting would have been unacceptable to the Regents if one of them had been portrayed drunk. One might go on discussing each of these points for pages. (Men in seventeenth-century Holland wore their hats on the side of their heads in order to be thought of as adventurous and pleasure-loving. Heavy drinking was an approved practice. Etcetera.) But such a discussion would take us even farther away from the only con-

frontation which matters and which the author is determined to evade.

In this confrontation the Regents and Regentesses stare at Hals, a destitute old painter who has lost his reputation and lives off public charity; he examines them through the eyes of a pauper who must nevertheless try to be objective; i.e., must try to surmount the way he sees as a pauper. This is the drama of these paintings. A drama of an "unforgettable contrast."

Mystification has little to do with the vocabulary [20] used. Mystification is the process of explaining away what might otherwise be evident. Hals was the first portraitist to paint the new characters and expressions created by capitalism. He did in pictorial terms what Balzac did two centuries later in literature. Yet the author of the authoritative work on these paintings sums up the artist's achievement by referring to

> Hals's unwavering commitment to his personal vision, which enriches our consciousness of our fellow men and heightens our awe for the ever-increasing power of the mighty impulses that enabled him to give us a close view of life's vital forces.

That is mystification.

In order to avoid mystifying the past (which can equally well suffer pseudo-Marxist mystification) let us now examine the particular relation which now exists, so far as pictorial images are concerned, between the present and the past. If we can see the present clearly enough, we shall ask the right questions of the past.

Today we see the art of the past as nobody saw it before. We actually perceive it in a different way.

This difference can be illustrated in terms of what was thought of as perspective. The convention of perspective, which is unique to European art and which was first established in the early Renaissance, centres everything on the eye of the beholder. It is like a beam from a lighthouse—only instead of light travelling outwards, appearances travel in. The conventions called those appearances *reality*. Perspective makes the single eye the centre of the visible world. Everything converges on to the eye as to the vanishing point of infinity. The visible world is arranged for the spectator as the universe was once thought to be arranged for God.

According to the convention of perspective there is no visual reciprocity. There is no need for God to

situate himself in relation to others: he is himself the situation. The inherent contradiction in perspective was that it structured all images of reality to address a single spectator who, unlike God, could only be in one place at a time.

After the invention of the camera this contradiction gradually became apparent. 25

> I'm an eye. A mechanical eye. I, the machine, show you a world the way only I can see it. I free myself for today and forever from human immobility. I'm in constant movement. I approach and pull away from objects. I creep under them. I move alongside a running horse's mouth. I fall and rise with the falling and rising bodies. This is I, the machine, manoeuvring in the chaotic movements, recording one movement after another in the most complex combinations.
>
> Freed from the boundaries of time and space, I coordinate any and all points of the universe, wherever I want them to be. My way leads towards the creation of a fresh perception of the world. Thus I explain in a new way the world unknown to you.[2]

The camera isolated momentary appearances and in so doing destroyed the idea that images were timeless. Or, to put it another way, the camera showed that the notion of time passing was inseparable from the experience of the visual (except in paintings). What you saw depended upon where you were when. What you saw was relative to your position in time and space. It was no longer possible to imagine everything converging on the human eye as on the vanishing point of infinity.

This is not to say that before the invention of the camera men believed that everyone could see every-

Still from *Man with a Movie Camera* by Vertov (1895–1954).

thing. But perspective organized the visual field as though that were indeed the ideal. Every drawing or painting that used perspective proposed to the spectator that he was the unique centre of the world. The camera—and more particularly the movie camera—demonstrated that there was no centre.

The invention of the camera changed the way men saw. The visible came to mean something different to them. This was immediately reflected in painting.

For the Impressionists the visible no longer presented itself to man in order to be seen. On the contrary, the visible, in continual flux, became fugitive. For the Cubists the visible was no longer what

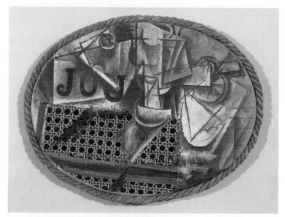

Still Life with Chair Caning by Picasso (1881–1973).

2. This quotation is from an article written in 1923 by Dziga Vertov, the revolutionary Soviet film director.

confronted the single eye, but the totality of possible views taken from points all round the object (or person) being depicted [*Still Life with Chair Caning*, page 685].

The invention of the camera also changed the way in which men saw paintings painted long before the camera was invented. Originally paintings were an integral part of the building for which they were designed. Sometimes in an early Renaissance church or

chapel one has the feeling that the images on the wall are records of the building's interior life, that together they make up the building's memory—so much are they part of the particularity of the building [below].

The uniqueness of every painting was once part of the uniqueness of the place where it resided. Sometimes the painting was transportable. But it could never be seen in two places at the same time. When the camera reproduces a painting, it destroys the uniqueness of its image. As a result its meaning changes. Or, more exactly, its meaning multiplies and fragments into many meanings.

This is vividly illustrated by what happens when a painting is shown on a television screen. The painting enters each viewer's house. There it is surrounded by his wallpaper, his furniture, his mementos. It enters the atmosphere of his family. It becomes their talking point. It lends its meaning to their meaning. At the same time it enters a million other houses and, in each of them, is seen in a different context. Because of the camera, the painting now travels to the spectator rather than the spectator to the painting. In its travels, its meaning is diversified.

One might argue that all reproductions more or less distort, and that therefore the original painting is still in a sense unique. Here [right] is a reproduction of the *Virgin of the Rocks* by Leonardo da Vinci.

Having seen this reproduction, one can go to the National Gallery to look at the original and there discover what the reproduction lacks. Alternatively one can forget about the quality of the reproduction and simply be reminded, when one sees the original, that it is a famous painting of which somewhere one has already seen a reproduction. But in either case the uniqueness of the original now lies in it being *the original of a reproduction*. It is no longer what its image shows that strikes one as unique; its first meaning is no longer to be found in what it says, but in what it is.

This new status of the original work is the perfectly rational consequence of the new means of reproduction. But it is at this point that a process of mystification again enters. The meaning of the original work no longer lies in what it uniquely says but in what it uniquely is. How is its unique existence evaluated and defined in our present culture? It is defined as an object whose value depends upon its rarity. This market is affirmed and gauged by the price it fetches on the market. But because it is nevertheless "a work

Church of St. Francis of Assisi.

Virgin of the Rocks by Leonardo da Vinci (1452–1519). Reproduced by courtesy of the Trustees, The National Gallery, London.

Before the *Virgin of the Rocks* the visitor to the 35 National Gallery would be encouraged by nearly everything he might have heard and read about the painting to feel something like this: "I am in front of it. I can see it. This painting by Leonardo is unlike any other in the world. The National Gallery has the real one. If I look at this painting hard enough, I should somehow be able to feel its authenticity. The *Virgin of the Rocks* by Leonardo da Vinci: it is authentic and therefore it is beautiful."

To dismiss such feelings as naive would be quite wrong. They accord perfectly with the sophisticated culture of art experts for whom the National Gallery catalogue is written. The entry on the *Virgin of the Rocks* is one of the longest entries. It consists of fourteen closely printed pages. They do not deal with the meaning of the image. They deal with who commissioned the painting, legal squabbles, who owned it, its likely date, the families of its owners. Behind this information lie years of research. The aim of

of art"—and art is thought to be greater than commerce—its market price is said to be a reflection of its spiritual value. Yet the spiritual value of an object, as distinct from a message or an example, can only be explained in terms of magic or religion. And since in modern society neither of these is a living force, the art object, the "work of art," is enveloped in an atmosphere of entirely bogus religiosity. Works of art are discussed and presented as though they were holy relics: relics which are first and foremost evidence of their own survival. The past in which they originated is studied in order to prove their survival genuine. They are declared art when their line of descent can be certified.

Virgin of the Rocks by Leonardo da Vinci (1452–1519). Louvre Museum.

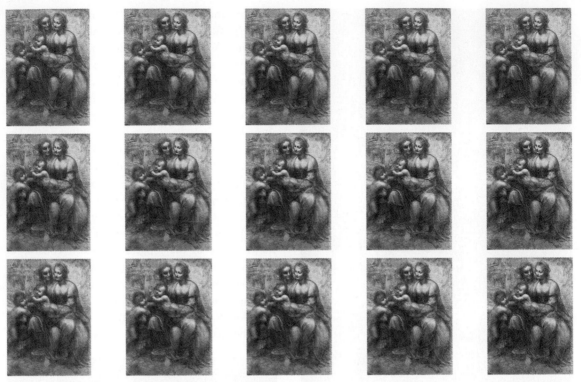

The Virgin and Child with St. Anne and St. John the Baptist by Leonardo da Vinci (1452–1519). Reproduced by courtesy of the Trustees, The National Gallery, London.

the research is to prove beyond any shadow of doubt that the painting is a genuine Leonardo. The secondary aim is to prove that an almost identical painting in the Louvre is a replica of the National Gallery version [see bottom, page 687].

French art historians try to prove the opposite.

The National Gallery sells more reproductions of Leonardo's cartoon of *The Virgin and Child with St. Anne and St. John the Baptist* [above] than any other picture in their collection. A few years ago it was known only to scholars. It became famous because an American wanted to buy it for two and a half million pounds.

Now it hangs in a room by itself. The room is like a chapel. The drawing is behind bullet-proof perspex. It has acquired a new kind of impressiveness. Not because of what it shows—not because of the meaning of its image. It has become impressive, mysterious, because of its market value.

The bogus religiosity which now surrounds original works of art, and which is ultimately dependent upon their market value, has become the substitute for what paintings lost when the camera made them reproducible. Its function is nostalgic. It is the final empty claim for the continuing values of an oligarchic, undemocratic culture. If the image is no longer unique and exclusive, the art object, the thing, must be made mysteriously so.

The majority of the population do not visit art museums. The following table [right] shows how closely an interest in art is related to privileged education.

The majority take it as axiomatic that the museums are full of holy relics which refer to a mystery which excludes them: the mystery of unaccountable wealth. Or, to put this another way, they believe that original masterpieces belong to the preserve (both materially and spiritually) of the rich. Another table indicates what the idea of an art gallery suggests to each social class.

Venus and Mars by Botticelli (1445–1510). Reproduced by courtesy of the Trustees, The National Gallery, London.

In the age of pictorial reproduction the meaning of paintings is no longer attached to them; their meaning becomes transmittable: that is to say it becomes information of a sort, and, like all information, it is either put to use or ignored; information carries no special authority within itself. When a painting is put to use, its meaning is either modified or totally changed. One should be quite clear about what this involves. It is not a question of reproduction failing to reproduce certain aspects of an image faithfully; it is a question of reproduction making it possible, even inevitable, that an image will be used for many different purposes and that the reproduced image, unlike an original work, can lend itself to them all. Let us examine some of the ways in which the reproduced image lends itself to such usage.

Reproduction isolates a detail of a painting from the whole. The detail is transformed. An allegorical figure becomes a portrait of a girl [see left].

When a painting is repro- 45 duced by a film camera it inevitably becomes material for the film-maker's argument.

National proportion of art museum visitors according to level of education: Percentage of each educational category who visit art museums

	Greece	Poland	France	Holland
With no educational qualification	0.02	0.12	0.15	—
Only primary education	0.30	1.50	0.45	0.50
Only secondary education	0.5	10.4	10	20
Further and higher education	11.5	11.7	12.5	17.3

Source: Pierre Bourdieu and Alain Darbel, *L'Amour de l'art,* Editions de Minuit, Paris 1969, Appendix 5, table 4.

Of the places listed below which does a museum remind you of most?

	Manual workers	Skilled and white collar	Professional and upper managerial
	%	%	%
Church	66	45	30.5
Library	9	34	28
Lecture hall	—	4	4.5
Department store or entrance hall in public building	—	7	2
Church and library	9	2	4.5
Church and lecture hall	4	2	—
Library and lecture hall	—	—	2
None of these	4	2	19.5
No reply	8	4	9
	100 (n = 53)	100 (n = 98)	100 (n = 99)

Source: As left, Appendix 4, table 8.

Procession to Calvary by Breughel (1525–1569).

A film which reproduces images of a painting leads the spectator, through the painting, to the film-maker's own conclusions. The painting lends authority to the film-maker. This is because a film unfolds in time and a painting does not. In a film the way one image follows another, their succession, constructs an argument which becomes irreversible. In a painting all its elements are there to be seen simultaneously.

The spectator may need time to examine each element of the painting but whenever he reaches a conclusion, the simultaneity of the whole painting is there to reverse or qualify his conclusion. The painting maintains its own authority.

Paintings are often reproduced with words around them.

Wheatfield with Crows by Van Gogh (1853–1890).

This is a landscape of a cornfield with birds flying out of it. Look at it for a moment. Then see the painting below.

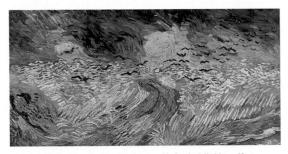

This is the last picture that Van Gogh painted before he killed himself.

It is hard to define exactly how the words have changed the image but undoubtedly they have. The image now illustrates the sentence.

In this essay each image reproduced has become 50 part of an argument which has little or nothing to do with the painting's original independent meaning. The words have quoted the paintings to confirm their own verbal authority. . . .

Reproduced paintings, like all information, have to hold their own against all the other information being continually transmitted [see top, page 691].

Subject and significance in
Titian's Death of Actaeon

Heritage exploits the authority of art to glorify the present social system and its priorities.

The means of reproduction are used politically and commercially to disguise or deny what their existence makes possible. But sometimes individuals use them differently [see top, page 692].

Adults and children sometimes 55 have boards in their bedrooms or living-rooms on which they pin pieces of paper: letters, snapshots, reproductions of paintings, newspaper cuttings, original drawings, postcards. On each board all the images belong to the same language and all are more or less equal within it, because they have been chosen in a highly personal way to match and express the experience of the room's inhabitant. Logically, these boards should replace museums.

What are we saying by that? Let us first be sure about what we are not saying.

We are not saying that there is nothing left to experience before original works of art except a sense of awe because they have survived. The way original works of art are usually approached—through museum catalogues, guides, hired cassettes, etc.—is not the only way they might be approached. When the art of the past ceases to be viewed nostalgically, the

Consequently a reproduction, as well as making its own references to the image of its original, becomes itself the reference point for other images. The meaning of an image is changed according to what one sees immediately beside it or what comes immediately after it. Such authority as it retains, is distributed over the whole context in which it appears [below].

Because works of art are reproducible, they can, theoretically, be used by anybody. Yet mostly—in art books, magazines, films, or within gilt frames in living-rooms—reproductions are still used to bolster the illusion that nothing has changed, that art, with its unique undiminished authority, justifies most other forms of authority, that art makes inequality seem noble and hierarchies seem thrilling. For example, the whole concept of the National Cultural

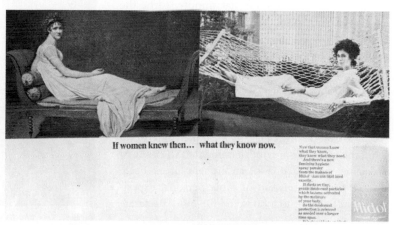

If women knew then... what they know now.

works will cease to be holy relics—although they will never re-become what they were before the age of reproduction. We are not saying original works of art are now useless.

Original paintings are silent and still in a sense that information never is. Even a reproduction hung on a wall is not comparable in this respect for in the original the silence and stillness permeate the actual material, the paint, in which one follows the traces of the painter's immediate gestures. This has the effect of closing the distance in time between the painting of the picture and one's own act of looking at it. In this special sense all paintings are contemporary. Hence the immediacy of their testimony. Their historical moment is literally there before our eyes. Cézanne made a similar observation from the painter's point of view. "A minute in the world's life passes! To paint it in its reality, and forget everything for that! To become that minute, to be the sensitive plate . . . give the image of what we see, forgetting everything that has appeared before our time . . ." What we make of that painted moment when it is before our eyes depends upon what we expect of art, and that in turn depends today upon how we have already experienced the meaning of paintings through reproductions.

Nor are we saying that all art can be understood spontaneously. We are not claiming that to cut out a magazine reproduction of an archaic Greek head, because it is reminiscent of some personal experience, and to pin it to a board beside other disparate images, is to come to terms with the full meaning of that head.

The idea of innocence faces two ways. By refusing to enter a conspiracy, one remains innocent of that conspiracy. But to remain innocent may also be to remain ignorant. The issue is not between innocence and knowledge (or between the natural and the cultural) but between a total approach to art which attempts to relate it to every aspect of experience and the esoteric approach of a few specialized experts who are the clerks of the nostalgia of a ruling class in decline. (In decline, not before the proletariat, but before the new power of the corporation and the state.) The real question is: to whom does the meaning of the art of the past properly belong? To those who can apply it to their own lives, or to a cultural hierarchy of relic specialists?

Woman Pouring Milk by Vermeer (1632–1675).

The visual arts have always existed within a certain preserve; originally this preserve was magical or sacred. But it was also physical: it was the place, the cave, the building, in which, or for which, the work was made. The experience of art, which at first was the experience of ritual, was set apart from the rest of life—precisely in order to be able to exercise power over it. Later the preserve of art became a social one. It entered the culture of the ruling class, whilst physically it was set apart and isolated in their palaces and houses. During all this history the authority of art was inseparable from the particular authority of the preserve.

What the modern means of reproduction have done is to destroy the authority of art and to remove it—or, rather, to remove its images which they reproduce—from any preserve. For the first time ever, images of art have become ephemeral, ubiquitous, insubstantial, available, valueless, free. They surround us in the same way as a language surrounds us. They have entered the mainstream of life over which they no longer, in themselves, have power.

Yet very few people are aware of what has happened because the means of reproduction are used nearly all the time to promote the illusion that nothing has changed except that the masses, thanks to reproductions, can now begin to appreciate art as the cultured minority once did. Understandably, the masses remain uninterested and sceptical.

If the new language of images were used differently, it would, through its use, confer a new kind of power. Within it we could begin to define our experiences more precisely in areas where words are inadequate. (Seeing comes before words.) Not only personal experience, but also the essential historical experience of our relation to the past: that is to say the experience of seeking to give meaning to our lives, of trying to understand the history of which we can become the active agents.

The art of the past no longer exists as it once did. 65 Its authority is lost. In its place there is a language of images. What matters now is who uses that language for what purpose. This touches upon questions of copyright for reproduction, the ownership of art presses and publishers, the total policy of public art galleries and museums. As usually presented, these are narrow professional matters. One of the aims of this essay has been to show that what is really at stake is much larger. A people or a class which is cut off from its own past is far less free to choose and to act as a people or class than one that has been able to situate itself in history. This is why— and this is the only reason why—the entire art of the past has now become a political issue. ○

Many of the ideas in the preceding essay have been taken from another, written over forty years ago* by the German critic and philosopher Walter Benjamin.

His essay was entitled The Work of Art in the Age of Mechanical Reproduction. *This essay is available in English in a collection called* Illuminations *(Cape, London, 1970).*

---

* Now over seventy years ago [eds.].

SCOTT MCCLOUD

"When I was a little kid I knew exactly what comics were," Scott McCloud writes in his book *Understanding Comics: The Invisible Art* (1993). "Comics were those bright, colorful magazines filled with bad art, stupid stories and guys in tights." But after looking at a friend's comic book collection, McCloud became "totally obsessed with comics" and in the tenth grade decided to become a comics artist.

In 1982, McCloud graduated with a degree in illustration from Syracuse University. "I wanted to have a good background in writing and art and also just liberal arts in general because I thought that just about anything can be brought to bear in making comics." Later McCloud worked in the production department of DC Comics until he began publishing his two comic series, "Zot!" (1984) and later "Destroy!!"

In *Understanding Comics*, a caricature of McCloud leads readers through an insightful study of the nature of sequential art by tracing the history of the relationship between words and images. "Most readers will find it difficult to look at comics in quite the same way ever again," wrote cartoonist Garry Trudeau of McCloud's work. In 2000, he published *Reinventing Comics,* which he describes as "the controversial 242-page follow-up" to *Understanding Comics.* Recently McCloud has been working with comics in the digital environment. His web site is at scottmccloud.com. "Show and Tell" is the sixth chapter in *Understanding Comics.*

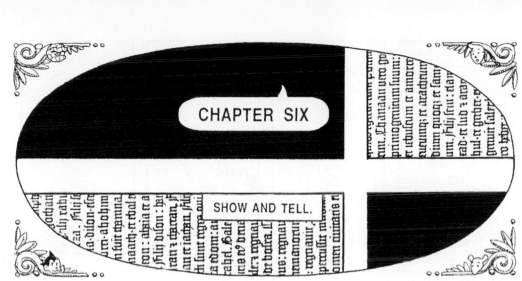

CHAPTER SIX

SHOW AND TELL.

THIS IS MY ROBOT.

WHAT CAN YOU *TELL* US ABOUT YOUR ROBOT, TOMMY?

WELL, UH... I LIKE IT 'CAUSE... 'CAUSE, UH...

IT'S GOT ONE OF *THESE* THINGS.

WHAT IS *THAT,* TOMMY?

138

IT'S THIS *THING* AND IF YOU *PULL* IT, IT GOES LIKE *THIS*.

KUNK!

THE HEAD FLIPS BACK.
...?
YEAH.

AND... AND *THEN* YOU CAN DO *THIS* AND IT GOES *UP* AND YOU FLIP *THIS*.

I DID IT WRONG. WAIT.

LOOK, IT'S A *AIRPLANE* NOW!

THANK YOU, TOMMY.

WE *ALL* STARTED OUT LIKE THIS, *DIDN'T WE?* USING WORDS AND IMAGES *INTERCHANGEABLY*. IT DIDN'T REALLY MATTER *WHICH* WE USED, SO LONG AS IT *WORKED*.

PSST! HEY, TOMMY!

HEE! HEE!

IT'S CONSIDERED *NORMAL* IN THIS SOCIETY FOR CHILDREN TO COMBINE WORDS AND PICTURES, SO LONG AS THEY *GROW OUT OF IT*.

TOMMY

139

TRADITIONAL THINKING HAS LONG HELD THAT TRULY *GREAT* WORKS OF ART AND LITERATURE ARE ONLY POSSIBLE WHEN THE TWO ARE KEPT AT ARM'S LENGTH.

WORDS AND PICTURES *TOGETHER* ARE CONSIDERED, AT BEST, A *DIVERSION* FOR THE *MASSES*, AT WORST A PRODUCT OF *CRASS COMMERCIALISM.*

AS CHILDREN, OUR FIRST BOOKS HAD *PICTURES GALORE* AND VERY FEW *WORDS* BECAUSE THAT WAS "EASIER."

THEN, AS WE GREW, WE WERE EXPECTED TO GRADUATE TO BOOKS WITH MUCH *MORE* TEXT AND ONLY *OCCASIONAL* PICTURES --

--AND FINALLY TO ARRIVE AT *"REAL"* BOOKS -- THOSE WITH NO PICTURES *AT ALL.*

OR PERHAPS, AS IS SADLY THE CASE THESE DAYS, TO NO *BOOKS* AT ALL.

140

MEANWHILE, WORDS AND *MOVING* PICTURES HAVE HALF THE WORLD IN THRALL TO THEIR CHARMS, BUT MUST STRUGGLE TO MAKE *THEIR* POTENTIAL UNDERSTOOD.

WORDS AND PICTURES ARE AS POPULAR AS EVER, BUT THIS WIDESPREAD FEELING THAT THE COMBINATION IS SOMEHOW *BASE* OR *SIMPLISTIC* HAS BECOME A *SELF-FULFILLING PROPHECY.*

THE ROOTS OF THIS ATTITUDE RUN PRETTY *DEEP.*

AS NEAR AS WE CAN TELL, PICTURES *PREDATE* THE WRITTEN WORD BY A *LARGE MARGIN.* HERE ARE SOME BIG HITS FROM THE GOLDEN AGE OF CAVE PAINTING, ABOUT 15,000 YEARS AGO.

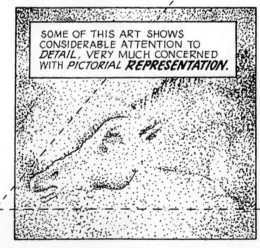

SOME OF THIS ART SHOWS CONSIDERABLE ATTENTION TO *DETAIL,* VERY MUCH CONCERNED WITH *PICTORIAL* **REPRESENTATION.**

BUT OTHERS WERE VERY *ICONIC,* ACTING AS **SYMBOLS** RATHER THAN *PICTURES*-- MORE LIKE A *PRIMITIVE LANGUAGE!*

141

AS MENTIONED IN OUR *LAST CHAPTER,* THE EARLIEST *WORDS* WERE, IN FACT, *STYLIZED PICTURES.*

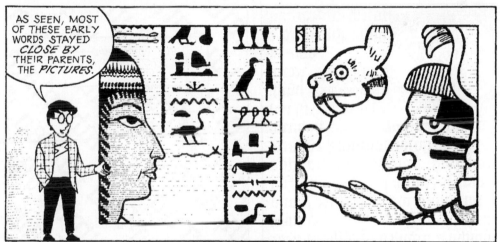

AS SEEN, MOST OF THESE EARLY WORDS STAYED *CLOSE BY* THEIR PARENTS, THE *PICTURES.*

IT DIDN'T TAKE *LONG,* THOUGH-- RELATIVELY SPEAKING -- BEFORE ANCIENT WRITING STARTED TO BECOME MORE *ABSTRACT.*

SOME WRITTEN LANGUAGES SURVIVE TO THIS DAY, BEARING TRACES OF THEIR ANCIENT PICTORIAL HERITAGE.

* SEE PAGE 129.

142

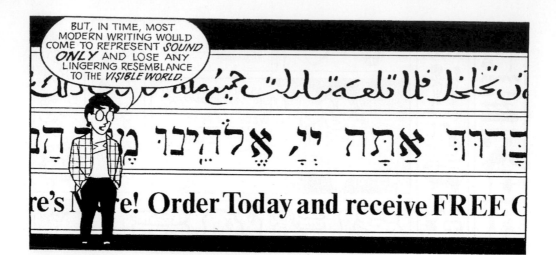

> BUT, IN TIME, MOST MODERN WRITING WOULD COME TO REPRESENT *SOUND ONLY* AND LOSE ANY LINGERING RESEMBLANCE TO THE *VISIBLE WORLD.*

re's More! Order Today and receive FREE G

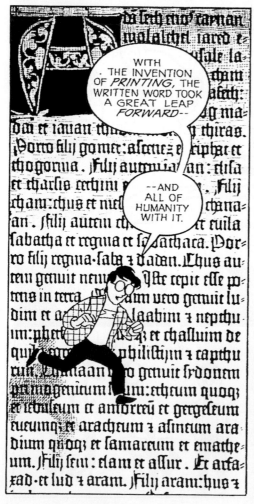

> WITH THE INVENTION OF *PRINTING,* THE WRITTEN WORD TOOK A GREAT LEAP *FORWARD*--

> --AND ALL OF HUMANITY WITH IT.

> BUT WHERE HAD THE *PICTURES* ALL GONE?

> WORDS AND PICTURES DID STILL *COEXIST* AT THIS STAGE IN WESTERN CIVILIZATION.*

> BUT *THOSE* INSTANCES WERE BECOMING THE *EXCEPTION,* NOT THE *RULE.*

143

*IN ILLUMINATED MANUSCRIPTS, FOR EXAMPLE.

MORE *IMPORTANTLY*, WHEN THEY ***WERE*** COMBINED, AS IN THIS *GERMAN* COMIC FROM THE 1400's, WORDS AND PICTURES STAYED *SEPARATE*, REFUSING TO *MIX*-- LIKE *OIL AND WATER*.

THE WRITTEN WORD WAS BECOMING MORE *SPECIALIZED*, MORE *ABSTRACT*, MORE *ELABORATE*--

--AND *LESS AND LESS LIKE PICTURES*.

PICTURES, MEANWHILE, BEGAN TO GROW IN THE *OPPOSITE* DIRECTION: LESS *ABSTRACT* OR *SYMBOLIC*, MORE *REPRESENTATIONAL* AND *SPECIFIC*.

FACSIMILE DETAILS OF PORTRAITS BY DURER (1519) REMBRANDT (1660) DAVID (1788) AND INGRES (1810-15).

144

John Keats   1819
Ode on a Grecian Urn

1

Thou still unravish'd bride of quietness,
  Thou foster-child of silence and slow time,
Sylvan historian, who canst thus express
A flowery tale more sweetly than our rhyme:
What leaf-fring'd legend haunts about thy shape
  Of deities or mortals, or of both,
    In Tempe or the dales of Arcady?
    What men or gods are these? What maidens loth?
What mad pursuit? What struggle to escape?
  What pipes and timbrels? What wild ecstasy?

BY THE EARLY 1800's, WESTERN ART AND WRITING HAD DRIFTED ABOUT AS FAR APART AS WAS *POSSIBLE*.

ONE WAS OBSESSED WITH *RESEMBLANCE, LIGHT* AND *COLOR,* ALL THINGS *VISIBLE*...

...THE *OTHER* RICH IN *INVISIBLE* TREASURES, SENSES, EMOTIONS, SPIRITUALITY, PHILOSOPHY...

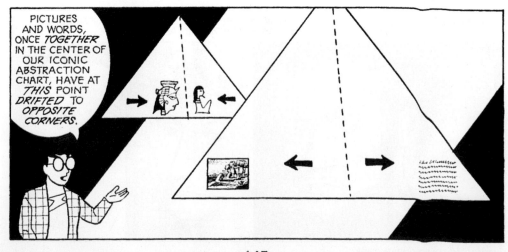

PICTURES AND WORDS, ONCE *TOGETHER* IN THE CENTER OF OUR *ICONIC ABSTRACTION* CHART, HAVE AT *THIS* POINT *DRIFTED* TO *OPPOSITE* CORNERS.

145

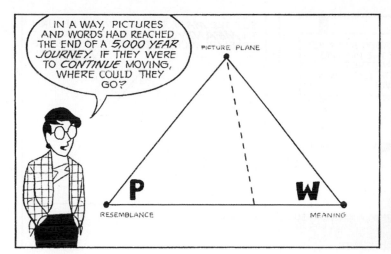

IN A WAY, PICTURES AND WORDS HAD REACHED THE END OF A *5,000 YEAR JOURNEY.* IF THEY WERE TO *CONTINUE* MOVING, WHERE COULD THEY GO?

PICTURE PLANE

P   **W**

RESEMBLANCE   MEANING

FOR *PICTURES,* THERE WAS ONLY *UP!*

IMPRESSIONISM SENT WESTERN ART TOWARD THE *ABSTRACT VERTEX,* BUT IN A WAY THAT *CLUNG* TO WHAT THE *EYE* SAW.

P

IMPRESSIONISM, WHILE IT COULD BE THOUGHT OF AS THE FIRST *MODERN* MOVEMENT, WAS MORE A *CULMINATION* OF THE *OLD,* THE *ULTIMATE STUDY* OF LIGHT AND COLOR.

FACSIMILE DETAIL OF "A SUNDAY AFTERNOON ON THE ISLAND OF LA GRANDE JATTE" BY GEORGES SEURAT.

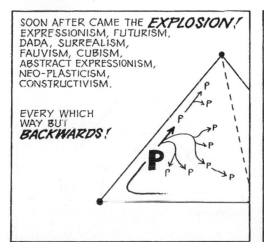

SOON AFTER CAME THE *EXPLOSION!* EXPRESSIONISM, FUTURISM, DADA, SURREALISM, FAUVISM, CUBISM, ABSTRACT EXPRESSIONISM, NEO-PLASTICISM, CONSTRUCTIVISM.

EVERY WHICH WAY BUT *BACKWARDS!*

P

STRICT REPRESENTATIONAL STYLES WERE OF LITTLE IMPORTANCE TO THE NEW SCHOOLS. *ABSTRACTION,* BOTH ICONIC AND *NON*-ICONIC MADE A SPECTACULAR *COMEBACK!*

FACSIMILE DETAILS OF PORTRAITS BY PICASSO, LEGER AND KLEE.

146

MONDRIAN A LA McCLOUD.

SOME ARTISTS HEADED *UPWARD* TO THE *SUMMIT* OF THE PICTURE PLANE, WANTING NEITHER *RESEMBLANCE* NOR EXTERNAL *"MEANING."*

BUT THE *MAIN* THRUST WAS A RETURN TO *MEANING* IN ART, *AWAY* FROM RESEMBLANCE, BACK TO THE REALM OF *IDEAS.*

RESEMBLANCE · MEANING

MEANWHILE, THE WRITTEN WORD WAS ALSO CHANGING. POETRY BEGAN *TURNING AWAY* FROM THE ELUSIVE, *TWICE-ABSTRACTED* LANGUAGE OF OLD TOWARD A MORE *DIRECT,* EVEN *COLLOQUIAL,* STYLE.

John Keats · 1819
Ode on a Grecian Urn

I

Thou still unravish'd bride of quietness,
Thou foster-child of silence and slow time,
Sylvan historian, who canst thus express
A flowery tale more sweetly than our rhyme:
What leaf-fring'd legend haunts about thy shape
Of deities or mortals, or of both,
In Tempe or the dales of Arcady?
What men or gods are these? What maidens loth?

Walt Whitman · 1890
Facing West from California's Shores

Facing west, from California's shores,
Inquiring, tireless, seeking
what is yet unfound,
I, a child, very old, over waves, towards the
house of maternity, the
land of migrations, look afar
Look off the shores of my Western sea, the
circle almost circled:
For starting westward from Hindustan,
from the vales of Kashmere, From Asia,
from the north, from the God, the sage,
and the hero, From the south, from the
flowery peninsulas and the spice islands,
Long having wandered since, round the
earth having wandered,
Now I face home again,
very pleased and joyous;
(But where is what I started for,
so long ago?
And why is it yet unfound?)

IN PROSE, LANGUAGE WAS BECOMING EVEN MORE DIRECT, CONVEYING MEANING *SIMPLY* AND *QUICKLY,* MORE LIKE *PICTURES.*

"MEANING" WAS NOT *ABANDONED* BY *ANY MEANS,* BUT AUTHORS WERE DEFINITELY MOVING *LEFT* --

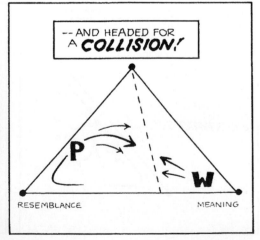

-- AND HEADED FOR A *COLLISION!*

RESEMBLANCE · MEANING

147

DADA POSTER FOR THE PLAY
"THE BEARDED HEART"

FACSIMILE OF "ORIENTAL SWEE'NESS" (1938) BY PAUL KLEE.

PAINTINGS INCREASINGLY TOOK ON *SYMBOLIC,* EVEN *CALLIGRAPHIC,* MEANINGS...

WHILE SOME ARTISTS ADDRESSED THE IRONIES OF WORDS AND PICTURES *HEAD-ON!*

148

AND IN *POPULAR* CULTURE THE TWO FORMS COLLIDED *AGAIN AND AGAIN* WITHOUT ANY PRETENSES OF *"HIGH"* ART.

NOWHERE IS THIS COLLISION MORE THOROUGHLY EXPLORED THAN THE MODERN COMIC. AND IT'S NOT A RECENT OBSESSION.

LET'S GO BACK TO THE EARLY 1800's BEFORE ANY OF THIS HAPPENED, WHEN WORDS AND PICTURES HAD DRIFTED AS FAR APART AS *POSSIBLE.*

UP TO THAT POINT, *EUROPEAN BROADSHEETS* HAD OFFERED *REMINDERS* OF WHAT WORDS AND PICTURES COULD DO WHEN COMBINED.

BUT AGAIN IT WAS *RODOLPHE TÖPFFER* WHO FORESAW THEIR *INTERDEPENDENCY* AND BROUGHT THE FAMILY *BACK TOGETHER* AT LAST.

M. CRÉPIN ADVERTISES FOR A TUTOR, AND MANY APPLY FOR THE JOB.

TRANSLATION BY E. WIESE.

I'M SURE THAT THESE IDEAS WERE THE *FURTHEST THING* FROM TÖPFFER'S MIND WHEN HE PUT *PEN TO PAPER*--

--BUT THE FACT THAT THE MODERN COMIC WAS BORN JUST AS ART AND WRITING WERE PREPARING TO CHANGE DIRECTION IS AT LEAST *INTRIGUING.*

AND PERHAPS THIS COMMON THREAD OF *UNIFICATION* DID GROW OUT OF A *SHARED INSTINCT* OF THE DAY...

...AN INSTINCT WHICH SAID THAT WE HAD REACHED THE END OF A *LONG JOURNEY* AND THAT IT WAS TIME AT LAST TO *HEAD FOR HOME.*

* NOT AS MUCH AS WE LIKE TO *THINK* IT HAS, ANYWAY.

150

THE ART FORM OF COMICS IS MANY CENTURIES OLD, BUT IT'S *PERCEIVED* AS A RECENT INVENTION AND SUFFERS THE CURSE OF *ALL* NEW MEDIA,

THE CURSE OF BEING JUDGED BY THE STANDARDS OF THE OLD.

EVER SINCE THE INVENTION OF THE WRITTEN WORD, NEW MEDIA HAVE BEEN *MISUNDERSTOOD*.

CAREFUL, JACOB! IF YOU KEEP DOING THIS, YOU'LL STOP USING YOUR *MEMORY!*

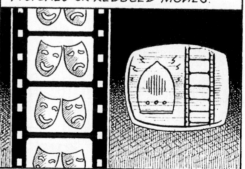

EACH NEW MEDIUM BEGINS ITS LIFE BY IMITATING ITS *PREDECESSORS*. MANY EARLY MOVIES WERE LIKE FILMED *STAGE PLAYS*, MUCH EARLY *TELEVISION* WAS LIKE *RADIO WITH PICTURES* OR *REDUCED MOVIES*.

FAR TOO MANY COMICS CREATORS HAVE NO HIGHER GOAL THAN TO MATCH THE ACHIEVEMENTS OF OTHER MEDIA, AND VIEW ANY CHANCE TO *WORK* IN OTHER MEDIA AS A *STEP UP.*

AND *AGAIN*, AS LONG AS WE VIEW COMICS AS A *GENRE* OF WRITING OR A *STYLE* OF GRAPHIC ART THIS ATTITUDE MAY *NEVER* DISAPPEAR.

151

WORDS AND PICTURES IN COMBINATION MAY NOT BE MY *DEFINITION* OF COMICS, BUT THE COMBINATION HAS HAD *TREMENDOUS INFLUENCE* ON ITS *GROWTH.*

com·ics (kom'iks) n. p... ...form, used with a singula... Juxtaposed pictoria... ...her images in deliberate ...ence, intended to conve... ...n and/or to prod... ...response in th... **2.** Superheroes ...costumes, fight... villains who want... ...he world in violent... ...use.

A HUGE RANGE OF HUMAN EXPERIENCES CAN BE *PORTRAYED* IN COMICS THROUGH EITHER WORDS OR PICTURES.

AS A RESULT--AND DESPITE ITS MANY *OTHER* POTENTIAL USES -- COMICS HAVE BECOME *FIRMLY IDENTIFIED* WITH THE ART OF *STORYTELLING.*

AND *INDEED,* WORDS AND PICTURES HAVE *GREAT* POWERS TO TELL STORIES WHEN CREATORS FULLY EXPLOIT THEM *BOTH.*

DADA

BIOGRAPHY HORROR

ROMANCE SURREALISM

BLANK VERSE HISTORICAL FICTION

EPIC POETRY FOLK TALES

SEQUENTIAL ART EROTICA

SOCIAL ALLEGORY MYSTERY

ADAPTATIONS RELIGIOUS TOPICS

STREAM OF CONSCIOUSNESS

SATIRE

AND SO FAR, WE'VE ONLY SEEN THE *TIP OF THE ICEBERG!*

AS CHILDREN, WE "SHOW AND TELL" *INTERCHANGEABLY,* WORDS AND IMAGES COMBINING TO TRANSMIT A *CONNECTED SERIES OF IDEAS.*

IT'S GOT ONE OF *THESE* THINGS

THE DIFFERENT WAYS IN WHICH WORDS AND PICTURES CAN *COMBINE* IN COMICS IS VIRTUALLY *UNLIMITED.*

BUT LET'S TRY TO BREAK IT DOWN INTO SOME DISTINCT *CATEGORIES.*

152

153

154

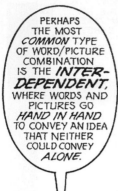

PERHAPS THE MOST *COMMON* TYPE OF WORD/PICTURE COMBINATION IS THE *INTER-DEPENDENT*, WHERE WORDS AND PICTURES GO *HAND IN HAND* TO CONVEY AN IDEA THAT NEITHER COULD CONVEY *ALONE*.

MEANWHILE...

DID ANYONE *SEE* YOU?

THIS IS ALL I NEED TO *STOP* HIM!

I ASK YOU, DOES THIS GUY LOOK LIKE A *C.E.O.* TO *YOU*??

"AND JUST *GUESS* WHO DROVE UP IN BOB'S TRUCK AN HOUR LATER!"

HEY, MARGE!

OH, MY *GOD!*

HE'S LYING.

UH-HUH.

"AFTER COLLEGE, I PURSUED A CAREER IN *HIGH FINANCE*."

HURRY UP, WILLYA?!

INTERDEPENDENT COMBINATIONS AREN'T ALWAYS AN *EQUAL BALANCE* THOUGH AND MAY FALL *ANYWHERE* ON A SCALE BETWEEN TYPES ONE AND TWO.

GENERALLY SPEAKING, THE MORE IS SAID WITH *WORDS*, THE MORE THE PICTURES CAN BE FREED TO GO EXPLORING AND *VICE VERSA*.

$$\frac{P}{W}$$

$$\frac{W}{P}$$

155

IN COMICS AT ITS *BEST,* WORDS AND PICTURES ARE LIKE *PARTNERS* IN A *DANCE* AND EACH ONE TAKES TURNS *LEADING.*

WHEN *BOTH* PARTNERS TRY TO LEAD, THE COMPETITION CAN *SUBVERT* THE OVERALL GOALS...

YOW!

...THOUGH A LITTLE *PLAYFUL COMPETITION* CAN SOMETIMES PRODUCE *ENJOYABLE RESULTS.*

BUT WHEN THESE PARTNERS EACH *KNOW* THEIR ROLES--

--AND *SUPPORT* EACH OTHER'S *STRENGTHS--*

--COMICS CAN MATCH *ANY* OF THE ART FORMS IT DRAWS SO MUCH OF ITS STRENGTH FROM.

156

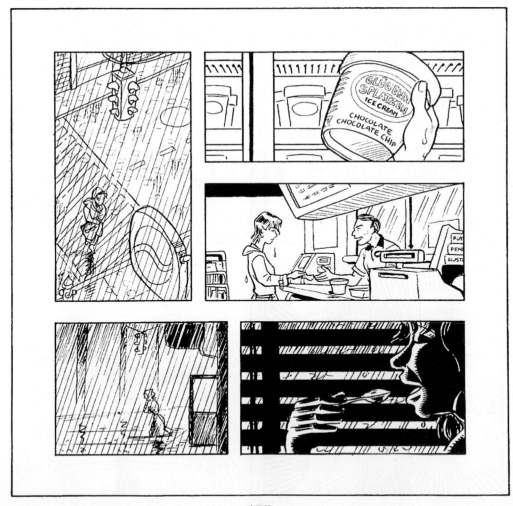

157

WHEN A SCENE SHOWS YOU ALL YOU *"NEED"* TO KNOW, LIKE *THIS* ONE, THE LATITUDE FOR *SCRIPTING* GROWS *ENORMOUSLY.*

IT COULD BECOME AN *INTERNAL MONOLOGUE.*

I MAY BE ALONE LIKE THIS FOR A VERY LONG TIME.

(INTERDEPENDENT)

PERHAPS SOMETHING WILDLY *INCONGRUOUS*

"MISSION CONTROL, MISSION CONTROL, DO YOU READ ME?"

(PARALLEL)

MAYBE IT'S ALL JUST A BIG *ADVERTISEMENT!*

YOU'LL *Love* THE TASTE!

(INTERDEPENDENT)

OR A CHANCE TO RUMINATE ON *BROADER TOPICS:*

THIS IS THE WAY THE WORLD ENDS...

THIS IS THE WAY THE WORLD ENDS...

(INTERDEPENDENT)

158

ON THE *OTHER* HAND, IF THE **WORDS** LOCK IN THE *"MEANING"* OF A SEQUENCE, THEN THE *PICTURES* CAN REALLY TAKE OFF.

P

W

SAME SCENE NOW, BUT THIS TIME ALL IN *WORDS!*

I CROSSED THE STREET TO THE CONVENIENCE STORE. THE RAIN SOAKED INTO MY BOOTS.

I FOUND THE LAST PINT OF CHOCOLATE CHOCOLATE CHIP IN THE FREEZER.

THE CLERK TRIED TO PICK ME UP. I SAID *NO THANKS.* HE GAVE ME THIS CREEPY LOOK...

I WENT BACK TO THE APARTMENT--

--AND FINISHED IT ALL IN AN HOUR.

ALONE AT LAST.

159

IF THE ARTIST WANTS TO, HE/SHE CAN NOW SHOW ONLY *FRAGMENTS* OF A SCENE.

(WORD SPECIFIC)

OR MOVE TOWARD GREATER LEVELS OF *ABSTRACTION* OR *EXPRESSION*.

(AMPLIFICATION)

PERHAPS THE ARTIST CAN GIVE US SOME IMPORTANT *EMOTIONAL* INFORMATION.

(INTERDEPENDENT)

OR SHIFT AHEAD OR BACKWARDS IN TIME.

(WORD SPECIFIC)

160

THE PICTURE PLANE

P W

RESEMBLANCE   MEANING

HOWEVER MUCH WE MAY *CHART* THESE THINGS, THEY'RE ALL *ULTIMATELY* BEST LEFT TO THE CREATOR'S *INSTINCTS.*

THE MIXING OF WORDS AND PICTURES IS MORE *ALCHEMY* THAN SCIENCE.

SOME OF THE SECRETS OF THOSE *FIRST* ALCHEMISTS MAY HAVE BEEN LOST IN THE ANCIENT PAST.

BUT WE HAVE SOME POWERFUL MAGIC RIGHT HERE IN THE *20TH CENTURY,* TOO!

THE RICHNESS OF MODERN LANGUAGE IS AN *IRREPLACEABLE COMMODITY!*

THIS IS AN *EXCITING TIME* TO BE MAKING COMICS, AND IN MANY WAYS I FEEL VERY *LUCKY* TO HAVE BEEN BORN WHEN I WAS.

STILL, I DO FEEL A CERTAIN *VAGUE LONGING* FOR THAT TIME OVER *50* CENTURIES AGO--

-- WHEN TO TELL WAS TO *SHOW*--

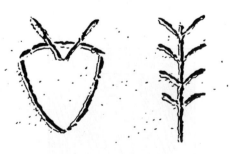

--AND TO SHOW WAS TO *TELL.*

161

Many writers create pictures with words; many artists convey a complicated idea in a single image; and, increasingly, many people use words and images in combination to create meaning. As you become better readers of the diverse texts in *Seeing & Writing 3* and better writers, we hope that you also will become more conversant with the distinctions between types of texts and among the different genres. The following eight groups of suggestions offer possible strategies for helping you begin to approach a range of verbal and visual texts: images, essays, advertisements, poetry, paintings, photographs, short stories, and mixed media.

Reading an Image

Seeing & Writing 3 features many different types of images, including photographs, ads, paintings, prints, and film stills. The following gives general guidelines for reading and making meaning of various kinds of images.

Determine the initial source of the image.

In some cases, images that appear to be photos are actually stills or frames from films. This means that the shot is cut from a larger whole, which might change the meaning (e.g., the stills from *Pocahontas* and *Smoke Signals* in Chapter 5, p. 439). In other cases, images that appear to be photos may be paintings (e.g., Alfred Leslie's *Television Moon* in Chapter 1, p. 90). In other cases, images are clearly photos or paintings.

Viewers should consider the context and construction of each image. In looking at a movie still, it is important to have an understanding of the film, as this is probably assumed by the artist. You should also be aware of the different limitations and opportunities available to photographers as opposed to painters. Photographers can and often do enhance and transform their shots, but initially they begin with an image that captures a specific and finite moment in time. Painters may capture the mood of a moment, but not with the click of a shutter. A photographer is expected, on some level, to be "true" to his or her subject; a painter is not. Thus, when a photographer alters the image, the reader should ask why—as she should when a painter attempts to exactly re-create life.

Determine what is the figure and what is the background.

These are terms from Gestalt theories of visual organization. They are useful in determining the most important object in an image. The figure is what draws the viewer's attention; the background is its immediate context. Just as a story might have a protagonist, a visual image has a figure—what the viewer should follow through the narrative of the image. This figure might be a building, a person, or an object. The background is all else.

Often the viewer's eye works almost unconsciously to find the figure in a visual image. For example, it is fairly easy to determine that the figure in Mark Peterson's *Image of Homelessness* (p. 180) is the homeless man in the appliance box. The viewer intuits this information because in many ways the photo is a standard, centered portrait. However, in an image like Brian Ulrich's *Granger, IN* (p. 191), it might take a moment to think through what the figure is. Depending on how the viewer defines the figure, he or she may read the photo quite differently.

Determine the narrative of the image.

Every image is communicating something to the viewer. Our culture is driven by narrative, driven by a desire to draw connections. Those who study visual perception and literacy even refer to people as homo significans—"meaning makers." So, the easiest way to first read an image is to determine its story, its message. What are the denotative and connotative meanings of the objects, people, and places within the image? Where are the items in the image placed in relationship to each other? In our drive to make meaning, we often connect elements that are in close proximity and establish relationships between or among them. This is just as true for objects (e.g., the items in Roe Ethridge's photo in Chapter 1, p. 27) as it is for people (e.g., the people standing around a table in Tina Barney's photo on p. 494). Viewers, just like readers, prefer an interpretation that offers closure.

Because viewers come from different backgrounds and read with different perceptions, the narrative of an image may be perceived differently by different viewers. In some cases, such as with images we think of as "art," these varying perspectives add depth to a reading. However, in other cases, such as with images we think of as "ads," the varying perspectives can destroy a product. For example, Martin Parr might be quite pleased if a variety of viewers were to find a variety of narratives in his *USA. Arizona. Grand Canyon* (p. 231). But if some viewers were to read the Pirelli Tire ad (p. 384) as a parody of masculinity rather than as a paean to it, the Pirelli ad agency might soon find itself out of a job.

Break the image into visual fields, looking for focal points. Images direct a viewer's eyes. Some aspects of the image draw our attention, whereas others recede. Our initial impulse is to focus on the center of an image because it offers balance, but often an artist shifts the viewer's focus through the use of color, light, or line. If the viewer can locate the composition's focal point (or points), this can serve as a clue to interpreting the image. It might help first to divide an image by finding its horizontal or diagonal line. Sometimes this line is self-evident, as in Richard Misrach's *Golden Gate* series (pp. 139–47), where there is an actual horizon. At other times this line is not as self-evident but still present, as in the P-F

shoes ad (p. 58), where it is the textual line "Everything you do is more fun with 'P-F.'" Such lines direct the viewer's attention, leading it up or down or across, and they also provide smooth movement within an image, which is crucial for the visual perception of most viewers.

If the viewer's initial reaction is to stare at the center of an image, then the artist must have some reason for fighting this impulse. The viewer should think about how the focal point (its position, its composition, its identity) helps to construct the meaning of the image. For example, in Martin Parr's photo *Greece, Athens, Acropolis* (p. 241), the viewer can try to focus on the crowd that is slightly in the foreground, but the crowd at the left edge of the picture captures the viewer's eye, creating a sense of movement and drawing the viewer into the activity.

Look for patterns of color, shape, or shadow in the image. Viewers organize information by establishing relationships of similarity, by looking for patterns. And patterns may be established by repeating a color or a shape, by repeating the use of light or dark. Just as a writer might use alliteration or rhyming to draw a reader's attention to connections in a poem, a visual artist uses repetition to draw a viewer's eye. The question is, "Why is my eye being drawn in this way?" The pattern may hint at the image's meaning—or part of that meaning—or it may be a pattern wholly imposed by a viewer longing for closure.

Advertising images rely heavily on repeated patterns to convey and then hammer home their message. So, for example, a viewer can easily find a repetition of shape in the Volkswagen *Drivers Wanted* ad (pp. 104–105). The curved Volkswagen Beetle is pictured at the end of a series of photographs of square everyday objects. The message is simple: The Volkswagen Beetle is a refreshingly distinctive vehicle in a world constrained by the conventional square. Yet patterns are not exclusively the domain of commercial art. Instead, they may be traced within one painting, like the blue tones in Edward Hopper's *House by the Railroad* (p. 150), or across a series of images to determine an artistic style, like the heavy shadows on the faces of Nancy Burson's *He/She* series (pp. 370–75).

Look for visual manifestations of metaphor, metonymy, or symbolism. Visual artists employ many of the same devices that verbal artists use. Thus, when a viewer considers an image, he or she should look for metaphor, metonymy, and symbol. Whereas readers frequently find metaphor, viewers frequently find metonymy. The concept of "part for whole" is particularly well suited to a visual medium. Thus, an artist might show only a fragment of a larger object in order to send a message to a reader. For example, Danwen Xing's photograph (p. 459) presents only a fraction of the "e-trash" dump. By focusing on detail, Xing brings the viewer's attention to what cannot be seen; the viewer is left to imagine how vast the dump must be outside of the frame.

Viewers should also look for symbolic images, often referred to as cultural icons. A culture often has a visual shorthand language, and within this language certain images have specific, shared meanings: for example, the American flag, a cowboy, Elvis Presley, Marilyn Monroe. These symbolic images may be used in a way that is true to their accepted cultural currency or in a way that subverts this cultural meaning. For example, the Graphis image entitled *Man Turning into a Barcode* (p. 22) plays on our cultural understanding of the bar code. Such codes mark commercial products, track inventory, and encode prices. So, when a person turns into a bar code, what happens to him? He is now a product, a piece of inventory just like, say, a bottle of mouthwash.

Remember that a complete reading should account for all design elements that were within the control of the artist. Viewers should remember that all images are composed. The elements within them are like the elements in a poem. When a reader analyzes a poem, she accounts not just for the language of the poem but also for the capitalization, the punctuation, the arrangement into lines and stanzas, and so on. When a viewer analyzes an image, she should think about it in essentially the same way, asking the following questions about its design:

> Is there any obvious distortion in the image (things taller, smaller, flatter, fatter, brighter, darker, etc.)? How does this distortion relate to or shape the meaning of the image?
>
> Is there anything only partially within the frame of the image? Why?
>
> What is the perspective of the image? Is the viewer placed above the image, below it, or at the same level? How is this related to the meaning of the image?
>
> What is the size of the image? Is it a miniature or a magnification? How does this relate to the message?

An active reader remembers how the artist has chosen to present his or her final image: photo or painting, watercolor or oil, black and white or color. These statements hold true for painters, graphic designers, and photographers. For example, one of the most popular contemporary photographers, Lorna Simpson, often dramatically enlarges her photos and has them printed to feltboard. In this case, a viewer wishing to read the images needs to also account for the manner in which a photo printed on felt is very different from a photo printed to glossy paper. The picture of the painting by Chuck Close that is reproduced in this textbook (p. 132) is small; but in a museum a viewer looking at a painting by Close would see a massive work, usually 7 feet by 8 feet. The size of this work is crucial to reading it.

Reading an Essay

Each essay in *Seeing & Writing 3* is part of a larger whole—a textbook—composed of written and visual texts. Each essay should be read not only for what it says but also for how it is laid out (how words and images are distributed) and how it fits into the entire chapter. What inferences can be made about *Seeing & Writing 3* from the way the texts are presented? Looking at essays as physical objects can be an important step in seeing (and developing one's own) written texts with a fresh eye.

The core activity of reading an essay involves being a careful observer, first getting the facts straight through a series of precise observations.

Exactly what happens in the essay? What process occurs between the opening and the closing paragraphs?

Where does the voice of the essay originate? (Who is speaking?) In what tone does the voice speak? What kind of language does it use?

Where does the essay take place? What details are given to help the reader visualize the world of the essay?

What images or ideas predominate? What patterns or shifts in images or ideas occur during the course of the essay?

What is the purpose of the text? Is it to describe, to argue, to tell a story, to explain, to compare—or a combination of these?

The more accurate and plentiful a reader's observations are about a given text, the more opportunities there will be to construct and defend meaningful inferences.

Reading an Advertisement

There are many examples of advertisements in *Seeing & Writing 3,* spanning a wide range of products and pitches from throughout the twentieth century. The advertisement as a genre has probably existed for as long as the market economy has; a combination of words and pictures is used for a single purpose, no matter the product—to entice consumers to buy. Because ads often must make their points in a page or two, they combine visual and verbal strategies to shape the most powerful message possible in the briefest amount of space. Most of us encounter more advertisements in a day than any other kind of text; the following questions will facilitate critical reading of these texts.

What is foregrounded in the frame of the advertisement? Where is the viewer's eye drawn first? In the Kodak advertisement in Chapter 3 (p. 322), the photograph in the top half of the frame and the phrase "Keep the story with a KODAK" are roughly equal in drawing our attention. Our eye goes only secondarily to the rest of the print on the page. Thus, the association of Kodak with home photography is made visually.

How much of the advertisement's message is delivered through words and how much through images? What is the proportion of one to the other? In the 1990 U.S. Army ad (p. 402), most of the message is conveyed through the images: A woman first appears looking serious in her uniform, yet feminine with her make-up; then, in a second image, we see her dressed up and laughing on a date. The text appeals to an American woman's desire to be strong and independent without compromising her femininity.

Are the connotations of the language congruent with the connotations of the images? The image of children holding guns dominates the Collaborate/Amnesty International *Imagine* campaign ad on page 601. The word "imagine" draws our eye, and the text continues in smaller print with "nothing to kill or die for." In this case, the contradiction between the text and the reality of the image lends the message a sense of urgency.

In what ways does the advertisement appeal to a specific type of viewer? The purpose of advertisements is to market something to a particular audience. The Visa advertisement in Chapter 5 (p. 467), with a young man holding a guitar, clearly has a youthful appeal.

What is the underlying logic of the advertisement? What does it suggest? This logic is created by the pairing of the image and the product. In Baby Phat's advertisement (pp. 490–91), for example, the underlying logic is that as a customer of the Baby Phat brand you participate in the outlook and lifestyle of Kimora Lee Simmons, the founder of Baby Phat, pictured in the ad.

Reading a Poem

In a letter to a publisher friend, the celebrated American poet Robert Frost offered the following engaging definition of poetry: "A poem starts with a lump in the throat, a homesickness, or a lovesickness. It is a reaching out toward expression, an effort to find fulfillment. A complete poem is one where an emotion has found its thought and the thought has found the words. . . . My definition of poetry (if I were forced to give one) would be this: words that have become deeds."

Poetry is one of the oldest and most imaginative and intense forms of verbal communication. In *A Handbook to Literature,* William Harmon and Hugh Holman define poetry as "a term applied to the many forms in which human beings have given rhythmic expression to their most imaginative and intense perceptions of the world, themselves, and the relation of the two" (p. 384). As these definitions underscore, imagination, emotion, and aesthetic values, along with such characteristics as rhythm and the use of intense and concrete images, help to mark one's experience of reading poetry. So, too, the language of poetry is, as the eminent English poet John Milton noted, "simple, sensuous, and im-passioned." Poetry is also a form of communication that accentuates the sound of the speaker's voice, his or her tone of voice. To read poetry effectively, one might well follow the suggestion of Robert Frost and read with what he calls the "hearing imagination." The poet, much like other artists and musicians, is especially sensitive to artistic expressions of states of consciousness. This sensitivity to beauty, as the British poet Percy Bysshe Shelley noted, "turns all things to loveliness; it exalts the beauty of that which is most beautiful, and it adds beauty to that which is most deformed /. . . strips the veil of familiarity from the world and lays bare the naked and sleeping beauty, which is the spirit of its forms." One teacher, Charles Hood of Antelope Valley College, defines poetry as "a tango with death. . . ."

Because the language of poetry can be expected to be more economical than that of prose writers, every word in a poem bears the pressure of meaning and significance. So, too, many readers argue that poetry is meant to be experienced as much as it is meant to be read. The questions that follow will help readers, especially those who are unfamiliar with the genre, to come to a better understanding and appreciation of this ancient form of verbal art.

How does the poem look on the page? A reader doesn't need a detailed knowledge of poetics to make careful observations about a poem's shape—its length, the arrangement of lines, or any other visual detail. In "Edward Hopper and the House by the Railroad (1925)" by Edward Hirsch (p. 151), the length of the stanzas and the placement of the stanzas on the page suggest a balanced structure, which is fitting since the poem describes a house.

Who is the speaker of the poem? Although readers often feel mystified by poems, if they imagine the speaker they may get some clues. In Jacinto Jesús Cardona's

"Bato con Khakis" (p. 337), the speaker remembers how, as a younger man, he admired the elusive cool of the other boys in his neighborhood. Recalling his desire to emulate them, the poet evokes his feelings at the time, even switching to the present tense to admit, "cool bato I am not." But by writing the poem, Cardona has already answered his youthful question, "Could I be the bookish bato?"

What kinds of images are present in the poem? The images in poems can be literal, representing the world as it appears, or they can be figurative, capturing the world as it feels. In "Himalaya" (p. 629), Abdessalam Mansori tries out a number of unlikely images to describe his experiences. The liquid inside a tomato becomes a figure for sadness, and a cactus grows "all alone / in the center of the ocean." By placing familiar sights in unusual contexts, Mansori encourages us to look at them more closely.

What does the poem sound like? Poems are made for breath and air, and often reading them aloud aids in understanding. This can be a way to investigate the tone of a poem as a means to discovering its meanings. For example, reading aloud David Mura's "Fresh from the Island Angel" (p. 422) will call attention to the effect of his many fragments. Using frequent full stops, Mura assumes the young woman's voice, enacting her pauses and hesitations. In the final stanza, the short sentences become more declarative as each stands alone on its line. The reader can feel, through the recitation of the poem, the progress from the tentative tone of the opening questions to the mournful certainty of the ending.

What is the world of the poem like? Does it have a setting? Is it in a landscape? Does it have characters? Different poems foreground different elements. Jane Yolen's "Grant Wood: American Gothic" (p. 513)

takes its setting from the painting, but she mentions details of the house and of the characters' dress only to instruct the reader to ignore them. The "broach at the throat, / the gothic angel wing / of window" are unimportant; what is essential to Yolen is the character of these two people, which she imagines "looks out at you" from their eyes.

Reading a Painting

Each painting in *Seeing & Writing 3* is part of a visual genre that shares certain conventions and goals. Painting, along with sculpture, has historically been associated with high art and the individual style and vision of the artist; one of the oldest visual genres, it has developed through many schools of representative and abstract styles of expression. The following questions will help you read paintings in a meaningful way even if you have no previous experience in studying the genre conventions of painting.

What is the style of painting? A viewer doesn't need to be well versed in art history to determine whether a painting is more or less realistic. To begin reading a painting, he or she must understand what the painter wants to convey: a realistic depiction of a person, place, or thing; a purely personal impression of it; or something in between. For example, Edward Hopper's *House by the Railroad* (p. 150) is clearly recognizable as a house by a railroad even though Hopper imbues the painting with a haunting feeling and a strong sense of isolation.

What is the tone of the painting? Just as a writer uses words, a painter uses color and light. Thus a painting might be airy and inviting, with little shading and bright colors. An example is Alice Davis's dunes painting (p. 50), which conveys a sense of the light, airy—and perhaps lonely—seaside landscape. Alternatively a painting might be dark and foreboding, with lots of shadow and dark shades. An example is Alfredo Esquillo Jr.'s *MaMcKinley* (p. 458).

What is the size of the painting? In an illustrated textbook, the size of an original painting is quite difficult to discern. However, an image's size makes a significant impression on a viewer. Consider the images by Chuck Close and Edward Hopper that are included in this textbook (pp. 132–33, 150). Seen in a museum, Close's painting is nearly four times as large as Hopper's—although in Close's work we see only a head and in Hopper's we see an entire house. An artist often uses size to convey a message. For example, during the Renaissance loved ones gave each other small miniature portraits to wear on garments to indicate intimate relationships. The size permitted this message to be shared.

How does the subject of the painting relate to the manner in which the artist depicts it? Like all art, paintings can affect the way their viewers see the world. For example, through his depiction of the Grand Canyon, Thomas Moran helped shape the world's view of this part of America—as both reality and myth. In *The Chasm of the Colorado* (p. 226) Moran's approach to his subject is reverential, and he expects his audience to share this feeling because the grandeur of nature is worthy of their respect. In contrast, Alfred Leslie plays with his audience's expectations of painting and photography by re-creating a very ordinary household scene in *Television Moon* (pp. 90–91).

What perspective is used in the painting? The perspective situates the viewer and can be used to convey or negate depth. For example, in *House by the Railroad* (p. 150), Edward Hopper relies on perspective to create a sense of isolation. In contrast, many primitive or folk art styles of painting, such as the one used by César A. Martínez (p. 336), eschew perspective and offer simple, flat images. These underscore a sense of primitive purity and honesty. Readers should also be alert to paintings that add depth where one might not expect it (e.g.,

the reflections in the window in Richard Estes's *Central Savings*, p. 72) or deny depth where one does expect it (e.g., the flat-looking image by James Rosenquist, p. 633). Often, these works use perspective to add an extra layer of meaning.

Reading a Photograph

Like the paintings, the photographs in *Seeing & Writing 3* are part of a visual genre that shares certain conventions and goals. This genre has existed for a little over a century and is commonly recognized as setting the standard for realistic representation, replacing painting as the most accurate means of recording an image. Generally, photographs can be divided into one of two broad categories: documentary photographs, such as those that accompany a news story, that seek to accurately show what a person, place, or event actually looks like; and creative photographs, such as advertising or artistic photos, in which the person, place, event, or photograph has been staged to some degree in order to achieve a certain effect. The Looking Closer section for Chapter 7, "The Ethics of Representation" (pp. 657–76), examines the blurring of the lines between these two types of photographs. The following questions will help you interpret photographs even if you are unfamiliar with the genre conventions of photography.

Is the photo a news, commercial, or art image? The distinctions are becoming increasingly blurred, but a reader should still understand the initial purpose of the photo if only to get a sense of its context. For example, viewers may be expected to spend only a few seconds scanning a newspaper photo but minutes or hours studying an art photo in a gallery. A photographer's beliefs about how the image will be received by an audience affect the way in which he or she composes the image. Viewers might consider how Adbusters' *Follow the Flock* (p. 595) differs dramatically from

James Nachtwey's photo of Ground Zero (p. 304) largely because of their contexts and purposes: One spoofs advertising, the other presents a historic moment.

Is the photo in black and white or color? Black and white photos, such as Andrew Savulich's snapshots (pp. 274–77), hold a documentary connotation. Often these may be news photos, and the simplicity of black and white (initially a limitation of the printing press) conveys a sense of straightforward truth. Other photos may not be news images but are associated with the same connotations, such as Jim Goldberg's *USA, San Francisco* (p. 485). Color photos may more accurately reflect the images we associate with real life, but often they are regarded as commercial.

Does the image in the photo seem to have been altered in any way? Photography seems like an art that captures exactly what the photographer sees: a moment in time. However, it is easy to airbrush out cosmetic defects, rearrange subjects, enhance colors and shading, or add digital effects. Often these changes are difficult to discern. Viewers should consider the purpose of a photo when asking whether effects might have been added and how to interpret their use. For example, a model in an ad or fashion editorial is unlikely to appear "as is," and most readers understand that the model's image will be modified before it is published. However, fewer readers expect that news images, such as that of the flag-raising on Iwo Jima (p. 296), will be altered.

How is the image framed in the photo? Just like text on a page, an image in a photo might be centered, offset to the left, or offset to the right. Traditionally a straight, centered shot has been used for portraits. Offset shots are often used to suggest motion by drawing the viewer's eye along a horizontal or diagonal line, as in Martin Parr's *Paris, 18th District* (p. 239).

Sometimes these images also suggest entrapment by crowding the subject against one of the photo's edges. In addition, photos have a vertical axis that can either open up or close down an image. If a photographer heavily shades the top of an image it can appear to be pressing down on the photo subject, whereas if the image is bright, the effect can be the opposite. For example, the woman in Richard Billingham's *Untitled* (p. 620) offers an imposing top element that crowds the composition.

How is the photo cropped? Often what is left out of a photo is as important as what is included in it. A photo may have been cropped (or cut) to eliminate elements that would distract from the subject or to refocus the subject. For example, Joe Rosenthal's picture (p. 296) has focused the viewer's attention on the flag-raising as a symbol of victory by eliminating anything distracting.

Reading a Short Story

The short story spans works such as biblical narratives and Chaucer's tales, and it gained ground especially in the twentieth century as a dominant literary genre. Generally a short story can be defined as a brief fictional prose narrative; the term is often applied to any work of narrative prose fiction that is shorter than a novel. A short story is usually a connected narrative that has an identifiable plot, structure, characters, setting, and point of view. Short stories are usually easier to read than other verbal texts. The following questions will help you think critically about the formal elements of the story.

What is the point of view of the story? Who is the narrator, and from what perspective is he or she speaking? In "This Is Earl Sandt" (p. 266), Robert Olen Butler tells the story from the first-person point of view as a witness of the plane crash. The narrator describes the events as he watched them unfold in the early twentieth century.

This treatment establishes the setting of the story and, because airplanes represent a new, thrilling technology to the narrator, the crash is an even more powerful and mysterious event.

What is the setting of the story? Where does it take place? What are the characteristics of that place? Eudora Welty's "The Little Store" (p. 155) takes place in Jackson, Mississippi, and as the title suggests, the store is the setting. This location becomes emblematic of the lives that play out in the small community during the narrator's childhood. As Welty states, "We weren't being sent to the neighborhood grocery for facts of life, or death. But of course those are what we were on the track of, anyway" (para. 30).

Who are the characters in the story? To whom is the story happening? How are the characters affected? The very short story "Vivian, Fort Barnwell" by Ethan Canin (p. 323) has few characters—primarily the narrator and his wife. However, it is about characters that are not present—his mother and grandmother. The story is about the narrator's realization that a photograph he has always treasured is not of his mother but of his grandmother. What he thought was his very clear memory of the day and place in the photograph turns out to be faulty. He questions, "My God, you're right. How could that have happened?" (para. 4). Indeed, the family history embodied in family snapshots may not be "true" as we remember.

What happens in the story? What is the main action? What happens in "I Stand Here Ironing" by Tillie Olsen (p. 66) is simple and profound. As she irons a dress, the narrator's thoughts dwell upon her troubled daughter and how her family has arrived at its present situation. The story's action does not move beyond the woman's ruminating as she irons.

What are the significant images in the story? How do things look? Eudora Welty's "The Little Store" (p. 155) is about what a child sees and fails to see. Although Welty's descriptions utilize the five senses, some of the most revealing involve sight. The description of the cheese being "as big as a doll's house" (para. 16) firmly puts readers in the child's point of view. The narrator's descriptions provide readers with a sense of character as well as a sense of place.

What changes or transformations occur (or fail to occur) during the course of the narrative? Amy Tan's "Fish Cheeks" is a narrative of a young Chinese American girl who struggles to come to terms with her Chinese heritage; she wants to assimilate completely into American culture. She describes the evening when an American family came to her childhood home for dinner and, to her horror, her own family boldly embraced their Chinese culture. By the end of the narrative, she gains just a sense of what would become an important lesson—that she must be proud of who she is.

Reading Mixed Media

Mixed media is generally used to describe the work of contemporary artists who employ unusual combinations of material to achieve a desired effect (sometimes appealing to senses of smell, taste, and touch as well as sight). Materials used in the texts in *Seeing & Writing 3* that are labeled as mixed media include wood, "found" ordinary objects, photographs, newspapers, videos, and other unusual or unexpected building blocks combined and presented in extraordinary ways. (Mixed media is often used when a piece doesn't fall into a "pure" category such as painting or photography.)

What material has been used in the creation of the work? Why might the artist have used this particular combination of materials? Often the original source of some part of the artwork—text from a newspaper, for example—has been deliberately chosen to make a particular point and must be considered in reading the work as a whole. The artist Sally Mankus (not represented in *Seeing & Writing 3*), for example, lifts rust, carbon, and marking from charred surfaces (mainly bakeware). She writes that "objects (pans, pot lids, napkins, etc.) and materials (rust, carbon) used are so common they become symbols in a universal language."

Is any part of the work a "found" object?
Mixed media works often include "found" objects, that is, things that have been incorporated into an original piece or simply appropriated for art. When artists use found objects, they are commenting on the role of these products within our culture. For example, Pepón Osorio's *Badge of Honor* (pp. 94–95 and 97) includes actual posters of basketball players and suggests how such figures can become father figures.

Is the work realistic, or is it abstract and impressionistic? Any work of art falls along this spectrum. For example, Duane Hanson's *Tourists* (p. 313) is so realistic that many museum visitors may fail to understand it is a sculpture. In part, this realism is the message. We know these people and immediately recognize their qualities. In contrast, Pepón Osorio's *Badge of Honor* (pp. 94–95 and 97) is not as realistic. Instead, the exaggerated opulence of the boy's room invites viewers to contrast it with the father's stark cell.

If the work is three dimensional, what does the third dimension add to the piece? Unless otherwise enhanced, photography and painting are primarily two-dimensional media. Most mixed media offers viewers a third dimension, which might make the work tactile or might add realism. For example, Duane Hanson's *Tourists* (p. 313) would not have the same impact of automatic recognition ("I've seen that couple!") if it were just a photo of tourists.

If the work includes text, what is the relationship between the text and the image/body of the piece? Mixed media pieces sometimes take the form of a collage of image and text. The text comments on the work, helping to frame the viewer's reading. For example, Barbara Kruger's *Untitled* (p. 635) foregrounds the word *picture*—which describes both the work itself and the subject of the work. Yet because the viewer's eye is probably first drawn to the word, not the image, *Untitled* may be offering another interpretation to the viewer: A word can supersede an image.

GLOSSARY

abstract art visual art that explores meaning through shape, color, and texture rather than a realistic representation of scenes or objects.

abstract expressionism an abstract art movement in which the act of expressing emotions was considered as important as the resulting work. Abstract expressionists applied paint rapidly to the canvas, believing that the spontaneity of this technique released creativity.

ad-libbing speaking or performing spontaneously, without preparation.

allusion an indirect, brief, or casual reference to a person, place, event, object, or artwork. Allusion draws on a body of images or stories shared by the audience and allows a short phrase to bring up a whole set of associated information.

ambiguity the potential for being reasonably understood in more than one way. Both literature and the visual arts use ambiguity to express the inherent richness and complexity of the world. In advertising, ambiguity can be used to create deception without actually lying.

analogy use of a comparison to extend knowledge of something new by its similarity to something already known. Analogy can be explanatory, as in comparing ice skating with in-line skating. Comparing the "war on drugs" with Prohibition is an example of using analogy to further an argument.

analysis the process of breaking something complex into its parts, examining each part and the relations among the parts, and coming to a better understanding of the whole. An analytical essay reconstructs the whole in an orderly way to facilitate understanding.

argument a claim advanced with its supporting reasons, or evidence. The claim addresses a single point ("the town should fund a night school"). The reasons may be facts ("25 percent of high school students in this town drop out without graduating") or values ("everyone deserves equal treatment"), but they must lead logically to the conclusion without intellectual dishonesty. In an argument essay, the claim is the thesis statement; it is presented early and followed by a summary of the argument. Each of the reasons is then developed, with supporting information where it is needed. In addition to advancing sufficient reasons to support its claim, a good argument assesses and refutes claims opposed to it. An effective argument essay takes into account the audience's values and knowledge base.

assertion a claim or statement of belief. To be useful in discourse, an assertion needs supporting evidence. An unsupported assertion is merely an expression of opinion.

assumption a claim accepted without the necessity of proof or other support. While assumptions are necessary devices in all arguments, many faulty arguments depend on assumptions that, once accepted, require the acceptance of the conclusions. Analysis of an argument should always include a clear statement of its assumptions.

audience the intended recipient of a communication or work of art. Audiences differ as to their values, assumptions, knowledge bases, needs, desires, tastes, and styles. Having a clear picture of the intended audience is an essential task for a writer.

brainstorming recording thoughts as they occur, with no regard for their relation to each other. When writers brainstorm, they often leap from one thought to another without exploring the connections between ideas. Brainstorming unleashes creativity by temporarily removing the censor or editor that restricts us to considering only what we already know.

cause and effect an analysis that focuses on why something happens (cause) and what happens as a result (effect). Explorations of cause and effect can be quite complex since some events have many contributing causes, not all of them close to the event itself. Unless a causal mechanism is demonstrated, the mere association of events (coincidence) is not grounds for concluding a cause and effect relationship.

character the combination of features or qualities that distinguishes a person, group, or object from another; a person (or occasionally an animal or inanimate object) in a literary or dramatic work.

claim a statement made with the intention that it be accepted as true. In an argument essay, the claim is expressed as the thesis statement.

classification the act of sorting things based on shared characteristics. The characteristics can be physical (the class of all round things), social (the class of middle income people), personal (the class of things I don't like), and so on. The items in one class may or may not also belong to other classes.

cliché a figure of speech or a graphic expression that has lost its capacity to communicate effectively because of overuse. A cliché fails in two ways: first, because the point of figurative language is to convey something more richly than literal words can, and second, because the empty phrase is like a dead space. Because a sentence that uses cliché was not worth writing carefully, it probably is not worth reading carefully. To avoid cliché, use figures of speech that arise from concrete, specific experience. Picture in your mind what you want the reader to see and make sure your language calls up that picture effectively.

color in seeing, color is seeing the different ranges of the electromagnetic spectrum that are reflected by pigments or transmitted by light. In art, the use of color is a deliberate choice. In writing, color is adding emotional content to a factual account, a technique that is sometimes considered distorting.

comic a story told in drawings, hand-lettered dialogue, and very short bits of written narrative. Not all comics are intended to be funny; Art Spiegelman's *In the Shadow of No Towers* (p. 300) is a comic tale based on his experience in New York City on and following 9/11.

compare and contrast a systematic exploration of the ways in which two or more things are alike and the ways in which they are different. A writer might use this technique to show that two apparently dissimilar things are alike in some important way or to point out important differences between two related things.

composition the act of arranging parts so that they form a meaningful or pleasing whole. A written or graphic composition requires thought and planning of the sequential or spatial relationship of its elements to produce this meaningful unity. See each chapter's "Visualizing Composition" for explanations and illustrations of specific elements of composition: "Close Reading" (p. 72), "Tone" (p. 209), "Structure" (p. 295), "Purpose" (p. 386), "Audience" (p. 467), "Metaphor" (p. 545), and "Point of View" (p. 642).

connotation the associations and emotional impact carried by a word or phrase in addition to its literal meaning. A minivan, an SUV, and a Volkswagen Bug are all vehicles, but specifying one of them as a character's means of transportation tells us about more than just the cubic feet of interior capacity.

context the part of a text or statement that surrounds a particular word or image and helps determine its meaning; the interrelated conditions within which something exists or occurs (historical, cultural, and environmental setting).

Context is essential to the full understanding of a text or event. See each chapter's "Context" for further illustration and explanation of context.

contrast to make use of strong differences in art or in argument. Advertising often uses contrast by pointing out the differences between a product and its competitors.

critical reading the act of analyzing, interpreting, and evaluating verbal or graphic text. A critical reading of a text includes close reading, note taking, contextualizing, rereading, and connecting. Most texts provoke some emotional response; critical reading explores this emotional response rather than simply accepting it as true.

critical thinking the practice of subjecting claims to close examination and analysis.

cropping to make smaller by cutting so that some of the original photo is lost. Cropping is part of the photographer's act of framing an image.

deduction in logic, a form of argument in which *if* the premises are true, then the conclusion *must be* true as well. To dispute a conclusion arrived at using deduction, you must show that at least one of the premises is false. (Compare with "Induction.")

definition an explanation of the meaning of a word, phrase, or concept. A definition essay is an extended exploration both of the class to which something belongs and of the ways it differs from other things in that class.

demographic statistical characterization of a population by age, marital or household status, education, income, race, ethnicity, and so on, used for planning and marketing purposes.

description an account of an event, object, person, or process. A writer uses description to convey a vivid and accurate mental image to the reader. Description requires attention to sensory details—sights, smells, sounds, tastes, touch. *Subjective description* includes an account of the writer's inner experience of the thing being described.

design to work out the plan for an event, object, or process. Design combines purpose with an understanding of the ways things work. It marks the difference between a random collection and a purposeful composition.

diction stylistic choice of words and syntax, as between high (educated and formal) and low (ordinary and popular), between abstract and concrete, between specific and general. In "The Little Store" (p. 155), Eudora Welty uses a distinctively southern diction: "[W]here our house was when I was a child growing up in Jackson, it was possible to have a little pasture behind your backyard where you could keep a Jersey cow, which we did. My mother herself milked her." In "Cool Like Me" (p. 440), Donnell Alexander alternates street diction—"I'm the kinda nigga who's so cool that my neighbor bursts into hysterical tears whenever I ring her doorbell after dark"—with more conventional usage— "But her real experience of us

is limited to the space between her Honda and her front gate."

digital imaging creating or altering images electronically. Before the use of digital imaging, photographic evidence was considered a reliable record of events. Since digital technology can generate quite realistic images of things that have no real-world counterpart, photographs have lost this status.

documentary photography photography that pays close attention to factual detail. Although it captures an image of what actually is, it still uses such compositional techniques as framing and cropping. Documentary photography often has a social commentary intent, but not always. The photographers Jim Goldberg (p. 485), Mario Testino (p. 430), and James Nachtwey (p. 304) each have a particular sense of what the form is about.

draft a preliminary or intermediate version of a work. A first draft forges the results of research, planning, note taking, brainstorming, and freewriting into the beginning of a cohesive whole. Further drafts refine the thesis, improve the organization, and add transitions.

emphasis bringing increased attention to a point or element to convey its importance. Repetition and prominent placement add emphasis, as do the use of italics, larger type, color, and bold contrast.

euphemism an expression used in place of a word or phrase that is considered harsh or unpleasant—for example, using *passed away* for *died.*

evidence information presented in support of a claim. To be convincing, the information must be from a reliable source and adequately documented.

exposition an essay that explains difficult material. In addition to analysis, exposition uses familiar illustrations or analogies. K. C. Cole's "A Matter of Scale" (p. 128) is an example of exposition.

figurative language language that is not literally true but is used to express something more richly and effectively than literal language can. In "Seeing" (p. 108), Annie Dillard calls an island *tear-shaped,* conveying in two words an image that would require a much longer physical description if described literally.

font the design of lettering used in text. Fonts can be formal, elegant, traditional, modern, casual, silly, or purely functional. Choice of font is a subtle but critical design element.

found objects ordinary objects, not originally intended as art, that are found, chosen, and exhibited by an artist.

framing to construct by fitting parts into a whole; to design, shape, construct; to put into words, to formulate; to contrive the evidence against an innocent person; to enclose in, or as if in, a frame. Framing is one of the compositional elements of a photo or other graphic image.

freewriting also called *nonstop writing,* a strategy in which the writer writes without pausing to consider grammar, sentence structure, word choice, and spelling.

graphic design the application of design principles to articles intended for commercial or persuasive purposes. Virtually every printed or broadcast item encountered—packaging, signage, sets and backdrops, book covers, magazines—has been graphically designed to maximize the effectiveness of its message.

graphic elements separate pieces that are assembled into a whole in a graphic composition.

high art art whose techniques require formal education and whose purpose is primarily aesthetic. In contrast, *craft* may be decorative but is mainly functional, and *folk* or *popular art* requires little formal training.

hyperbole an obvious and intentional exaggeration—for example, using *starving* for *hungry.*

hypothesis an explanation that accounts for the known facts and makes further predictions that logically must be true if the explanation is true. These predictions can be tested, and the hypothesis is disconfirmed if they are false.

identity a unified, persistent sense of who a person uniquely is; the inner experience of one's self.

idiom a style of expression peculiar to an individual or a group. Idiomatic expressions may make no sense literally—for example, "to have it in for someone" or "to give someone a piece of your mind."

illustration / illustrative essay a design or picture in a print medium used to explain the text.

image a thing that represents something else; a symbol, an emblem, a representation. Also, the picture called into a reader's mind by a writer's use of descriptive or figurative language.

induction method of reasoning from experience, from observed facts to a generalized pattern; scientific reasoning is inductive. *Inductive generalization* is the conclusion that the next item in a series will be like the items already observed. The strength of an inductive conclusion depends on the size of the sample observed and the uniformity of the sample. (Compare with "Deduction.")

inference an intellectual leap from what one sees to what those details might suggest; a conclusion drawn from available facts. An interpretation of a text is an inference, a conclusion about what the text means based on detailed observations about it.

installation a planned, deliberate arrangement of art works in a space.

invention the development of a device or process not previously in use.

irony a humorous aspect of writing that calls attention to the difference between the actual result of a sequence of events and the expected result; an expression that says one thing while intending to convey its opposite.

layout the process of arranging printed or graphic material on a page; the overall design of a page, including such elements as type size, typeface, titles, and page numbers.

media the methods by which things are transmitted; in particular, the mass media—newspapers, magazines, movies, television and radio broadcasts, and recordings—that transmit ideas and images to the culture at large.

medium the material or technique used by an artist; by extension, the material or technique that carries a message, including print and airwaves.

metaphor a word or phrase that means one thing but is used to describe something else in order to suggest a relationship between the two; an implied comparison. See "Visualizing Composition: Metaphor" (p. 545) for more examples.

metonymy a figure of speech in which one word or phrase substitutes for another closely associated with it—for example, *Washington* for *U.S. government.*

mixed media using two or more media in one composition, as in a collage, a sound and light show, or a combination of sculptures and plantings.

narrative a verbal or graphic account of the events of a story. More than just a listing of occurrences, narrative provides a cohesive unity to a description of events.

narrator the person telling a story, from whose point of view it has cohesive unity. The narrator can be a character in the story or an observer who takes no part in the action.

observation the act, practice, or power of noticing; a comment or remark based on something observed. In rhetoric, an observation is a neutral statement supported by specific evidence about something in a text.

ode a formal poem in praise of something noble.

parody a mocking imitation that exaggerates some quality in the original. Parody is used to entertain, unlike satire, whose general purpose is to stimulate reform.

personification a metaphor in which something nonhuman is given human attributes. In "Edward Hopper and the House by the Railroad (1925)" (p. 151), Edward Hirsch gives a house a facial expression, feelings, and even the moral capacity to do "something against the earth."

perspective the physical or figurative point from which the artist or writer sees the subject; also, the effect of that standpoint on what the writer or artist sees and conveys. The size, relation, and even existence of both physical and conceptual things seem different depending on where, in relation to a scene, one stands to observe.

persuasion the act or process of moving someone to a decision or a position.

photo-essay a collection of photographs composed to develop a point or a theme in the manner of a written essay.

photojournalism reporting on events through the use of photographs.

point of view the angle of vision, the perspective from which writers and artists see—and present—a subject. This perspective may be expressed—simply and literally—as the physical stance they establish in viewing a subject. In writing, point of view may also be revealed through the tone of voice, or attitude, that the writer expresses in addressing a subject. See "Visualizing Composition: Point of View" (p. 642) for more examples.

pop art an art movement that used familiar images from the mass culture to blur the distinction between high art and popular expression. James Rosenquist (p. 633) is an example of a Pop artist.

portfolio a collection representative of an artist's work; in particular, a collection of closely related images. See the portfolios of Gueorgui Pinkhassov (p. 74), Joel Sternfeld (p. 192), Andrew Savulich (p. 274), Nancy Burson (p. 370), Nikki S. Lee (p. 407), and Tibor Kalman (p. 546) for examples of this kind of representation.

portraiture a posed representation of a specific person or group of persons. In addition to showing a physical likeness, a portrait conveys the subject's personality. Historically, portraits included clothing, jewelry, and settings that showed the subject's relative social standing.

premise a statement that forms the basis of an argument and leads to the conclusion; one of the reasons why a claim should be accepted.

public art art that is paid for with tax dollars, installed in public places, and intended for a wide audience. The Vietnam Veterans Memorial in Washington, D.C., is an example of public art.

purpose the goal a writer has in mind; the effect a writer intends to have on the audience. A writer's purpose is the *why* behind the text. See "Visualizing Composition: Purpose" (p. 386) for more examples.

representation a depiction, portrayal, or reproduction that brings to mind a thing or person.

revision the act of rewriting an initial draft of a text, toward a final version. Revising includes both large-scale revisions such as restructuring or rewriting and smaller-scale revisions such as editing for grammar and syntax.

rhetoric writing or speaking for the purpose of communication or persuasion, with attention to audience and purpose; the principles, technical terms, and rules developed for the practice of rhetoric.

satire a literary composition that criticizes vice through the use of ridicule. Satire is a form of political speech whose intent is to provoke change.

simile a figure of speech that compares two unlike things using the words *like, as, as if,* or *as though*. In "Seeing" (p. 108), Annie Dillard uses simile when she writes that a drawing "looked as though five shining, real quarter horses had been corraled by mistake with a papier-mâché moose."

staged photography a work in which the photographer arranges the elements of a picture deliberately, in contrast to a candid shot or a documentary photograph.

stereotype an uncritical generalization, which can be either positive or negative. The word *stereotype* comes from the form or mold used by artisans to create a repeating pattern. To hold a stereotyped idea of a population is to act as if all of its members were stamped out of a mold instead of being complex, highly variable individuals.

still life a form of painting that represents a composed arrangement of ordinary objects. The act of making art out of the ordinary challenges the viewer to look more deeply and carefully at the everyday.

structure the way in which the parts in a system are put together; the planned framework of a piece of writing. See "Visualizing Composition: Structure" (p. 295) for more examples.

style a writer's distinctive way of using words to achieve particular effects. Style includes diction, syntax, figures, imagery, and tone.

syllogism a valid argument containing two premises and a conclusion. If both premises are true, then the conclusion is true. But if one of the premises is false, there is no way to judge the conclusion.

symbolism the use of something tangible, material, or visible to stand for and express what is intangible, spiritual, or invisible—for example, the eagle standing for the qualities that make up U.S. national culture.

syntax the study of the rules whereby words or other elements of sentence structure are combined to form grammatical sentences; the pattern of formation of sentences or phrases in a language. Syntax implies a systematic, orderly arrangement.

texture as an element of art, the surface feel—smooth, rough, soft, and so on. The texture may be actual or simulated.

thesis statement an explicit statement of the purpose of an essay; in an argument essay, the claim that is being advanced and will be supported.

tone the feelings conveyed by the writer's choice of words. In "No Place Like Home" (p. 183), David Guterson conveys disapproval with his choice of descriptive words—"expensive mountain bikes," "conspicuously devoid of gas stations." See "Visualizing Composition: Tone" (p. 209) for more examples.

typography the design, style, and arrangement of printed material. Careful choice of fonts establishes tone. The relative sizes of fonts; use of color, italics, and bold; and the arrangement of blocks of text and white space guide a reader's attention. Digital technology has made typography options widely available and has increased the effectiveness of text as a communication.

visual literacy the ability to read and write in a purely visual medium; the ability to decode the meaning delivered by visual texts, as through design, typography, and images.

voice the sound of the text in the reader's mind, as well as the sense of the person it conveys. Voice results from the distinctive blend of diction and syntax, the resulting rhythms and sounds, and the use of images and idioms. A voice that is natural and authentic sounds consistent to the reader, but a voice that is put on gives itself away in false notes.

RHETORICAL TABLE OF CONTENTS

DESCRIPTION

ACKNOWLEDGMENTS

Chapter 1
Verbal Texts

Bill Bryson. "Introduction." From *A Short History of Nearly Everything* by Bill Bryson. Copyright © 2003 by Bill Bryson. Used by permission of Broadway Books, a division of Random House, Inc. All rights reserved.

K.C. Cole. "A Matter of Scale." From *The Universe and the Teacup: The Mathematics of Truth and Beauty* by K.C. Cole. Copyright © 1998 by K.C. Cole. Reprinted by permission of Harcourt, Inc.

Annie Dillard. "Seeing." From *Pilgrim at Tinker Creek* by Annie Dillard. Copyright © 1974 by Annie Dillard. Reprinted by permission of HarperCollins Publishers Inc.

Brian Doyle. "Joyas Volardores." From *The American Scholar*, Autumn 2004, vol 73, #4. Copyright © 2004 by the author. Reprinted by permission of the publisher.

Jan Greenberg. "Diamante for Chuck." From *Heart to Heart* by Jan Greenberg. Copyright © 2001. Reprinted with the permission of Harry Abrams, Inc.

Joseph Jacobs. "Pepón Osorio — Badge of Honor." Originally published in the Newark Museum exhibition catalog, 1996. Copyright © 1996. Reprinted with the permission of The Newark Museum Association.

Peter Menzel. "The Wu Family." © *Material World: A Global Family Portrait* (Sierra Club Books, 1994). Courtesy Peter Menzel Photography.

Steven Millhauser. "The Fascination of the Miniature." Copyright © 1983 by Steven Millhauser. First appeared in *Grand Street* (Summer 1983). Reprinted by permission of International Creative Management, Inc.

Tillie Olsen. "I Stand Here Ironing." From *Tell Me A Riddle* by Tillie Olsen. Copyright © 1956, 1957, 1960, 1961 by Tillie Olsen. Introduction by John Leonard. Used by permission of Elaine Markson Agency.

Henry Petroski. "The Pencil." From *The Pencil* by Henry Petroski. Copyright © 1999 by Henry Petroski. Used by permission of Alfred A. Knopf, a division of Random House, Inc.

Carl Sagan. "Reflections on a Mote of Dust." Excerpt from a commencement address delivered on May 11, 1996. Copyright © The Estate of Carl Sagan. Reprinted with permission of The Estate of Carl Sagan.

John Updike. "An Oil on Canvas." Reprinted from *The American Scholar*, Volume 73, No. 4, Autumn 2004. Copyright © 2004 by the author.

Larry Woiwode. "Ode to an Orange." Originally published in *Harper's*, 1985. Copyright © 1985 by Larry Woiwode. Reprinted by permission of Donadio & Olson, Inc.

Visual Texts

Mom Ironing, 1997. Tracey Baran. © Tracey Baran, Courtesy Leslie Tonkonow Artworks + Projects, NY.

Orange Crate Labels. Courtesy of California Orange Growers.

Self Portrait, 2000–2001. Chuck Close. Oil on canvas, 9′ × 7′ (2.74 × 2.12m). Photograph by: Ellen Page Wilson, Courtesy PaceWildenstein. © Chuck Close, Courtesy PaceWildenstein, NewYork.

Self Portrait, 2000-2001, detail. Chuck Close. Oil on canvas, 9′ × 7′ (2.74 × 2.12m). Photograph by: Ellen Page Wilson, Courtesy PaceWildenstein. © Chuck Close, Courtesy PaceWildenstein, New York.

Bullet Through the Apple, 1964. Harold Edgerton. © Harold & Esther Edgerton Foundation, 2005, courtesy of Palm Press, Inc.

Central Savings. Richard Estes. Courtesy of The Nelson-Atkins Museum of Art, Kansas City, Missouri (Gift of the Friends of Art) F75-13.

Roe Ethridge Portfolio. *Kitchen Table*; *Refrigerator*; *The Jones's Sun Room*; *Ryder Truck at the Jones's*; *Chairs and Boxes*; *Basement Carpet*. Roe Ethridge. Courtesy of Roe Ethridge.

The Wu Family. Photographs by Leong Ka Tai from *Material World: A Global Family Portrait* by Peter Menzel (Sierra Club Books, 1994). Courtesy Leong Ka Tai.

Television Moon. Alfred Leslie. © Alfred Leslie. Reprinted with permission.

Pencil, 2000. Abelardo Morell. Courtesy of the artist and Bonnie Benrubi Gallery, NYC.

MTV's Real World still. Courtesy of The Everett Collection, Inc.

Pale Blue Dot, Voyager 1. NASA/JPL/Voyager.

Badge of Honor, 1995. Pepón Osorio. © Pepón Osorio. Courtesy Ronald Feldman Fine Arts, New York.

Pepón Osorio Self-Portrait. Courtesy Ronald Feldman Fine Arts, NY.

Gueorgui Pinkhassov Portfolio. *Pregame Prayer, Billy Ryan High School, Denton, Texas*; *Salat-ul-zuhr (Noon) Prayers, Mardigian Library, University of Michigan–Dearborn*; *Shacharit (Morning) Prayer Kew Gardens Hills, Queens*; *Day of Miracles Ceremony, Land of Medicine Buddha, Soquel, California*; *Bedtime Prayer, The Robertson Family, Frisco, Texas*;

Satnam Waheguru (Noon) Prayers, Minar's Taj Palace, New York. Gueorgui Pinkhassov. Courtesy Gueorgui Pinkhassov/Magnum Photos.

Retrospect: Advertising on the Run. The Picture Desk, Inc./The Advertising Archive Ltd.

Have One Brand. Sequoia Citrus Association. Courtesy the Bancroft Library, University of California, Berkeley.

terraFutura #9. Bryan Steiff. Courtesy of Bryan Steiff.

Drivers Wanted (Squares). Malcolm Venville. © 2002 courtesy Volkswagen of America, Inc.

It's ugly, but it gets you there. Courtesy Volkswagen of America, Inc.

Man v. Ant. Willard Wigan. Courtesy of Willard Wigan.

Yahoo! screenshot. Courtesy of Yahoo!

Chapter 2
Verbal Texts

"Civic Duty." From *Newark Evening News*, March 30, 1964. Reprinted with permission.

David Guterson. "No Place Like Home: On the Manicured Streets of a Master-Planned Community." Copyright © 1991 by David Guterson. Originally appeared in *Harper's Magazine*. Reprinted by permission of Georges Borchardt, Inc. for the author.

Edward Hirsch. "Edward Hopper and the House by the Railroad (1925)." From *Wild Gratitude* by Edward Hirsch. Copyright © 1985 by Edward Hirsch. Used by permission of Alfred A. Knopf, a division of Random House, Inc.

Eric Liu. "The Chinatown Idea." Originally published in *The Accidential Asian* by Eric Liu. Copyright © 1998 by Eric Liu. Reprinted with the permission of the author.

Shawn Macomber. "The Chasm between Grand and Great: Next to Hoover Dam, the Grand Canyon Is a Hole in the Ground." From *The Los Angeles Times*, August 17, 2004, Tuesday Home Edition. Copyright © 2004 by Shawn Macomber. Reprinted by permission of the author, a freelancer who runs the website www.returnoftheprimitive.com.

Norman Mailer. "Three Minutes or Less." © by Norman Mailer. Reprinted with the permission of the Wylie Agency Inc.

Bill McKibben. "Worried? Us?" From *Enough: Staying Human in An Engineered Age* by Bill McKibben. Copyright © 2003 by Bill McKibben. Reprinted by permission.

Bharati Mukherjee. "Imagining Homelands." Originally published in *Letters of Transit: Reflections on Exile,*

Identity, Language and Loss, edited by Andre Aciman. Copyright © 1999 by Bharati Mukherjee. Reprinted by permission of the author.

"What Kind of People Are We?" From The New York Times, March 28, 1964. Copyright © 1964 by The New York Times Company. Reprinted with permission.

Scott Russell Sanders. "Homeplace." First published in Orion (Winter 1992). From Staying Put by Scott Russell Sanders. © 1992 by Scott Russell Sanders. Reprinted by permission of the author.

Eudora Welty. "The Little Store" and excerpt from "Storekeeper, 1935." From The Eye of the Story: Selected Essays and Reviews by Eudora Welty. Copyright © 1978 by Eudora Welty. Used by permission of Random House, Inc.

E.B. White. "Once More to the Lake." From One Man's Meat by E.B. White. Text copyright © 1941 by E.B. White. Copyright renewed. Reprinted with permission of Tilbury House Publishers, Gardner, Maine.

Visual Texts

Grand Canyon National Park, from Yavapai Point, 1942. Ansel Adams. Collection Center for Creative Photography, University of Arizona © Trustees of the Ansel Adams Publishing Trust.

Amazon.com screenshot. Courtesy of Amazon.com.

Friends still. Courtesy of Everett Collection, Inc.

Tourists, 1989. Woody Gwyn. From the Private Collection of Steven Ratner.

House by the Railroad. 1925. Edward Hopper. Digital Image ® The Museum of Modern Art/Licensed by SCALA/Art Resource, NY.

The Far Side. Gary Larson. © 1991 Farworks, Inc. All Rights Reserved. Used with permission.

Watts 1963. Kerry James Marshall. Courtesy of the Jack Shainman Gallery.

Golden Gate series. Richard Misrach. Courtesy Richard Misrach.

The Chasm of the Colorado, 1873–74. Thomas Moran. Oil on canvas, 84³/₈ × 144³/₄ in, (214.3 × 367.6 cm). Lent by the U.S. Department of the Interior, Office of the Secretary. Smithsonian American Art Museum, Washington, DC/Art Resource, NY.

Bharati Mukherjee portrait. Courtesy of Jerry Bauer.

Earth at Night. Courtesy of National Geographic.

Tourists at the Grand Canyon. Bill Owens. Courtesy of Bill Charles Inc.

USA. Arizona. Grand Canyon. Martin Parr. Courtesy Martin Parr/Magnum Photos.

Image of Homelessness. Mark Peterson. Courtesy of Redux Pictures.

Santa Fe Railroad ad. Published in Fine Arts Journal, January 1909.

Joel Sternfeld Portfolio. Courtesy of the artist and Luhring Augustine.

Turn Left or Get Shot. © Bettmann/Corbis.

Granger, IN, 2003. Brian Ulrich. From Copia series. Courtesy Brian Ulrich.

65 East 125th Street, Harlem series. Camilo José Vergara. Courtesy of Camilo José Vergara.

Storekeeper, 1935. Eudora Welty Collection, Mississippi Department of Archives and History.

Chapter 3

Verbal Texts

Dorothy Allison. "This Is Our World." Originally published in Double Take magazine, Summer, 1998. Copyright © 1998 by Dorothy Allison. Reprinted by permission of Frances Goldin Literary Agency, Inc.

Tom Brokaw. "An Ode to Loved Labors Lost." From The New York Times, September 1, 2003. Copyright © 2003 The New York Times Company. Reprinted with permission.

Robert Olen Butler. "This Is Earl Sandt." © 2004 Robert Olen Butler. Used by permission of Grove/Atlantic, Inc.

Ethan Canin. "Vivian, Fort Barnwell," by Ethan Canin. Copyright © 1998 by Ethan Canin. First published in Doubletake. Reprinted by permission of the author.

Babbette Hines. "Picture Perfect," from Photobooth. Copyright © Princeton Architectural Press 2002. Reprinted by permission of Babbette Hines.

N. Scott Momaday. "The Photograph." From The Man Made of Words by N. Scott Momaday. Copyright © 1998 by the author. Reprinted by permission of St. Martin's Press, LLC.

James Nachtwey. "Ground Zero." From American Photo, 13.1 January/February 2002. Reprinted by permission.

Joe Rosenthal. "Flag Raising on Iwo Jima, February 23, 1945." From Faces of the 20th Century: Master Photographers and Their Work, Abbeville Press.

Susan Sontag. "On Photography." From "In Plato's Cave." As published in On Photography by Susan Sontag. Copyright © 1977 by Susan Sontag. Reprinted by permission of Farrar, Straus & Giroux, LLC.

"Interview with Art Spiegelman" by Nina Siegal. From The Progressive, January 2005. Copyright © The Progressive. Reprinted with permission from The Progressive, 409 East Main Street, Madison, WI 53703. www.progressive.org.

Amy Tan. "Fish Cheeks." Copyright © 1987 by Amy Tan. By permission of the Sandra Dijkstra Literary Agency.

Sarah Vowell. "The First Thanksgiving." From The Partly Cloudy Patriot by Sarah Vowell. Copyright © 2002 by Sarah Vowell. Reprinted with the permission of Simon & Schuster Adult Publishing Group.

Visual Texts

ABC News still. Courtesy of ABC News.

Portrait of Art Spiegelman. Bob Adelman. © Bob Adelman.

AlterNet.org screenshot. Reprinted with Permission of the Independent Media Institute.

Father and Son; Beach Flower. Mike Bragg. Courtesy of Mike Bragg.

Flag Raising, World Trade Center, 2001. Associated Press photograph by Thomas E. Franklin.

Tourists. Duane Hanson. Courtesy of National Galleries of Scotland.

From Photobooth. Babbette Hines. Courtesy of Babbette Hines.

Los Angeles Times, December 16, 2004. Reprinted with Permission.

Sharbat Gula, 1985; Sharbat Gula, 2002. Photographs by Steve McCurry. Courtesy of Magnum Photos, Inc.

No One Ever Poses with Their Toaster. Courtesy of Mercedes-Benz.

Crushed Car. Photograph by James Nachtwey. © James Nachtwey/VII Photo, Paris.

Snapshots Freeze the Moment. Radio Captures the Story. National Public Radio, Inc. Reprinted with permission.

New York Times, December 16, 2004. © 2004 The New York Times Company. Reprinted with Permission.

Martin Parr Portfolio. Courtesy of Martin Parr/Magnum Photos Inc.

Superbowl XXXVI, 2002. Photograph by David J. Philip. Courtesy Associated Press/Wide World Photos.

Marines Raising the Flag on Mount Suribachi, Iwo Jima. Photo by Joe Rosenthal. Joe Rosenthal. Courtesy of AP/Wide World Photos.

Andrew Savulich Portfolio. Courtesy Andrew Savulich.

From Birthday Party (Muenster), 1997. Yutaka Sone. Birthday Party by Yutaka Sone. VHS video tape; 1 Beta submaster; 1 certificate. 22 minutes. Edition of 5. SONYU0052. Photograph Credit Roman Mensing/

artdoc.de; Thorsten Arendt/artdoc.de; Christina Dilger/artdoc.de. Courtesy of David Zwirner, New York.

In the Shadow of No Towers. Art Spiegelman. From *In The Shadow of No Towers* by Art Spiegelman, © 2004 by Art Spiegelman. Used by permission of Pantheon Books, a division of Random House, Inc.

A Young Man Gathering Shopping Carts, Huntington, New York, July 1993, from *Stranger Passing* by Joel Sternfeld. Courtesy of Joel Sternfeld/Luhring Augustine, NY.

Seattle Central Library. Lara Swimmer. © Lara Swimmer/Esto.

Three-Cent Iwo Jima Stamp, 1945. U.S. Postal Service. AP/Wide World Photos.

USA Today, December 16, 2004. Reprinted with Permission.

Yearbook Photos. Courtesy of Classmates Media, Inc.

Chapter 4
Verbal Texts

Chris Ballard. "How to Write a Catchy Beer Ad." From *The New York Times Magazine*, January 26, 2003. Copyright © 2003 by The New York Times. Reprinted by permission.

Susan Bordo. "Never Just Pictures." Courtesy of Susan Bordo and University of California Press.

Jacinto Jesús Cardona. "Bato con Khakis." From *Heart to Heart: New Poems Inspired by Twentieth Century American Art* by Jacinto Jesus Cardona. © 2001 by Jacinto Jesús Cardona. Reprinted by permission of the author.

Judith Ortiz Cofer. "The Story of My Body." From *The Latin Deli: Prose and Poetry* by Judith Ortiz Cofer. Copyright © 1993 by Judith Ortiz Cofer. Reprinted by permission of The University of Georgia Press.

"An Interview with Judith Ortiz Cofer" by Stephanie Gordon. From *AWP Chronicle*, October/November 1997 issue, pp. 1–9. Copyright © Stephanie Gordon. 1997. Reprinted with permission of the author.

Jamaica Kincaid. "Girl." From *The New Yorker*, and from *At the Bottom of the River* by Jamaica Kincaid. Copyright © 1983 by Jamaica Kincaid. Reprinted by permission of Farrar, Straus & Giroux, LLC.

Katha Pollitt. "Why Boys Don't Play With Dolls." First published in *The New York Times Sunday Magazine*. Copyright © Katha Pollitt. Reprinted by permission of the author.

Marjane Satrapi. Introduction to *Persepolis: The Story of a Childhood* by Marjane Satrapi, translated by Mattias Ripa & Blake Ferris. Copyright

© 2003 by L'Association, Paris, France. Used by permission of Pantheon Books, a division of Random House, Inc.

Jane Slaughter. "A Beaut of a Shiner." From *The Progressive*. Copyright © 1987 by Jane Slaughter. First published by *The Progressive*. © 1987 by Jane Slaughter. Reprinted by permission of the author.

Visual Texts

Extreme Makeover. ABC Photography/New Media. © ABC Photography Archives.

Asics ad. © Asics Tiger Corporation, 1998. Reprinted with permission.

How Joe's Body Bought Him Fame Instead of Shame. © Charles Atlas, Ltd. Reprinted with permission.

From the *He/She* series. Nancy Burson. Copyright © 1996–97 by Nancy Burson.

Untitled (Cheerleading #81), 2002; Untitled (Football #75), 2002. Brian Finke. © Brian Finke. Courtesy of ClampArt, New York City.

Kids Couture. Marianne Ghantous, 2002. Courtesy of Thierry Van Biesen and Tank Magazine.

Ashleigh, 13, with Her Friend and Parents, Santa Monica. Lauren Greenfield. Courtesy Lauren Greenfield Photography/VII photo.

Li'L Sis, 1944. William H. Johnson. Smithsonian American Art Museum. Washington, DC/Art Resource, NY.

Untitled (Your body is a battleground), 1989. Barbara Kruger. Collection: Eli Broad Family Foundation. Santa Monica, California. Courtesy Mary Boone Gallery, New York.

Self-Portrait, 1980 series. Robert Mapplethorpe. © The Estate of Robert Mapplethorpe/Art & Commerce Anthology. Used by Permission.

Bato con Khakis, 1982. César A. Martínez. From *Heart to Heart*, ed. Jan Greenberg and Harry N. Abrams, 2001. Courtesy of César A. Martínez.

Pirelli Tire ad featuring Carl Lewis. Courtesy of The Advertising Archive.

Queer Eye for the Straight Guy still. Courtesy of Everett Collection.

The Veil, from *Persepolis: The Story of a Childhood* by Marjane Satrapi, translated by Mattias Ripa & Blake Ferris. © 2003 by L'Association, Paris, France. Used by permission of Pantheon Books, a division of Random House, Inc.

Portrait of Judith Ortiz Cofer. Photograph by and Courtesy of Steve Sortino.

Nature vs. Nurture cartoon. Art Spiegelman. Copyright © 1997 Art Spiegelman. First appeared in The New Yorker. Reprinted with permission of the Wylie Agency Inc.

There's Something about a Soldier, U.S. Army ad. United States Government. Reprinted with permission.

Washingtonpost.com screenshot. Courtesy of Newsweek Interactive.

Chapter 5
Verbal Texts

Donnell Alexander. "Cool Like Me." Copyright © Donnell Alexander. Reprinted by permission of Featurewell.

Stanley Crouch. "Goose-Loose Blues for the Melting Pot." From *Reinventing the Melting Pot: The New Immigrants and What It Means to Be American,* edited by Tamar Jacoby. Copyright © 2004 by Tamar Jacoby. Reprinted by permission of Basic Books, a member of Perseus Books, LLC.

Annie Dillard. "How to Live." First appeared in *Image: A Journal of Arts and Religion* #32, Spring 2002. Copyright © 2002 by Annie Dillard. Reprinted by the permission of Russell & Volkening, as agents for the author.

Paul Fussell. "A Touchy Subject." From *Class: A Guide Through the American States System* by Paul Fussell. Copyright © 1983 by Paul Fussell. Reprinted with the permission of Simon & Schuster Adult Publishing Group.

Harris Poll. "Belief in God, and Other Supernatural Forces, Places, and Events" and "Where Will You Go When You Die?" From The Harris Poll #41, August 12, 1998. Copyright © 1998 Harris Interactive, Inc. Reprinted by permission of Harris Interactive. All rights reserved.

Gish Jen. "Coming into the Country." From *The New York Times*, May 7, 2000, p. 27, section 6. Copyright © The New York Times Company. Reprinted with permission.

Nicholas D. Kristof. "Believe It, or Not." From the *New York Times*, August 15, 2003. Copyright © 2003 by The New York Times Company. Reprinted with permission.

David Mura. "Fresh from the Island Angel." From *Angels for the Burning* by David Mura. Copyright © 2004 by David Mura. Reprinted with the permission of BOA Editions, Ltd. www.boaeditions.org.

"National Museum of the Middle Class Opens in Schaumberg, IL." *The Onion*. Volume 40 Issue 44, November 3, 2004. Reprinted with permission of *The Onion*. Copyright 2004, by Onion, Inc. www.theonion.com.

Pew Global Attitudes Project. "Age and Social Values." From "Views of a Changing World." As posted on www.people-press.org. June 2003. Reprinted by permission of The Pew Research Center.

Robert Shireman. "10 Questions College Officials Should Ask about Diversity." First published in *The Chronicle of Higher Education*, August 15, 2003, pp. B10, B12. Copyright © 2003 Robert Shireman. Reprinted with the permission of the author.

Gilbert Vicario. "Interview with Nikki S. Lee." From *Projects* by Nikki S. Lee. Hatje Cantz Publishers, Germany. Distributed in the USA by Distributed Art Publishers, Inc. Interview © 2001 Gilbert Vicario and Nikki S. Lee.

Visual Texts

How Mali Lost Her Accent, 1991. Pacita Abad. © 2005 Pacita Abad.

MTV TRL with P. Diddy and B5. Evan Agostini. Courtesy Evan Agostini/Getty Images.

Baby Phat advertisement by Kimora Lee Simmons. Courtesy of Kellwood Company.

The Reunion, 1999. Tina Barney. Courtesy of Janet Borden, Inc.

Blackplanet.com screenshot. Courtesy of Blackplanet.com. © Community-Connect.com.

The Louisville Flood, 1937. Courtesy Margaret Bourke-White/Getty Images.

Da Ali G Show still. Jeff Riedel Studio.

MaMcKinley, 2001. Alfredo Esquillo Jr., Philippines. Courtesy John Batten Gallery, Hong Kong.

Fifth Avenue, 1984. Bruce Gilden. Courtesy of Bruce Gilden/Magnum Photos.

USA, San Francisco, 1979; *USA, San Francisco, 1982*; *USA, San Francisco, 1982*. Jim Goldberg. From *Rich and Poor: Photographs by Jim Goldberg*. Random House, 1985. Jim Goldberg/Magnum Photos.

Portrait of Nikki Lee. Photograph by Donald Graham.

Untitled, from the series *Maehyang-ri*, 1999. Yongsuk Kang. Courtesy Yongsuk Kang.

Nikki S. Lee Portfolio. © Nikki S. Lee, Courtesy Leslie Tonkonow Artworks + Projects, NY.

The Life of Buffalo Bill film poster. Autry National Center, Los Angeles.

Down and Out in Discount America cover, by *Nation* magazine, January 3, 2005. Reprinted with permission from *Nation* magazine. For subscription information, call 1.800.333.8536. Portions of each week's *Nation* magazine can be accessed at thenation.com.

Pocahontas film still. © Disney Enterprises, Inc.

Redskin film poster, 1929. *Redskin*, starring Richard Dix. Paramount Pictures.

Religious Adherents as a Percentage of All Residents, 2000. Reprinted with permission from Religious Congregations and Membership in the United States: 2000. (Nashville: Glenmary Research Center, 2002). ©Association of Statisticians of American Religious Bodies. All rights reserved.

German Indians: *Knife Thrower*, 1998. Andrea Robbins and Max Becher. Chromogenic print. Courtesy of Sonnabend Gallery.

Bratatata, 2001 (detail). Miguel Angel Rojas. Courtesy of Casas Riegner Gallery, Columbia.

24 People for Whom I Have Been Mistaken, 1999. Roger Shimomura. Collection of David E. Schwartz.

Smoke Signals film still. © Miramax Films. Jill Sabella / Everett Collection. Screenplay by Sherman Alexie. Chris Eyre, director. Actors: Adam Beach and Evan Adams. Reprinted by permission.

Doubles, Lima; *Shalom and Linda, Paris*. Mario Testino. Reprinted for and on behalf of Mario Testino/Art Partner, NY.

It's Your Life. Courtesy of Visa.

Friendship after September 11, 1 (2001). Saira Wasim. Collection of Banik Koli. Courtesy of Saira Wasim.

Untitled, from the series *disCONNEXION*, 2003. Danwen Xing, China. Chromogenic color print. Courtesy Danwen Xing.

Chapter 6

Verbal Texts

Guy Davenport. "The Geography of the Imagination." From *The Geography of the Imagination: 40 Essays* by Guy Davenport. Copyright © 1981. Reprinted with the permission of Bonnie Jean Cox.

Kari Lynn Dean. *She Can't Smile without You*. Reprinted with permission from *Wired* magazine, October, 2004.

Anne Fadiman. "A Piece of Cotton." Originally appeared in the Winter 2002 issue of *The American Scholar*. Copyright © 2002 by Anne Fadiman. Reprinted by permission of Lescher & Lescher, Ltd. All rights reserved.

Neal Gabler. "Inside Every Superhero Lurks a Nerd." Originally published in the *New York Times*, May 12, 2002. Copyright © 2002 by Neal Gabler. Reprinted with permission of the Elayne Markson Agency.

Chip Kidd. "Super." From *2wice* magazine, volume 2, no. 2, p. 25. Copyright © 1998 2wice. Reprinted by permission of the 2wice Arts Foundation, Inc.

Tom Perrotta. "The Cosmic Significance of Britney Spears." From *GQ* magazine, December 2001. Copyright © Tom Perrotta, 2001. Reprinted by permission of Lippincott Massie McQuilkin as agents for the author.

Keith Phipps. "Chip Kidd Interview." From *The Onion*, Volume 40, No. 22. Copyright © 2004 by Onion, Inc. Reprinted with permission of The Onion A.V. Club. www.theonionavclub.com.

Paul Rand. "Logos, Flags, and Escutcheons." From *AIGA Journal of Graphic Design*, Vol. 9, No. 3, 1991. © 1991 Paul Rand. Reprinted by permission of Mrs. Paul Rand.

Sally Stein. "Passing Likeness: Dorothea Lange's 'Migrant Mother' and the Paradox of Iconicity." From *Only Skin Deep: Changing Visions of the American Self*, edited by Coco Fusco & Brian Wallis. Copyright © 2003 International Center of Photography Published by Harry N. Abrams, Inc. Publishers, New York. Reprinted with the permission of the author.

Gilbert Vicario. "Interview with Nikki S. Lee." From *Projects* by Nikki S. Lee. Copyright © 2001 Gilbert Vicario and Nikki S. Lee. Reprinted by permission of Gilbert Vicario.

Richard B. Woodward. "Wonder." From *2wice* magazine, Volume 2, No. 2, p. 16. Copyright © 1998 2wice. Reprinted by permission of the 2wice Arts Foundation, Inc.

Jane Yolen. "Grant Wood: American Gothic." From *Heart to Heart*, published by Harry N. Abrams, Inc. Copyright © 2001 by Jane Yolen. Reprinted by permission of Curtis Brown, Ltd.

Visual Texts

Follow the Flock. Adbusters Media Foundation. Courtesy www.adbusters.org.

American Dream Team. Scottie Pippen, Michael Jordan, and Clyde Drexler, 1992. Courtesy AP/Wide World Photos.

Bathroom Signs Portfolio. From *Colors 1000 Signs*, Taschen Books.

Our Lady of Good Children, 1847–1861. Ford Madox Brown. Tate Gallery, London/Art Resource, NY.

Madonna and Child. 1940s. Jean Cocteau. © 2006 Artists Rights Society (ARS), New York/ADAGP, Paris.

The Vanishing Race, 1907. Edward S. Curtis. National Anthropological Archives, Smithsonian Institution, Washington, D.C.

Mural, Sunnyside, Queens, 2001. Erni, Smith, and Lady Pink. Reprinted with permission.

A Child Is Born, 1999. Michael Escoffery. Private Collection. Michael Escoffery/Art Resource, NY.

Chip Kidd. Courtesy of Marianne Ettlinger.

Holy Family with Saints Margaret and Francis, 1578. Lavinia Fontana. Gift of William and Selma Postar, 2001. 104. Courtesy Davis Museum and Cultural Center, Wellesley College, Wellesley, MA.

Florence Thompson and her daughters. Modesto, CA, by Bill Ganzel, http://www.ganzelgroup.com. From *Dust Bowl Descent*, by Bill Ganzel, 1984.

Ray Charles Google logo. Courtesy of Google © 2005.

What Is America? Jesse Gordon. From New York Times Op-Art, July 3, 2000.

Life in Hell. Matt Groening. © 1985 by Matt Groening.

Lizzy Gardiner, 1995 Academy Awards. Photo © Dan Groshong/SYGMA. Courtesy of American Express/Sandra Marsh Management.

Duck-Rabbit image by Joseph Jastrow, courtesy of John F. Kihlstrom, University of California, Berkeley (http:Socrates.berkeley.edu/'kihlstrm/JastrowDuck.htm).

Tibor Kalman portfolio. *Michael Jackson; Arnold Schwartzenegger; Spike Lee; Queen Elizabeth II*. From *Colors* magazine, #4, "Race." Reprinted by permission.

E and F from *She Can't Smile without You*. L. L. Kontsevich, Ph.D. & C. W. Tyler, Ph.D., 2004. Vision Research, 44, 1493–1498.

Hopi Indian Man, 1926. Dorothea Lange, Oakland Museum of California, City of Oakland. Gift of Paul S. Taylor.

Migrant Mother, Nipomo, California series, 1936. Dorothea Lange. Courtesy the Dorothea Lange Collection, Oakland Museum of California.

Woman and Child, 1921. Fernand Léger. Gift of Professor and Mrs. John McAndrew in honor of Alfred H. Barr, Jr. 1954.9. Courtesy Davis Museum and Cultural Center, Wellesley College, Wellesley, MA.

Mona Lisa, 1503–06. Leonardo da Vinci. The Bridgeman Art Library/Getty Images.

B, C, and D from *She Can't Smile without You*. Courtesy of Margaret Livingstone, Harvard Medical School.

Madonna Nursing the Child, 895 or 898 c.e. The Pierpont Morgan Library/Art Resource, NY.

Master of the Virgin of Vysehrad, *Virgin and Child*, after 1355. National Gallery, Prague, Czech Republic. Erich Lessing/Art Resource, NY.

What Makes a Symbol Endure? Courtesy of Mercedes-Benz USA, Inc. Montvale, NJ. A Daimler Chrysler Company, www.mbusa.com.

Making Faces, 2004. Jason Mercier. Courtesy of Jason Mercier.

American Gothic. Gordon Parks. Courtesy Gordon Parks/Corbis.

Madonna del Granduca, 1505. Raphael. Galleria Palatina, Palazzo Pitti, Florence, Italy. Alinari/Art Resource, NY.

The Adventures of Superman. © DC Comics. Licensed by Warner Bros. Entertainment Inc. All Rights Reserved.

Superman: The Movie (2 images). © Film Export A.G. Licensed by Warner Bros. Entertainment Inc. All Rights Reserved.

Lemon. Courtesy Volkswagen of America, Inc.

210 Coca-Cola Bottles, 1962; *Two Hundred Campbell's Soup Cans*, 1962. Andy Warhol. © 2000 Andy Warhol Foundation for the Visual Arts/ARS, New York and The Andy Warhol Foundation, Inc./Art Resource, NY.

Wonder Woman (U.S. TV series). © Warner Bros. Entertainment Inc. and DC Comics. All Rights Reserved.

Wonder Woman Archives Volume 1. © 1998 DC Comics. All Rights Reserved. Used with permission.

American Gothic. Painting by Grant Wood. Courtesy Chicago Institute of Art.

Chapter 7
Verbal Texts

Isabel Allende. "Omayra Sanchez." From *Talking Pictures*: *People Speak about the Pictures That Speak to Them* by Marvin Heiferman. Chronicle Books, 1994. Copyright © 1994 by Isabel Allende. Reprinted by permission of the author.

Nick Hornby. "Richard Billingham." From *Writers and Artists*: *Modern Painters* by Dorling Kindersley. Copyright © 2001 by Penguin Books Ltd. Reprinted by permission of Penguin Books Ltd.

Michael Kimmelman. "150th Anniversary: 1851–2001: The Assignment Is to Get the Story, but the Image Can Rise to Art." From *The New York Times*, November 14, 2001. Copyright © 2001 by The New York Times Company, Inc. Reprinted with permission.

John Long. "Ethics in the Age of Digital Photography." First published in *Challenging Images*. Copyright © 2002. Reprinted by permission of the author.

Carla Marinucci. "Doctored Kerry Photo Brings Anger, Threat of Suit." From the *San Francisco Chronicle*, February 20, 2004, p. A. Copyright © 2004 San Francisco Chronicle. Reprinted by permission of Copyright Clearance Center.

Susan Sontag. Excerpt from *Regarding the Pain of Others* by Susan Sontag. Copyright © 2003 by Susan Sontag. Reprinted by permission of Farrar, Straus and Giroux, LLC.

Kelly K. Spors. "Where All School Photos Are Above Average." From *Wall Street Journal*, pp. d1–d2. Copyright © 2003 by the Dow Jones Company and the Wall Street Journal. Reprinted by permission of the publisher via rightslink.com.

Michael Stephens. "Expanding the Language of Photographs." From *Media Studies Journal*, Spring 1997. Copyright © 1997 Media Studies Journal. Reprinted by Permission of The Freedom Foundation.

Edward Tufte. "PowerPoint Is Evil." From *Wired Magazine*, Issue 11.09 (September 2003). Reprinted by permission of Graphics Press, LLC. P.O. Box 430, Cheshire, CT, 06410.

WritersCorps Portfolio. Poems courtesy of Katherine Gin and students of WritersCorps, San Francisco.

Visual Texts

American Idol still. Courtesy of Everett Collection.

Untitled photographs. Richard Billingham. © Richard Billingham. Courtesy Anthony Reynolds Gallery, London.

Iraqi man at a regroupment center for POWs, Najaf, Iraq, March 31, 2003. Jean-Marc Bouju. Jean-Marc Bouju/AP/Wide World Photos.

Omaha Beach, June 6, 1944. Robert Capa. © Robert Capa/Magnum Photos.

Members of the 129th Rescue Squadron, Moffitt Federal Airfield, CA. Photo by Lance Cheung.

Death Penalty Y/N (Yes/No). Courtesy of Collaborate, San Francisco, for Rock the Vote. Creative Director/Copywriter: Robin Raj; Art Director: Kurt Lighthouse/Daniel Jung; Photography: Getty Images.

Imagine series. Collaborate. Courtesy of Collaborate, San Francisco © 2003 for Amnesty International. Creative Director/Copywriter: Robin Raj; Art Director: Kurt Lighthouse; Photography: Magnum.

Rodolfo Monteil (Defend the Earth). Courtesy of Collaborate, San Francisco, for Amnesty International and Sierra Club. Creative Director/Copywriter: Robin Raj; Art Director: Kurt

Lighthouse; Photography: Keba Konte.

Greenhouse Dog, 1951. Photo provided by the Defense Threat Reduction Agency.

Omayra Sanchez, Colombia, 1985. Frank Fournier. ©1985 Frank Fournier/Contact Press Images.

Jane Fonda Protesting. Owen Franken. © Owen Franken/Corbis.

Home of a Rebel Sharpshooter, Gettysburg, July, 1863. Alexander Gardner. From *Gardner's Photographic Sketchbook of the American Civil War 1861–1865*. Division of Rare & Manuscript Collections, Carl A. Kroch Library, Cornell University Library.

Untitled. Barbara Kruger. Courtesy Mary Boone Gallery, New York.

John Kerry at the Register. 1971. Ken Light. © Ken Light/Corbis.

Breaching Great White Shark. Charles Maxwell. © Charles Maxwell. Reprinted with permission.

The Men of the 308th, the "Lost Battalion," April 28, 1919. © Corbis.

PowerPoint Presentation for the Gettysburg Address. Peter Norvig. Courtesy of Peter Norvig/Google.

Tommy/Parents. The Anti-Drug. Courtesy of Office of National Drug Control Policy/Partnership for a Drug-Free America.

(This Is) Your Brain on Drugs. By Warren Berger. From *Advertising Today*, 2001. © Partnership for a Drug-Free America.

Frank Fournier. Michelle Poiré. © 2004 Michelle Poiré/World Picture News.

Bootiful. Rankin. Courtesy Rankin/Icon International.

Professional Courtesy, 1996. James Rosenquist. Licensed by VAGA, New York, NY.

Nicole Benson. Dean Stewart. © Dean Stewart Photography.

PowerPoint Is Evil. From *The Cognitive Style of PowerPoint* by Edward Tufte/Graphics Press.

Children Fleeing a Napalm Strike, Vietnam, 1972. Nick Ut. AP/Wide World Photos.

Wolfschmidt's Vodka. Reprinted with permission.

WritersCorps Portfolio. Images courtesy of Katherine Gin and students of WritersCorps, San Francisco.

Appendix A

Verbal Texts

John Berger. "Chapter 1." From *Ways of Seeing* by John Berger. Copyright © 1972 by John Berger. Used by permission of Viking Penguin, a division of Penguin Group (USA) Inc.

Visual Texts

Venus and Mars. Sandro Botticelli. National Gallery, London, Great Britain.

Procession to Calvary, 1546. Brueghel, Pieter the Elder. Kunsthistorisches Museum, Vienna, Austria. Photo Credit: Erich Lessing/Art Resource, NY.

Regentesses of the Old Men's Alms House. Hals. © Hals Museum. Reprinted by permission of Frans Halsmuseum.

Regents of the Old Men's Alms House. Hals. © Hals Museum. Reprinted by permission of Frans Halsmuseum.

Virgin and Child with St. Anne and St. John the Baptist. Leonardo da Vinci. National Gallery, London, Great Britain. Photo Credit: Art Resource, NY.

Virgin of the Rocks. Leonardo da Vinci. c. 1483. Louvre, Paris, France. Photo Credit: Scala/Art Resource, NY. Photo credit: Alinari/Art Resource, NY.

Virgin of the Rocks. Leonardo da Vinci. c. 1491–1508. National Gallery, London, Great Britain. Photo Credit: Art Resource, NY.

Key of Dreams. René Magritte. © 2006 C. Herscovici, Brussels/Artists Rights Society (ARS), New York. *Le Clef des Songes (The Key of Dreams)*. Coll. Wormland, Munich, Germany. Photo credit: Bridgeman-Giraudon/Art Resource, NY.

Scott McCloud. From *Understanding Comics* by Scott McCloud. Copyright © 1993, 1994 by Scott McCloud. Reprinted by permission of Harper-Collins Publishers.

Still Life with Chair Caning, 1912. Pablo Picasso. © Copyright ARS/NY. Photo Credit: Bridgeman-Giraudon/Art Resource, NY.

Wheatfield with Crows. Vincent van Gogh. Van Gogh Museum, Amsterdam, The Netherlands. Photo Credit: Art Resource, NY.

Woman Pouring Milk. Vermeer. © Raymond Schoder/CORBIS.

INDEX OF VERBAL AND VISUAL TEXTS

A NOTE ON THE TYPE

Seeing & Writing 3 was designed
at 2x4 by Katie Andresen
assisted by Kiki Katahira, using
a mixture of historical and contemporary typefonts. Chapter
heads, headnotes, and questions
appear in Bryant (2002) designed by Eric Olson. Heads for
the text selections are set
in Electra (1935–49), drawn by
the renowned American designer
William Addison Dwiggins.
The primary text font is Minion
(1989) by Robert Slimbach.

A NOTE ABOUT THE COVER

Artist Peter Arkle drew on his
observations of people and
places on college campuses
to create the cover illustration
for *Seeing & Writing 3*. Arkle's
interpretations of the themes
of *Seeing & Writing* are also
included throughout the book.
Please visit seeingandwriting.com
for an interview with Peter Arkle
as well as for interactive exercises on the cover art.

seeingandwriting.com

Visit the *Seeing & Writing 3* companion web site for materials to supplement the text, including guided visual exercises based on specific selections in the book, annotated research links for authors and selections, unabridged interviews with authors and artists, and general composition resources.

Resources for instructors include downloadable course materials, sample syllabi, and access to a new online community where instructors can share teaching assignments, post class ideas, and exchange feedback about working with *Seeing & Writing.*

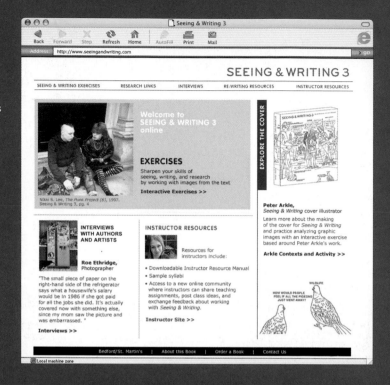